THE GREAT *Composers*

THE GREAT Composers

An illustrated encyclopedia of the lives and works of the world's best-loved composers

WENDY THOMPSON

HERMES HOUSE

This edition published in 2001 by Hermes House

Hermes House is an imprint of Anness Publishing Limited
Hermes House, 88–89 Blackfriars Road, London SE1 8HA

Published in the USA by Hermes House
Anness Publishing Inc., 27 West 20th Street
New York, NY 10011

A CIP catalogue record for this book is available
from the British Library

Publisher: Joanna Lorenz
Managing Editor: Judith Simons
Project Editor: Felicity Forster
Editor: Beverley Jollands
Designer: Michael Morey
Jacket Design: SteersMcGillan
Picture Researcher: Cathy Stastny
Editorial Reader: Penelope Goodare
Production Controller: Don Campaniello

Jacket Picture Credits: AKG, London (Beethoven, Brahms, Mozart)
The Art Archive (Bach, Strauss)

1 3 5 7 9 10 8 6 4 2

HALF TITLE PAGE: Johann Sebastian Bach playing at the court of Frederick the Great in 1747.
FRONTISPIECE: An idealized artist's impression of Mozart conducting parts of his Requiem from his deathbed.
TITLE PAGE: Ludwig van Beethoven in later life, composing at the piano in his Viennese apartment.

LEFT: Detail of a boys' choir from the Seven Joys of the Virgin Altarpiece (c.1480) by the anonymous Master of the Holy Parent.
OPPOSITE: A musical party, painted by Per Hillestrom (1732–1816)

Contents

Pro Sacro Die Ascensionis Dni
tem ad te uenio non rogo ut tollas eos de mundo sed ut ser
ues eos a malo ae u ia ae u ia
In die ascensionis
Viri galilei quid admiramini aspicientes
in celum ae u ia quemadmodum uidistis eum ascenden
tem in celum ita ueniet ae u ia ae u ia ae u ia ps
Cumque intuerentur in celum euntem illum ecce duo uiri as
Omnes gentes plaudite manibus iubilate
deo in uoce exultationis
titerunt iuxta illos in uestibus albis qui et dixerunt
A e
u ia
Ascendit deus in iubila tio ne
Et dominus in uoce tu be
A e
u ia
A o

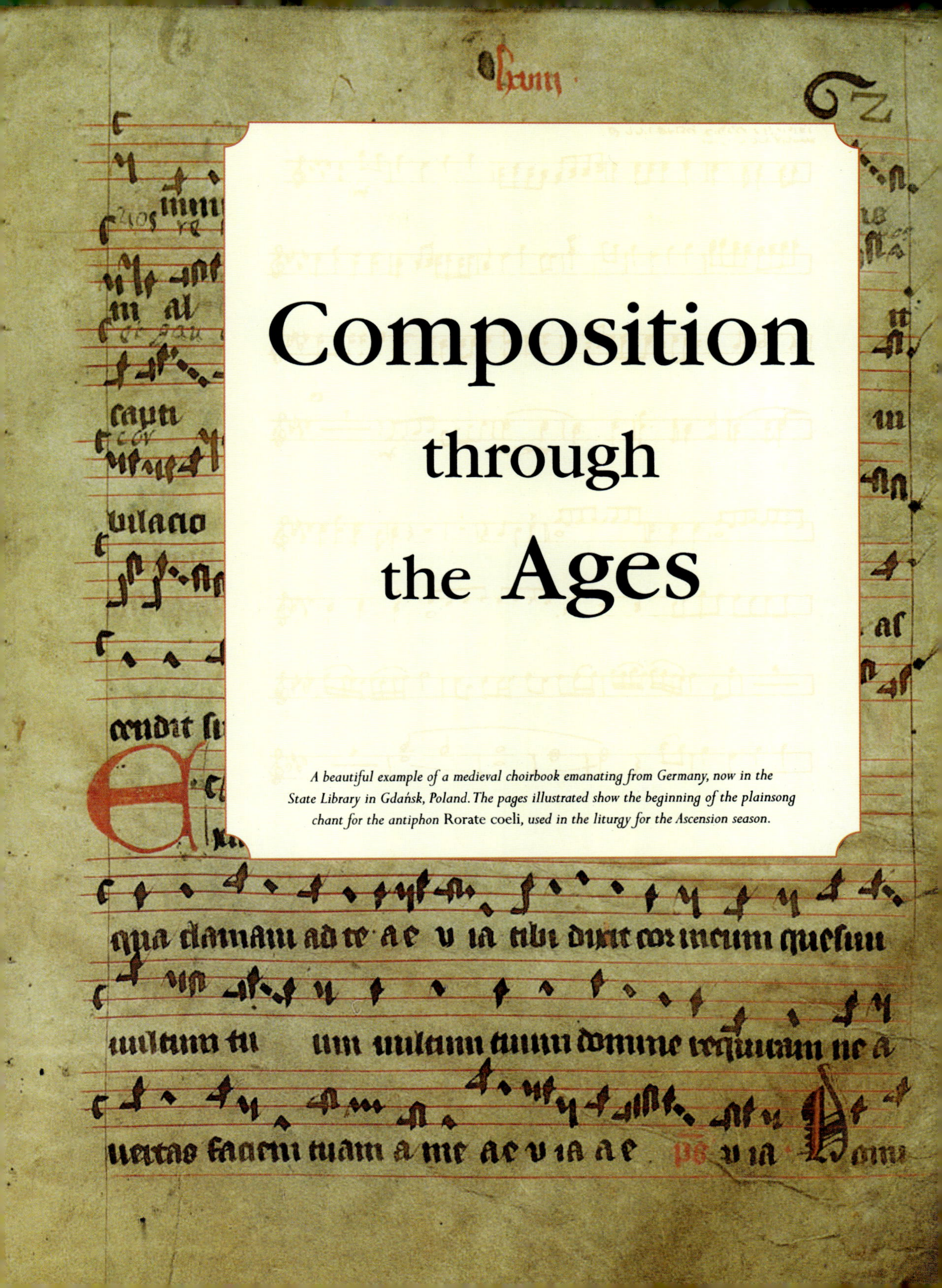

Composition through the Ages

A beautiful example of a medieval choirbook emanating from Germany, now in the State Library in Gdańsk, Poland. The pages illustrated show the beginning of the plainsong chant for the antiphon Rorate coeli, *used in the liturgy for the Ascension season.*

Music as a Language

We – are we not formed, as notes of music are,
For one another, though dissimilar?

PERCY BYSSHE SHELLEY (1792–1822), "EPIPSYCHIDION"

Musical composition is one of the most mysterious of all art forms. People who can easily come to terms with a work of literature or a painting are still often baffled by the process by which a piece of music – appearing in material form as notation – must then be translated back into sound through the medium of a third party – the performer. Unlike a painting, a musical composition cannot be owned (except by its creator); and although a score may be published, like a book, it may remain incomprehensible to the general public until it is performed. Although a piece may be played thousands of times, each repetition is entirely individual, and interpretations by different players may vary widely.

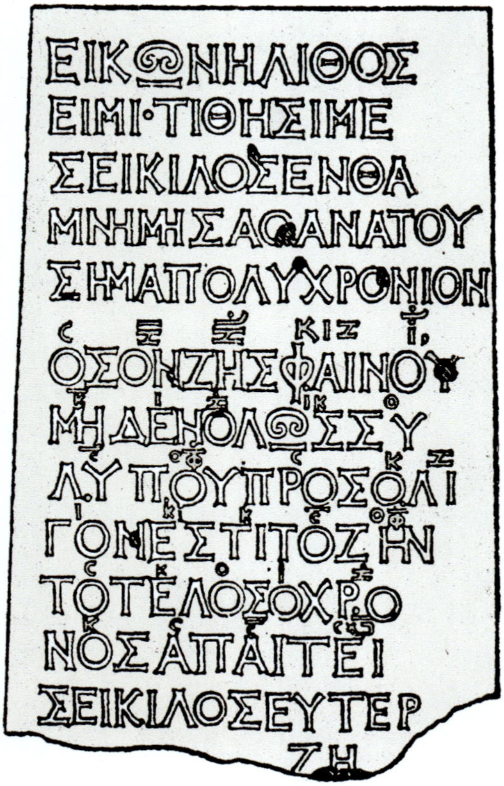

ABOVE: An early example of musical notation, a 3rd-century BC Greek song. The letters above the text indicate the notes.

Origins of musical notation

The earliest musical compositions were circumscribed by the range of the human voice. People from all cultures have always sung, or used primitive instruments to make sounds. Notation, or the writing down of music, developed to enable performers to remember what they had improvised, to preserve what they had created, and to facilitate interaction between more than one performer. Musical notation, like language, has ancient origins, dating back to the Middle East in the third millennium BC. The ancient Greeks appear to have been the first to try to represent variations of musical pitch through the medium of the alphabet, and successive civilizations all over the world attempted to formulate similar systems of recognizable musical notation.

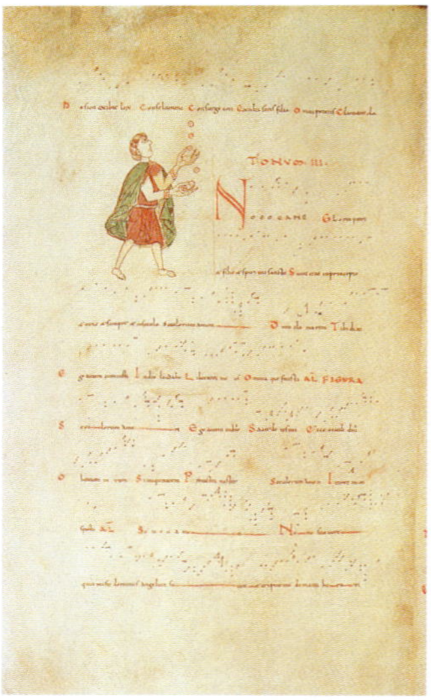

ABOVE: An early example of neumatic notation, from a German illustrated liturgical manuscript.

Neumatic notation

The earliest surviving Western European notational system was called "neumatic notation" – a system of symbols which attempted to portray the rise and fall of a melodic line. These date back to the 9th century AD, and were associated with the performance of sacred music – particularly plainsong – in monastic institutions. Several early manuscript

ABOVE: Guido d'Arezzo (c.977–1050), who devised the hexachord. His statue stands outside the Uffizi Gallery in Florence.

sources contain sacred texts with accompanying notation, although there was no standard system. The first appearance of staff notation, in which pitch was indicated by noteheads on or between lines with a symbol called a clef at the beginning to fix the pitch of one note, was in the 9th-century French treatise *Musica enchiriadis*. At the same time, music for instruments (particularly organ and lute) was beginning to be written down in diagrammatic form known as tablature, which indicated the positions of the player's fingers.

Guido d'Arezzo

The 11th-century Italian monk Guido d'Arezzo invented the "solmization" system – the precursor of "tonic solfa" – in which various syllables were used to indicate pitches in a musical scale. He also invented the "Guidonian Hand", in which the tips and joints of the five fingers were used as an aid to remembering the various notes. At the same time, attempts were being made to indicate rhythm in performance, by varying the length and angle of the tails of the neumes, and the earliest polyphony (the simultaneous performance of more than one melodic line) was being explored.

The modal system

From around 400 BC until AD 1500, European music was built on modes. In the 4th century BC, the Greek mathematician Pythagoras worked out a scale roughly corresponding to the (modern-day) white keys of the piano, and two centuries later this scale was being used by the Greeks in seven different ways. The early Christian church adopted four so-called "authentic" modes (corresponding to white-note scales beginning on D, E, F and G), and under the 6th-century Pope Gregory, four more modes were added for the performance of plainsong.

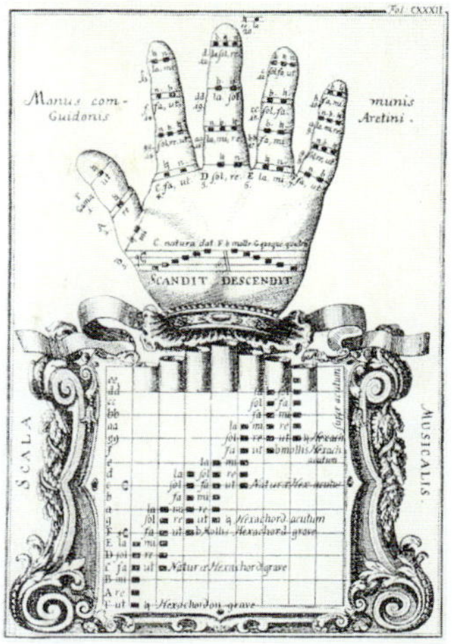

ABOVE: The so-called "Guidonian Hand", Guido d'Arezzo's device for showing the notes of the scale.

In 1547, the Swiss monk Henricus Glareanus postulated the theory of 12 modes, giving them somewhat inauthentic Greek names:

- Dorian (range D–D)
- HypoDorian (range A–A)
- Phrygian (range E–E)
- HypoPhrygian (range B–B)
- Lydian (range F–F)
- HypoLydian (range C–C)
- Mixolydian (range G–G)
- HypoMixolydian (range D–D)
- Aeolian (range A–A)
- HypoAeolian (range E–E)
- Ionian (range C–C)
- HypoIonian (range G–G)

ABOVE: Pope Gregory (c.540–604), who gave his name to "Gregorian" plainsong melodies for liturgical use.

Of these, the Aeolian and Ionian modes later became the basis of the minor and major scales respectively, which have since underpinned Western European music. The modes finally gave way to the keys we know today with the development of harmony in the late Renaissance period.

Emergence of Composers

Lovely forms do flow
From conceit divinely framed;
Heaven is music.

THOMAS CAMPION (1567–1620), "OBSERVATIONS IN THE ART OF ENGLISH POESIE"

Much medieval music survives in manuscript anthologies, some copied by monks for a particular monastery, others – often exquisitely illuminated – commissioned by an aristocratic patron. The earliest surviving ones date from the 10th century. Among the most famous manuscripts are two 15th-century English sources, the Old Hall Manuscript and the Eton College Choirbook. There are also two French sources dating from around 1470, the beautiful heart-shaped *Chansonnier cordiforme* and the *Mellon chansonnier*. Many pieces in these manuscripts are anonymous, but some were attributed to individual composers.

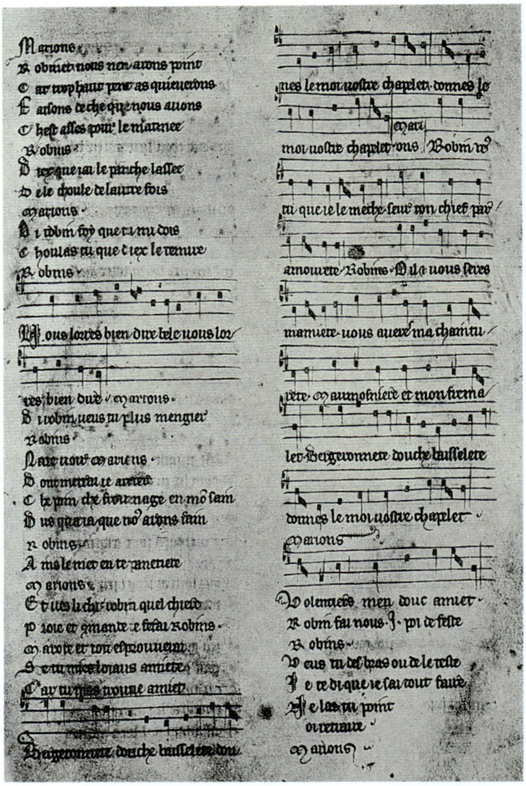

ABOVE: An example of the ars antiqua *– a page from the* Jeu de Robin et Marion *by Adam de la Halle (1230–c.1288).*

Ars antiqua

The Parisian composers Léonin and Pérotin were among the finest exponents of the style called *ars antiqua*, or "ancient style", a method of harmonizing plainsong melodies by adding between one and three secondary voices to the main vocal line, moving in parallel motion. This was known as *conductus*, and was an early form of polyphony – a compositional technique in which several melodic lines are combined, moving independently (as opposed to homophony, in which the voices move together, forming blocks of harmony). European music was dominated by the polyphonic principle from the 13th to the 16th centuries.

By the 13th century, musical notation had become more sophisticated and standardized, with only the finer points of rhythmic notation still open to interpretation. *Conductus* was gradually superseded by a new form known as the motet, a sacred Latin song, usually with a Biblical text, in which other voices moved in counterpoint to the main tune. The motet has remained a standard form of liturgical music.

Ars nova

At the same time, secular songs, such as those sung by French troubadours and *trouvères*, were being written down. Their flexibility and tunefulness led to the development of a new style (*ars nova*) in the 14th century, initiated by the theorist Philippe de Vitry. The music of the *ars nova*, which flourished particularly in France and Italy, had greater rhythmic vitality, and composers such as Guillaume de Machaut began to experiment with new techniques such as isorhythm, in which the same rhythmic pattern appears in successive repetitions of the melody, but not necessarily using notes of the same value. Many motets of the period were based on this technique, and on a *cantus firmus* – a familiar tune (either a plainsong melody or a folk song) which underpinned a polyphonic composition

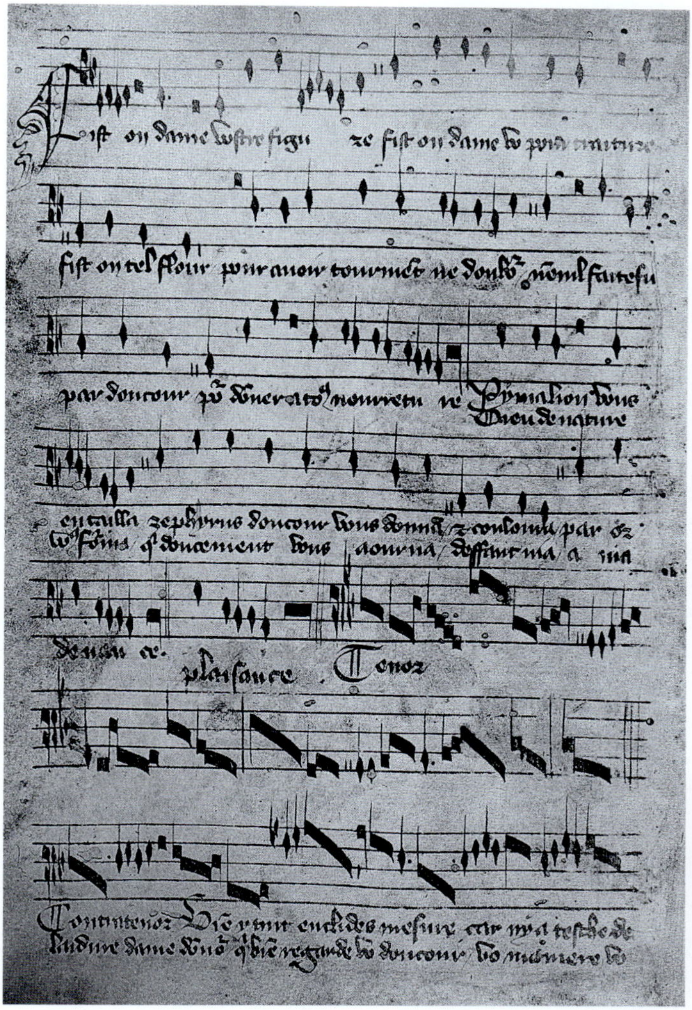

ABOVE: An example of ars nova *notation – an anonymous 14th-century French virelai (song). Note the increasing complexity of the notation.*

by appearing throughout, usually in the tenor line.

By 1500 the system of Western European musical notation had become largely standardized, and from then onwards it became increasingly sophisticated and refined. The 16th century (the High Renaissance) was dominated by the principle of polyphony, brought to a height of perfection by composers such as Palestrina in Italy, Lassus in Germany, Victoria in Spain, and William Byrd in England.

Radical change of style

Around 1600, a musical sea-change occurred, partly as a reaction against polyphony, partly as a result of the secularization of society, and the increasing sophistication of musical instruments. This was the invention of "monody", a new style in which the old principle of equal voices moving in counterpoint gave way to a single vocal line accompanied by instruments. While the tenor line still carried the main tune of a composition, it was now underpinned by a "ground bass", or *basso continuo* – a strong bass line played on keyboard and reinforced by cello and other bass instruments, which provided a harmonic foundation. The new style – the basis of all Baroque music – originated in Florence, where the composer Giulio Caccini published a famous collection of monodies, *Nuove musiche*, in 1602. The invention of monody coincided with the birth of a new secular musical genre, opera. The concept of a drama set to music, performed by costumed singers with instrumental accompaniment, originated in Florence with early examples by Peri and Caccini. Its greatest early exponent was Claudio Monteverdi.

ABOVE: An exquisitely illuminated page from the 15th-century Squarcialupi codex *showing Francesco Landini (c.1325–97) with the score of his madrigal* Musica son.

Baroque Forms

[Opera is] one of the most magnificent and expenseful diversions the wit of man can invent.

JOHN EVELYN (1620–1706), DIARY, 1645

Music in the Baroque era (c.1600–1750) was dominated by an insatiable demand for recreational art-forms. The great aristocratic and royal households, which could support their own orchestras, also employed composers to supply a constant need for new works. In 18th-century Europe, the growing size and wealth of the new middle classes led to a gradual democratization of musical appreciation and the advent of public performances in new concert halls and opera houses.

ABOVE: A sumptuous court entertainment of 1747 in the Teatro Argentina in Rome to celebrate the marriage of the son of Louis XV.

Music and drama

Opera became a favourite entertainment at the many princely courts which dotted Europe; the first public opera house opened in Venice in 1637, followed by others in major European cities. New musical forms were developed to suit the genre, including recitative and aria: the recitative allowed the singer (accompanied only by keyboard) to advance the story rapidly; while the aria, accompanied by the orchestra, allowed for expansive and lyrical reflection on a given situation or emotion.

The Baroque era was dominated by *opera seria*, based on plots drawn from ancient mythology, legend or history, with heroic characters fulfilling their destinies according to approved behavioural concepts. The most prolific 17th-century opera composers included Alessandro Scarlatti and Antonio Vivaldi in Italy, Reinhard Keiser in Germany, and Jean-Baptiste Lully in France.

But by far the greatest exponent of Italian *opera seria* was Handel, who managed to make his characters express real human emotions. His operas have survived, while works by his contemporaries have been consigned to history. *Opera seria* lasted into Mozart's time, but by then audiences were demanding a lighter, more naturalistic type of drama, often dealing with comic subject-matter, which flowered in the hands of Gluck and especially Mozart.

Oratorio

Despite initial resistance, not even the church could remain unaffected by these new developments. A sacred – and normally unstaged – type of musical drama called oratorio, using the same musical forms as opera, but based on biblical stories, came into being. Most opera composers (such as Scarlatti and Vivaldi) also wrote oratorios, but again it was Handel's fine examples which have survived to the present day. Bach's *St John* and *St Matthew Passions*, relating the story of Christ's death according to the Gospels, belong to this genre.

Instrumental forms

A growing demand for purely instrumental music led to the development of other new forms, such as the sonata. This was conceived both as a form suitable for church performance – the *sonata da chiesa*, which the Italian composer Corelli developed as a standard four-movement form – and its lighter counterpart the *sonata da camera*, which had an unspecified number of dance-like movements. Dance types – gavotte, minuet, courante, allemande, gigue – found their way into instrumental compositions, and their enormous variety formed the basis of the Baroque suite, perfected by Bach and Handel.

Another new form was the concerto, a genre pioneered by Giovanni Gabrieli in the late 1500s, in which a small group of instruments (later one solo instrument) is contrasted with the main body of the orchestra (the earlier form is known as a *concerto grosso*). While Renaissance music had exalted the principle of equality, Baroque music thrived on contrast.

Transition to Classicism

The still, sad music of humanity.
WILLIAM WORDSWORTH (1770–1850), "TINTERN ABBEY"

Baroque music reached its zenith in the works of Bach and Handel. Bach concentrated on sacred music, notably in his many cantatas – dramatic works for voices and instruments intended for church performance; Handel worked in both secular and sacred genres, writing Italian operas and English oratorios. The opening instrumental overtures, or "sinfonias", of such pieces gradually expanded into the 18th-century symphony, which eventually settled into a standard four-movement form with an opening fast movement, a lyrical slow movement, a short dance movement (usually a minuet and trio) and a fast finale. This was the form which Joseph Haydn perfected in over 100 examples, together with another new instrumental genre, the string quartet, written for two violins, viola and cello.

ABOVE: A group of musicians playing stringed and keyboard instruments at the court of the Duke of Modena in the late 17th century, painted by Antonio Gabbiani (1652–1726).

Sonata form

These works, together with the Classical sonata itself, were dominated by the structural principle of "sonata form", in which an opening exposition, usually presenting two main, contrasting themes, is succeeded by a central "development" section, in which the themes are subjected to a variety of treatments. Then comes a "recapitulation", in which the opening themes are repeated (often in shortened or slightly varied form), followed by a short "coda" to round off the movement.

Haydn's great Viennese contemporaries Mozart and Beethoven consolidated and developed the symphony and string quartet, as well as the solo concerto – which was now becoming primarily a vehicle for one virtuoso performer. As the 18th-century harpsichord gave way to the more powerful and reliable pianoforte, the piano concerto – and the solo piano sonata – became favoured forms from Mozart's time onwards.

ABOVE: An 18th-century concert with wind, string and keyboard players held at a private Italian palazzo (probably in Venice).

The Romantic Heyday

There is nothing stable in the world; uproar's your only music.
JOHN KEATS (1795–1821)

While Napoleon Bonaparte swept across Europe, toppling the decadent aristocratic rulers of the *ancien régime*, Beethoven's powerful musical vision heralded a new age of individualism. His massive *Eroica* Symphony (No. 3) pushed Classical symphonic form to its limits, while his Sixth (*Pastoral*) Symphony showed how music could be used to illustrate humanity's relationship with nature (a favourite concept of the Romantic era, as illustrated in the art and literature of the period). Meanwhile, as aristocratic patronage declined, the burgeoning middle classes began to demand music on a domestic scale for private enjoyment – a market filled by the music of

ABOVE: One of the seminal literary works of Romanticism – an artist's impression of Goethe's Faust in his study, painted in 1829.

Schubert, Schumann, Chopin, Mendelssohn and Brahms, who produced songs with piano accompaniment, chamber music (for combinations of string and wind instruments) and solo piano pieces.

The rapid expansion of the orchestra during this period, together with the invention of new instruments such as the clarinet and the improvement of existing ones, particularly woodwind and brass, led to the creation of much larger ensembles with increased power, colour and tonal range. These demanded new types of music on a vastly expanded scale. In line with the expansionist vision of the 19th century, the symphonic canvases of Schumann, Brahms, Bruckner and Mahler became

ABOVE: A typical Romantic seascape: Moonrise over the Sea, *by Caspar David Friedrich (1774–1840).*

ABOVE: An impression of Wotan from Wagner's massive operatic cycle Der Ring des Nibelungen *(1853–74).*

ABOVE: The Russian composer Nikolay Rimsky-Korsakov was the most prominent member of "The Mighty Handful". His nationalistic works include Voskresenaya *(*Russian Easter Festival Overture*) and the opera* Sadko, *a setting of Russian folk legends.*

ever more inflated; while Wagner's massive "music-dramas", culminating in the epic saga *Der Ring des Nibelungen*, first performed complete in 1876, pointed the way forward to the "music of the future".

Rise of nationalism

While Germany led the musical world in symphonic terms, composers such as Smetana and Dvořák in Bohemia, Glinka, Borodin and Rimsky-Korsakov in Russia, Grieg in Norway and Chopin in Poland were beginning to discover an individual musical culture by introducing the colourful inflections of their native folk music into standard musical genres. Liszt, the Hungarian composer and virtuoso pianist, tackled the symphony from a different angle, inventing the one-movement symphonic "tone-poem" (usually inspired by a poetic, artistic or literary idea); this form was later adopted by Richard Strauss.

For much of the 19th century, England languished as "the land without music" until it was rescued from oblivion on the one hand by the enchantingly witty "Savoy Operas" of Gilbert and Sullivan, and on the other by the genius of Edward Elgar, the first major British composer since Purcell. Italy, however, continued to consolidate its reputation as the operatic centre of the world, with masterpieces by Rossini, Donizetti, Bellini, Verdi and Puccini.

ABOVE: A poster advertising three operas by Gilbert and Sullivan – The Gondoliers, The Mikado *and* The Yeomen of the Guard *– produced by the D'Oyly Carte Opera Company.*

Dawn of a New Age

Music should not decorate, it should be truthful.

ARNOLD SCHOENBERG (1874–1951)

ABOVE: An example of Expressionist art – The Dream *by Franz Marc (1880–1916).*

The harmonic tonal framework established during the Baroque and Classical eras remained common musical currency until the turn of the 20th century, when the fluid, impressionistic style of the French composer Claude Debussy began to loosen the hold of tonality. At the same time, the German Expressionist composer Arnold Schoenberg was working independently on a completely new harmonic system, based on the principle of the equality of the 12 notes of the Western scale. Schoenberg's 12-note system, which destroyed the traditional ascendancy of traditional harmony, had many detractors, and he is still considered a "difficult" composer even today, but it had enormous influence on future composers, such as his followers Berg and Webern, and the French composers Boulez and Messiaen.

The innovations of both Debussy and Schoenberg, combined with the raw, exotic harmonies and rhythms of Russian folk music, melded in the works of Stravinsky, the dominant figure of 20th-century music. From his early scores for Diaghilev's Ballets Russes – *The Firebird, Petrushka* and *The Rite of Spring* – to the 12-note music written towards the end of his long life, Stravinsky produced a string of original masterpieces, constantly re-inventing his style to accommodate changing tastes. His compatriots Prokofiev and Shostakovich made significant contributions to 20th-century music – Prokofiev in the fields of ballet, opera and the concerto; Shostakovich most notably in his 15 symphonies and 15 string quartets.

Central Europe produced two other major 20th-century figures, both continuing their respective countries' nationalist traditions: the Hungarian Béla Bartók (who was not only a composer, but a major folk song collector), and the Czech Leoš Janáček, whose operas are now acclaimed as masterpieces.

Political events in Europe in the mid 20th century drove many fine composers (including Schoenberg and Bartók) into exile in America. But the USA had its own home-grown innovators: while Aaron Copland and Leonard Bernstein celebrated mainstream American culture in their hugely popular and accessible works, composers such as Charles Ives and John Cage experimented with new compositional techniques, ranging from aleatory music (which depends on chance) to polytonality (music played in different keys at the same time), and even to complete silence.

As new instruments, including electronic ones, have evolved, new systems of notation have developed to cope with them. In the final decade of the 20th century, many composers abandoned traditional methods of writing music with pen and paper in favour of computer-generated scores, enabling them to produce both scores and parts rapidly and efficiently.

Music of the Future

What we need is a music of the earth, everyday music...
music one can live in like a house.

JEAN COCTEAU (1889–1963), "LE COQ ET L'ARLEQUIN"

The dawn of the 21st century finds so-called "classical" music with many questions to answer. There is no longer any one "system" to follow: the forms and musical styles of previous generations, which formed the bedrock of every composer's vocabulary, have been discarded. Composers now have to either re-invent them, or find an entirely original voice. Some – Harrison Birtwistle, Peter Maxwell Davies, George Benjamin and Thomas Adès in Britain; Steve Reich and John Adams in the USA; Hans Werner Henze in Germany; Luciano Berio in Italy; Sofia Gubaidulina in Russia – are succeeding; others are now seen as derivative or of fringe interest only.

ABOVE: Composition 1999-style, using midi-keyboard and a computer.

Since the 1950s a chasm has opened between "serious" composers and their public. The vast majority of people listen to rock music and other popular forms, and regard classical music as an exclusive and élitist genre, of which they know nothing; while even lovers of classical music often find themselves bewildered by the new sounds produced by contemporary composers, and prefer the music of previous eras. But the 20th century certainly produced its fair share of composers whose music will endure and perhaps in time will become more popular, while young, exciting talents are still bursting on to the scene. And not all new music is inaccessible: as Schoenberg himself remarked, "There is still plenty of good music to be written in C major!"

ABOVE: The British composer Michael Nyman at a 1991 recording session in London.

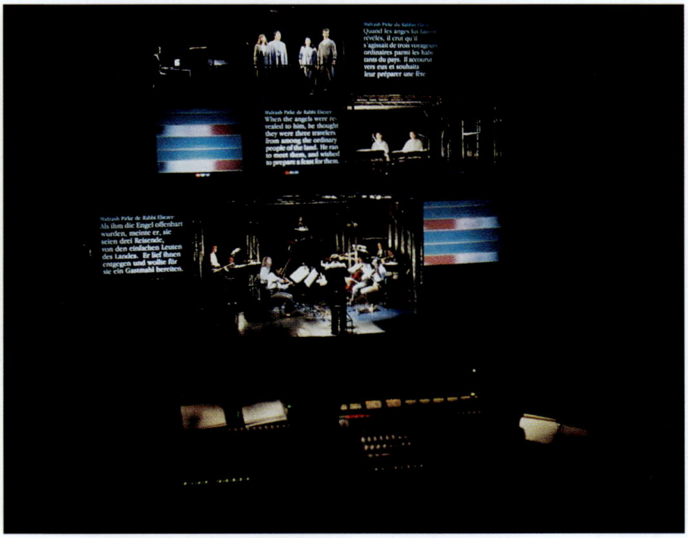

ABOVE: A scene from Steve Reich's music-theatre work The Cave *(1989–93). Reich's music has connections with pop and rock music, a factor that contributes to its popularity.*

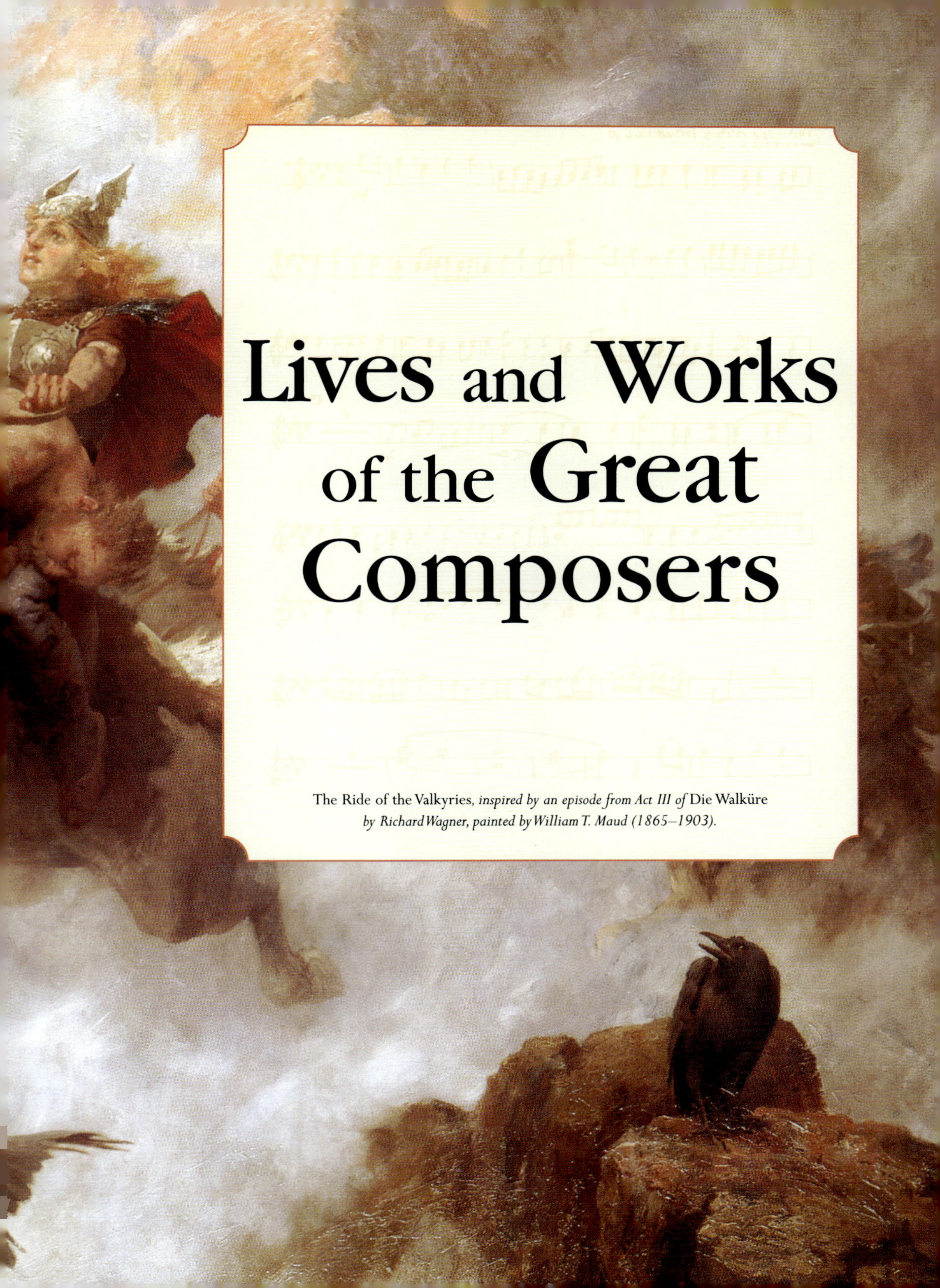

Lives and Works of the Great Composers

The Ride of the Valkyries, *inspired by an episode from Act III of* Die Walküre *by Richard Wagner, painted by William T. Maud (1865–1903).*

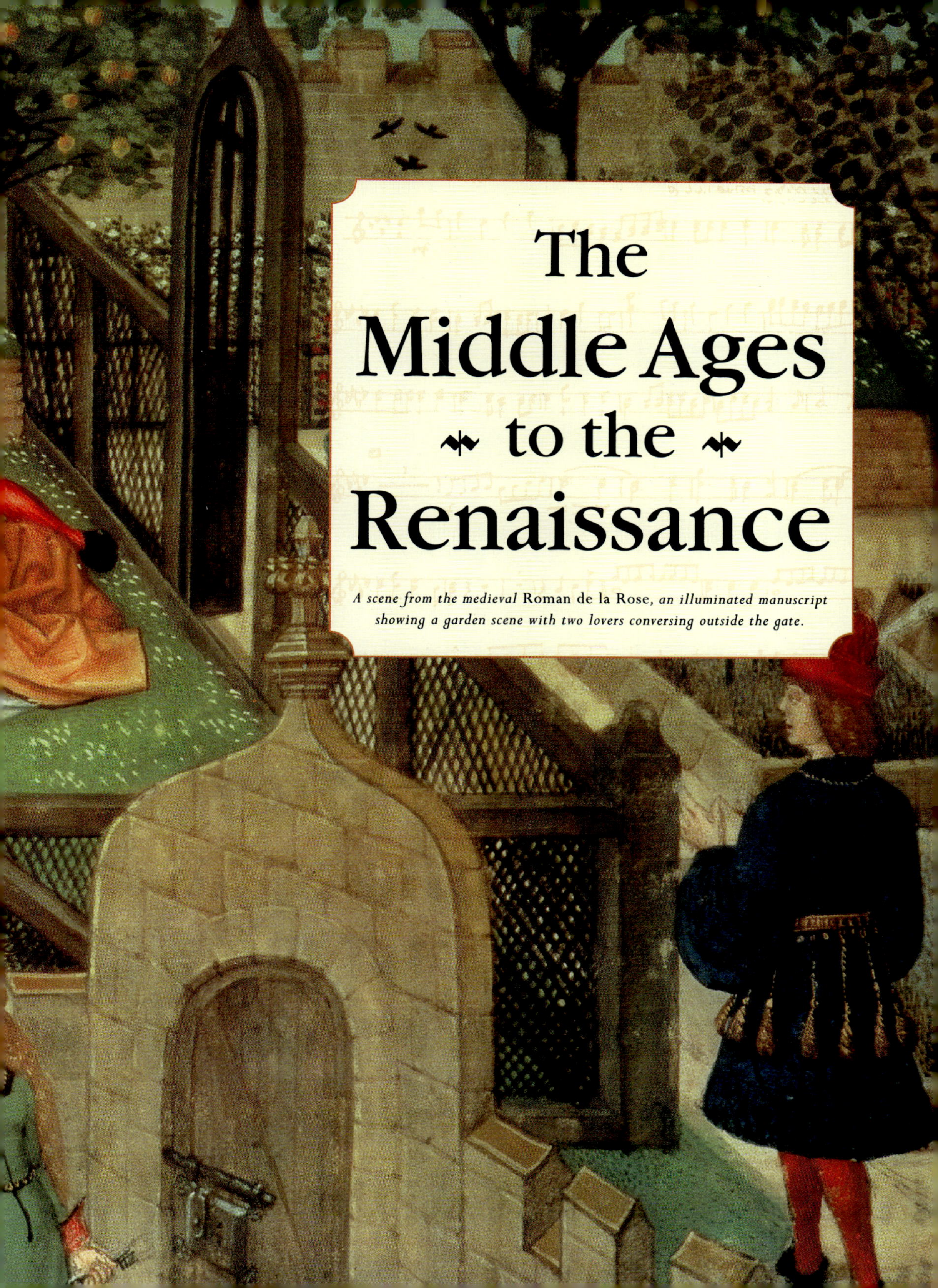

The Middle Ages to the Renaissance

A scene from the medieval Roman de la Rose, *an illuminated manuscript showing a garden scene with two lovers conversing outside the gate.*

Medieval and Polyphonic Music

The sound of the cornet, flute, harp, sackbut, psaltery, dulcimer, and all kinds of music.

Daniel, 3:3

Until the 20th century, there was a general perception that the history of music began with Bach. Only with the huge growth in musical research and scholarship, together with the explosion of the "early music movement" in the later decades of the 20th century, did many lost masterpieces of the medieval and Renaissance periods come to light, prompting a re-evaluation of their composers' achievements.

Sacred music

Music in the Middle Ages was largely the preserve of the church. Surviving medieval sources were mostly produced by monastic scribes, and kept in monastery libraries. While secular music existed, much of it was improvised, so the earliest music to survive was generally intended for sacred use.

ABOVE: A page from an illuminated Flemish medieval psalter dating from c.1470.

ABOVE: French church singers dating from the 14th century, the time of the innovative composer Guillaume de Machaut.

The names of individual composers become scarcer the further back into history we travel. Among the earliest musicians who may be singled out from the 12th and early 13th centuries are the French composers Léonin and Pérotin, who were associated with the newly built cathedral of Notre-Dame in Paris. A spate of enormously popular recordings has recently revealed the visionary music of the 12th-century nun Hildegard of Bingen, who not only has the distinction of being one of the earliest known composers, but was also a woman working in a field where women have traditionally not been prominent. She is now something of a feminist icon. Performances and recordings by early music groups have also uncovered a wealth of music by unnamed composers derived from medieval manuscript sources, such as the 13th-century Spanish *Cantigas* of Alfonso X.

Polyphony

The French composer Guillaume de Machaut was the single most important musical figure of the 14th century. His many innovations included being the first to compose a complete setting of the Ordinary of the Mass, the first to write music in four parts (which became the

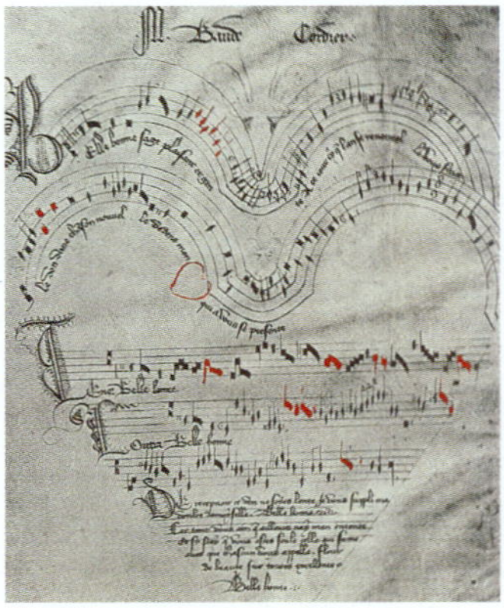

ABOVE: A heart-shaped score, in red and black ink, of a three-part French chanson Belle, bonne *by Baude Cordier (fl.1390s).*

ABOVE: An illumination from a 15th-century manuscript showing secular musicians playing a variety of instruments – crumhorn, fiddle, lute, bagpipes, nakers (drums) and triangle.

standard polyphonic combination), and one of the first to set the typical secular poetic forms of his day: *ballade*, *rondeau* and *virelay*.

For the next century, the musical centres of gravity remained the courts and churches of northern France and Flanders, which produced the sacred and secular works of the Flemish composers associated with the court of the dukes of Burgundy: Dufay, Ockeghem, Josquin des Prez and their contemporaries. However, many drew inspiration from prolonged visits to Italy, where musical activity flourished at important courts such as those of Ferrara and Mantua.

The harmonious exercises in perspective of Renaissance architects such as Filippo Brunelleschi (1377–1446), evident in Florentine churches such as San Lorenzo and Santo Spirito, or the wonderful ducal palace at Urbino, found a musical counterpart in Renaissance polyphony. Music, too, acquired new depth and perspective. While three Flemish composers had dominated the 15th century, the polyphonic art of the High Renaissance was perfected by a trio of musicians – Palestrina from Italy, Lassus from Flanders, and Victoria from Spain – who all spent long periods in Italy.

The polyphonic principle continued to dominate 16th-century music, from the Masses and motets written for performance in the great Catholic churches of France, Italy, Spain and southern Germany, to the equivalent settings of both Catholic and Protestant liturgies by the English composers Tallis and Byrd, and the enchanting secular partsongs of the Elizabethan madrigal school. Meanwhile the plangent songs and solo lute music of Dowland looked forward to a new age of individualism.

ABOVE: The nave and choir of the church of Santo Spirito in Florence, designed by Filippo Brunelleschi in the mid 15th century. This church is a classic Renaissance masterpiece of perspective.

Hildegard of Bingen

A feather on the breath of God.

HILDEGARD

This remarkable woman was one of the earliest known composers. A contemporary of the famous medieval lovers Abélard and Héloïse, who also ended their lives in monastic institutions, Hildegard was born into a noble German family. As the tenth child she was considered a tithe and therefore due to the church, and was dedicated to religious service. When she was eight years old, she was sent as a novice to the Benedictine monastery of Disibodenberg.

ABOVE: A modern plaque in the German town of Bingen commemorating its famous Abbess, Hildegard of Bingen.

In 1136 Hildegard became an abbess in her own right, and around the age of 50 she founded a nunnery near Bingen in the Rhine Valley. She died at the advanced age of 81, and her name was put forward by several popes as a candidate for canonization. Though never formally canonized, she is often referred to as a saint, and has a feast-day which is particularly celebrated in Germany.

ABOVE: An illustrated 13th-century manuscript depicting The Vision of St Hildegard, *compiled 50 years after her death in 1179.*

Mysticism and music

Hildegard was a visionary, and soon gained a widespread reputation as a prophetess. Popes, emperors, monarchs, archbishops and clergymen of all kinds flocked to Bingen to consult this "Sybil of the Rhine". Between 1141 and 1170 she recorded her mystical experiences; she also wrote two important works on natural history and medicine, and a great deal of lyric and dramatic poetry, collected together in a volume called *Symphonia armonie celestium revelationum*.

Most of her poetry is liturgical, including antiphons, sequences and hymns designed for performance on the feast-days of particular saints. Among her work is the earliest known surviving morality play, *Ordo virtutum*, which describes the 16 Virtues battling with the Devil for a human soul. This and many of her poems have music attached, written in German neumatic notation. Unlike much music of this period, Hildegard's melodies are not drawn from monastic plainsong, but are strikingly original, and sometimes highly complex and decorative.

Many of her works have been performed and recorded during the recent revival of interest in early music: the album released under the title *A Feather on the Breath of God* (1984) has enjoyed huge popularity.

Life and works

NATIONALITY: German

BORN: Böckelheim, 1098; **DIED:** Bingen, 1179

SPECIALIST GENRES: Plainsong settings of her own poetry.

MAJOR WORK: *Ordo virtutum*; *Symphonia armonie celestium revelationum*.

The Notre-Dame School

Who could retain a grievance against the man
with whom he had joined in singing before God?

St Ambrose (c.339–97)

Léonin and Pérotin – sometimes referred to as Master Leoninus and Master Perotinus – were the best-known of a group of composers who worked in medieval Paris in the late 12th and early 13th centuries. This was the age of King Philippe-Auguste (Philippe II), during whose reign, from 1180 to 1223, the medieval kingdom of France was consolidated. Little is known of the lives of Léonin and Pérotin, but both are associated with the cathedral of Notre-Dame de Paris, whose foundations were laid in the mid 1160s, and its high altar consecrated in 1182.

ABOVE: An initial letter from an illuminated French psalter dating from the 13th century – the time of Léonin and Pérotin.

Léonin

The major work attributed to Léonin was the *Magnus liber* ("great book") designed for use by the choir of the new cathedral. He is mentioned by an anonymous 13th-century theorist as "the best composer of organum for the amplification of divine service", suggesting that he wrote polyphonic settings for two independent voices of parts of the liturgy intended for performance on the main feast-days of the church's year. Léonin may also have been among the first to indicate rhythm as well as pitch in his musical notation. His vocal writing was imaginative, free-flowing and improvisatory in style.

Lives and works

Nationality: French

Active: Léonin, c.1163–90; Pérotin, c.1200

Specialist genres: Early polyphonic sacred music.

Major works: *Magnus liber*, motets and graduals.

Pérotin

Some time after Léonin's death, Pérotin, who may have been his pupil, seems to have revised and shortened the *Magnus liber*. Pérotin remains a shadowy figure. He may have been born around 1160, and died some time between 1205 and 1225. Some scholars have suggested that he may have worked at the royal parish church of St Germain-l'Auxerrois, near the Tuileries Palace, since there is no direct evidence that he worked at Notre-Dame.

Pérotin was active in the creation of the four-voice motet, an ecclesiastical musical form which survives to the present day. His contribution towards the development of three- and four-voice polyphony was one of the most important steps forward in musical history. Of his works, two graduals in four voices for the Christmas season survive, as do about a dozen liturgical works in three voices, and about 160 *clausulae* – polyphonic passages written for insertion into liturgical plainsong to vary the texture.

ABOVE: A view of medieval Paris showing the cathedral of Notre-Dame, where Léonin and Pérotin worked, from the 15th-century Book of Hours of Etienne Chevalier.

Guillaume de Machaut

...the morning star of song, who made
his music heard below.

ALFRED, LORD TENNYSON (1809–92), "A DREAM OF FAIR WOMEN"

A near contemporary of Geoffrey Chaucer (c.1340–1400), whose poetry he influenced, Guillaume de Machaut was one of the most important composers of the 14th century. Not only did he compose more than anyone else of his period, but his works are enormously varied in style and form.

He seems to have spent much of his life in Rheims, in northern France, where he died. He entered the service of John, King of Bohemia, around 1323, and in the manner of a courtier of the time, travelled around Europe in the royal retinue until the king was killed at the Battle of Crécy in 1346. Meanwhile, however, John's patronage had enabled Machaut to procure several lucrative canonries at major northern French cathedrals. After John's death, Machaut continued to serve the French nobility, including the future King Charles V (for whose coronation he composed a Mass) and John, Duke of Berry.

ABOVE: A contemporary portrait of Guillaume de Machaut (1300–77), one of the earliest surviving portraits of a composer.

Ars nova

Machaut's output is equally divided between sacred and secular music. His most famous piece is the *Notre-Dame Mass*, and he wrote over 20 motets, but also a large quantity of secular songs – ballades, rondeaux and virelays, which were the principal vocal types of the time. His works are representative of the French *ars nova*, or new style, and are often very rhythmically complex.

ABOVE: A joust, watched by ladies. Many of Machaut's songs dealt with courtly love.

Life and works

NATIONALITY: French

BORN: Machaut, c.1300; **DIED:** Rheims, 1377

SPECIALIST GENRES: Sacred and secular vocal music of the *ars nova*.

MAJOR WORKS: *Notre-Dame Mass*; motets; secular songs.

ABOVE: The score of a Machaut motet, an example of the 14th-century ars nova *style.*

Guillaume Dufay

L'homme armé doibt on doubter. (Fear the armed man.)

ANONYMOUS, 15TH-CENTURY FOLK SONG

The pre-eminence of northern France and Flanders in the development of compositional technique continued into the 15th century, in the person of Guillaume Dufay. Born near Brussels around the turn of the century, the illegitimate son of a priest, he became a choirboy at Cambrai Cathedral and, around 1420, he entered the service of the powerful Italian Malatesta family. He seems to have returned from Italy to hold posts in several churches in and around Cambrai in the mid 1420s, but in 1428 he became a singer in the papal choir in Rome. While in Italy, he evidently worked for several other noble families, including the Este family of Ferrara and the dukes of Savoy. He returned north to Cambrai around 1436, when he became a canon at the cathedral, but he maintained his ties with Italy, spending seven years in Savoy in the 1450s. He died at Cambrai and was buried in a chapel in the cathedral.

ABOVE: Guillaume Dufay depicted in a French manuscript dating from 1440 called Le champion des dames.

Cantus firmus

Dufay was the most celebrated composer of his time: other budding composers flocked to Cambrai to seek his advice. His surviving compositions – about 200 in all – show his absolute mastery of the major forms of his time, together with an attractive and fluent talent for melody. Many of his works are harmonizations of liturgical chants, but eight complete Masses survive, along with Mass fragments, hymns, antiphons and motets. Many of his works are based on a *cantus firmus* – either a plainsong melody or a popular secular tune, such as the folk song *L'homme armé* (*The Armed Man*), on which Dufay based his most famous Mass. (The same tune was used in this way by many other composers of the 15th, 16th and 17th centuries.) Dufay also wrote over 80 songs – probably for his Italian patrons – for voices accompanied by instruments. He was apparently the first to write a Requiem Mass, completed just four years before his own death, but the manuscript of this work has been lost.

Life and works

NATIONALITY: Flemish

BORN: near Brussels, 1397; **DIED:** Cambrai, 1474

SPECIALIST GENRES: Polyphonic sacred and secular forms.

MAJOR WORKS: Motets; Masses; songs.

ABOVE: A Dance of the Shepherds *depicted in a 15th-century Book of Hours (of Charles d'Angoulême), now held in the Bibliothèque Nationale in Paris.*

Johannes Ockeghem

He alone of all singers is free from all vice and abounds in all virtues.

FRANCESCO FLORI (DIED 1588)

Among the composers who visited Dufay at Cambrai was the Franco-Flemish composer Johannes (or Jean d') Ockeghem, then aged around 50, and destined to succeed Dufay as the most celebrated composer of his period.

Ockeghem's early life, and even his birthplace and date, are shrouded in obscurity. The earliest mention of him is as a singer at Notre-Dame in Antwerp in 1443; shortly afterwards he entered the service of Charles I, Duke of Bourbon, at Moulins in France. In the early 1450s he was employed by Charles VII of France as a chaplain, and probably remained in the royal service until his death. He died at an advanced age in Tours, where he had been for many years, and by royal appointment, treasurer of St Martin's Church. He appears to have been admired as much for the kindness and generosity of his character as for the "extraordinary sweetness and beauty" of his music, and his death was mourned in flowery verbal and musical tributes from fellow musicians and poets.

ABOVE: Johannes Ockeghem directing a choir of monks in the Gloria of one of his Masses.

ABOVE: Ockeghem's last royal patron, Charles VIII of France (reigned 1477–98). He had worked for three French kings.

Contrapuntal innovation

Relatively few of Ockeghem's compositions have survived, among them 14 Masses, a polyphonic Requiem Mass (which is the earliest surviving example), nine motets and a handful of secular chansons. His Masses are the most important of their time. The earlier ones are based, like Dufay's, on an existing melody, either sacred or secular; but the later ones are more experimental. Instead of keeping the *cantus firmus* in the tenor part, Ockeghem shares it between the voices, producing a texture of great contrapuntal complexity. He was also the first composer known to have used the melodies of his own songs as the *cantus firmus* of a Mass setting (a technique known as "parody mass", used in his Masses *Fors seulement*, *Au travail suis* and *Ma maistresse*). Several of his works, notably the *Missa prolationum*, do not rely on a *cantus firmus*, but are freely constructed from an intricate combination of rhythmic and melodic fragments.

Life and works

NATIONALITY: Flemish

BORN: ?Dender, c.1410; **DIED:** Tours, 1497

SPECIALIST GENRES: Polyphonic sacred works.

MAJOR WORKS: 14 Masses.

Josquin des Prez

Josquin is master of the notes; others are mastered by them.

MARTIN LUTHER (1483–1546)

Among the tributes paid to Ockeghem was the beautiful elegy *Nymphes des bois*, written by the final member of the great 15th-century trio of Franco-Flemish composers. Josquin des Prez, who may have been Ockeghem's pupil, can lay claim to being the finest composer of the High Renaissance. Possibly born in Picardy, he may have begun his career as a choirboy in the collegiate church at St Quentin, but then went to Milan, where he sang in the cathedral choir and also worked for the Sforza family.

In the late 1480s he was a member of the papal choir. Around 1500 he was working both for the French court and for the dukes of Ferrara, but when plague broke out in Ferrara in 1503 he fled north, becoming provost of the church of Notre-Dame in Condé. He died there in August 1521 and was commemorated by a flood of verbal and musical homages. Josquin's fame as a composer during his lifetime is attested by three individual publications of his Masses in the early 1500s by the Venetian printer Petrucci. Publications devoted to the works of one composer were extremely rare at the time.

ABOVE: A woodcut of Josquin des Prez (c.1440–1521).

Matching music to words

Like Mozart some three centuries later, Josquin took the common musical currency of his time and refined it into pure gold. He was one of the first composers to relate his music closely to the text: his word-setting is infinitely sensitive, dramatic and highly expressive, while his use of complex musical techniques is handled in a masterly but unobtrusive way. His early Masses were based on *cantus firmus* techniques, but the later ones, such as *Ave Maris Stella*, *L'homme armé* and *Pange lingua*, use a variety of unifying devices including parody technique and motto themes.

Life and works

NATIONALITY: Flemish

BORN: ?Picardy, c.1440; **DIED:** Condé, 1521

SPECIALIST GENRES: Polyphonic sacred works and secular songs.

MAJOR WORKS: 19 Masses, including *Pange lingua* and *De beata virgine.*

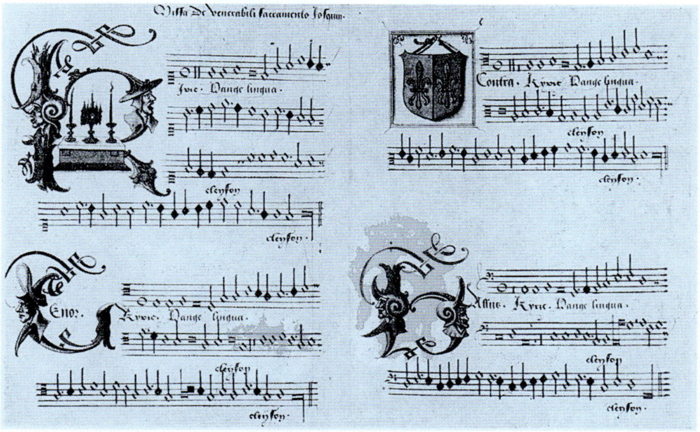

ABOVE: A page from a 16th-century missal showing part of Josquin's Mass Pange lingua *(*Sing, my tongue*).*

Giovanni Pierluigi da Palestrina

The most frivolous and gallant words are set to exactly the same music as those of the Bible… the truth is that he could not write any other kind of music.

HECTOR BERLIOZ (1803–69), "MEMOIRS"

Palestrina's name has become synonymous with textbook perfection in the field of harmony and counterpoint, and his reputation long outlived him. He began his career in Rome as organist and choir-master.

In 1552, under the patronage of his former bishop, now Pope Julius III, Palestrina became choir-master at the Julian Chapel, the training school for the Sistine Choir. After three years he was dismissed by a new pope because he was married, but in the same year he succeeded Lassus as choir-master of the church of St John Lateran. He resigned after a dispute over money matters in 1560, and returned to S. Maria Maggiore, but during the last two decades of his life he worked once more at the Julian Chapel.

In the 1570s Palestrina lost his brother, two of his sons, and finally his wife in plague epidemics, which led him to consider entering the priesthood. However, in 1581, just eight months after his first wife's death, he married a wealthy widow, who assured his financial security.

ABOVE: A contemporary painting of Giovanni Pierluigi da Palestrina, who worked mostly in Rome.

ABOVE: An artist's impression of Palestrina at work, composing one of his many Masses.

Masses and motets

Palestrina worked against the background of the Counter-Reformation. The Council of Trent had initiated ecclesiastical reforms, which decreed that sacred music should be kept simple so that the words could be heard clearly. Elaborate polyphony and the extensive use of instrumental accompaniment was discouraged. Palestrina's Masses and motets are all constructed with an ear to clarity of textual declamation: the vocal lines flow freely and the intertwining parts create their own beauty, enhancing rather than obscuring the meaning of the words.

Over 100 of Palestrina's Masses survive, including the famous *Missa Papae Marcelli*, together with about 375 motets for between four and 12 voices and many other liturgical works, including Magnificat and Lamentation settings. However, as his career demonstrates, he achieved a balance between the sacred and the secular. While much of his music was written to the glory of God, some is based on secular models; and his many published collections include two books of madrigals.

Life and works

NATIONALITY: Italian

BORN: Palestrina, c.1525; **DIED:** Rome, 1594

SPECIALIST GENRES: Polyphonic sacred music.

MAJOR WORKS: *Missa Papae Marcelli* (1567); *Missa Assumpta est Maria* (1567); *Missa brevis* (1570); Stabat Mater (1590).

Orlande de Lassus

Orlandissimo Lassissimo amorevolissimo.

LASSUS'S SIGNATURE ON A LETTER TO DUKE WILHELM V, c.1575

The Flemish composer Orlande de Lassus (sometimes known by the Italian form of his name, Orlando di Lasso) was a contemporary of Palestrina: they died in the same year. Lassus spent his early years travelling in Sicily and Italy attached to the households of various Italian nobles. His earliest collections of compositions – madrigals, songs and motets – were published in Antwerp and Venice when he was in his early 20s, and in 1556 he joined the court of Duke Albrecht V of Bavaria in Munich, as a singer in the ducal chapel.

ABOVE: The Flemish composer Orlande de Lassus (c.1532–94), painted in 1580 by Johann von Achen.

Court music

By 1563 Lassus had risen to become the duke's *maestro di cappella*, a position he held until his death. His duties included providing sacred music for the chapel's services, and secular music for the court's entertainment on occasions such as state visits, banquets and hunting parties. In 1569 he provided the music for the sumptuous festivities surrounding the marriage of Duke Wilhelm V of Bavaria to Renée of Lorraine. Lassus continued to travel widely, particularly in France and Italy, but his base remained Munich for the last 34 years of his life, towards the end of which he suffered from depression and became preoccupied with sacred works. Two of his sons became musicians. His own fame had spread far and wide, and he was one of the most respected and prolific composers of his time. About 2000 of his compositions survive.

His supreme mastery of the art of polyphony is demonstrated in his Masses, motets, settings of the Passions and other liturgical works, including the fine *Psalmi Davidis poenitentiales* (*Seven Penitential Psalms of David*) published in 1584 but written around 1563. He was equally skilled in the lighter, more lyrical style, exemplified in his Italianate madrigals and French chansons.

Life and works

NATIONALITY: Flemish

BORN: Mons, c.1532;
DIED: Munich, 1594

SPECIALIST GENRES: Polyphonic sacred and lyrical secular music.

MAJOR WORKS: *Psalmi Davidis poenitentiales* (1584); "Tristis est anima mea" (1568); "Adoremus te, Christe" (1604) and many other motets.

ABOVE: The Royal Chapel in Munich, c.1565, where Lassus worked as maestro di cappella. *He is the bearded figure dressed in yellow.*

Tomás Luis de Victoria

...in solemn beauty like slow old tunes of Spain.

John Masefield (1878–1967)

Victoria (also known as Tommaso Ludovico da Vittoria) stands beside Palestrina and Lassus as one of the finest composers of the 16th century. He was born into a distinguished family in Ávila, where he was a choirboy at the cathedral (one of his uncles was a canon there), and attended a highly regarded Jesuit school. In 1563 he was sent to the Jesuit Collegio Germanico in Rome, where he may have studied composition with Palestrina. Eight years later he himself became a music teacher there, finally leaving in early 1577, by which time he had been ordained as a priest. He took up a chaplaincy at San Girolamo della Carità, but also drew income from five benefices back in Spain, granted to him by Pope Gregory XIII.

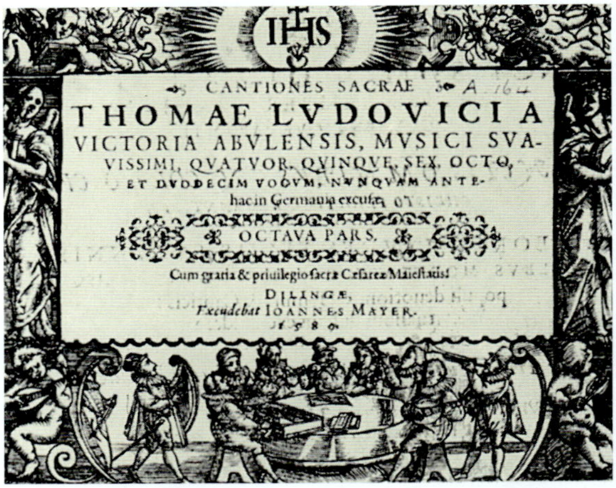
IHS

CANTIONES SACRAE

THOMAE LVDOVICI A VICTORIA ABVLENSIS, MVSICI SVAVISSIMI, QVATVOR, QVINQVE, SEX, OCTO, ET DVODECIM VOCVM, NVNQVAM ANTEhac in Germania excusæ.

OCTAVA PARS.

Cum gratia & priuilegio sacræ Cæsareæ Maiestatis.

DILINGÆ, Excudebat IOANNES MAYER.

1589

ABOVE: The title page of a book of Tomás Luis de Victoria's motets, published in 1589 as Cantiones sacrae *(Sacred Songs).*

Madrid

In the early 1580s Victoria decided that he wanted to return to Spain, and King Philip II appointed him chaplain to his sister, the Dowager Empress Maria, at the Madrid convent where she lived. Victoria served the empress from 1587 until her death in 1603, and subsequently remained at the convent until his own death, refusing many tempting offers from other Spanish cathedrals. From 1592–5 he revisited Rome to supervise the printing of a book of Masses, and also attended Palestrina's funeral.

Though Victoria wrote only sacred music, as befitted his priestly vocation, his works are far from solemn, revealing a naturally sunny disposition. His 20 Masses were all published in his lifetime: many of them are based on his own motets, antiphons and psalms, while the *Missa pro victoria* is a battle Mass based on a popular French chanson called *La guerre* (*The War*). There are also 16 extant Magnificat settings, many other shorter liturgical works, and a much-admired sequence of music for Holy Week, including nine expressive Lamentations.

ABOVE: King Philip II of Spain (1527–98), painted c.1575.

Life and works

Nationality: Spanish

Born: Ávila, c.1548; **died:** Madrid, 1611

Specialist genres: Richly polyphonic sacred works.

Major work: Requiem Mass for the Dowager Empress Maria (1603); 20 Masses; 16 Magnificats.

Thomas Tallis

As he did live, so also did he die,
In mild and quiet sort (O! happy man)
TALLIS'S EPITAPH

During his long and productive lifetime, the English composer Thomas Tallis served four monarchs: Henry VIII, Edward VI, Mary Tudor and Elizabeth I. Though born a Catholic, he managed to survive an extremely dangerous age of religious upheaval and persecution, mainly by adapting his musical style to suit the circumstances, and by keeping a low personal profile.

ABOVE: Thomas Tallis shared with Byrd the right to print music and music paper.

Royal monopoly

Probably a native of Kent, Tallis's first recorded post was as organist of the Benedictine Priory in Dover. He then joined the choir of Waltham Abbey, near London, around 1538. The Abbey was dissolved in 1540, during Henry VIII's reign, and Tallis became a lay clerk at Canterbury Cathedral. From around 1543 until his death he shared the position of organist and composer to the Chapel Royal with his pupil, William Byrd.

In 1575 Tallis and Byrd received a patent from Elizabeth I granting them a 21-year monopoly on printing music and music paper in England. Their first publication was a joint collection of 34 *Cantiones sacrae* (sacred songs) in five and six parts.

Textual clarity

Tallis is chiefly remembered for his church music, setting text in both Latin and English, depending on the prevailing religious climate. One notable feature of his style was a move away from florid, elaborate counterpoint towards simpler, syllabic declamation in which the text could be clearly heard: in this respect he was pointing the way forward to the Baroque era.

His mastery of contrapuntal techniques is amply demonstrated in his breathtaking 40-part motet *Spem in alium*, which opens in 20-part imitation. The hymn tune known as "Tallis's Canon" (later set as a hymn tune to the words "Glory to thee, my God, this night") was written for Archbishop Parker's *Metrical Psalter* of 1567, and another tune was used by Vaughan Williams as the basis for his *Fantasia on a Theme of Thomas Tallis* (1910).

LEFT: Queen Elizabeth I, by George Gower (1540–96). During the Elizabethan period (1558–1603) Tallis wrote his later works, such as the Whitsuntide anthem O Lord give Thy Holy Spirit.

Life and works

NATIONALITY: English

BORN: ?Kent, c.1505; **DIED:** Greenwich, 1585

SPECIALIST GENRES: Polyphonic motets in Latin and English.

MAJOR WORKS: Motet *Spem in alium* (c.1570); *Lamentations of Jeremiah; Cantiones sacrae.*

William Byrd

How daintily this Byrd his notes doth vary,
As if he were the Nightingale's own brother.
ANONYMOUS, FROM THE PREFACE TO "PARTHENIA", 1613

Apart from Tallis, the other giant of 16th-century English music was his pupil, William Byrd. In 1563, aged about 20, Byrd was appointed organist and master of the choristers at Lincoln Cathedral. He married in 1568 and had several children. In 1570 he became a Gentleman of the Chapel Royal in London, while also making the acquaintance of various powerful nobles, to whom he dedicated compositions.

ABOVE: William Byrd was a Catholic composer who managed to survive persecution at the time of Elizabeth I.

Catholicism

His noble patrons undoubtedly helped to protect Byrd through difficult times, when he became known as a Roman Catholic recusant and continued to risk prosecution by writing Masses for undercover use by prominent Catholic families. His three fine Latin Masses, in four, three and five parts respectively, were published openly in the 1590s, but after his publication between 1605–10 of the *Gradualia* (a huge collection of music for use with the Catholic liturgy), possession of the volume became a criminal offence.

ABOVE: A magnificently inlaid virginal, once owned by Queen Elizabeth I. Byrd wrote a great deal of virginal music.

Songs and instrumental music

Between 1588 and 1611, Byrd published three collections of *Psalmes, Songs and Sonnets*, miscellaneous collections of English anthems, secular partsongs, madrigals and pieces for viol consort. His instrumental music was particularly fine: he was a master of the art of consort music (particularly fantasias for viols), and of keyboard music, especially the pavans and galliards so much loved by Queen Elizabeth I and her court. His keyboard music appeared in various collections intended for aristocratic use, including the *Fitzwilliam Virginal Book, My Lady Nevell's Book* and *Parthenia*, a printed collection issued in 1613 jointly with John Bull (1563–1628) and Orlando Gibbons (1583–1625).

Byrd's later years were spent at an Essex mansion, where he died. His Latin church music lay forgotten until the mid 19th century, although his Anglican anthems remained constantly popular. His madrigals and lively keyboard music were rediscovered in the early 20th century. At least two of the English madrigalists were his pupils, and his influence on English music was profound.

Life and works

NATIONALITY: English

BORN: ?Lincoln, c.1543; **DIED:** Stonden Massey, Essex, 1623

SPECIALIST GENRES: Sacred music, songs, madrigals, keyboard works, consort pieces for viols.

MAJOR WORKS: Masses, three Latin and one English; *Cantiones sacrae* (1575); 140 keyboard pieces, including *The Queenes Alman* and *Wolsey's Wilde*.

Carlo Gesualdo

...music oft hath such a charm
To make bad good, and good provoke to harm.

WILLIAM SHAKESPEARE (1564–1616), "MEASURE FOR MEASURE"

Gesualdo, Prince of Venosa, occupies a unique place in the history of music: he was both a composer (albeit an amateur one) and a murderer. He came of an aristocratic Neapolitan family: his mother was a niece of Pope Pius IV and the sister of a prominent cardinal, and his uncle was Archbishop of Naples – a potent and dangerous brew of religion and politics which characterized the highest levels of contemporary Italian society.

Scandal

In 1586, after the death of his elder brother left Gesualdo heir to the family title, he married his beautiful cousin Maria d'Avalos, daughter of the Marquis of Pescara. Four years later he caught his wife with her aristocratic lover and had them both stabbed to death. The double murder caused a storm of protest, and Gesualdo retired to his country estates, and devoted himself to composition.

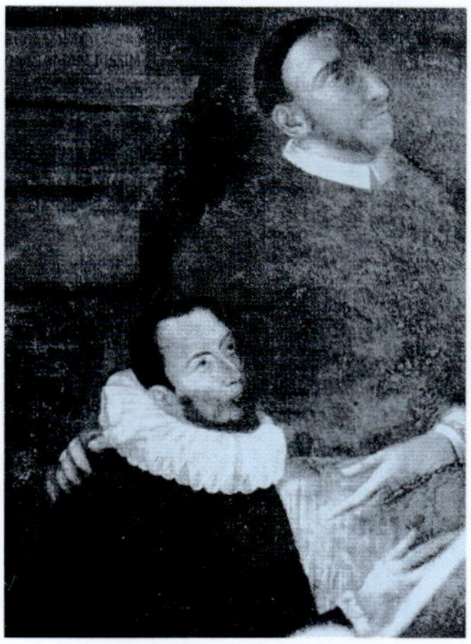

ABOVE: Carlo Gesualdo, Prince of Venosa (kneeling), with his uncle, Carlo Borromeo, Archbishop of Naples.

In 1594 he visited Ferrara, where he married Leonora d'Este, the niece of Alfonso, Duke of Ferrara. This second marriage also proved unsuccessful. Leonora soon tired of her gloomy husband's introspective and melancholy nature, and after their only son died in childhood, Gesualdo increasingly withdrew from the world. He died on the edge of madness, a lonely and embittered man.

Harmony and dissonance

Gesualdo's place in musical history is assured by his six collections of madrigals. Many of these illustrate dolorous texts (containing many references to pain, death and sorrow) with extraordinarily advanced chromatic harmony – perhaps reflecting his tortured mental state. Four centuries later, Gesualdo's love of dissonant harmony excited the interest of Stravinsky; but he had little immediate influence, being seen as an extreme example of the "mannerist" style in music. Nevertheless, he is one of the composers who bridged the divide between Renaissance and Baroque.

Life and works

NATIONALITY: Italian

BORN: Naples, c.1560; **DIED:** Naples, 1613

SPECIALIST GENRES: Secular vocal music.

MAJOR WORKS: Six books of madrigals.

ABOVE: A painting showing the view of the shoreline at Naples, by Gaspar van Wittel (1653–1736), now in the Palazzo Pitti in Florence.

English Madrigal School

He would sing of her with falls
Used in lovely madrigals.

ELIZABETH BARRETT BROWNING (1806–61), "A PORTRAIT"

The madrigal – a setting of a (usually secular) text for several voices – developed in Italy towards the end of the 13th century, but flowered some 300 years later in the hands of both Flemish and Italian composers, including Gesualdo and Luca Marenzio (1553–99). During the reign of Elizabeth I (1558–1603) this immensely popular form was imported to England by Italian composers working at the English court. The publication in 1588 of the Italian collection *Musica transalpina* inspired native composers to follow the Italian example.

Thomas Morley

Among these was Byrd's pupil, Thomas Morley (1557–1602), who may have been a friend of Shakespeare (his famous setting of "It was a Lover and his Lass" was probably written for the original production of *As You Like It* in 1599). In 1601 Morley edited *The Triumphs of Oriana*, a celebrated anthology of madrigals by the best composers of the time in honour of the Queen, to which he himself contributed "Arise, Awake" and "Hard by a Crystal Fountain".

ABOVE: An English masque at the time of Elizabeth I, with musicians playing lute, viols, gittern and flute, and singing madrigals.

Thomas Weelkes

Morley's friend Thomas Weelkes (c.1576–1623) was another contributor to the same anthology (with the madrigal "As Vesta was from Latmos Hill Descending"). He was an organist and composer, who published three books of madrigals between 1597 and 1600. His accomplished compositions include "O Care, Thou Wilt Despatch Me", "Thule, the Period of Cosmography" and "Like Two Proud Armies", as well as some fine church music.

John Wilbye

Wilbye (1574–1638) published two madrigal collections in 1598 and 1614; he is regarded as one of the greatest exponents of the genre. His madrigals include the powerfully expressive "Draw on, Sweet Night", "Sweet Honey-sucking Bees" and "Weep, Weep, Mine Eyes".

ABOVE: One of John Dowland's songs, from The First Booke of Songes or Ayres of Foure Partes, *with tablature for the lute (1597).*

John Dowland

At the same time, the solo song with lute accompaniment was coming into its own in England. Dowland (c.1563–1626), its finest exponent, was the royal lutenist to the court of James I. Among his greatest works are the affecting songs "Flow my Tears", "Sweet, Stay Awhile" and "In Darkness Let Me Dwell", together with his 1604 collection of lute pieces *Lachrimae* (*Tears*).

Other Composers of the Era

Modern church music is so constructed that
the congregation cannot hear one distinct word.

DESIDERIUS ERASMUS (1466–1536)

Many composers made outstanding contributions to the development and vitality of polyphonic music during this period. Notable for his chansons and motets, Gilles Binchois (c.1400–60) was organist at Mons Cathedral, and a member of the Burgundian court chapel from 1430. He may also have served as a soldier, fighting with the occupying English army at the time of Joan of Arc. His death was lamented in works by both Ockeghem and Dufay (in a rondeau – a form much cultivated by Binchois). His secular songs embody the courtly tradition of the time, and his sacred music represents a consolidation of the Burgundian style.

ABOVE: Gilles Binchois (right) with his great contemporary and fellow composer Guillaume Dufay, c.1440.

Binchois's contemporary, John Dunstable (c.1390–1453), was the leading English composer of his time. Also an astrologer and mathematician, Dunstable travelled widely in Europe in the service of his aristocratic patrons, and enjoyed an international reputation. He was a master of isorhythmic technique, and his Masses and motets greatly influenced Dufay.

ABOVE: The English Agincourt Song, *celebrating Henry V's victory at Agincourt (1415), dating from the time of Dunstable.*

The 15th-century Flemish composer Jacob Obrecht (c.1451–1505) divided his time between the Netherlands and Ferrara, where he died of the plague. He often used secular tunes as the basis for his Masses and motets (a technique he bequeathed to Josquin des Prez), and was one of the first known composers to employ number symbolism in his music.

Antiphony

Another Flemish-born composer, Adriaan Willaert (c.1490–1562), played a significant role in the transition between Renaissance and Baroque styles. One of the earliest madrigal composers, he became choir-master at St Mark's in Venice in 1527, where he established the principle of writing antiphonal music for double choirs, a form well suited to the special acoustic properties of the Byzantine-style basilica.

Willaert's work greatly influenced Giovanni Gabrieli (1557–1612), who became organist at St Mark's in 1585, inheriting the post from his uncle Andrea (c.1510–86), who had been Willaert's pupil. Giovanni initiated the tradition of writing Venetian motets with instrumental accompaniment. He perfected antiphonal technique both in his motets and his purely instrumental music. The first set of his *Sacrae symphoniae*, 1597, contains the famous *Sonata pian' e forte* for groups of brass instruments.

ABOVE: The Flemish composer Adriaan Willaert, who served as music director at St Mark's Cathedral, Venice, for over 30 years.

The Baroque Era

A concert given to the Procurators of Venice by the girls of an 18th-century Venetian orphanage. Vivaldi taught at such an institution.

Harmony and Ornament

Architecture in general is frozen music.

FRIEDRICH VON SCHELLING (1775–1854)

ABOVE: Baroque flamboyance at its height – the interior of St Peter's Basilica in Rome in 1730.

The term "Baroque", which is derived from *barroco*, the Portuguese word for a misshapen pearl, was originally used – in a pejorative sense – to describe the flamboyant, ornate architecture found in German, Austrian and Italian churches of the 17th century, which were designed as a reaction to the cool classicism of Renaissance architecture. One of the most prominent Baroque architects was the Italian sculptor Gianlorenzo Bernini (1598–1680), who worked principally in Rome. His work exhibits the fluid, dynamic shapes, theatricality and illusion that characterize the style.

In music, the Baroque period covers the years from c.1600–1750, during which Renaissance polyphony gave way to a new, highly ornamental style with a strong harmonic basis. Most Baroque music – from operatic arias to *concerti grossi* for groups of instruments – was supported by a *basso continuo*, a firm bass line played on keyboard and reinforced on cello or bass, which provided a harmonic foundation.

ABOVE: An opera theatre in Munich, Germany, in 1665.

Opera

The Baroque period saw the introduction of several new forms, mostly developed in Italy. In the late 16th century, a group of poets and musicians formed an association in Florence called the Camerata, and several of their members – the poet Ottavio Rinuccini (1562–1621) and the composers Jacopo Peri (1561–1633) and Giulio Caccini (c.1550–1618) – collaborated to produce the earliest music-dramas, or operas. The new form was taken up and transformed by the genius of Claudio Monteverdi, whose three surviving operas are the earliest still to be regularly performed today.

Opera spread like wildfire, with demand coming not only from aristocratic patrons, but also from newly opened public opera houses. Monteverdi's pioneering work was carried on by composers such as Vivaldi and Alessandro Scarlatti in Italy, Hasse in Germany, Lully, Charpentier and Rameau in France, and the German-born Handel in England. Alongside secular operas (usually based on plots derived from ancient history or mythology), a similar sacred form – oratorio – developed, using the same forms and styles as opera, but based on biblical stories. Oratorio flourished both in the Catholic South and the

ABOVE: A realistic depiction of an 18th-century private concert against an allegorical background, one of a set of four Fine Arts designs by Giuseppe Zocchi (1711–67).

Protestant North, where Heinrich Schütz pioneered it in Germany, paving the way for the great sacred works of J. S. Bach. It reached its apogee in the works of Handel, written in English, of which *Messiah* has been the most frequently performed.

Instrumental forms

The Baroque period also saw a huge demand for instrumental music, particularly concertos, *concerti grossi*, sonatas and suites, and almost all major composers worked in these new forms. Again, they flourished in Italy in the hands of Corelli, Vivaldi and Alessandro Scarlatti, but were equally popular in Germany. Bach's *Brandenburg Concertos* and Handel's sets of *concerti grossi* brought the genre to its peak, while the solo concerto and solo sonata underwent further metamorphosis in the Classical era. Meanwhile Alessandro Scarlatti's son Domenico, an exact contemporary of Bach and Handel, defied convention by removing to the Portuguese and Spanish courts, where he developed his own highly individual form of keyboard sonata.

Bach and Handel

In musical terms, the Baroque era reached its height in the works of Bach and Handel. Both were reared in the German Protestant tradition, but their careers took very different paths.

Bach concentrated on church music, whether for voices and instruments (in the form of the church cantata, a kind of unstaged mini-drama performed during the Sunday services), or for instruments alone (particularly solo organ). His Passion settings brought a German tradition to its peak, and his monumental Mass in B minor took the form to an unprecedented level.

Handel flourished in a more cosmopolitan environment, first in Italy and then in England, where he stepped neatly into the void left by the early death of Henry Purcell. Handel's many Italian operas, written for London theatres, have recently resumed their place in the repertoire, while his English oratorios have always been a well-loved feature of the British choral tradition.

ABOVE: The Rehearsal, *with viols, flute, oboe and voice, by Etienne Jeaurat (1699–1789).*

Claudio Monteverdi

Claudio Monteverdi, in moving the affections…
becomes the most pleasant tyrant of human minds.

AQUILINO COPPINI, 1608

Monteverdi was a composer of enormous significance in the history of music. Like his contemporary Heinrich Schütz in Germany, he bridged the worlds of the High Renaissance and the Baroque era. He can also be compared to Stravinsky: during the course of long lives both men showed an endless capacity to re-invent and adapt their musical styles according to changing tastes.

ABOVE: Claudio Monteverdi (1567–1643), painted around 1640 by Bernardo Strozzi.

Early years

Monteverdi began his career as a chorister at the cathedral in his birthplace, Cremona. By the age of 16 – already a fine instrumentalist – he had published a volume of three-part motets and a book of sacred madrigals. In 1587 he published his first volume of secular madrigals, followed by a second volume in 1590. Around that time he found a job as a string player at the ducal court in Mantua, and by the time his third madrigal collection appeared in 1592 his fame as a composer was spreading rapidly. He married in 1599 and had three children, of whom two sons survived: the elder became a musician, the younger a doctor.

Triumph and tragedy

In 1601 Monteverdi became *maestro di cappella* at the Mantuan court, where he published two more madrigal collections over the next four years. In 1607 he made his first foray into the new genre of opera with *L'Orfeo*, which was performed in Mantua in February. Seven months later his wife died after a long illness, leaving Monteverdi a grief-stricken widower with two small children.

He was obliged to pull himself together enough to finish his second opera, *L'Arianna*, which was performed in May 1608 to celebrate the marriage of the Gonzaga heir, Francesco, to Margaret of Savoy. (Only one aria from this opera has survived.) During rehearsals another tragedy struck when Caterina Martinelli, the young principal singer and a close friend of Monteverdi, died of smallpox. Monteverdi then suffered a complete collapse, although his glorious setting for voices and instruments of the *Vespro della beata vergine* (*Vespers of the Blessed Virgin*, 1610) dates from this unhappy period.

ABOVE: The interior of the Teatro Olimpico in Vicenza, designed by Andrea Palladio (1508–80).

Venice

After making several attempts to leave the service of the Gonzagas, Monteverdi was finally dismissed in

Life and works

Nationality: Italian

Born: Cremona, 1567; **died:** Venice, 1643

Specialist genres: Opera, madrigals, motets.

Major works: Nine books of madrigals; *Vespro della beata vergine* (1610); *La favola d'Orfeo* (1607); *Il ritorno d'Ulisse in patria* (1640); *L'incoronazione di Poppea* (1642).

ABOVE: A scene from a 1975 production of Monteverdi's L'incoronazione di Poppea *(1642), shortly after its re-introduction to modern audiences.*

1612, and in 1613 became *maestro di cappella* at St Mark's Cathedral in Venice, where he remained for the rest of his life. He also continued to write ballets and operas for the Mantuan court, but many of his scores were destroyed when Austrian troops sacked the palace in 1630. In the same year Venice was ravaged by plague, and shortly afterwards Monteverdi renounced the world and took holy orders.

In 1637, after the first public opera house opened in Venice, he was commissioned to write several operas. The two that survive – *Il ritorno d'Ulisse in patria* (*The Return of Ulysses*) and *L'incoronazione di Poppea* (*The Coronation of Poppea*) – are masterpieces of the genre in their superb characterization and instinctive feel for dramatic effect. The final scene of *L'incoronazione di Poppea*, despite celebrating the union of two ambitious and deeply unpleasant people, contains one of the most intensely passionate love duets in all opera.

The works of Monteverdi's Venetian years include three more madrigal collections. Book 8 of 1638, entitled *Madrigali guerrieri et amorosi* (*Songs of War and Love*), contains substantial dramatic works such as *Il ballo delle ingrate*, and the famous *Combattimento di Tancredi e Clorinda*, a graphic description of a duel between the Christian knight Tancred and the pagan Clorinda, who is disguised as a man. As a whole, the madrigal collections show Monteverdi moving with the times, from typically Renaissance polyphonic pieces in the earlier volumes (one of the most beautiful and frequently performed of these is the five-voice *Zefiro torna*, a setting of words by Petrarch), to highly expressive dramatic works for solo voices with instrumental accompaniment in the later ones. All his music, early or late, is characterized by qualities of emotional intensity, depth of expression and understanding of human nature comparable with those that inform the works of Shakespeare.

ABOVE: The sinfonia da guerra *(*Battle Sinfonia*) from the score of Monteverdi's* Il ritorno d'Ulisse in patria *(1640).*

MONTEVERDE * CLAVDIO

FIORI POETICI
Raccolti nel Funerale
DEL MOLTO ILLVSTRE;
E Molto Reuerendo
SIGNOR CLAVDIO
Monte verde
Maestro di Cappella della Ducale di S. Marco.
Consecrati
DA D. GIO: BATTISTA
Marinoni, detto Gioue:
Maestro di Cappella del Domo di Padoua
ALL' ILLVSTRSSIMI
& Eccellentissimi
SIG. PROCVRATORI
Di Chiesa di S. Marco.

In VENETIA, Presso Francesco Miloco.
Con Lic. de Sup. MDCXLIV.

ABOVE: The title page of a collection of poetical tributes in commemoration of Monteverdi's death, published in 1644.

Heinrich Schütz

The most spiritual musician the world has ever seen.

ALFRED EINSTEIN (1880–1952)

The achievements of J. S. Bach would not have been possible without the ground-breaking work of his illustrious predecessor, Heinrich Schütz. Born into a middle-class family of innkeepers in Saxony, Schütz became the most esteemed German composer of the 17th century. During two prolonged visits to Italy – the first, made while he was still a law student, enabling him to study in Venice with Giovanni Gabrieli – Schütz absorbed the Italian style, which he then amalgamated with the very different musical tradition of his native Germany.

ABOVE: A portrait of Heinrich Schütz (1585–1672), by his contemporary Christoph Spetner.

Dresden *Kapellmeister*

On his return from Italy in 1613 after Gabrieli's death, Schütz became organist and then *Kapellmeister* at the electoral court in Dresden, the most important musical centre in Protestant Germany. He published his first important compositions in 1619. These were a collection of settings for voices (some with instrumental interludes in the Venetian style) of the Psalms of David, described as "various motets and concertos". In the same year he married Magdalena Wildeck, daughter of a court official. Their happy union, which produced two daughters, was tragically brief: Magdalena died in 1625, and the grief-stricken composer never remarried. He outlived both his children: the elder died at the age of 16, and the younger in 1655, aged 31.

Schütz's court duties included writing music for official events, such as weddings and funerals. For the wedding of the elector's daughter to the Landgrave of Hessen-Darmstadt in 1627, he wrote the first German opera, setting the same libretto (*Dafne*) which the Italian composer Jacopo Peri had set 30 years earlier. Unfortunately the music has not survived.

ABOVE: Schütz's birthplace in Bad Köstritz, Germany. The building is now a museum devoted to the composer.

In 1628 Schütz paid a second visit to Italy, where he met Monteverdi. This contact with recent musical developments bore fruit in a second published collection of vocal and instrumental music, *Symphoniae sacrae*. But there were troubles at home: Germany had entered the Thirty Years

War, and the Elector of Dresden found himself unable to pay his employees. Schütz escaped for two years to the court of the Crown Prince of Denmark, for whose wedding festivities he provided elaborate musical entertainments. But despite constant financial problems, he remained in the service of the Dresden court (apart from two more visits to Denmark) until 1657, when he was pensioned off. After his retirement he continued to write works for the electoral chapel until his death at the age of 87.

ABOVE: Gondolas moored near the Rialto Bridge in Venice, where Schütz studied with Giovanni Gabrieli.

Schütz's music

Although Schütz was an enormously prolific composer, many of his manuscripts were destroyed by fire or the ravages of war. Even so, some 500 works survive. *Die Geburt unsers Herren Jesu Christi* (*The History of the Birth of Jesus Christ*), performed at Christmas Vespers at the Dresden court in 1660, is the earliest known German setting of the Nativity story in which the words of the Evangelist – or Narrator – are sung in recitative, rather than chanted as in earlier settings. His settings of the four Passions, together with innumerable psalm and motet settings and Italianate madrigals, influenced later composers such as Bach. Although Schütz's music fell out of fashion fairly rapidly, it was rediscovered in the 20th century, and championed by performers such as Roger Norrington in Britain, who founded first the amateur Heinrich Schütz Choir in 1962, and then the professional Schütz Choir of London.

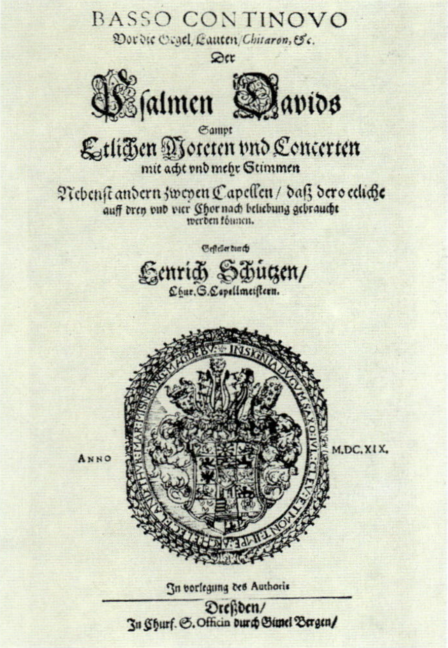

BASSO CONTINOVO
Vor die Orgel, Lauten, *Chitaron*, &c.
Der
Psalmen Davids
Sampt
Etlichen Moteten und Concerten
mit acht und mehr Stimmen
Nebenst andern zweyen Capellen / daß dero etliche auff drey und vier Chor nach beliebung gebraucht werden können.
Gestellet durch
Henrich Schützen/
Chur. S. Capellmeistern.
ANNO M.DC.XIX.
In vorlegung des Authoris
Dreßden/
In Churf. S. Officin durch Gimel Bergen/

ABOVE: The title page of Schütz's Psalmen Davids, *settings of the Psalms for voices and instruments published in 1619.*

Life and works

NATIONALITY: German

BORN: Köstritz, 1585; **DIED:** Dresden, 1672

SPECIALIST GENRES: Sacred vocal and instrumental music, including oratorios and Passions.

MAJOR WORKS: *Psalmen Davids* (1619); *Cantiones sacrae* (1625); opera *Dafne* (1627); *Symphoniae sacrae* (1629, 1647, 1650); *Sieben Worte Jesu Christi am Kreuz* (*Seven Words of Christ on the Cross*, 1645); Christmas Oratorio (1660); Passions according to Matthew, Mark, Luke and John (1664–6).

Jean-Baptiste Lully

The musician is to follow the poet's direction, only in my opinion, Lully is to be exempted, who knows the passions and enters further into the heart of man than the authors themselves.

SEIGNEUR DE SAINT-EVREMOND (1610–1703)

The founder of French opera owed his success partly to his exceptional talent, and partly to his ruthless, ambitious nature – only Wagner has rivalled Lully in sheer single-mindedness of purpose and grandiose vision. His career mirrored that of his patron, the "Sun King" Louis XIV (1643–1715), perhaps the greatest European monarch of his age, who saw his own glory reflected in the sumptuous entertainments devised by his clever court composer.

King and composer enjoyed a close, symbiotic relationship: indeed Lully's death, in 1687 at the age of only 55, marked the zenith of the Sun King's reign. Thereafter it was a long, slow story of royal decline, marked by personal misfortunes and military defeats.

ABOVE: Louis XIV's court composer, Jean-Baptiste Lully (1632–87).

The ambitious page

The son of a humble Florentine miller, Lully's singing voice was spotted at the age of 13 and he was taken to Paris and employed as a pageboy to a distant member of the royal family. Having perfected his own talents for dancing and playing the violin, he applied himself to social climbing, and quickly got his first royal appointment. His job was to write music for the lavish court ballets, and to drill the orchestra which accompanied them, the *Vingt-quatre violons du roi*. He soon established himself as a strict disciplinarian with a quick temper – later in life, as director of the opera house in Paris, he allegedly punched his pregnant leading lady in the stomach, causing her to miscarry, rather than jeopardize his productions.

ABOVE: The courtyard of Louis XIV's palace at Versailles, the envy of many other European monarchs. Many of Lully's court ballets and comedy-ballets were performed here.

ABOVE: A 17th-century engraving of Lully in his role as director of the royal orchestra.

Life and works

Nationality: Italian

Born: Florence, 1632;
died: Paris, 1687

Specialist genres: Court ballets, comedy-ballets, opera.

Major works: 36 court ballets; 14 *comédies-ballets,* including *Les fâcheux* (1661) and *Le bourgeois gentilhomme* (1670); 16 *tragédies-lyriques*, including *Alceste* (1674), *Atys* (1676), *Amadis* (1684), *Roland* (1685) and *Armide* (1686).

ABOVE: An original stage design by Jean Berain for Lully's tragédie-lyrique, Armide, *first performed at the Académie Royale de Musique in Paris in 1686.*

Lully's ruthless nature suited his purposes well. He made an expedient marriage in order to disguise his homosexuality – a predilection which the king (a great lover of women) abhorred – and consolidated his position at court by choosing as his bride the daughter of the court composer, Michael Lambert. Meanwhile he cultivated the playwright Molière (1622–73), with whom he collaborated on several *comédies-ballets* (a hybrid form – half play, half ballet) for the entertainment of the court. The most famous of these was *Le bourgeois gentilhomme* (1670).

Opera at Versailles and Paris

Lully's next move, in 1672, was to take advantage of the bankruptcy of a fellow musician who had obtained a royal licence to import Italian opera. Lully seized the licence for himself, and while continuing to supply music for lavish court entertainments at the magnificent new palace of Versailles, he established a virtual monopoly over operatic productions, opening his own opera house in a disused tennis court in Paris. The following year he turned his old friend Molière's troupe of actors out of their centrally sited theatre in the Palais Royal, and took it over, with the king's permission, rent-free.

Over the next 14 years, Lully and the poet Philippe Quinault (1635–88) produced a succession of brilliant operas in an entirely new and original style. These "lyric tragedies" were based on subjects drawn from mythology and legend (such as *Isis*, *Thésée*, *Phaëton* and *Armide*), worked into plots which subtly flattered Louis XIV – his victories, his devotion to duty and his personal concept of glory. Audiences of the time loved them – as did the king. Lully had struck gold, and made a huge fortune.

ABOVE: A costume design for a character in Armide, *regarded as Lully's masterpiece.*

A bizarre end

Lully's court position required him to compose sacred music for the royal chapel, and while conducting a Te Deum written to celebrate Louis XIV's recovery from illness, he accidentally struck his foot with the heavy stick he used to mark the beat by banging it on the floor. Gangrene set in, but Lully refused to have the toe amputated.

As he lay dying, he was visited by a priest. In a final dramatic gesture to mark his penitence, Lully threw his last opera manuscript on to the fire, and received absolution. After the priest had gone, a horrified friend asked Lully why he had wantonly destroyed his last great work. "Don't worry," whispered the dying man, "I've got another copy!"

Arcangelo Corelli

I never met with any man that suffered his passions to hurry him away so much whilst he was playing on the violin as the famous Arcangelo Corelli, whose eyes will sometimes turn as red as fire.

FRANÇOIS RAGUENET (C.1660–1722)

While 17th-century German composers were bringing the art of organ-playing to a peak of perfection, Italy remained pre-eminent for nurturing the art of the violin. With the products of an unsurpassed school of instrument-makers – the Amati and Guarneri families, Stradivari, Gasparò da Salo and Maggini – at their disposal, Italian performers could hardly fail to establish a European reputation as masters of their art. One of the most influential of these – both in terms of violin technique and musical style – was Arcangelo Corelli.

Success as a performer

Corelli came from Fusignano, a town between Bologna and Ravenna. He took music lessons from a priest in nearby Faenza, and in 1666 arrived in Bologna, where he studied the violin with several fine players. By 1675 he had made his professional debut in Rome where, over the next few years, he established himself as a brilliant performer, taking part in the elaborate church performances commissioned by Rome's decadent but artistically inclined prelates, and in secular performances at the theatres. In 1679 he became chamber musician to the exiled Queen Christina of Sweden, to whom he dedicated his first compositions, a set of 12 *sonate da chiesa*.

Before long, the ambitious violinist had decided to replace his patron with a more influential one: Cardinal Pamphili, one of the richest men in Rome. From 1684 onwards Corelli began to play regularly at musical events organized by Pamphili, while introducing his own works – including a set of chamber trios

ABOVE: Arcangelo Corelli, probably painted by the Flemish artist Jan Frans van Douven around 1700.

LEFT: A highly romanticized impression (1913) of the violin maker Antonio Stradivari in his workshop at Cremona, by Edgar Bundy (1862–1922).

RIGHT: The Hellier *Stradivarius, made in 1679.*

VIOLINO PRIMO.

SONATE

A trè, doi Violini, e Violone, ò Arcileuto, col Basso per l'Organo,

CONSECRATE

ALLA SACRA REAL MAESTA'

DI

CRISTINA ALESSANDRA

REGINA DI SVEZIA, &c.

DA ARCANGELO CORELLI DA FVSIGNANO,

Detto il Bologneſe.

OPERA PRIMA.

IN ROMA, Per il Mascardi. 1685. Con Licenza de' Superiori.

ABOVE: The title page of Corelli's Op. 1 trio sonatas, published in 1685 with a dedication to Queen Christina of Sweden.

dedicated to Pamphili – at the musical academies held on Sunday afternoons at the cardinal's sumptuous palazzo. His social climbing bore fruit, and in July 1687 he was formally engaged as the cardinal's music master, and given a suite of rooms in the palace.

Orchestral compositions

In 1690 Pamphili moved to Bologna, but Corelli declined to follow him. Instead, he was engaged by a rival cardinal, the young Pietro Ottoboni, nephew of Pope Alexander VIII, another ostentatious patron of the arts. Corelli and Ottoboni became good friends, and Corelli dedicated a second set of chamber trios to him in 1694. He also began to write orchestral works (sinfonias and concertos), which attracted much attention. He was described as "the famous violinist...the Orpheus of our time," whose works were "prized and esteemed".

In 1702, however, his self-esteem was shaken when he visited Naples to play in the opera orchestra, taking with him two Roman players since he distrusted the abilities of the Neapolitans. To his surprise, he found that the despised southerners could actually play quite well, while he himself had embarrassing difficulty with a particular passage that his hosts managed fluently.

In 1707 Corelli met Handel (who was working in Rome), and played in a performance of an early Handel oratorio. Shortly afterwards he retired from playing to devote himself to composition. His health deteriorated, and he died early in 1713. He was buried in the Pantheon. His reputation both as performer and composer long outlived him: his compositions were reprinted many times and sold all over Europe. They were particularly popular in England and Germany, where they influenced many later composers, including Handel, Telemann and Bach.

Life and works

NATIONALITY: Italian

BORN: Fusignano, 1653; **DIED:** Rome, 1713

SPECIALIST GENRES: Violin music, sinfonias, concertos.

MAJOR WORKS: Four sets of 12 trio sonatas; 12 solo sonatas; 12 *concerti grossi*.

ABOVE: Queen Christina holding court. She is talking with the French philosopher René Descartes (painting by Dumesnil the Younger, 1698–1781).

Henry Purcell

Mr Purcell, in whose person we have at length found an Englishman equal with the best abroad.

JOHN DRYDEN (1631–1700)

Unlike some European countries, which enjoyed a strong and continuing musical tradition from the Renaissance onwards, England – while strong on literature – has suffered from a distinctly patchy musical heritage. After the Elizabethan flowering, only a few distinctive figures emerged in the early 17th century – notably the Lawes brothers, Henry (1596–1662) and William (1602–45), and later John Blow (1649–1708); but England produced no composer of European stature until the brilliant but tragically short-lived Henry Purcell.

Occasional music

Purcell began his career as a chorister in the Chapel Royal; in 1679 he succeeded Blow as organist of Westminster Abbey. He seems to have married around 1680, and had several children, of whom a son and a daughter survived him. In 1682 he was appointed an organist of the Chapel Royal, and a year later became organ-maker and keeper of the king's instruments.

His court appointments were renewed after Charles II's death, and he continued to produce many odes and welcome songs (cantata-like compositions) for occasions such as royal birthdays, marriages and New Year's Day. Most of these "occasional" works are now among the least known of his output, but the 1692 Ode for St Cecilia's Day, *Hail, Bright Cecilia*, is one of his best-loved works.

ABOVE: A 19th-century lithograph of Henry Purcell by Alfred Lemoine (1824–81).

LEFT: William III (1650–1702) and his wife Mary II (1662–94), who reigned jointly as King and Queen of England from 1689.

Life and works

NATIONALITY: English

BORN: London, 1659; **DIED:** London, 1695

SPECIALIST GENRES: Opera and incidental music for the stage, odes, anthems, instrumental music.

MAJOR WORKS: *Dido and Aeneas* (1689); *King Arthur* (1691); *The Fairy Queen* (1692); *Hail, Bright Cecilia* (1692); *Come, Ye Sons of Art* (1694); Te Deum and Jubilate in D (1694); Funeral music for Queen Mary (1695).

LEFT: The opening of Purcell's Golden Sonata *for two violins and* basso continuo.

RIGHT: The frontispiece to the text of Purcell's 1683 Ode to St Cecilia, Welcome to all the pleasures.

A

Musical Entertainment

PERFORM'D

On NOVEMBER XXII. 1683.

IT BEING THE

Festival of St. CECILIA, *a great Patroness of* Music;

WHOSE

MEMORY is ANNUALLY honour'd by a public *Feast* made on that Day by the MASTERS and LOVERS of Music, as well in *England* as in Foreign Parts.

LONDON,

Printed by *J. Playford* Junior, and are to be sold by *John Playford* near the *Temple* Church, and *John Carr* at the *Middle-Temple* Gate, 1684.

Stage works

During the last decade of his life, Purcell combined his court duties with writing music for the stage. Opera as such did not exist in England at the time, but between 1690 and 1695 Purcell provided incidental music for five major "semi-operas" put on at London theatres: Betterton's *Dioclesian, King Arthur* and *The Indian Queen* (with texts by John Dryden), *The Fairy Queen* and *The Tempest* (both loosely based on Shakespeare).

Purcell's most famous stage work, however, is the opera *Dido and Aeneas*, long thought to have been written around 1689 for a girls' school in Chelsea, but possibly dating from several years earlier. He also provided individual musical items for over 40 other plays by the most notable playwrights of the time. The Rondeau from his music for Aphra Behn's 1695 play *Abdelazer* was used by Benjamin Britten as the theme of his *Young Person's Guide to the Orchestra* (1946).

Purcell's legacy

Apart from his dramatic music, Purcell wrote many exquisite anthems, a Magnificat and a Te Deum, a vast number of solo songs and partsongs (some with extremely bawdy texts which have only recently been permitted to surface), instrumental music including fantasias for viol consort, a set of 12 trio sonatas for two violins and continuo, a set of 10 sonatas "in four parts", clearly influenced by Corelli, and some charming keyboard music, including eight suites. Among his last works was the moving Funeral Music for Queen Mary, written for the young and much-mourned queen: within a short while Purcell had followed her to the grave at the age of only 36. The music he had written for the queen was played at his own funeral.

Purcell's genius lay in his unique response to the setting of English words, whether sacred or secular, his gift for appealing melody, his assimilation of elements from both Italian and French music – notably Corelli's violin writing, and Lully's unusual effects (the "Frost Scene" from *King Arthur*, in which each note is sung with a shiver, was borrowed from a similar scene in Lully's opera *Isis*) – and his forward-looking treatment of the orchestra, particularly the strings.

Though regarded as a "one-off" genius, the end of a tradition rather than an initiator, Purcell is still held in high esteem. *Dido and Aeneas* is often performed, and in the last decade of the 20th century, particularly during the tercentenary celebration of his death, most of his music was made widely available through high-quality performances and recordings.

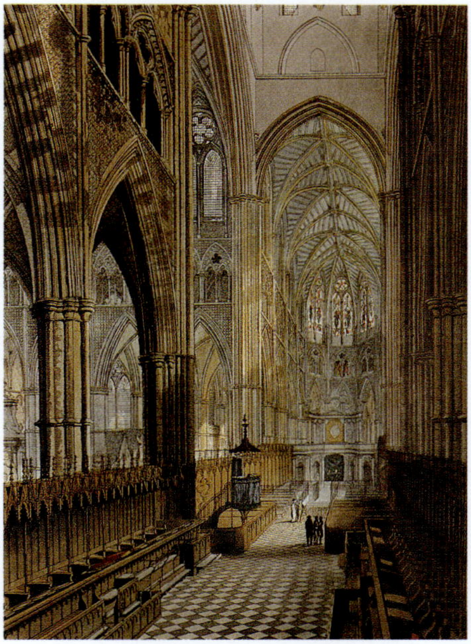

ABOVE: The choir of Westminster Abbey, where Purcell was buried at the foot of the organ.

Antonio Vivaldi

He is an old man, who has a prodigious fury for composition. I heard him undertake to compose a concerto, with all the parts, with greater despatch than a copyist can copy it.

CHARLES DE BROSSES, 1739

For many people, the name Vivaldi is associated with just one piece of music – *Le quattro stagioni* (*The Four Seasons*) – which has been recorded countless times. But many other gems of Vivaldi's output are worth exploring: he was one of the most prolific and influential composers of his time, and without his contribution to the development of concerto form, the instrumental music of later composers such as Bach would have been the poorer.

ABOVE: The violinist and composer Antonio Vivaldi (1678–1741), painted in 1723 by François Morellon La Cave.

The Red Priest

Vivaldi was born (during a minor earthquake) in Venice, to a baker turned professional violinist, with whom the young Antonio studied. In 1693 he began to train for the priesthood, while still living at home and continuing his violin studies. He was ordained in 1703, and his startling red hair earned him the nickname of *il prete rosso* (the Red Priest), but the ecclesiastical life did not entirely suit him, and several times he found himself at odds with the church authorities.

In the year of his ordination, Vivaldi was appointed violin teacher at the Conservatorio dell'Ospedale della Pietà, a Venetian orphanage which housed and educated young girls. Music was held in high esteem there, and its reputation was such that many leading performers took part in its concerts. Vivaldi was required to teach and rehearse the students and to maintain the instruments. His initial appointment lasted six years, during which time he published a set of 12 trio *sonate da camera* and a set of solo violin sonatas. He had already begun to write concertos, which became his favourite medium.

ABOVE: Vivaldi's family home on the Fondamenta del Dose in Venice.

Vivaldi's concertos

In all Vivaldi wrote well over 200 violin concertos, around 27 cello concertos, around a dozen for flute, three for

ABOVE: A page from the cello part of Vivaldi's collection of concertos L'estro armonico.

piccolo, 20 for oboe, 37 for bassoon (an instrument for which few other composers have written concertos), and many more double and multiple concertos, of which the E minor concerto for four violins, Op. 3 No. 4, is very well known.

The fanciful titles of some of his concertos gave Vivaldi plenty of opportunity for descriptive writing. As well as the famous *Four Seasons*, programmatically depicting seasonal activities such as skating on the ice (winter), hunting (autumn), and listening to birdsong (spring), their titles include *La tempestà di mare* (*Storm at Sea*), *L'amoroso* (*The Lover*), *La caccia* (*The Hunt*) and *Il corneto di posta* (*The Posthorn*).

A set of 12 concertos for one, two or four solo violins was published in Amsterdam in 1711 under the title *L'estro armonico*, and instantly sold all over Europe (Bach made keyboard transcriptions of five of them). Another set of 12 *(La stravaganza)* appeared in 1714, and from then on Vivaldi's music was much in demand (the collection

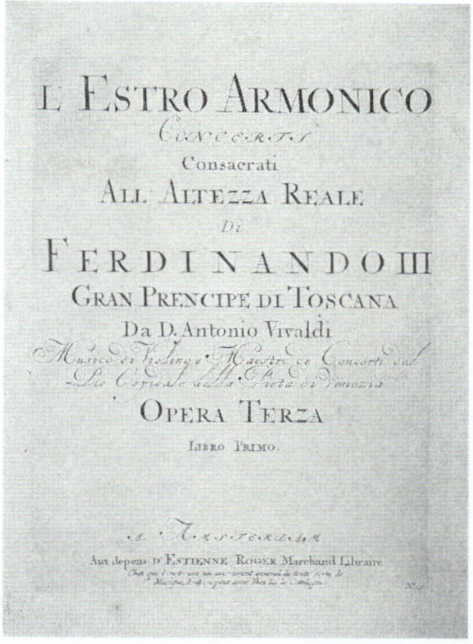
L' ESTRO ARMONICO
Concerti
Consacrati
ALL' ALTEZZA REALE
Di
FERDINANDO III
GRAN PRENCIPE DI TOSCANA
Da D. Antonio Vivaldi
OPERA TERZA
LIBRO PRIMO
Aux depens D'ESTIENNE ROGER Marchand Libraire

ABOVE: The title page of Vivaldi's L'estro armonico, *published 1711 with a dedication to the Grand Duke of Tuscany.*

containing *The Four Seasons* was published in 1725). He also wrote around 60 *concerti grossi* for strings and bass.

In 1711 Vivaldi returned to the Pietà, where he took the opportunity to write sacred as well as instrumental music. His cheerful *Gloria* is still much performed today. He was associated with the institution until his death, although his frequent absences were not popular. He also began to write operas (about 45 in all) for various Italian courts and opera houses, including Mantua, Venice and Rome. Several have recently been revived, although interest still tends to be academic.

Fall from grace

Vivaldi spent much of the last two decades of his life on the move. Around 1725 he became involved with his singing pupil, Anna Giraud. The church authorities cannot have been pleased with the whiff of scandal surrounding the "Red Priest" and in 1737 he was censured for unpriestly conduct. In 1741 Vivaldi undertook a mysterious journey to Vienna (perhaps connected with Anna's work as an opera singer). He arrived on 28 June, and a month later he was dead, apparently of unknown causes. His arrogance and egotism had made many enemies, but his posthumous influence was immense.

Life and works

NATIONALITY: Italian

BORN: Venice, 1678; **DIED:** Vienna, 1741

SPECIALIST GENRES: Instrumental music, especially violin concertos.

MAJOR WORKS: Over 400 concertos published in sets, including *L'estro armonico* (1711); *Il cimento dell'armonia e dell'inventione* (1725 – 12 concertos of which the first four are *Le quattro stagioni*).

ABOVE: The Piazza San Marco in Venice, painted in 1723 during Vivaldi's lifetime by the Italian artist Canaletto.

Johann Pachelbel

A perfect and rare virtuoso.

Daniel Eberlin (1647–c.1715)

Johann Pachelbel, an important predecessor of J. S. Bach, is remembered today chiefly for a single composition, known as "Pachelbel's Canon" (of which many versions – including rock – now exist). But in his day he was much admired for his contribution to German Protestant church music, particularly for the organ.

Born in Nuremberg, he began his career as organist at St Stephen's Cathedral in Vienna. In 1677 he became organist at Bach's birthplace, the Thuringian town of Eisenach, but a year later he moved a few miles east to Erfurt, where for the next 12 years he was organist at the Predigerkirche. There he came into contact with members of the Bach family (he was godfather to one of J. S. Bach's sisters, and taught his elder brother Johann Christoph, who in turn taught Johann Sebastian).

ABOVE: The title page of Pachelbel's Hexachordum Apollinis, *printed in Nuremberg in 1699, six "arias" for organ or harpsichord, with variations.*

ABOVE: A 1732 engraving of a concert with organ, strings, wind and brass instruments. Pachelbel specialized in organ church music.

While at Erfurt, Pachelbel married, only to lose his wife and their baby son two years later in a plague epidemic. He remarried in 1684, and raised a family of seven children. He then spent two years as court organist at Stuttgart, and three as town organist at Gotha, before finally moving back to his own birthplace as organist of St Sebald's Church.

Pachelbel's music

The organ chorales composed by Pachelbel – complex polyphonic pieces based on Protestant hymn tunes – had enormous influence on those of Bach. He was also a master of various other keyboard genres of the time, including toccatas, *ricercari*, fantasias, chaconnes and variations – his *Hexachordum Apollinis* (1699) is a group of six arias with variations for organ or harpsichord, each in one of five keys making up a perfect fifth.

Pachelbel also wrote six suites for two violins and keyboard, the masterly and justly famous Canon (a set of 28 canonic variations originally scored for three violins and bass), motets, sacred concertos and 11 fine settings of the Magnificat for chorus and instruments, intended for the Vesper services in Nuremberg.

Life and works

Nationality: German

Born: Nuremberg, 1653;
died: Nuremberg, 1706

Specialist genres: Organ music.

Major works: Canon and Gigue in D major; six suites for two violins; organ chorales.

Dietrich Buxtehude

I should place an organist who is master of his instrument at the very head of all virtuosi.

LUDWIG VAN BEETHOVEN (1770–1827)

The Danish organist and composer Dietrich Buxtehude was an almost exact contemporary of Pachelbel, and like him, proved a formative influence on J. S. Bach. Probably of German origin, he was born some time around 1637 in the duchy of Holstein, where his father was a schoolmaster and organist. In 1668 Buxtehude himself became organist at St Mary's Church in Lübeck, in north Germany. This appointment was one of the most important and lucrative in Germany, and competition was fierce (even though one of the stranger conditions attached to it was that the successful candidate should marry a daughter of his predecessor). This Buxtehude did – although Handel apparently declined an offer of the post nearly 40 years later when confronted with the necessity of marrying Buxtehude's own ageing daughter.

ABOVE: A painting by Johannes Voorhout depicting the friendship between Dietrich Buxtehude and his colleague J. A. Reincken (at the harpsichord).

Buxtehude remained at Lübeck for the rest of his life. His duties at St Mary's required him to play and compose music for the main services, but he also reinstated an old tradition of giving substantial concerts in the church on the five Sundays before Christmas, just after the afternoon service. These *Abendmusiken*, as they were called, became famous, as was Buxtehude's extraordinarily accomplished organ-playing. In the winter of 1705–6, the young J. S. Bach is reputed to have walked from Thuringia to Lübeck just to hear the great man play.

ABOVE: St Mary's Church in Lübeck, where Buxtehude was organist for nearly 40 years, and where Bach heard him play.

Buxtehude's music

Buxtehude left a substantial body of compositions, including cantatas, several oratorio-like works intended for the *Abendmusiken*, many organ works including chorale preludes, fantasias, fugues and variations based on chorale themes, as well as some lighter chamber and keyboard music. His organ works, which had enormous influence on Bach, exploit the characteristic range of tone-colour of north German organs of the period, and liberate the pedal from its traditional role as harmonic foundation – some of Buxtehude's pedal parts require virtuoso footwork in their own right.

Life and works

NATIONALITY: Danish

BORN: Oldesloe, c.1637; **DIED:** Lübeck, 1707

SPECIALIST GENRES: Organ music, cantatas for the German Protestant liturgy.

MAJOR WORKS: 120 sacred cantatas and other vocal pieces; many organ works; chamber and keyboard music.

Johann Sebastian Bach

Johann Sebastian Bach has done everything completely,
he was a man through and through.

FRANZ SCHUBERT (1797–1828)

For many music-lovers, the music of J. S. Bach fulfils a profound spiritual need: it has a timeless, other-worldly quality which could only come from a composer who felt himself close to God. Just as Bach's birthplace was overshadowed by the Wartburg mountain, topped by the fortress in which Martin Luther hammered out the fundamental principles of Protestant theology, so his life was dominated by his devotion to the Lutheran faith, and his music was dedicated to its service.

ABOVE: Johann Sebastian Bach, four years before his death, in a painting by E. G. Haussmann.

Early years

Unlike many of his more cosmopolitan contemporaries, Bach spent his entire career in Germany – mostly in the central regions of Thuringia and Saxony. He was born into a long dynasty of Thuringian organists and composers who worked as church organists and choir-masters, municipal musicians, and at the many small princely or ducal courts which flourished in the region. Bach's father, Ambrosius, was himself employed as a musician by the town council of Eisenach, where Johann Sebastian was born on 21 March 1685.

After losing both parents by the age of ten, Bach was sent to live at Ohrdruf with his married elder brother, Johann Christoph, who was organist there. It seems likely that Johann Christoph helped with his young brother's musical training, but once Johann Sebastian reached the age of 15, there was no longer room for him in the Ohrdruf household, and he obtained a free place at St Michael's

ABOVE: The house where Bach is believed to have been born in the Rittergasse in Eisenach, Thuringia, now a Bach museum.

RIGHT: A room in Bach's probable birthplace, containing contemporary instruments.

LEFT: A view of Eisenach, with the Wartburg Castle on the hill behind.

RIGHT: Thomaskirche in Leipzig, where Bach was an organist and choir-master, and where he was subsequently interred.

School in Lüneburg, 320km (200 miles) away in north Germany. There he benefited from a solid musical education and sang in the choir, but his formal education came to an end in 1702.

Arnstadt and Mühlhausen

At the age of 17, Bach returned to his native Thuringia to look for a job. After a temporary spell as a violinist at the Weimar ducal court, he was appointed organist at the New Church in Arnstadt, not far from Weimar. There he started to compose in earnest, and in the winter of 1705–6 he made his legendary pilgrimage (allegedly on foot) to Lübeck, 420km (260 miles) to the north, to hear the celebrated organist Dietrich Buxtehude.

After his return to Arnstadt, Bach's relationship with the church council deteriorated (he had a stubborn and at times arrogant streak, which caused problems with all his employers), and in the summer of 1707 he left to take up a new post as organist at the imperial free city of Mühlhausen, some 58km (36 miles) to the north-west. His salary was now such that he felt able to marry his second cousin, Maria Barbara Bach. But although his personal life had settled down, Bach quickly became dissatisfied with conditions at Mühlhausen, and in 1708 he moved again, this time to the ducal court at Weimar.

ABOVE: Bach directing a concert in 1714 at the Court Chapel in Weimar, where he worked from 1708 until 1717.

Life and works

NATIONALITY: German

BORN: Eisenach, 1685; **DIED:** Leipzig, 1750

SPECIALIST GENRES: Sacred music for the German Protestant liturgy, especially cantatas, instrumental and keyboard music.

MAJOR WORKS: *Brandenburg Concertos* (1721); 4 orchestral suites; 7 harpsichord concertos; 3 violin concertos; *Goldberg Variations* (1722); *The Well-Tempered Clavier* (1722–44); over 200 cantatas; *St John Passion* (1723); *St Matthew Passion* (1729); *Christmas Oratorio* (1734); *Italian Concerto* (1735); *The Musical Offering* (1747); Mass in B minor (1749); *The Art of Fugue* (1750).

Weimar

In the early 18th century Weimar was just another small, provincial town – its period of glory was to come some 80 years later, when its residents would include Goethe, Wieland and Schiller. Bach's job was as organist at the ducal chapel in the castle, but six of his children – including the future composers Wilhelm Friedemann (1710–84) and Carl Philipp Emmanuel (1714–88) – were christened at the City Church of St Peter and Paul during the Weimar years.

It was here that Bach began composing cantatas in earnest for performance at court, and he also provided instrumental music for the court orchestra. His early years at Weimar were happy and productive but, after 1713, relations with his employer, Duke Wilhelm Ernst, began to deteriorate and in 1717 Bach accepted the job of *Kapellmeister* to the court of Prince Leopold of Anhalt-Cöthen. The duke was so reluctant to let him go that he placed him under house arrest for a month. Eventually, in December 1717, the Bach family was allowed to leave.

ABOVE: *A romanticized artist's impression of Bach's visit to Frederick the Great at the palace of Sans Souci in Potsdam, May 1747.*

ABOVE: *Bach's eldest son, Wilhelm Friedemann (1710–84), painted around 1760. Like his father, he was a composer.*

Cöthen

While most of Bach's compositions up to 1717 had been organ works and sacred cantatas, he now exploited the instrumental resources available to him at the Cöthen court. Most of his work there was secular, since the Calvinist Prince Leopold required little sacred music. Among the works he composed during this period were the six *Brandenburg Concertos* for various instrumental combinations, together with concertos for violin (including the famous Double Concerto in D minor), orchestral suites, sonatas for harpsichord, violin, and flute, the suites for solo cello and the sonatas and partitas for solo violin. These works show that Bach had thoroughly absorbed the Italian style, through intensive study of works by Corelli and Vivaldi.

Remarriage

In May 1720, while Bach was away at a spa with his employer, Maria Barbara died suddenly. Bach remarried the next year: his bride, Anna Magdalena Wilcken (1701–60), proved a great asset to her husband, both domestically and professionally (the daughter of a musician, she was a singer, harpsichordist and music copyist). She inherited Bach's four surviving

ABOVE: *The trumpeter Gottfried Reiche (1667–1734), who played the high clarino parts in Bach's works in Leipzig.*

children, to whom she added another 13, including another future composer, Johann Christian (1735–82), later known as the "English Bach", since he spent much of his career there. Shortly after their marriage Bach began to compile two *Clavierbüchlein* (*Little Keyboard Books*) for his wife, which contain, among other works, the 15 Inventions and Sinfonias and several preludes and fugues, which were later assembled with others as *Das wohltemperierte Clavier* (*The Well-Tempered Clavier*).

ABOVE: A page from the manuscript score of Bach's St Matthew Passion, *first performed in Leipzig on Good Friday in 1729.*

In 1721 Prince Leopold of Anhalt-Cöthen married his cousin, and life changed irrevocably at the Cöthen court. The frivolous new princess was uninterested in music, and Bach soon felt obliged to move on – probably with some regret. In June 1722 the post of Kantor of the Thomasschule in Leipzig became vacant. The town council wanted Telemann, but he could not be released from his job at Hamburg, and so, after much deliberation, they appointed Bach. On 22 May 1723 he moved into his new quarters in the Thomasschule, where he stayed until his death 27 years later.

Leipzig

Bach's years at Leipzig, where he was required not only to teach, but to supply music for the town's two principal churches, St Thomas and St Nicholas, were relatively uneventful, but were punctuated by acrimonious disagreements with the council over pay and conditions. Nonetheless, they were amazingly fruitful. One of his principal jobs was to write, rehearse and direct cantatas for the Sunday services at the two churches, and his output included around 250 of these substantial works for voices, chorus and orchestra, mostly based on well-known Protestant chorale tunes.

In addition, he produced two magnificent settings of the Passion story, according to St Matthew and St John, the Mass in B minor, the *Christmas Oratorio*, and other major sacred works, into which he poured all the resources of vocal and instrumental writing available to him. Towards the end of his life, several books of keyboard music were published, but Bach's fame remained local. Among his last major works were the *Goldberg Variations* for harpsichord, allegedly written for an aristocratic insomniac; *Das musicalisches Opfer* (*The Musical Offering*, based on a fugue subject devised by Frederick the Great when Bach visited him at Potsdam in 1747), and the almost visionary *Kunst der Fuge* (*The Art of Fugue*), a complex series of canons on which Bach worked during the last years of his life, when his sight began to fail. He was almost totally blind when he died, leaving his widow in dire financial straits.

By the time of Bach's death, musical fashions were fast changing, and his music was perceived as antiquated. During his lifetime he had been more celebrated as an organist than as a composer. Unlike Mozart or Beethoven, he had little posthumous influence until Mendelssohn rediscovered his choral masterpieces in the 19th century, and his works began to be performed once more. He is now revered as one of the greatest of all composers.

ABOVE: A romanticized 19th-century impression of the Bach family at their morning prayers.

George Frideric Handel

Handel understands effect better than any of us – when he chooses, he strikes like a thunderbolt.

WOLFGANG AMADEUS MOZART (1756–91)

Handel and Bach were born in the same year, in much the same area of central Germany – Halle, Handel's birthplace in Saxony, is about 160km (100 miles) north of Thuringia. Both men lived to a reasonable old age, and both had lost their sight when they died. But their respective careers could not have been more different.

ABOVE: George Frideric Handel (1685–1759). He never appeared in public without his voluminous wig.

Early years

While Bach was content to live and work within the musical tradition of his family, Handel had to struggle to make a career in music. His father wanted his son to study law, and tried to stifle the boy's interest in music. But Handel persisted, and was eventually allowed to study music as part of his general education. Only after his father's death did he take it up full-time and in 1703, aged 18, he set out for Hamburg in search of employment.

ABOVE: An anonymous painting of Hamburg, one of the most important of the Hanseatic ports, in 1700.

Hamburg

One of Hamburg's attractions was as a flourishing centre of opera. Germany's first commercial opera house had opened there in 1678, and had scraped along financially under a succession of entrepreneurial directors with flair but no money. Here Handel found an ideal proving-ground for his early attempts at the genre which would dominate his life. But he refused the offer of a permanent post, and instead departed for Italy – the birthplace of opera.

The Italian experience

Handel travelled to Italy under the patronage of Prince Ferdinando de'Medici, and in 1707 his first mature opera, *Rodrigo*, was produced at a Florentine theatre. It was a success, earning Handel the favours of the grand duke's mistress, the singer Vittoria Tarquini. Perhaps wisely, Handel quickly departed for Rome, where he found employment at the court of Cardinal Pietro Ottoboni, the immensely wealthy papal vice-chancellor. There he met celebrated musicians including Corelli and the Scarlattis, and tried his hand at music for the unfamiliar Catholic liturgy, including a setting of the Vespers. His first oratorio, a setting of the Resurrection story, was performed with great splendour on Easter Sunday 1708 at the Palazzo Bonelli.

From Rome Handel travelled on to Naples and then to Venice, where his opera *Agrippina* was performed during

ABOVE: The square in front of St Peter's Basilica in Rome, painted in 1754 by G. P. Pannini.

ABOVE: A romantic impression depicting Handel making music at the keyboard with his friends.

the 1710 carnival season. Then, ever eager for new experiences, he returned north to Hanover, to be appointed *Kapellmeister* to the elector at a good salary and with the promise of a year's sabbatical leave. He took it immediately, and promptly left with an invitation to London. His transformation from a German to an English composer had begun.

England

In Queen Anne's England, Handel stepped into a musical vacuum left by the deaths of John Blow and his gifted pupil Henry Purcell. He decided to fill it by satisfying the growing middle-class demand for opera. His opera *Rinaldo* scored a huge success at the Queen's Theatre in London, both musically and dramatically. Audiences were particularly intrigued by a dramatic masterstroke – the release of a flock of sparrows onstage to lend verisimilitude to the aria "Augelletti" ("Little Birds"). But Handel was under an obligation to return to Hanover, where he spent some 15 months perfecting his instrumental compositions – overtures and *concerti grossi*.

In the autumn of 1712 Handel obtained another period of leave from the indulgent Elector of Hanover, and returned to London, where his next opera, *Il pastor fido* (*The Faithful Shepherd*), was put on at the Haymarket Theatre. This time the public was disappointed. As one critic put it: "The habits [costumes] were old. The opera short." Handel immediately hit back with a full-length, five-act opera, based on the Greek myth of Theseus. At the same time he began to fulfil royal commissions, supplying royal odes and a triumphantly received Te Deum and Jubilate to celebrate the Treaty of Utrecht, which ended the War of the Spanish Succession.

Life and works

NATIONALITY: German

BORN: Halle, 1685;
DIED: London, 1759

SPECIALIST GENRES:
Italianate operas, English oratorios.

MAJOR WORKS:
Water Music (1717); *Acis and Galatea* (1718) and 45 other operas; *Chandos Anthems* (1717–20); 12 *concerti grossi* (1739); *Messiah* (1742); 15 other oratorios; *Music for the Royal Fireworks* (1749).

Life under a new king

Handel had absented himself from his duties in Hanover for two years when in 1714 he received a rude shock: Queen Anne died childless, and the English throne passed to his neglected former employer the Elector of Hanover, now George I of England. It is said that the famous *Water Music*, written to accompany the king's triumphal procession up the Thames, was composed as a peace-offering (although it was probably written three

ABOVE: Handel playing one of his organ concertos at the Covent Garden Theatre in London.

years after George's accession). In any case, Handel was quickly forgiven, and remained a favoured royal composer for the rest of his life. He also acquired a new patron, the Duke of Chandos, for whose magnificent estate in Edgware Handel wrote the 11 *Chandos Anthems*, a Te Deum, the masque *Acis and Galatea*, and his first attempt at an English oratorio, *Esther*.

The Royal Academy

In 1719 the grandly named Royal Academy of Music came into being. This institution, supported by a group of 62 royal and noble subscribers, aimed to establish a regular opera company in London, with Handel as its composer-in-residence. Over the next eight years he supplied some 14 Italian operas for the company, including *Radamisto, Rodelinda, Admeto, Giulio Cesare* and *Tamerlano*, and engaged some of the finest European singers to perform them. These included the great castrato Senesino, a man possessed of a "powerful, clear, equal and sweet contralto voice", and the sopranos Francesca Cuzzoni and Faustina Bordoni, all engaged at astronomical salaries. Apart from the entertainment of the operas themselves, London society was soon treated to the diverting spectacle of the two rival divas fighting on stage while Senesino spent his time sulking in the background.

Change to oratorio

George I died in 1727. For his successor, George II's, coronation Handel provided four anthems (including *Zadok the Priest*, which has been sung at British coronations ever since). By this time the Academy was in deep financial trouble, and Handel's own financial losses – combined with waning public enthusiasm for this "exotic and irrational entertainment", the unexpected popularity of John Gay's satirical *Beggar's Opera* in 1728, and a complete breakdown in health – prompted a change of direction. He was already

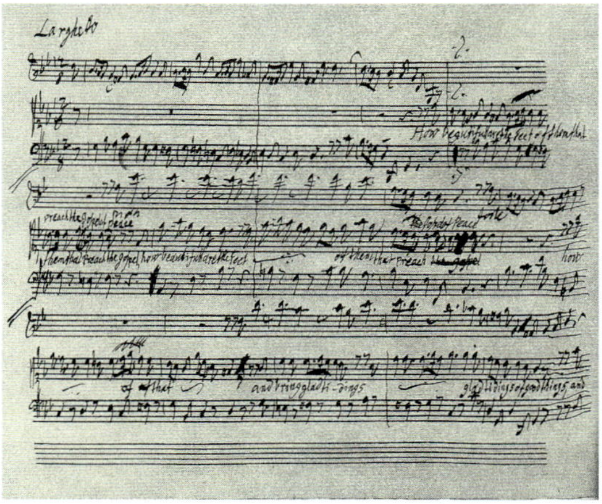

LEFT: The aria "How beautiful are the feet" from Handel's autograph score of Messiah.

RIGHT: Handel's choir singing an oratorio by Willem de Fesch, as drawn by Hogarth in 1731.

writing instrumental music, especially organ concertos, for the London pleasure gardens, but although he continued to write Italian operas, including *Ariodante* and *Serse*, until 1740, he needed a new genre. He found it in the English oratorio, beginning with *Deborah*, *Athaliah*, *Saul* and *Israel in Egypt* in the 1730s, but reaching its apogee in *Messiah*, written for performance in Dublin in 1742.

In setting these Biblical stories, Handel adapted elements from Italian opera, particularly the recitative-aria format; but reduced the soloists' importance in order to give more prominence to the chorus and orchestra. This clever ploy ensured the survival of his oratorios as a mainstay of the repertoire of British choral societies. *Messiah* was followed by some 15 further oratorios, including *Samson* (1741–2), *Semele* (1743), which is more of an opera than an oratorio, *Judas Maccabaeus* (1746), *Alexander Balue* and *Joshua* (1747), *Solomon* (1748) and *Jephtha* (1751), all of which are still regularly performed.

ABOVE: Handel's memorial in Westminster Abbey, London.

Last years

Handel's fortunes were mixed in the last years of his life. He had amassed considerable wealth despite his losses, and used some of it to support philanthropic causes, such as the Foundling Hospital. In April 1749 he fulfilled his last royal commission: music to accompany a grand firework display in London's Green Park to mark the Peace of Aix-la-Chapelle – an occasion marred when the firework pavilion burnt to the ground. But Handel's *Music for the Royal Fireworks* ranks with the *Water Music* among his most popular instrumental compositions.

Two years later his sight was failing. A painful operation to cure cataracts proved useless, and for the last seven years of his life he was totally blind. But the people of his adopted land had taken him to their hearts, and while Bach's death went largely unremarked, Handel was buried with full honours in Westminster Abbey. His epitaph summed up his extraordinary achievement:

The most Excellent Musician
any Age ever produced:
Whose Compositions were
a Sentimental Language
rather than mere Sounds;
And surpassed the Power of Words
In Expressing the various Passions
of the Human Heart.

ABOVE: A contemporary artist's view of the structure erected in Green Park for the 1749 firework display celebrating the Peace of Aix-la-Chapelle.

ABOVE: The Handel Centenary Commemoration concert (1785) in Westminster Abbey.

Domenico Scarlatti

Scarlatti frequently told M. L'Augier that he was sensible he had broke through all the rules of composition...

CHARLES BURNEY (1726–1814), "GENERAL HISTORY OF MUSIC"

The son of the composer Alessandro Scarlatti, Domenico probably began his musical training with his father. At the age of 16 he was appointed organist in the Neapolitan royal chapel, where his father was *maestro di cappella,* but in the spring of 1705 Alessandro ordered his son to seek his fortune in the northern Italian cities of Florence and Venice, describing him in a letter of recommendation as "a young eagle whose wings are grown: he must not remain idle in the nest, and I must not hinder his flight". In fact, Alessandro continued to interfere with his son's career until Domenico obtained legal independence in 1717, at the advanced age of 32.

In 1709 Domenico entered the service of the exiled Polish Queen Maria Casimira in Rome, where he encountered other up-and-coming musicians, including his contemporary, Handel. After a spell as *maestro di cappella* at the Julian Chapel in the Vatican, he decided to leave Italy for Portugal, and from 1719 until 1728 he worked in Lisbon.

Keyboard sonatas

Scarlatti's duties in Lisbon included teaching the king's musical daughter Maria Barbara. When the princess married the Crown Prince of Spain and moved to Madrid in 1728, Scarlatti accompanied her. He remained in her service for the rest of his life, and it was for her that he wrote the 550 or so one-movement keyboard sonatas on which his fame rests.

These sonatas are unique in the keyboard repertoire. Apart from their unusual binary format, they explore new playing techniques, including hand-crossing and rapid note repetition. Each sonata, which Scarlatti himself described as "an ingenious jesting with art", focuses on a particular technical problem, and many incorporate special effects in imitation of Spanish idioms, such as the thrumming of guitars and the clicking of castanets.

ABOVE: A contemporary portrait in oil of Domenico Scarlatti by Antonio de Velasco.

LEFT: The Harpsichordist, *by Edith Hipkins (1885), now in the Royal Academy of Music in London.*

Life and works

NATIONALITY: Italian

BORN: Naples, 1685; **DIED:** Madrid, 1757

SPECIALIST GENRES: Virtuoso harpsichord music.

MAJOR WORKS: 550 keyboard sonatas.

Jean-Philippe Rameau

The expression of thought, of sentiment, of the passions, must be the true aim of music.

RAMEAU

The French composer Jean-Philippe Rameau is now chiefly remembered for his operas, but like Janáček, he was a late starter in the operatic field. Born two years before the great Bach-Handel-Scarlatti triumvirate, he spent the earlier part of his career working as an organist, moving between various major towns in central France and Paris, where he eventually settled in 1722. In that year he published a textbook on harmony, *Traité de l'harmonie*, which established him as one of the most innovative and controversial musical theorists of his age.

Over the next 25 years or so Rameau worked principally as a harpsichord teacher, and his volumes of enchanting "character" pieces for keyboard in the tradition of François Couperin became very popular. In 1730 he found a wealthy patron, the tax-collector Le Riche de la Pouplinière, who introduced him to the playwright Abbé Simon-Joseph Pellegrin. Rameau's first opera, *Hippolyte et Aricie,* to a libretto by Pellegrin, was produced at the Paris Opéra in October 1733. It established the composer as a worthy successor to Lully in the operatic field.

ABOVE: Jean-Philippe Rameau with his violin, a famous portrait by Joseph Aved (1702–66).

ABOVE: Sophie Arnould (1740–1802), one of the most celebrated French opera singers of Rameau's time.

Rameau went on to write some 30 stage works – full-blown *tragédies-lyriques* in the Lullian mould such as *Castor et Pollux*, *Dardanus* and *Les boréades*; opera-ballets (operas with a substantial dance element, often written to celebrate royal victories or marriages), such as *La princesse de Navarre*, *Les fêtes de Polymnie* and *Zaïs*; and straightforward ballets such as *Pygmalion*. All are characterized by sensitive handling of the text, whether comic, sentimental or tragic; colourful and innovative use of the orchestra (especially evident in the many brilliant and lively dances); and expressive and powerful choral writing.

War of the Buffoons

In the early 1750s Rameau (or rather his supporters) became embroiled in the celebrated *"Querelle des bouffons"* – a war of words between admirers of Rameau's traditional French style, and those of the newly imported Italian style of Pergolesi. In the long run, the Italians won, and Rameau's operas finally dropped out of fashion. They were resurrected some 200 years later by William Christie's *Les arts florissants* in France and the British conductors John Eliot Gardiner and Nicholas Kraemer.

Life and works

NATIONALITY: French

BORN: Dijon, 1683; **DIED:** Paris, 1764

SPECIALIST GENRES: Opera and opera-ballets in the French style.

MAJOR WORKS: *Les Indes galantes* (*The Courtly Indies*, 1735); *Castor et Pollux* (1737); *Pièces de clavecin* (1741).

Other Composers of the Era

The Italian style and the French style have for long divided the Republic of Music in France.

FRANÇOIS COUPERIN (C.1626–61)

The Baroque era produced a plethora of minor composers, many of whom are remembered today only for a handful of works.

ABOVE: Gregorio Allegri (1582–1652), noted particularly for his nine-part Miserere.

Italy

Among these was the Italian priest and singer Gregorio Allegri (1582–1652), who worked at the Sistine Chapel in Rome. His chief claim to fame is the nine-part Miserere which he wrote for the exclusive use of the chapel, and which was jealously guarded until the young prodigy Mozart wrote it out from memory after hearing it twice on a visit in 1770.

Giacomo Carissimi (1605–74), who worked in Rome as choir-master to Queen Christina of Sweden, adapted Monteverdi's operatic style to the sacred oratorio, of which he wrote over a dozen, together with many motets and cantatas. He was the last composer to use the ancient folk tune "L'homme armé" as the musical basis for a Mass setting.

ABOVE: Alessandro Scarlatti (1660–1725), father of Domenico, and a noted composer in his own right.

Carissimi's pupil Alessandro Scarlatti (1660–1725) also worked for Queen Christina, and spent his life moving between Rome and Naples in the service of court and church. More than half of his 115 operas survive, but only a handful, including *La Griselda* (1721), have been revived. Scarlatti invented the *da capo* aria, with its long introduction and closing orchestral *ritornello*. He is credited with introducing recitative accompanied by orchestra rather than keyboard, and invented the "Italian overture", a two-part slow-fast orchestral introduction to a dramatic work, which later developed into the symphony. He also wrote a large volume of sacred music, and around 700 chamber cantatas.

The Venetian composer Tomaso Albinoni (1671–1751) is now more famous for one work which he did not compose – the Adagio for organ and strings constructed from musical fragments by Remo Giazotto in 1945 – than for his genuine 81 operas, 99 sonatas, 59 concertos and nine sinfonias. His solo concertos for oboe (the earliest known) and trumpet, and some of his *concerti grossi*, are now back in the repertoire.

ABOVE: Giovanni Battista Pergolesi (1710–36), a highly talented composer who died young of tuberculosis.

Giovanni Battista Pergolesi (1710–36) died of tuberculosis at the age of only 26. Many of his works were lost, but he is remembered for a brilliant comic opera, *La serva padrona*

ABOVE: An atmospheric contemporary portrait of the great Italian violinist and composer Giuseppe Tartini (1692–1770).

(*The Maid as Mistress*, 1733), a Stabat Mater (1736), and for tunes he probably did not write (but which were ascribed to him after his death because of his popularity) which Stravinsky recycled in his ballet *Pulcinella* (1920).

Like Corelli, Giuseppe Tartini (1692–1770) is remembered for his daringly original violin music. A brilliant virtuoso, he wrote 42 violin

ABOVE: Johann Hasse (1699–1783), upon hearing the 15-year-old Mozart, remarked "This boy will cause us all to be forgotten."

sonatas of immense technical difficulty (the most famous is the *Devil's Trill*, said to have been played to him in a dream by the Devil), 135 violin concertos, and many other instrumental pieces.

France

In France, the vacuum left by Lully's death in 1687 was filled by Marc-Antoine Charpentier (c.1645–1704), who began his career as music master and court singer to the Duchesse de Guise. From 1672 until 1686 he was also associated with Molière's troupe, writing music for the original production of *Le malade imaginaire*, among other works. He wrote a great deal of fine sacred music: 10 Magnificats, 37 antiphons, 84 psalms, over 200 motets and four Te Deums (one of which is now often performed) for Sainte-Chapelle on the Ile de Paris. Among his many fine stage works, *Les arts florissants* (1685–6) has lent its name to one of the foremost modern French ensembles playing music of the Baroque period.

Another French composer, François Couperin (c.1626–61), worked for the courts of Louis XIV and Louis XV. Born into a famous musical dynasty (his uncle Louis was a fine composer for organ and harpsichord), François became organist at the royal chapel. His harpsichord works (four published volumes contain around 230 pieces) are masterpieces of delicacy and musical description; many have enigmatic titles. He also wrote several instrumental suites in the fashionable style of Corelli.

Germany

The composer Johann Hasse (1699–1783) concentrated on opera, becoming director of the Dresden court opera. In 1763 he moved to Vienna, where he continued to write *opere serie* on texts by Metastasio, even though fashions were changing.

ABOVE: François Couperin, known as "Le grand" ("the Great"), one of the finest composers of keyboard music of his time.

Georg Philipp Telemann (1681–1767) spent most of his career as music director to the Hamburg churches. Probably the most prolific composer in the history of music (his output includes 600 overtures, 40 operas, 44 Passion settings and a huge quantity of instrumental music), he was in his day more highly regarded than Bach. His instrumental music is still popular today.

ABOVE: Georg Philipp Telemann (1681–1767) holds the record as the most prolific composer of all time.

The Classical Period

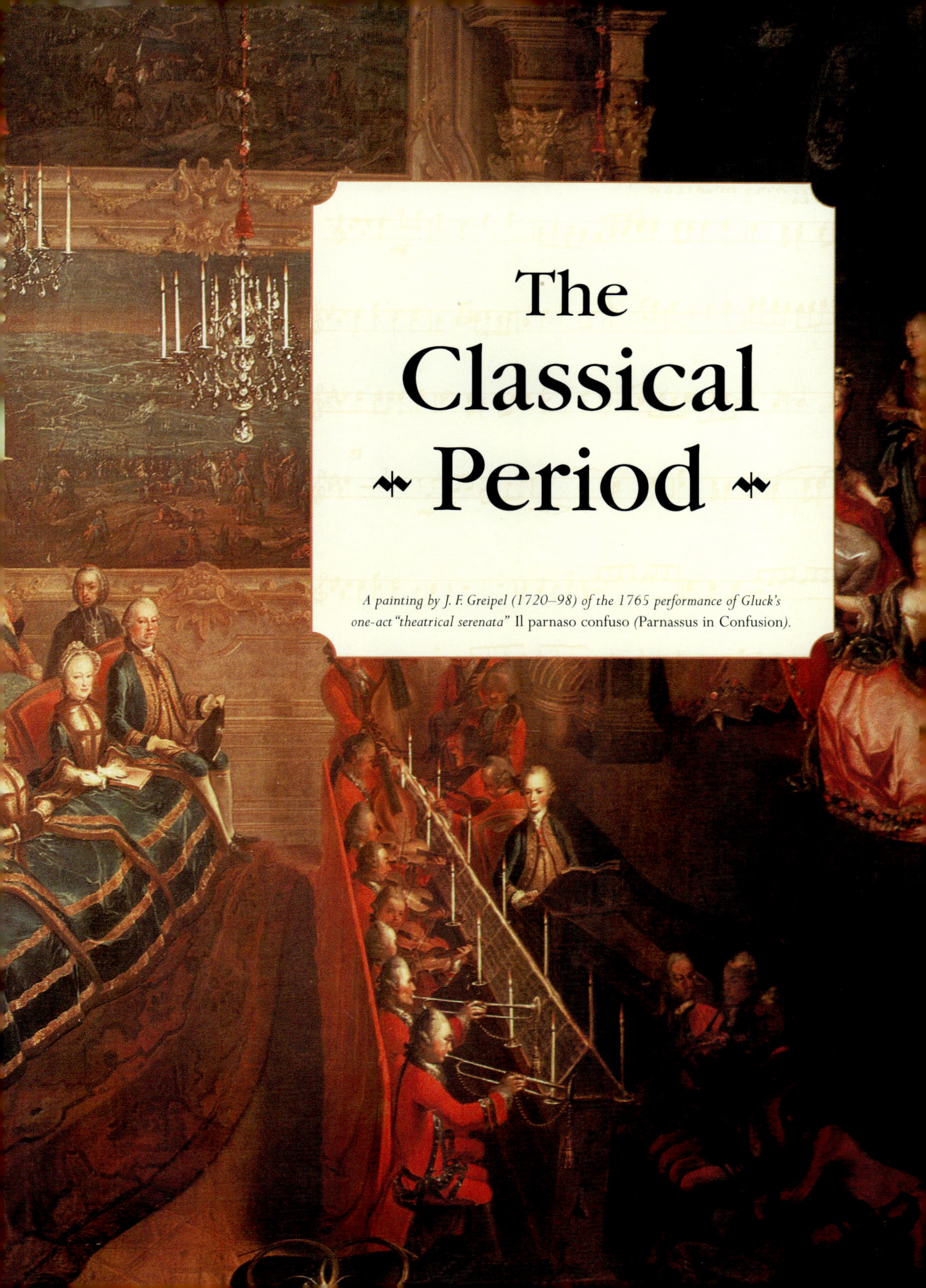

A painting by J. F. Greipel (1720–98) of the 1765 performance of Gluck's one-act "theatrical serenata" Il parnaso confuso *(*Parnassus in Confusion*).*

Music of the Enlightenment

Dust as we are, the immortal spirit grows
Like harmony in music.

WILLIAM WORDSWORTH (1770–1850), "THE PRELUDE"

By classical music, most people today mean serious music of any period, as opposed to jazz, pop, rock or other similar genres. But the term Classical is strictly applied to music written between about 1750–1830, corresponding to a period of classicism in art and architecture.

ABOVE: The building which inspired much 17th- and 18th-century neo-classical architecture – the Parthenon (Temple of Athena) on the Acropolis in Athens, built between 447 and 422 BC.

Classical style

During this period, the flamboyant, heavily ornate Baroque style of architecture (exemplified by the interior of the church of St Nicholas in Prague's Old Town, where Mozart played the organ on one of his visits) gave way to a cooler, more restrained style, based on the serene proportions of the ancient world. The 18th century was the age of the Grand Tour, when upper-class young men were despatched to Italy to study Greek and Roman architecture, as revealed through recent archaeological excavations.

Contemporary architects such as Robert Adam designed grand country houses with Classical façades, while the furniture designed by Sheraton and his colleagues took on a graceful, delicate look. In England, the fashion for the

ABOVE: A fine example of 18th-century neo-classical architecture – designs for Home House in Portman Square, London, by Robert Adam (1728–92).

ABOVE: Vienna in the 18th century – a view of one of its main streets, the Kohlmarkt. St Michael's Church can be seen on the right.

Classical look reached its height around the turn of the 19th century (the age of Jane Austen), continuing into the Regency period (1811–20). In France, particularly, there was a short period of transition between the Baroque and Classical styles known as Rococo, characterized by delicate but elaborate ornamentation, as seen in French furniture of the mid 18th century, and the paintings of artists such as Antoine Watteau (1684–1721) and François Boucher (1703–70).

ABOVE: A charming example of 18th-century Rococo art – The Dance *(c.1719) by Antoine Watteau (1684–1721), a favourite artist at the French court.*

Classical style in music

Musical tastes inevitably followed the decorative arts, and the florid, ornamental, technically intricate styles of late Baroque composers gave way to a new emphasis on clarity, order and balance, exemplified by the Classical symphony, string quartet and solo sonata. A few composers fitted the Rococo label, including C. P. E. Bach, François Couperin, the English composer William Boyce (1710–79), and Gluck and Rameau – both primarily opera composers – in some of their works. But generally speaking, the Classical period in musical history is dominated by four giants, all associated with Vienna, and sometimes collectively known as the First Viennese School. They were Haydn, Mozart, Beethoven and Schubert. Their works are still part of the core repertoire of classical music as a whole.

Music's place in society

The late 18th century was a period of great social upheaval. The breakdown of the old social order reached its culmination in the French Revolution (1789–99), and music ceased to be the exclusive preserve of pampered aristocrats or prelates. This radical social shift is reflected in the careers of the four great Classical composers.

Haydn, the oldest, spent his long career in the service of a single aristocratic family, who regarded him as a valued servant. Mozart began his career in a similar way, in the employment of the Archbishop of Salzburg, but when more lucrative court appointments eluded him, he took the radical step of trying a freelance existence, which allowed him personal liberty, but failed to provide sufficient financial security.

ABOVE: Private music-making – The Lost Chord *by Stephen Lewin (fl.1890–1910).*

Beethoven, in a similar situation, enjoyed the friendship and patronage of several wealthy noblemen, but he was not so fettered by 18th-century convention as Mozart. He understood his own worth as an individual, and his patrons played to his tune, not the other way round. Beethoven was one of the first composers to free himself from the idea of musician as servant, and to produce powerfully individualistic music which he himself promoted to an audience of the rising middle class.

Schubert, a native of Vienna, never tried to obtain a permanent job. A composer who stood on the threshold of the Romantic age, he wrote music out of personal choice, aimed at people like himself (he had a close circle of musically inclined friends). Much of his music – particularly his songs and chamber music – was intended for a domestic market, and none of his symphonies was professionally performed during his lifetime.

Christoph Willibald Gluck

Hearing "Iphigénie" I forget that I am in an opera house and think I am hearing a Greek tragedy.

BARON GRIMM

Gluck's career overlapped with that of Rameau, his senior by over 30 years, and like Rameau, he worked during the transitional period between Baroque and Classical styles, often known as the Rococo age. Born into a German family of foresters who lived in Upper Bohemia, he escaped being coerced into the family profession by running away from home when he was about 13. He went to Prague, and then to Vienna, where he was attached to a nobleman's household. When the nobleman moved to Milan, Gluck went with him, and it was in Italy that he realized his true profession – that of opera composer.

By 1744 eight of his operas had been produced in Italy, many based on libretti by the great Italian dramatist Pietro Metastasio. In 1745 Gluck went to London, where he found himself in competition with Handel (who is said to have remarked that "Gluck knows no more of counterpoint than my cook", though in fact he liked Gluck and arranged a concert with him). After leaving London, Gluck spent several peripatetic years travelling around Europe with an Italian opera company, before making an advantageous marriage and settling in Vienna. In 1754 the Empress Maria Theresa appointed him composer to the court theatre.

ABOVE: Christoph Willibald Gluck, painted by Duplessis in 1775, when Gluck was alternating between Vienna and Paris.

ABOVE: Gluck at the keyboard, by the French artist Eugène Delacroix.

"Reform" operas

Over the next few years Gluck evolved the operatic style which would make him famous. It was clear that *opera seria*, and its French equivalent, the *tragédie-lyrique*, had run their course. Audiences were beginning to demand different types of entertainment, portraying real people in real-life situations rather than cardboard-cutout ancient heroes. To Gluck's mind, opera had been taken over by the often absurd demands of star singers, who felt able to dictate their wishes to librettists and composers, usually in defiance of dramatic reason. In collaboration with the poet Raniero de Calzabigi (1714–95), and with the active encouragement of the Intendant of

ABOVE: The opening of Act II of Gluck's "azione teatrale", Orfeo ed Euridice.

Life and works

NATIONALITY: German

BORN: Erasbach, 1714; **DIED:** Vienna, 1787

SPECIALIST GENRES: Opera in Italian and French.

MAJOR WORKS: *Orfeo ed Euridice* (1762); *Alceste* (1767); *Iphigénie en Aulide* (1774); *Iphigénie en Tauride* (1779).

ABOVE: A design by V. D. Polenov (1844–1927) for Act I of Gluck's opera Orfeo ed Euridice, *for a performance of the French version in Moscow, 1897.*

the court theatres, Count Giacomo Durazzo, Gluck set out to "reform" operatic convention.

He began by writing a series of comic operas in the French style, including *La fausse esclave* and *L'île de Merlin* (1758), but his first major collaboration with Calzabigi and the choreographer Gasparo Angiolini was the ballet *Don Juan* (1761), a work of great dramatic force which influenced Mozart's opera *Don Giovanni* (1787). It was followed in 1762 by the opera *Orfeo ed Euridice* – the most expressive setting of this tragic love story since Monteverdi. Orfeo's aria "Che farò senza Euridice" is one of the most affecting operatic laments, while the scenes in Hades and Elysium (especially the famous "Dance of the Blessed Spirits") gave Gluck ample opportunity for dramatic instrumental and vocal effects, backed up by innovative staging.

In 1767, Gluck and Calzabigi produced the second of their "reform" operas, *Alceste*. In a famous preface to the score, Gluck laid out the principles of this new type of opera, free of the abuses "which have so long disfigured Italian opera and made of the most splendid and beautiful of spectacles the most ridiculous and wearisome". Gluck aimed to "restrict music to its true office of serving the poetry by means of expression and by following the situations of the story", seeking "a beautiful simplicity", free of unnecessary vocal display at the whims of individual singers. He also tried to make the overture an integral part of the drama. These principles governed his next Viennese opera, *Paride ed Elena* (*Paris and Helen*, 1770).

In 1774 Gluck moved to Paris, where over the next six years he wrote three new operas (two based on the story of Iphigenia, and *Echo et Narcisse*), as well as revisions (in French) of *Orfeo* and *Alceste*. He also found himself drawn into competition with the Italian composer Niccolò Piccinni (1728–1800). After *Echo et Narcisse* failed to please, Gluck returned to Vienna, where he died of the last of a series of strokes incurred, it was said, after drinking an after-dinner liqueur in defiance of his doctor's instructions.

ABOVE: The title page of the first edition of the score of Orfeo ed Euridice, *published in Paris in 1764.*

Joseph Haydn

So far as genius can exist in a man who is merely virtuous,
Haydn had it.

FRIEDRICH NIETZSCHE (1844–1900)

Joseph Haydn was the eldest and longest lived of the four great composers of the so-called "First Viennese School". Born when Bach and Handel were at the height of their fame, he outlived his friend Mozart by 18 years, and saw his former pupil Beethoven well established in his own career. It was Haydn who practically invented the Classical musical forms of symphony, concerto, string quartet and sonata. Mozart, Beethoven and Schubert all owed an incalculable debt to their genial, hard-working predecessor.

Haydn's life spanned a period of great social change. He was one of the last major musicians to work for a single aristocratic patron – in his case, the Hungarian Esterházy family, whose seat was the castle of Eisenstadt, some 80km (50 miles) from Vienna.

ABOVE: Joseph Haydn at the keyboard (c.1795) with the score of his penultimate symphony – the Drumroll *(No. 103).*

The arrangement worked quite well for Haydn – his employers treated him fairly – but in their eyes he was no better than a servant. His life-long desire for freedom was granted only towards the end of his long career, when he was effectively pensioned off and was able to travel and enjoy his spreading European reputation.

Early years

Haydn was one of 12 children born to the village wheelwright in Rohrau, about 50km (30 miles) south-east of Vienna. When he was only six, his budding musical talent was noticed by his family and neighbours, and a relative in Hainburg, who was a schoolmaster, offered to take the child as a boarder and begin his musical education. Shortly after his eighth birthday, Haydn was taken on as a choirboy at St Stephen's

LEFT: Prince Nikolaus Esterházy ("the Magnificent"), Haydn's patron and employer from 1762–90.

RIGHT: The courtyard of the Esterházy family palace at Eisenstadt, near Vienna, where Haydn worked.

ABOVE: A performance in 1775 of Haydn's opera L'incontro improviso (The Unforeseen Encounter), *in the theatre at Eszterháza. The composer is playing the harpsichord.*

Life and works

NATIONALITY: Austrian

BORN: Rohrau, 1732; **DIED:** Vienna, 1809

SPECIALIST GENRES: Symphonies, string quartets, opera, oratorios, Masses.

MAJOR WORKS: 15 surviving operas; 104 symphonies; violin and keyboard concertos; string quartets; keyboard sonatas; chamber music and songs; 12 Masses; Stabat Mater (1767); *Die Schöpfung* (1797–8); *Die Jahreszeiten* (1798–1801).

Cathedral in Vienna, under the harsh regime of the choir-master Karl Georg Reutter. Haydn said later in life: "I never had a proper teacher. I started with the practical side…I listened more than I studied, and tried to turn to good account all the things that impressed me."

Haydn left the choir in 1749, and for the next decade he eked out a meagre living in Vienna as a music teacher. His major breakthrough came when Prince Paul Anton Esterházy happened to hear a symphony of Haydn's and immediately offered the young composer a job. Haydn accepted, but first he took the disastrous step of getting married. His first love had become a nun, and perhaps out of a mistaken sense of duty to her father, Haydn agreed to marry her elder sister, Maria Anna Keller. His wife turned out to be bad-tempered, unattractive, and didn't care "whether her husband was a cobbler or an artist". She was also apparently unable to have children. During the years ahead Haydn found consolation with other women, but by the time his wife died in 1800 he was too old to think of remarriage.

ABOVE: The exquisite mirrored concert room at the summer palace of Eszterháza, built in the mid 1760s.

LEFT: A 19th-century edition of Haydn's Symphony No. 84 in E flat, first published as the fourth of the set of six Paris *Symphonies.*

RIGHT: A 19th-century artist's impression of Haydn and friends playing string quartets. Haydn was a good violinist.

Eisenstadt

In May 1761 Haydn took up his new post. His duties included training the choir and orchestra at Eisenstadt, maintaining all the instruments and music, and keeping discipline. He was also required to compose to order. Among the first works that Haydn wrote for his new patron were three symphonies called *Morning*, *Noon* and *Evening*, possibly intended to be played by the prince himself.

Less than a year later, Prince Paul Anton died. His successor, his brother Prince Nikolaus, was far more socially ambitious (he acquired the nickname "the Magnificent"), and soon Haydn found himself turning out a stream of music for his patron's entertainment: symphonies, concertos, string quartets, trios, and a vast quantity of chamber music for the prince's own instrument, the archaic, six-stringed baryton (similar to the viola d'amore).

ABOVE: A romantic impression of Haydn walking in the streets of Vienna carrying one of his scores under his arm.

Move to Eszterháza

In 1764 Nikolaus decided that Eisenstadt was no longer equal to his pretensions. He ordered the construction of a new summer palace – fit for a prince – on the shores of Lake Neusiedler. It had 126 lavishly decorated guest rooms, an art gallery, a concert hall, a ballroom and a 400-seat theatre. The Empress Maria Theresa attended a performance of one of Haydn's operas there in 1775, and declared: "If I want to hear a good opera, I go to Eszterháza." All in all, Haydn wrote some 25 operas for Eszterháza, including *L'infedeltà delusa* (*Infidelity Deluded*, 1773), *Il mondo della luna* (*The World on the Moon*, 1777) and *Armida* (1783).

While Haydn enjoyed the isolation of Eszterháza, where there was no one to bother him, and he was, as he said, "forced to become original", the other musicians hated it. Each year Prince Nikolaus found it harder to tear himself away from his fairy-tale palace, and he and his courtiers spent as little time at Eisenstadt as possible. But many of the court musicians had families in Vienna, and they begged Haydn to intercede with the prince.

His witty answer was the *Farewell* Symphony (No. 45), written in November 1772, in which one by one the musicians left the stage, packing up their instruments and blowing out their candles, until only two violins were left playing. The prince apparently took the hint.

The *Farewell* Symphony is one of a group of distinctive symphonies written during the 1770s in the fashionable, literary-influenced style known as *Sturm und Drang* ("storm and stress"). Many are in unusual keys, and exhibit a wide variety of moods. The same emotional style also influenced Haydn's other work of the period, including his highly original string quartets – of which he wrote 68 – and piano sonatas.

ABOVE: Haydn's last public appearance, at a performance of his oratorio The Creation *in the Great Hall of the University of Vienna on 27 March 1808, in honour of his 76th birthday.*

International fame

By the 1780s, Haydn's international reputation was spreading rapidly, and he managed to negotiate a new contract with his employer which allowed him to compose for other patrons, and to have his works published. In 1785 he became a Freemason, and around the same time he was commissioned to write several symphonies by a Parisian masonic lodge. The result was the "Paris" symphonies (Nos. 82–7) – several of which carry nicknames such as *The Bear*, *The Hen* and *The Queen* (a tribute to Marie Antoinette). Their success helped to consolidate his fame abroad.

ABOVE: A romantic impression of Haydn crossing the English Channel in the 1790s.

After the death of Prince Nikolaus Esterházy in 1790, Haydn was free to travel for the first time. He was persuaded by the impresario Johann Peter Salomon to visit London, where he was – to his surprise – fêted by the court and high society. In July 1791 Oxford University honoured him with the degree of Doctor of Music. His twelve "London" symphonies (Nos. 93–104, some again with nicknames including *The Surprise*, *The Miracle*, *The Military* and *The Clock*) met with great public enthusiasm. Haydn made a further trip to England in 1794–5, but resisted King George III's invitation to stay permanently.

Last years

Haydn returned to Vienna as *Kapellmeister* to a new Esterházy prince, Nikolaus II, who in contrast to his predecessors required only sacred music for his newly austere court. Between 1796 and 1802 Haydn produced six fine masses, including the *Missa in tempore belli* (*Mass in Time of War*) and the *Missa in Angustiis* (*Nelson Mass*), both reflecting the political turmoil of the Napoleonic wars. He also wrote two Handelian oratorios, *Die Schöpfung* (*The Creation*, 1798) and *Die Jahreszeiten* (*The Seasons*, 1801). These, his last major works, teem with vibrant detail and an undimmed creative impulse.

The increasingly frail composer made his last public appearance at a performance of *The Creation* at Vienna University in honour of his 76th birthday, and died at the end of May 1809, during the Napoleonic occupation of Vienna. The whole art-loving world of Vienna attended his memorial service, which included a performance of Mozart's Requiem. Eleven years later his remains were reinterred in the chapel at Eisenstadt.

Wolfgang Amadeus Mozart

Mozart is sunshine.

ANTONÍN DVOŘÁK (1841–1904)

The works of Mozart and Beethoven stand at the heart of Western art music. Until the mid 20th century, Beethoven was perhaps the more revered as a heroic figure, battling against personal misfortune to produce his visionary and powerfully original music; while Mozart's music tended to be dismissed as "galant" and superficial. But over the past half-century, the re-evaluation of Mozart, together with the performance and recording of many of his lesser-known works, has revealed a composer of inestimable profundity and infinite variety, whose music has enriched the lives of performers and listeners alike.

ABOVE: Wolfgang Amadeus Mozart, painted nearly three decades after his death by Barbara Krafft.

Family background

The "miracle whom God let be born in Salzburg" made his appearance on 27 January 1756, the last of seven children born to Leopold Mozart and his wife Anna Maria, and one of only two to survive infancy. Leopold Mozart – a talented violinist, and the author of a successful treatise on violin technique – played in the court orchestra of the Archbishop of Salzburg, one of the most powerful prelates in Austria.

Mozart's relationship with his father was central to his life. Leopold Mozart has been vilified as the archetypal domineering father, dragging his prodigiously talented son around the courts of Europe at an early age, not only subjecting him to the rigours of prolonged travel, but forcing him to display his skills on the keyboard to any bored aristocrat who would pay money to listen; then hectoring him when he grew older, trying to obstruct him from leaving a miserable existence in Salzburg for the excitements of Vienna, and interfering in his personal life. In fact, there is no evidence to suggest that Leopold was motivated by anything other than love and solicitude for his son. The Mozart family was

LEFT: Mozart's birthplace on the Getreidegasse in Salzburg, where the family lived from 1747 until 1773.

RIGHT: Mozart's father Leopold (1719–87), painted in 1756 – the year of his son's birth.

ABOVE: Mozart at the age of six in court dress, painted by P. A. Lorenzoni.

very close, and their voluminous correspondence is full of protestations of affection. Leopold's only concern was for Wolfgang's well-being and success. He was one of the few people who fully recognized his son's unique gift, and he took every step to prevent it being squandered.

Life and works

NATIONALITY: Austrian

BORN: Salzburg, 1756; **DIED:** Vienna, 1791

SPECIALIST GENRES: Opera, symphonies, piano concertos, string quartets, church music.

MAJOR WORKS: *Le nozze di Figaro* (1786); *Don Giovanni* (1787); *Così fan tutte* (1790); *Die Zauberflöte* (1791); 21 piano concertos; five violin concertos; concertos for clarinet and other wind instruments; 41 symphonies; 24 string quartets and other chamber music; 17 Masses.

Childhood

At the age of four, Wolfgang began to study keyboard and composition with his father. Wolfgang's elder sister Maria Anna (Nannerl) was also a talented pianist, though once she reached adulthood, the conventions of the time obliged her to confine her talents to the domestic sphere. Leopold saw it as his duty to exhibit his exceptional children to the world. When they were six and 11 respectively, he took them to perform before the Elector of Bavaria at Munich, and the Empress Maria Theresa in Vienna.

In 1763 the whole family undertook a trip to Paris and London, where Wolfgang played to both French and English monarchs. By this time he was already composing: four early keyboard sonatas were published in Paris, and he wrote his first symphonies in London. The family arrived back in Salzburg in November 1766. A further trip to Vienna failed to result in a hoped-for opera commission, but on returning home Mozart wrote one anyway, and *La finta semplice* (*The Pretend Simpleton*) was performed at the Archbishop's palace in May 1769.

ABOVE: A concert given by the young Mozart in the Redoutensaal (ballroom) of the Schönbrunn Palace in Vienna.

ABOVE: Leopold Mozart and his two talented children, Maria Anna and Wolfgang, 1763.

ABOVE: The young Mozart (aged six) being presented by Joseph II to his wife, the Empress Maria Theresa, at Schönbrunn Palace on 13 October 1762.

Years of travel

In December 1769 Leopold took Wolfgang to Italy for the first time. After visits to Milan, Florence, Rome and Naples, Mozart received his first opera commission. *Mitridate, rè di ponto* was performed at Christmas 1770 at the Milanese court; but although both it and a further opera, *Lucio Silla*, were well received, Mozart's request for a job was turned down.

Back in Salzburg, Mozart settled down reluctantly as *Konzertmeister* to the court orchestra of a new (and less tolerant) Archbishop, and continued to compose. In January 1775 he and his father travelled together for the last time, to Munich, for the performance of Mozart's comic opera, *La finta giardiniera* (*The Pretend Gardener*). Two years later he asked for another period of leave, for an extended trip to Paris. The Archbishop promptly dismissed him, and Leopold, realizing that his own position was now in jeopardy, decided not to go. Mozart set out with his mother as chaperone.

The trip was a disaster. After a prolonged stay in Mannheim, where Wolfgang fell madly in love with a young singer called Aloysia Weber, he was peremptorily ordered by Leopold on to Paris. There he found the sophisticated French capital totally uninterested in an unknown provincial composer, now too old to be interesting as a prodigy. Although the Paris experience did produce some fine works – the *Paris* Symphony (No. 31) and a concerto for flute and harp (both fashionable French instruments) – there was no financial gain and a severe loss, when Mozart's mother died suddenly. Saddened and disillusioned, Mozart returned home.

ABOVE: A romantic artist's impression of Mozart composing, painted around 1880 by Josef Büche.

Idomeneo

For the next 18 months he buried himself in his official court duties, writing sacred music for the Salzburg court, as well as symphonies, serenades, the Sinfonia Concertante for violin and viola (inspired by the French model) and a double piano concerto for himself and Nannerl. Then, in the summer of 1780, he was commissioned to write a new opera for Munich, on the subject of Idomeneus, king of Crete. *Idomeneo* is Mozart's first great opera – the first in which he demonstrated his extraordinary talent for bringing characters to life, allowing them to express real human emotions through the medium of music.

Vienna: early years

After being fêted in Munich, Mozart felt stifled by the petty humiliations of life in Salzburg. In March 1781 he was summoned to Vienna in the Archbishop's retinue, and took advantage of the rising antagonism between himself and his employer to engineer his own dismissal – albeit "with a box on the ear and a kick on the backside".

To Leopold's dismay, Mozart announced his intention of remaining in Vienna, where he would teach, compose, and give concerts. It was a bold idea, but ultimately an unsuccessful one. Austria was at war with the Turkish Empire, money was short, and fashions ephemeral, but for a few years, Mozart's novelty value paid dividends.

During his first year in Vienna he composed a group of three new piano concertos to play at his own subscription concerts, three magnificent wind serenades, and a new opera, *Die Entführung aus dem Serail* (*The Abduction from the Seraglio*), with a German text and spoken dialogue (a type known as a *Singspiel*). Its success

ABOVE: Mozart's first-floor apartment (with bay-window, second from right) in Vienna. He composed The Marriage of Figaro *there.*

was marred only by the laconic remark of the emperor that it seemed to have "too many notes".

Mozart also got married, much against his father's wishes. His bride, Constanze Weber, was the younger sister of his first love, Aloysia, who had turned him down. Constanze was an amateur singer: Mozart described her as "kind-natured…not ugly, but no beauty either". She has often been accused of ruining her husband's life by her bad housekeeping, but the accusation seems to have been unfounded, and the marriage – which produced two surviving sons (four other children died in infancy) – was very happy. When Leopold Mozart finally visited his son in 1785, he was much impressed with Wolfgang's fine apartment and high standard of living.

Vienna: middle years

For several years Mozart's new career proved successful. He had a busy teaching and concert programme, for which he turned out a string of piano concertos, raising the genre to new heights of virtuosity, passion and expression. Among these may be singled out the Concerto in D minor (K466), a highly emotional work in the *Sturm und Drang* ("storm and stress") style; and its companion in C major (K467), whose exquisite slow movement featured in the 1967 film *Elvira Madigan*.

ABOVE: Mozart's wife Constanze (1763–1842), painted by Hans Hansen in 1802, 11 years after Mozart's death. She remarried in 1809.

ABOVE: The final page from Mozart's own thematic catalogue of his works, which he kept from 1784 until his death. This page shows entries for the operas Die Zauberflöte *and* La clemenza di Tito, *the Clarinet Concerto and a Masonic cantata, finished in November 1791.*

ABOVE: Stage set for The Magic Flute*, designed by Simon Quadligo for a performance in Munich on 27 November 1818.*

Mozart's first love, however, was for opera – the genre which could make or break a composer – and in 1785 he began work on a daring new operatic venture, based on Pierre Beaumarchais's notorious French play *La folle journée, ou le mariage de Figaro*, which had been produced the previous year. This attack on aristocratic morals, disguised as a comedy, had already been banned in Vienna. Mozart's literary collaborator was the Italian adventurer, ex-priest and poet Lorenzo Da Ponte (1749–1838), with whom Mozart also worked on two later operas, *Don Giovanni* and *Così fan tutte*.

Le nozze di Figaro (*The Marriage of Figaro*) is one of the great monuments of Western art – a masterpiece of characterization, quicksilver wit and emotional depth. But Vienna failed to appreciate it. By this time, Mozart's arrogance had made him many enemies, including the powerful court composer, Antonio Salieri. Salieri and his friends were intensely jealous of Mozart's abundant talent, and did all they could to sabotage the opera's production. (Salieri may not literally have poisoned Mozart, as some later claimed, but he certainly stifled his rival's career.) However, the music-lovers of Prague, where Figaro was produced in 1787, took the opera to their hearts (the city went "Figaro-mad"), and immediately commissioned a new opera, *Don Giovanni*. Mozart's visit to Prague also produced a new symphony (No. 38), known as the *Prague*.

ABOVE: A seduction scene from Mozart's opera Don Giovanni *(1787).*

Vienna: last years

The final years of Mozart's brief life were a dismal catalogue of financial worry, constant moves to cheaper apartments, and failing health. He finally achieved his desire of a court appointment, but only as chamber composer, writing dance music for court balls, for a meagre salary. By June 1788 he was writing begging letters to his fellow Freemasons, asking for loans. *Don Giovanni* had been performed with even less success than *Figaro*.

In the summer of 1788, Mozart wrote his last three symphonies, including the *Jupiter* (No. 41), in the space of a few weeks; it is not known

ABOVE: A scene from Act II Scene 3 of the original 1791 production of The Magic Flute *at the Theater auf der Wieden in Vienna.*

if he ever heard them performed. A third opera written with Da Ponte, *Così fan tutte* (literally, "so do all women"), was premièred in the autumn of 1789, but the emperor died shortly afterwards and all theatres were closed. Two trips to Berlin and Frankfurt to give concerts failed to make any money, and by the end of 1790 Mozart was deeply depressed.

In the spring of 1791, he busied himself with dance music and pieces for mechanical organ and glass harmonica, several works for clarinet, including a fine concerto and quintet, and also with the serious and beautiful Piano Concerto in B flat (K595), a work tinged with melancholy. He also began work on another *Singspiel*, written for an actor-manager friend who ran a small suburban theatre. On the surface, *Die Zauberflöte* (*The Magic Flute*) appears to be an amusing pantomime with glorious music attached. But closer inspection reveals that the piece is infused with Masonic symbolism, including thinly disguised versions of Masonic rites and initiation ceremonies. Mozart was taking an enormous risk, and it has been suggested – probably wrongly – that he paid for his presumption with his life.

While working on *The Magic Flute,* he received two more commissions, one for an *opera seria*, *La clemenza di Tito* (*The Clemency of Titus*), which was produced in Prague in September 1791 and was to be the last major work of this type, and another for a Requiem Mass. The latter was commissioned anonymously, via an emissary dressed in grey, by a Viennese nobleman whose young wife had died. Mozart's own health was failing by this time, and as he worked on the Requiem, he became obsessed by the idea that it would be his own, and that he was being poisoned. In fact he had advanced kidney disease. He died on the morning of 5 December in his wife's arms. Because he left little money, he was given the cheapest possible funeral in an unmarked grave. Few mourners accompanied the cortège. The unfinished Requiem was completed after his death by Franz Süssmayr, one of his pupils.

ABOVE: A 19th-century artist's impression of Mozart's last hours, by Henry O'Neil (1817–80). The composer died in his wife's arms, aged 35.

Ludwig van Beethoven

Nature would burst should she attempt to produce nothing save Beethovens.

ROBERT SCHUMANN (1810–56)

Mozart died in Vienna in the late autumn of 1791, a victim of the stifling class conventions of the *ancien régime*. A year later, a 20-year-old named Ludwig van Beethoven arrived in Vienna, keen to make his name as a musician. By this time, the face of European society was changing fast. The French Revolution was in full swing, and Austria – horrified at the treatment meted out to the French monarchs, particularly Queen Marie Antoinette, a former Austrian archduchess – had declared war on France. For more than two decades, Europe would be ripped apart by war. While Mozart's life had remained largely unaffected by international politics, Beethoven's revolutionary artistic vision was shaped by the ideology and volcanic social change of the turbulent times in which he lived.

ABOVE: Ludwig van Beethoven (1770–1827), painted in 1823 by Ferdinand Georg Waldmüller.

ABOVE: Beethoven's birthplace in Bonn. He was born in the third-floor attic.

Early years

Beethoven was born into a musical family. His grandfather had been music director to the Archbishop-Elector of Cologne, and his father was also employed at the electoral court, though in the lowlier position of singer and instrumentalist. As with the Mozart family, the majority of the seven children born to Johann van Beethoven and his wife died in infancy. Three boys survived: Ludwig, born on 16 or 17 December 1770, and two younger brothers, Caspar Carl and Nikolaus.

Johann van Beethoven, an alcoholic bully, was determined that his eldest son should follow in the young Mozart's footsteps as a child prodigy. But Johann lacked Leopold Mozart's abilities as a teacher, and forced his son to practise the keyboard constantly at the expense of his general education. From around 1780 Beethoven received more kindly and sympathetic instruction from the court composer and organist Christian Neefe, who organized the publication of his pupil's first compositions – a set of keyboard variations. In 1783 a set of three piano sonatas appeared in print with a dedication to the elector, whose successor appointed Beethoven second court organist the following year.

In 1787 Neefe suggested that Beethoven should travel to Vienna to take lessons from Mozart, who was much impressed with the young man's talent. But Beethoven's trip was curtailed by news of his mother's serious illness: she died of tuberculosis in the summer of that year, leaving him to cope with his father's violence and alcoholism. At the age of 18 Beethoven assumed responsibility for the family affairs, being granted half his father's court salary as well as his own. He also found an influential patron, Count Ferdinand Waldstein, who persuaded the elector to allow Beethoven leave to study with Haydn in Vienna. The

Life and works

NATIONALITY: German

BORN: Bonn, 1770;
DIED: Vienna, 1827

SPECIALIST GENRES: Symphonies, piano concertos, string quartets, piano sonatas.

MAJOR WORKS: First period: Symphonies No. 1 (1800) and 2 (1802); six string quartets; Piano Sonatas No. 8 (*Pathétique*, 1799) and No. 14 (*Moonlight*, 1801).

Second period: Symphonies No. 3 (*Eroica*, 1803) to No. 7; *Kreutzer* Sonata for violin and piano (1803); *Fidelio* (1805); Violin Concerto (1806); *Razumovsky* Quartets (1806); Piano Concerto No. 5 (*Emperor*, 1809); *Archduke* Trio (1811).

Third period: *Diabelli Variations* (1823); last piano sonatas and string quartets; *Missa solemnis* (1823); Symphony No. 9 (*Choral*, 1824).

elector agreed, and in 1792 Beethoven arrived in Vienna, the city which became his permanent home.

Vienna

Beethoven found that his lessons with Haydn were not a great success, but he quickly began to make a name as a pianist, with a formidable reputation for improvisation. "He is greatly admired for the velocity of his playing, and astounds everybody by the way he can master the greatest difficulties with ease," a local paper reported. He also found a new and powerful patron, Prince Lichnowsky (in whose mansion he had an apartment), and despite his unprepossessing appearance – stocky, swarthy, with an ugly, red, pockmarked face – and rather boorish manners, he found himself tolerated by fashionable society.

He gave his first public concert, playing a new piano concerto of his own, at the Burgtheater on 29 March 1795, astonishing the audience with his fiery virtuosity and establishing a pattern which would continue for several years. By 1796 he had published a set of piano trios and three piano sonatas (a genre he would develop far beyond the Classical "galant" style of Mozart and Haydn), and had earned enough money to set himself up in his own apartment. Over the next four years he went on occasional concert tours, gave subscription concerts in Vienna, and issued his chamber works in print – sonatas for piano (including the magnificent *Pathétique* Sonata No. 8 in C minor), violin and cello, and the Op. 16 Quintet for piano and wind.

All these works show Beethoven's desire to push at the boundaries of conventional compositional technique, to expand sonata form, and to infuse his work with unheard-of drama and passion.

These principles were already evident in the first of his nine symphonies (written in 1800), which, while conforming to the standard Classical four-movement format, relies not so much on lyrical themes as on rhythmic dynamism and the development of short melodic fragments, or motifs. Clearly, the old courtly "minuet and trio" which traditionally constituted the third movement of a symphony had outlived its purpose: from the Second Symphony onwards Beethoven replaced it with a faster, more dynamic and rhythmically propelled scherzo, while retaining a tripartite structure with a slower, more lyrical central section. "There is something revolutionary about that music," remarked the emperor.

ABOVE: Beethoven, aged 17, playing to Mozart. Mozart declared that the young genius would "soon astonish the world".

ABOVE: A view of rural Heiligenstadt, where Beethoven escaped from city life to compose and recuperate, and where he wrote the "Heiligenstadt Testament".

The Heiligenstadt crisis

Around the turn of Beethoven's 30th year, just as his career seemed to be soaring, he was struck by an appalling personal crisis. He was forced to acknowledge the fact that he was going deaf. For several years he had tried to hide his hearing problems for both professional and social reasons, but it became clear that the affliction was incurable.

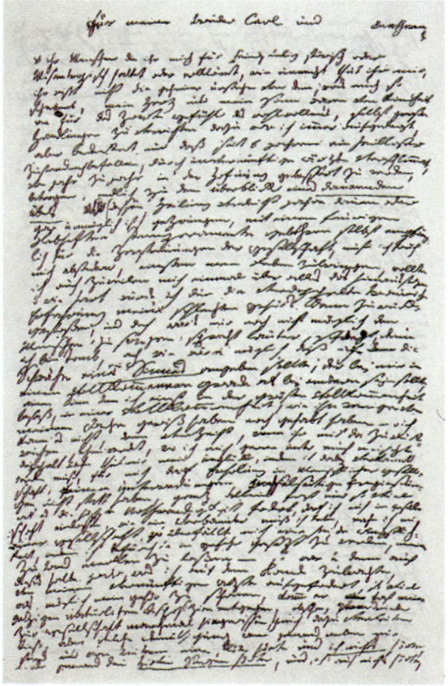

ABOVE: The "Heiligenstadt Testament", a letter written in 1802, in which Beethoven expressed his suicidal despair at his deafness.

In the summer of 1802 he reached a nadir of despair, while staying at the country retreat of Heiligenstadt, just outside Vienna. He wrote a long letter (known as the "Heiligenstadt Testament") to his brothers, in which he described his utter misery: "For me there can be no pleasure in human society, no intelligent conversation, no mutual confidences. I must live like an outcast." But though he had contemplated suicide, Beethoven concluded that he must henceforth live for his art: "It seemed impossible to leave the world before I had accomplished all I was destined to do." The letter was never sent, and was found among his effects after his death.

Years of struggle

Beethoven's inner struggle is reflected in the titanic works of the next few years. These included the massive *Eroica* Symphony (No. 3), originally dedicated to Napoleon, nearly twice as long as a conventional symphony, with a powerful and tragic funeral march as its slow movement; the Triple Concerto for piano, violin and cello; two piano sonatas (No. 21, the *Waldstein* and No. 23, the *Appassionata*); and his only opera, *Fidelio*.

The opera's plot was based on a French Revolutionary tale of a wife's heroic efforts to save her imprisoned husband. (For political reasons, Beethoven was obliged to move the action to 18th-century Spain.) By the time of the opera's production, in 1805, Napoleon's army had occupied Vienna and *Fidelio* received only two performances. It remains a lone masterpiece of its kind in Beethoven's output, perhaps lacking the innate sense of theatre of Mozart's mature operas, but containing memorable dramatic moments such as Leonora's great "Abscheulicher" aria, the quartet "Mir ist so wunderbar" and the moving chorus when the prisoners are brought from their cells and greet the light of day.

ABOVE: Napoleon Bonaparte (1769–1821), the original dedicatee of Beethoven's Symphony No. 3 (the Eroica*), but whom Beethoven despised when he proclaimed himself Emperor of France.*

ABOVE: The première of Beethoven's opera Fidelio *at the Theater an der Wien in Vienna, 1805. The opera was not an immediate success, owing to the French occupation.*

Disillusioned after *Fidelio*'s failure, Beethoven concentrated on instrumental pieces, producing a set of three string quartets dedicated to the Russian ambassador to Austria, Count Andreas Razumovsky, the Fourth Symphony, the Violin Concerto (again a lone masterpiece), and his Fourth Piano Concerto. Just before Christmas 1808 the Fifth and Sixth Symphonies, both revolutionary in concept, were premièred at the same concert. The Fifth, with its progression from tragedy to hope, has been interpreted as representing Beethoven's own struggle against adversity, and is one of the first symphonic works to recycle thematic material between movements. The Sixth (the *Pastoral*) is a harbinger of Romanticism. One of the earliest symphonic examples of "tone-painting", it illustrates scenes of Austrian country life, including a realistic thunderstorm, birdsong and a village festival.

By this time, Beethoven was enjoying a measure of financial security through the support of several wealthy patrons, including the Archduke Rudolph (to whom Beethoven dedicated his Fifth Piano Concerto, known as *The Emperor*). When Napoleon's troops invaded Vienna in 1809, the imperial family fled to safety: Beethoven celebrated their return from exile in 1810 with the Piano Sonata No. 26, *Das Lebewohl* (*The Farewell*). Seven years later Rudolph also received the dedication of the *Hammerklavier* Sonata (No. 29).

Disappointment in love

Apart from his deafness, Beethoven's life was marred by his failure to find a partner: the objects of his affection were usually either married, or else above him in social station (such as Countess Giulietta Guicciardi, the dedicatee of the *Moonlight* Sonata). An unsent letter written in 1812 reveals a deep attachment to an unspecified

ABOVE: The triumphant entrance of Napoleon's army into Vienna in 1805. The French occupation caused hardship for Viennese citizens.

ABOVE: Countess Giulietta Guicciardi, to whom the Moonlight *Sonata was dedicated.*

woman, "the immortal beloved", who may possibly have been Antonie Brentano, the wife of a Frankfurt businessman. She and Beethoven never met in later life, but many years later he dedicated to her his last work for piano, the *Diabelli Variations*.

Beethoven seems to have despised women of a lower social class: an attitude which led to acrimonious rows with his brothers over their "unsuitable" choice of wives. In 1820, after a long legal battle begun after his brother's death in 1815, he became sole guardian of his nephew Karl, perhaps fulfilling his own frustrated desire for an heir. Their relationship, however, proved a stormy one, and overshadowed the later years of Beethoven's life.

ABOVE: A 19th-century artist's impression of Beethoven (in later life) composing in his Viennese apartment. He was notably untidy.

Last years

In 1813 Beethoven celebrated Napoleon's defeat on the Iberian Peninsula with his *Battle Symphony*. Originally written for a mechanical instrument called the "panharmonicon", the piece is far inferior to the contemporary Seventh and Eighth

ABOVE: Beethoven's ear-trumpet lying on the manuscript of his Eroica *Symphony.*

ABOVE: The opening of the Theater in der Josefstadt in Vienna, 1822, for which Beethoven wrote the overture The Consecration of the House.

ABOVE: The Kärntnertor Theatre in Vienna, where the première of Beethoven's Ninth Symphony took place on 7 May 1824.

Symphonies. By this time Beethoven had more or less abandoned public performance, and by 1818 he was stone deaf.

He became increasingly withdrawn and anti-social, but continued to compose. Sacred music had never figured largely in his output, but in 1822 he completed the *Missa solemnis*, originally intended to celebrate Archduke Rudolph's enthronement as Archbishop of Olmütz. This great work, written "from the heart to the heart", ranks with Bach's B minor Mass as one of the crowning achievements of its composer's career. Sections of it were performed in May 1824 at a concert which included the première of the Ninth Symphony, the result of Beethoven's desire to write a "choral symphony with voices". Within a traditional symphonic framework (except that the scherzo is placed second), Beethoven burst the bonds of convention by introducing into the finale a setting for solo voices and chorus of Schiller's *An die Freude* (*Ode to Joy*), with its ecstatic vision of an international brotherhood of man.

Beethoven's last instrumental compositions – the last three piano sonatas and the late string quartets (including the six-movement Op. 130, with its immense fugal finale) – have always been regarded as embodying Western musical art at a peak of perfection. They are introspective works, not intended to be "understood" or applauded in the conventional sense. They are the work of a man who had withdrawn into an inner life, which could only be expressed through the medium of pure, abstract music.

In 1826 Beethoven's nephew Karl attempted suicide. By this time the composer (a heavy drinker) was already mortally ill with liver disease. After months of suffering, Beethoven died on 26 March 1827. In contrast to Mozart's low-key burial, 10,000 people are estimated to have watched Beethoven's funeral procession. The poet Franz Grillparzer delivered the funeral oration, in honour of "the man who inherited and enriched the immortal fame of Handel and Bach, of Haydn and Mozart... Until his death he preserved a father's heart for mankind. Thus he was, thus he died, thus he will live to the end of time."

ABOVE: A contemporary watercolour of Beethoven's funeral procession leaving the "House of the Black Spaniard", his last residence (to the right of the church).

Franz Schubert

If you go to see him during the day, he says "Hello, how are you? – Good!" and goes on working, whereupon you go away.

Franz von Schober (1798–1882)

On 29 March 1827, Beethoven was buried in the village cemetery of Währing, just outside Vienna. Among the torch-bearers in the funeral procession was a dark-haired, bespectacled young man of 30. His name was Franz Schubert, and he was paying homage to the member of his own profession he most revered. Less than two years later, Schubert's own body would be interred in the same cemetery, close to Beethoven's grave.

Unlike Beethoven, whose fame during his lifetime had spread all over Europe, Schubert's reputation was largely local. His composing career was short – a mere 15 years – and although he worked in the same genres as his three great predecessors, it was not his operas, or even his symphonies, but his more intimate works, particularly the songs and chamber music, which posthumously ensured his unique place in musical history.

By the time war in Europe ended with the Congress of Vienna (1815), European society had changed dramatically. A new generation of middle-class, independently minded citizens had sprung up, but conservative politicians, such as Prince Metternich in Vienna, attempted to maintain the status quo of the ruling classes and banish "subversive and revolutionary tendencies" by keeping the populace firmly under control through censorship and political repression.

ABOVE: Franz Schubert (1797–1828), aged about 28, painted by Wilhelm August Rieder around 1825.

People sought relief through social activity. Balls and parties became fashionable for the rich, while the less well-off built up a network of like-minded friends, meeting in private homes or at the local coffee houses. This was Schubert's social milieu.

Youth

Vienna was the centre of Schubert's universe. He was born on 31 January 1797 to a suburban schoolmaster, who taught all his children to play musical instruments. Franz learned the viola, and together with his father and brothers made up a string quartet. In 1808 he won a scholarship to the imperial seminary, where he had daily music lessons and played in the school orchestra. He also made several formative friendships, one with Joseph von Spaun, an ex-pupil and law student. By the time Schubert left school at the age of 16, he had already written a substantial quantity of music.

Schubert and Goethe

After his mother's death and his father's remarriage, Schubert spent some time as a teacher at his father's school. He also fell in love with a young singer named Therese

ABOVE: The great writer Johann Wolfgang von Goethe (1749–1832), the father of German Romanticism, painted c.1790.

Grob, who performed in his F major Mass in the autumn of 1814. Perhaps as a result of unrequited love, he began composing songs. His first efforts marked the beginning of a lifelong involvement with the poetry of Europe's most celebrated writer and the "father" of Romanticism, Johann Wolfgang von Goethe (1749–1832). Among these early songs was "Gretchen am Spinnrade" ("Gretchen at the Spinning Wheel"), from Goethe's *Faust*, a masterly characterization of the abandoned Margaret's distress.

The next year produced a huge crop of some 150 songs, many of them settings of Goethe's texts, such as the delicate ballad "Heidenröslein" ("Briar-rose"), and the stormy "Erlkönig" ("The Elf-king"), depicting a father's wild ride through the night to save his sick child from the grasp of Death. In spring 1816 Schubert's friend Spaun sent 28 Goethe settings to the poet, asking permission to dedicate them to him. Goethe, who loathed musical settings of his work, returned the volume without comment. Fortunately undeterred, Schubert went on to add another 100 songs – including the immortal settings of Goethe's "Nur wer die Sehnsucht kennt" ("Only he who knows yearning") and "Kennst du das Land" ("Do you know the country where lemon trees blossom?") – to his canon before the end of the year. In his 20th year he completed his Fourth and Fifth Symphonies, both very much in the Classical mould, for private performance by amateur orchestras.

Maturity

Schubert finally left the family home in December 1816, at the prompting of another close friend, Franz von Schober. A wealthy law student, Schober persuaded Schubert to abandon the drudgery of teaching and concentrate on composition (the song "An die Musik" – "To Music" – is a setting of a Schober poem). He also introduced Schubert to the singer Johann Michael Vogl, who became the leading interpreter of his songs. These continued to pour out throughout 1817, together with seven piano sonatas, heavily influenced by Beethoven.

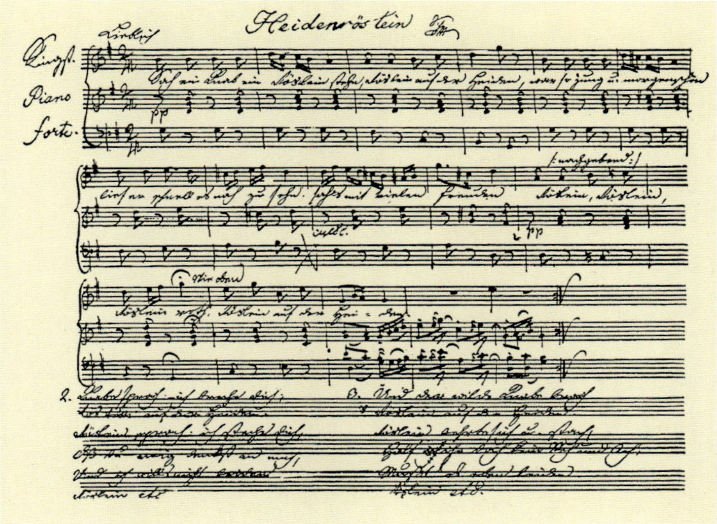

ABOVE: The autograph manuscript of Schubert's setting of Goethe's poem "Heidenröslein" ("Briar-rose"), one of his best-known early songs.

Life and works

NATIONALITY: Austrian

BORN: Vienna, 1797; **DIED:** Vienna, 1828

SPECIALIST GENRES: Songs, piano music, symphonies, chamber music.

MAJOR WORKS: Symphonies No. 8 (*Unfinished*, 1822) and No. 9 (*The Great*, 1828); String Quintet in C (1828); Piano Quintet in A (*The Trout*, 1819); Octet in F (1824); String Quartet No. 14 in D minor (*Death and the Maiden*, 1824); Fantasy in C major for piano (*The Wanderer*, 1822); Fantasy in F minor for piano duet (1828); over 600 songs; song-cycles *Die schöne Müllerin* (1823) and *Winterreise* (1827).

ABOVE: A view of a Viennese square in Schubert's time. Schubert spent all of his short life in Vienna.

ABOVE: An idealized portrait of the composer on his balcony, painted in 1917.

In 1818 Schubert's Sixth Symphony – a substantial work which shows Beethoven's influence – was performed (again by an amateur orchestra), and he spent five happy months on a Hungarian aristocratic estate as music teacher to the daughters of Count Esterházy of Galanta, concentrating on piano music for his young pupils. "I live and compose like a god", he told a friend.

ABOVE: Schubert playing the piano during an evening at Joseph von Spaun's.

Life in Vienna

The change of scene encouraged Schubert to broaden his horizons, and the next summer he and Vogl took a holiday in Steyr, where Schubert completed another piano sonata and the *Trout* Quintet, based on his own song "Die Forelle". From then onwards, Schubert's life took a regular shape. In Vienna, he was the focus of a close-knit group of talented young people – writers, poets and students – who enjoyed a happy and carefree existence, meeting at cafés, at parties in each other's homes or, in the summer, at a country estate owned by Schober's uncle. These informal gatherings, with games of charades, poetry readings and performances of Schubert's music, became known as "Schubertiaden". In the summers, Schubert and Vogl went on long walking tours of Upper Austria, where Schubert drew inspiration from the dramatic landscape.

The early 1820s brought mixed fortune. Vogl's performance of "Der Erlkönig" at a concert in the Burgtheater in 1821 brought public recognition for the as yet unpublished composer, but he had no experience of business matters, and when demand for his work rose, he rashly sold the copyrights of ten volumes of songs to the publisher Diabelli. And by 1823 it was clear that Schubert's operatic ambitions would never be realized. Of his 17 stage works, none achieved success, and only the charming and popular incidental music to *Rosamunde* has survived.

ABOVE: An excursion of the "Schubertians" from Atzenbrugg to Aumuhl, painted by Schubert's friend Leopold Kupelwieser. Schubert (wearing a top-hat) is walking behind the carriage.

Tragedy

The same year – 1823 – brought disaster. Schubert's hedonistic existence had left him suffering from syphilis, then a potentially fatal disease. At the height of his illness, he composed the two-movement *Unfinished* Symphony, restless and tragic in mood, as well as the great *Wanderer* Fantasy and the A minor Sonata, both for piano. He also composed his first song-cycle, a new genre consisting of a set of thematically linked songs based on a sequence of poems, telling a story. *Die schöne Müllerin* (*The Fair Maid of the Mill*) is a quintessentially Romantic tale of rejected love and death by drowning.

The last four years of Schubert's life were a constant struggle against

ABOVE: A "Schubertiad" (Schubert evening) in a Viennese salon. Schubert at the piano is accompanying the singer Johann Michael Vogl.

depression and illness, interspersed with frantic creative activity. As well as the Ninth Symphony (a work of Beethovenian proportions and unstoppable rhythmic impulse, which a Viennese orchestra declared "unplayable"), the works of these years included a great deal of chamber music: the Octet for wind and strings, string quartets in A minor and D minor (*Death and the Maiden*), two massive piano trios, and the three last piano sonatas (which Schumann memorably described as "purely and simply thunderstorms breaking forth with Romantic rainbows over slumbering worlds").

Last months

Schubert continued to compose songs until the end of his life. Some, such as the radiant "Ständchen" ("Serenade"), express a passionate delight in life; others – such as the bleak song-cycle *Winterreise* (*Winter Journey*), based on poems by Wilhelm Müller – plumb the depths of despair. Among the last was "Der Doppelgänger" – a terrifying setting of a poem by Heinrich Heine in which a young man sees his "double", foretelling his own death. It was a prophetic vision.

ABOVE: Schubert's spectacles lying on the manuscripts of some of his last works.

By September 1828, Schubert's health had worsened, and he moved in with his brother. That month he completed the sublime String Quintet in C major, followed in October by his last major work, *Der Hirt auf dem Felsen* (*The Shepherd on the Rock*), for soprano and piano with clarinet obbligato. He died of typhus on 19 November, aged 31, leaving only an unsurpassed musical legacy. His tombstone in the Währing cemetery carries the telling epitaph by Grillparzer: "The art of music has buried here a rich possession, but still fairer hopes."

Other Composers of the Era

Classicism is health, romanticism is sickness.

JOHANN WOLFGANG VON GOETHE (1749–1832)

Two sons of J. S. Bach bridged the gap between the Baroque and the Classical eras. Carl Philipp Emmanuel Bach (1714–88), born in Weimar, decided to follow a musical career, and in 1738 became keyboard player to the future Frederick the Great of Prussia. He remained in Berlin until 1767, when he succeeded Telemann as director of music at Hamburg. He is chiefly remembered for his inventive keyboard sonatas (of which he wrote over 200, for both "connoisseurs and amateurs"), which played a major role in the development of sonata form. His sinfonias, concertos and flute sonatas are also still performed today.

C. P. E. Bach taught the harpsichord to his younger brother Johann Christian Bach (1735–82). Bach's youngest son continued his studies in Italy, where he began a career as an opera composer, but moved to London in 1762 and remained there until his death, becoming known as "the English Bach". He was initially composer to the King's Theatre in London, and was later appointed music master to Queen Charlotte. His later operas were not very successful, but his instrumental works – particularly his skilfully crafted sinfonias and 40 or so piano concertos – had great influence on Haydn, Beethoven, and particularly Mozart, who met Bach when he visited London at the age of eight.

While British music in the 18th century was largely dominated by European imports, Thomas Arne (1710–78) was a notable home-grown exception. Arne's output was largely theatrical, including masques and operas (his 1740 masque *Alfred* contained the song "Rule, Britannia!"), but he also wrote some charming symphonies, keyboard concertos and sonatas, and songs, including "The British Grenadiers".

Muzio Clementi (1752–1832) was born in Rome, but lived mostly in England. A brilliant pianist, who later went into publishing and piano-making, he toured Europe as a virtuoso from 1781–83, but then settled in London, where he became a much sought-after teacher (his pupils included John Field). Clementi's own compositions, which include sonatas, sonatinas and studies for piano, are still used as teaching pieces.

ABOVE: Thomas Augustine Arne (1710–78), the composer of "Rule, Britannia!"

ABOVE: Carl Philipp Emmanuel Bach (1714–88), J. S. Bach's third son, who was an influential composer.

ABOVE: J. S. Bach's youngest son, Johann Christian Bach (1735–82), "the English Bach", who worked mostly in London.

ABOVE: Luigi Boccherini (1743–1805), who worked in Vienna and Madrid. He was a fine cellist.

Muzio Clementi's German contemporary, Johann Nepomuk Hummel (1778–1837), studied the piano with Mozart, and also worked for Haydn's employer Prince Esterházy. From 1819–37 he was *Kapellmeister* to the Weimar court. His fluent, tuneful works were very popular: his Trumpet Concerto (1803) is still much performed, as are his *Septet militaire* (1829) and a Piano Quintet of 1802. His piano concertos and sonatas influenced Chopin.

ABOVE: The Italian Domenico Cimarosa (1749–1801), court composer in St Petersburg and Vienna, playing the clavichord.

While the Classical period was dominated by the four Viennese giants, Italy continued to produce its fair share of talented composers. Among them was Luigi Boccherini (1743–1805), whose music is similar in style to Haydn's. He worked in Vienna from 1757–64, but in 1769 moved to Madrid as composer to the Spanish court. An enormously prolific composer, Boccherini left a vast output of chamber music, including 91 string quartets, 154 quintets and 60 trios, as well as symphonies, concertos and church music. His famous Minuet (featured in the 1955 British film *The Ladykillers*) comes from his String Quintet in E, Op. 13, No. 5.

Mozart's rival Antonio Salieri (1750–1825) worked principally in Vienna, where he was first an opera composer, and then court conductor. His operas, unlike Mozart's, have not survived, but he was an influential teacher; Beethoven, Schubert and Liszt were among his pupils.

ABOVE: The title page of a comic opera by Antonio Salieri, produced a few months after Mozart's Marriage of Figaro, *in 1785.*

Domenico Cimarosa (1749–1801) spent some time in St Petersburg as court composer to Catherine the Great of Russia, before succeeding Salieri as court *Kapellmeister* in Vienna. After 1792 he returned to his native Naples. Most of his 65 operas have been forgotten, with the single exception of the comic opera *Il matrimonio segreto* (*The Secret Marriage*, 1792). He also wrote an oboe concerto, around 30 keyboard sonatas, and other instrumental works.

His rival and contemporary Giovanni Paisiello (1740–1816) also worked in St Petersburg and Naples, producing over 100 operas as well as symphonies and piano concertos. His 1782 opera *Il barbiere di Siviglia* (*The Barber of Seville*), written when he was court composer to Catherine the Great, was at first more popular than Rossini's later version.

ABOVE: Giovanni Paisiello (1740–1816), one of the most successful opera composers of his time, painted by Elisabeth Vigée-Lebrun.

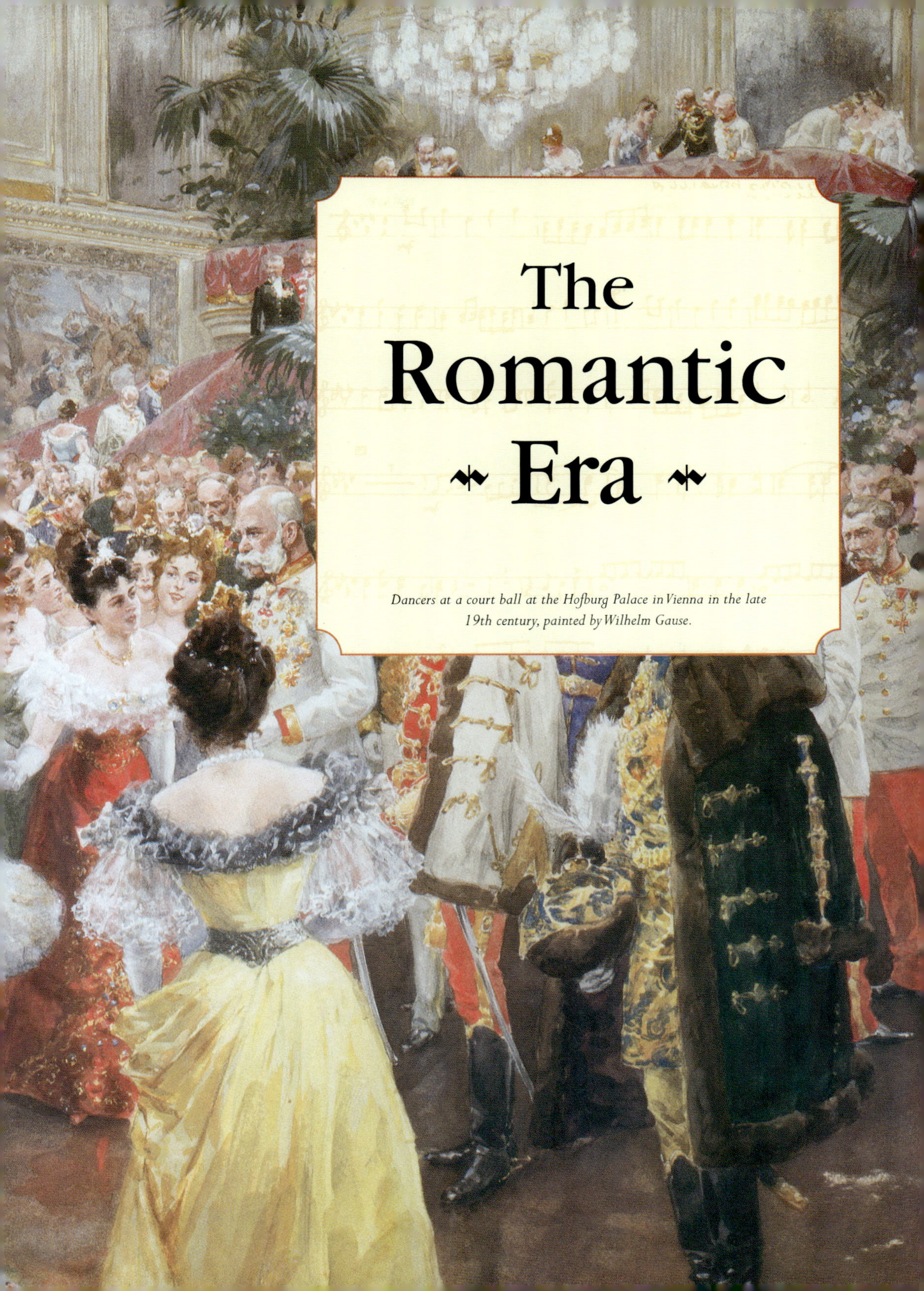

The Romantic Era

Dancers at a court ball at the Hofburg Palace in Vienna in the late 19th century, painted by Wilhelm Gause.

Drama and Poetry in Music

Music, moody food
Of us that trade in love.

William Shakespeare (1564–1616), "Antony and Cleopatra"

Schubert represented a turning-point in musical history. He inherited the Classical forms of his predecessors, but while his own musical style was essentially Classical, his inspiration looked forward to the age of Romanticism. One of the key features of Romantic music is its strong association with other art-forms, particularly literature or painting. Schubert responded instinctively to the poetry and drama of the great literary figures of his time: Goethe, Friedrich Schiller, Friedrich Rückert, Friedrich Klopstock, and Ludwig Hölty. Their writings, even when dealing with historical figures or events, expressed ordinary human emotions – love, happiness, sorrow – and the beauty of the natural world. One of the most potent examples of literary Romanticism was Goethe's epistolatory novel *Die Leiden des jungen Werthers* (*The Sorrows of Young Werther*), published in 1774. It was inspired by Goethe's own unrequited love for a friend's fiancée, and the news of another friend's suicide as a result of disappointed love. *Werthers* had an enormous influence on European youth, and the theme of frustrated passion became a common one in the literature of the period.

Untamed nature

The other great Romantic theme was a response to nature, especially in its wilder aspects. Earlier generations had sought to tame and cultivate the landscape; but in the late 18th century artists and writers – spurred on by Jean-Jacques Rousseau (1712–78) and his rejection of rationalism – reacted against the artificial moral code of Classical writers and philosophers, who believed in a neatly ordered world. Artists such as Théodore Géricault, J. M. W. Turner and Caspar David Friedrich began to depict the puny, helpless nature of human beings when pitted against terrifying natural phenomena such as avalanches or storms; while writers such as Lord Byron, William Wordsworth, Percy Bysshe Shelley and Sir Walter Scott identified human emotions with the turbulent moods of nature, and drew

ABOVE: This dramatic snow-capped landscape entitled Near Chamonix *was painted by James Stormont in the 19th century. Views such as this inspired many Romantic composers to write music that celebrated the beauty and ruggedness of nature.*

ABOVE: A caricature by Gustave Doré of Berlioz conducting at the Jardin d'Hiver (Winter Garden) in Paris, 1850.

inspiration from the rugged landscapes of northern Europe, especially Scotland, or from the remoter, brigand-infested parts of Italy and Greece.

Portrayal of emotion

This was the climate which produced the great musical masterpieces of early Romanticism. Among these are Schubert's song-cycles *Die schöne Müllerin*, in which the brook (represented in the piano accompaniment) becomes an equal partner in a drama of rejection and suicide; and *Winterreise* (*Winter Journey*), in which both singer and accompanist paint a vivid picture of wintry desolation, mirroring the bleak emptiness in the betrayed protagonist's soul.

Berlioz left no listeners in any doubt about the "programme" behind his orchestral masterpiece, the *Symphonie fantastique*, in which a young opium addict dreams he has killed his beloved and is led to the guillotine; while Mendelssohn's orchestral music records his vivid impressions of visits to Italy and Scotland. Much of Schumann's music was inspired by literary models; like Schubert, he had an immediate and passionate response to literature. At the same time, Liszt's newly invented "tone-poem" proved an ideal vehicle for musical responses to literature or art.

ABOVE: A painting by Edgar Degas (1876) of the divertissement in Meyerbeer's 1831 opera Robert le diable*, seen from the viewpoint of the orchestra.*

Virtuoso performers

The other hallmark of musical Romanticism was its emphasis on the individual – either the composer, fighting a lonely battle against incomprehension and intolerance, or the performer. The 19th century saw the rise of the star performer, and with it a division between creator and executant which became progressively more marked in the 20th century. Many 19th-century composers (Chopin, Liszt, Brahms, Paganini) carried on the tradition followed by Mozart and Beethoven in writing music for themselves to perform, but they also began to write for other virtuoso executants, such as the pianists Clara Schumann (1819–96), Eugen d'Albert (1864–1932) and his wife Teresa Carreño (1853–1917); the violinists Joseph Joachim (1831–1907), dedicatee of concertos by Brahms and Bruch, Ferdinand David (1810–73), for whom Mendelssohn wrote his concerto, and Pablo de Sarasate (1844–1908), for whom Lalo, Bruch and Saint-Saëns wrote concertos; and the clarinettist Richard Mühlfeld (1856–1907), for whom Brahms wrote his great chamber works for that instrument.

ABOVE: A poster advertising Massenet's opera Werther *(1887), based on Goethe's novel* The Sorrows of Young Werther.

Gioacchino Rossini

Rossini, in music, is the genius of sheer animal spirits.

LEIGH HUNT (1784–1859)

Towards the end of the 18th century, Italy was producing many composers of entertaining, accomplished, but undeniably ephemeral operas. Composers such as Giovanni Paisiello and Domenico Cimarosa wrote dozens of stage works, but very few survived for more than a season, and none could match the Italian masterpieces of Mozart. Opera in Italy had become stereotypical, subject to the tyrannical demands of audiences for a constant stream of hurriedly composed new works, and of singers for arias to show off their vocal technique, in defiance of dramatic exigencies. Italy needed an outstanding opera composer, and found one in the person of Gioacchino Rossini.

Rossini was the son of a horn player and a singer, and began to compose as a child. In 1806 he went to study at the Liceo Musicale in Bologna, and at the age of 15 was commissioned to write his first opera, *Demetrio e Polibio*. Further commissions followed, including several from the Teatro San Moïse in Venice for a series of one-act *farse* including *La scala di seta* (*The Silken Ladder*, 1811) and *Il Signor Bruschino* (1813).

Productive years

Rossini was able to work at high speed, and between 1810 and 1822 he turned out a steady flow of works, both comic and serious, for production in Venice, Milan, Naples and Rome, none of which took him more than a few weeks to write.

ABOVE: A portrait of Gioacchino Rossini (1792–1868), now in the Liceo Musicale in Bologna where he studied.

LEFT: The interior of the Teatro San Carlo in Naples, where several of Rossini's operas were first performed.

Life and works

NATIONALITY: Italian

BORN: Pesaro, 1792; **DIED:** Paris, 1868

SPECIALIST GENRES: Opera (both "serious" and comic).

MAJOR WORKS: *Il barbiere di Siviglia* (1816); *La cenerentola* (1817); *Semiramide* (1823); *Guillaume Tell* (1829); Stabat Mater (1832–41); *Petite messe solennelle* (1863).

Among them were the serious operas *Tancredi*, *Elisabetta, Regina d'Inghilterra* and *Otello* (based on Shakespeare's play), and the comic operas *L'italiana in Algeri* (*The Italian Girl in Algiers*), *Il barbiere di Siviglia* (*The Barber of Seville* – Rossini's comic masterpiece), *La cenerentola* (*Cinderella*), and *La gazza ladra* (*The Thieving Magpie*). Of these, *The Barber of Seville* (based on Beaumarchais's prequel to *The Marriage of Figaro*) was a disappointing failure at its Roman première in 1816, thanks to a catalogue of onstage disasters, though by its third performance it had recovered from its initial setback. In one version of a famous story about Rossini, who was a notorious gourmet, he was asked by a journalist whether it was true that he had cried in public only twice in his life – the first time after the première of *The Barber*, and the second when a particularly delicious piece of turkey stuffed with truffles had fallen in the river during a picnic. Rossini pondered, and then answered: "No, only once, and that was when the turkey fell in the river."

ABOVE: A set for an 1830 production of Rossini's opera Le siège de Corinthe (The Siege of Corinth) *at the Berlin State Opera.*

ABOVE: The title page of the fifth edition of the vocal score of Rossini's last opera, Guillaume Tell, *published in Paris.*

Rossini's greatest *opere serie* were written for the Teatro San Carlo in Naples between 1817 and 1823: they included *Mosè in Egitto* (*Moses in Egypt*), *La donna del lago* (based on Walter Scott's *The Lady of the Lake*), *Maometto II*, and *Semiramide*, the last of his Italian operas. In 1822 he married the singer Isabella Colbran, who had created the soprano roles in many of his operas, and after trips to Vienna and London, he settled in Paris as director of the Théâtre-Italien. He was still only 31 years old, rich and famous, with 34 operas to his credit.

Later life

Over the next six years he wrote several more operas for Paris, but after *Guillaume Tell* (*William Tell*), arguably his finest work, he effectively retired. In 1836 he returned to Italy, where he suffered prolonged periods of ill-health, but finally settled in Paris again with his second wife Olympe Pélissier, devoting himself to entertaining friends and eating (he invented, among other dishes, *tournedos Rossini*). The only musical products of his later life are the delightful series of salon pieces which he called "the sins of my old age", and two sacred works, a Stabat Mater and the *Petite messe solennelle*.

Rossini's music

In the operatic field, Rossini's innovations included the replacement of keyboard-accompanied recitative by orchestral accompaniment, the expansion of the chorus and its dramatic integration, the development of the coloratura aria, and the revitalization of *opera buffa*; his characters, such as Figaro and the delightful Rosina, are real people with whom audiences of all ages can identify. His brilliant opera overtures (characterized by their famous, whipped-up *crescendo* endings) are still often performed in the concert repertoire today.

ABOVE: An 1829 cartoon by A. E. Chalon of the character of Figaro, the hero of Rossini's Il barbiere di Siviglia.

Gaetano Donizetti

I wallowed in rapture.

MIKHAIL GLINKA (1804–57), ON HEARING "ANNA BOLENA"

Italian opera in the early 19th century was dominated by three composers: Rossini, who gave up composing in 1829; Bellini, who died at the early age of 33 in 1835; and Donizetti. These three laid the foundations for the work of Giuseppe Verdi.

Donizetti was born to a poor Bergamo family, but was fortunate to be able to attend a free music school in Bergamo founded and run by the opera composer and local *maestro di cappella* Johann Mayr (1763–1845). After two years of further study in Bologna, he began composing with astonishing speed and fluency. In 1822 he wrote a successful opera for production at the Teatro Argentina in Rome, and then moved to Naples, where over the next few years he turned out up to five operas a year. In 1828 he married Virginia Vasselli, a lawyer's daughter who died during a cholera epidemic nine years later – a tragedy from which Donizetti never recovered.

ABOVE: A portrait of Gaetano Donizetti, now in the Liceo Musicale in Bologna.

ABOVE: The "Swedish Nightingale" Jenny Lind as Marie, the heroine of Donizetti's La fille du régiment, *in an 1847 production.*

Maturity

In 1830 Donizetti achieved his first major international success with *Anna Bolena*. From then on he wrote for other operatic centres, including Milan, where he composed the enchanting comedy *L'elisir d'amore* (*The Love Philtre*), and the tragedy *Lucrezia Borgia*, performed at La Scala in December 1833. It was followed two years later by *Maria Stuarda*, based on Schiller's play about the Queen of Scots. Scotland also provided the impetus for Donizetti's greatest success, *Lucia di Lammermoor*, based on Walter Scott's tragic novel, which opened at the Teatro San Carlo, Naples, in 1835. (The heroine's famous "mad" scene was parodied over 50 years later by Gilbert and Sullivan in *Ruddigore*.)

In 1838 Donizetti moved to Paris, where his new works – including *La fille du régiment*, *Les martyrs* and *La favorite* – were hugely successful. But he was suffering from syphilis, and both his physical and mental faculties were in decline. In 1842 he was appointed *Kapellmeister* to the Austrian court, but his last operatic masterpiece, *Don Pasquale*, was produced at the Théâtre-Italien in Paris in 1843. He was eventually committed to a lunatic asylum, before being taken home to die in Bergamo.

Life and works

NATIONALITY: Italian

BORN: Bergamo, 1797; **DIED:** Bergamo, 1848

SPECIALIST GENRES: *Bel canto* opera.

MAJOR WORKS: *L'elisir d'amore* (1832); *Lucrezia Borgia* (1833); *Lucia di Lammermoor* (1835); *La fille du régiment* (1840); *Don Pasquale* (1843).

Vincenzo Bellini

Long, long melodies, such as no one has ever written before.

GIUSEPPE VERDI (1813–1901)

Vincenzo Bellini was the youngest member of the trio of early Romantic Italian opera composers. He was taught from an early age by his father and grandfather, both musicians, and at 18 went to study at the Royal Music Conservatory in Naples. The first of his ten operas was performed there in 1825, leading to further opera commissions from Naples and Milan.

Bellini achieved more or less instant success with *Il pirata*, produced at La Scala in 1827. It was written in collaboration with the librettist Felice Romani, who went on to supply the texts for six more Bellini operas, including *I Capuleti ed i Montecchi* (*The Capulets and the Montagues*, Venice, 1830), *La sonnambula* (*The Sleepwalker*) and *Norma* (both Milan, 1831), and *Beatrice di Tenda* (Venice, 1833). The failure of this last opera coincided with a rift with Romani, and the termination of a long-standing love affair with a married woman.

In the spring of 1833 Bellini visited London and Paris, where he was fêted, and made many valuable social contacts. The Théâtre-Italien in Paris commissioned his last opera, *I puritani* (*The Puritans*, based on Walter Scott's *Old Mortality*), which was performed with huge success in January 1835. Eight months later the composer was dead, after a violent attack of gastro-enteritis, less than two months short of his 34th birthday.

Coloratura

The hallmarks of Bellini's mellifluous, essentially lyrical art are expressive declamation and the close relationship of music and words. "Bellini's music comes from the heart and it is intimately bound up with the text," said Wagner. His operas, like those of Rossini and Donizetti, were written for the great voices of his time. They fell out of favour after the art of *bel canto* declined in the late 19th century, but enjoyed a revival in the 20th century with the emergence of a new breed of coloratura sopranos, such as Maria Callas (1923–77) and Joan Sutherland (born 1926). The aria "Casta diva" from *Norma* became one of Callas's showpieces.

ABOVE: Vincenzo Bellini (1801–35), a portrait now in the library of La Scala, Milan.

LEFT: The interior of La Scala (1819), where Bellini's Il pirata *was produced in 1827.*

Life and works

NATIONALITY: Italian

BORN: Catania, Sicily, 1801; **DIED:** Puteaux, near Paris, 1835

SPECIALIST GENRES: *Bel canto* opera.

MAJOR WORKS: *La sonnambula* (1830); *Norma* (1831); *I puritani* (1835).

Carl Maria von Weber

Weber, who seems to whisper in my ear like a familiar spirit,
inhabiting a happy sphere where he awaits to console me.

HECTOR BERLIOZ (1803–69)

Carl Maria von Weber, a leading pioneer of the German Romantic and nationalist movement, is chiefly remembered today for his opera *Der Freischütz* (*The Free Shooter*), the sparkling piano piece *Aufforderung zum Tanz* (*Invitation to the Dance*) which was orchestrated by Berlioz, the *Konzertstück* for piano and orchestra, and his brilliant works for clarinet.

Weber was born into a musical family in northern Germany, the son of a theatrical impresario and a singer. He took music lessons as a boy with Joseph Haydn's brother Michael in Salzburg, and by the age of 14 had already written his first opera. He completed his musical education in Vienna, and then spent over a decade working at various courts and municipal theatres in Germany (during which time he wrote many of his instrumental pieces) before being appointed director at the Prague Opera in 1813. During his tenure there he fell in love with the singer Caroline Brandt, but their tempestuous courtship lasted for four years before they were married.

ABOVE: A portrait of Carl Maria von Weber (1786–1826) by Caroline Bardua.

ABOVE: Costume designs for villains Samiel and Caspar in Der Freischütz *(1821).*

A new German opera

On Christmas Day 1816 Weber was appointed to the prestigious post of *Kapellmeister* at the Dresden court. His brief was to establish a national German opera to rival the current dominance of the Italians, and throughout his time at Dresden he had to contend with the overt hostility of the royal *Kapellmeister* (an Italian), as well as with the early symptoms of tuberculosis. Nevertheless he persevered with building up his opera company, and with the composition of his German opera *Der Freischütz.*

The première of *Der Freischütz* in Berlin on 18 June 1821 was

Life and works

NATIONALITY: German

BORN: Eutin, near Lübeck, 1786; **DIED:** London, 1826

SPECIALIST GENRES: German Romantic opera, works for clarinet.

MAJOR WORKS: Two clarinet concertos; Clarinet Quintet (1814); *Grand Duo Concertant* (1816); *Aufforderung zum Tanz* (1819); *Konzertstück* in F minor (1821); *Der Freischütz* (1821); *Euryanthe* (1823); *Oberon* (1826).

ABOVE: Berlin in Weber's time – a view of the Brandenburg Gate and the Pariser Platz.

a triumph. Compared with the stuffy court operas of the period, it was entirely fresh and riveting, based on a story drawn from German folklore, and with music strongly influenced by German folk song idioms – the music of the people. It is based on the tale of a young forester who tries to win the hand of his beloved by selling his soul to the Devil in return for seven magic bullets which cannot fail to hit their targets. This gave Weber the opportunity for a marvellous supernatural scene in the "Wolf's Glen", a gift to designers and producers, with spine-chilling music to match.

Although *Der Freischütz* went on to take Europe by storm, Weber's next two operas were less successful. Both *Euryanthe* and *Oberon*, while containing marvellous individual numbers (the overture to *Oberon* is a masterpiece), suffered from muddled, incomprehensible plots and little sense of drama. *Euryanthe* opened in Vienna in 1823, but was given only 20 performances.

ABOVE: The "Wolf's Glen" scene from Der Freischütz *– the 1982 production of Weber's famous opera performed at the Royal Opera House in Covent Garden, London.*

Last performances

Oberon, commissioned by the manager of the Covent Garden Theatre in London, was scheduled for performance in the spring of 1826. By the end of 1825 Weber knew that he was dying. Athough his wife and friends tried to dissuade him from travelling to London to conduct the opera, Weber was so worried about making financial provision for his young family that he insisted on making the journey.

He managed to conduct the première of *Oberon* on 12 April 1826, also undertaking many other concert engagements, but he was failing fast. He died at his lodgings in Great Portland Street in London on 5 June, aged only 39. Eighteen years later, Wagner, whose own early operas in the German Romantic style owed an enormous debt to Weber's pioneering work, had his predecessor's remains taken back to Dresden.

Giacomo Meyerbeer

Meyerbeer feels as Michelangelo felt.

GEORGES BIZET (1838–75)

While the operas of Rossini, Donizetti, Bellini and Weber have all to some extent held their place in the repertoire, those of Giacomo Meyerbeer have been revived only occasionally over the past century. In his own time, however, Meyerbeer was one of the most successful opera composers and one of the richest men in Europe. This inevitably provoked envious sniping from his less fortunate colleagues – particularly Wagner, who launched a vitriolic attack on Meyerbeer in his anti-Semitic pamphlet *Das Judenthum in der Musik* (1850).

ABOVE: Giacomo Meyerbeer (1791–1864), creator of French "grand opera". He and Berlioz shared a taste for the "monumental".

Child prodigy

Meyerbeer was a truly cosmopolitan figure. Born in Berlin, into the same affluent, cultured, Jewish milieu as his younger contemporary Mendelssohn, Jakob Liebmann Beer (as he was originally called) showed early promise as a pianist, appearing as soloist in a performance of a Mozart concerto at the age of 11. He began writing German operas while still in his teens.

From 1816 he spent nine years in Italy, where he wrote six operas in the style of Rossini. The last of these, *Il crociato in Egitto* (*The Crusader in Egypt*, 1824), was subsequently staged with equal success in London and Paris, where Meyerbeer met the librettist Eugène Scribe (1791–1861). From then onwards, Paris became the focus of Meyerbeer's activities, although he never lived there permanently. In the 1840s he was appointed *Generalmusikdirektor* in Berlin, where he wrote a *Singspiel* for the Swedish soprano Jenny Lind (1820–87).

Life and works

NATIONALITY: German

BORN: Vogelsdorf, near Berlin, 1791; **DIED:** Paris, 1864

SPECIALIST GENRES: French grand opera.

MAJOR WORKS: *Robert le diable* (1831); *Les Huguenots* (1836); *Le prophète* (1849); *L'Africaine* (1865).

Grand opera

Meyerbeer's reputation rests on the "grand operas" he created for the Paris Opéra in collaboration with Scribe, beginning with *Robert le diable* (*Robert the Devil*) in 1831, continuing with *Les Huguenots* and *Le prophète*, and ending with *L'Africaine* (premièred posthumously in 1865). All were staged with spectacular and innovative effects, such as storms, ships sinking on stage and massive crowd scenes.

Unlike Rossini, Meyerbeer was not a fast worker, and his productions were eagerly awaited. He wrote with specific voices in mind, and was always searching for new vocal and orchestral timbres.

ABOVE: Costume for the role of Marguerite de Navarre, worn at the première of Les Huguenots *in Paris on 29 February 1836.*

Niccolò Paganini

Paganini is the turning-point in the history of virtuosity.

Robert Schumann (1810–56)

The Italian violinist and composer Niccolò Paganini is still revered as the greatest virtuoso of all – a true "wizard of the violin" whose technical mastery has never been equalled. His brilliant Twenty-four Caprices for solo violin have spawned many imitations, and his concertos and variations are still part of the violin repertoire.

Born into a poor Genoese family, he was forced as a small child to practise the violin constantly by his bullying father. In 1795 he spent a year studying in Parma, and at 18 was appointed leader of the orchestra (and then solo violinist to the court) in Lucca. At one of his court concerts he improvised a musical "love scene" using only two strings of the violin, and he also wrote and performed a sonata entirely on the G string, demanding outstanding dexterity and accuracy.

From 1810 onwards, Paganini travelled Europe as a freelance virtuoso. After his 1813 debut concert at La Scala, Milan, a critic wrote: "He is without question the foremost and greatest violinist in the world. His playing is truly inconceivable. He performs certain passage-work, leaps, and double stops that have never been heard from any violinist…"

ABOVE: The legendary violinist Niccolò Paganini inspired composers and performers, including Schumann, Liszt and Chopin.

Life and works

Nationality: Italian

Born: Genoa, 1782; **died:** Nice, 1840

Specialist genres: Virtuoso violin music.

Major works: 24 Caprices for unaccompanied violin (1820); violin concertos and shorter works, including *Le streghe* (*Witches' Dance*) and *Moto perpetuo* (*Perpetual Motion*).

Pact with the Devil

The astonishing virtuosity of Paganini's playing, combined with his bizarre appearance – he was lean and gaunt, with a shock of long black hair, and very long, thin fingers – caused rumours that he was in league with the Devil. He never married, but a four-year relationship with a singer, Antonia Bianchi, produced one son, Achille, to whom he was devoted.

Between 1828 and 1834 Paganini's career as a touring virtuoso was at its height: he was acclaimed in Vienna, Berlin, Warsaw, Paris and London, but deteriorating health precipitated his retirement to Italy in 1834. Six years later he died of cancer of the larynx, but the church, having denounced him as a heretic, refused to allow his burial in consecrated ground. In 1845 his remains were transferred from the French Riviera to a private burial-ground in Parma, and were re-interred in Parma Cemetery in 1876. His Guarneri violin is preserved in the municipal museum in Genoa.

Paganini had enormous influence, both on composers (including Schumann), and performers: not only violinists, but also pianists. Both Liszt and Chopin were encouraged by his example to extend the frontiers of keyboard technique. Liszt's *Transcendental Studies* were directly inspired by Paganini's Caprices.

Hector Berlioz

Berlioz composes by splashing his pen over the manuscript and leaving the issue to chance.

FRÉDÉRIC CHOPIN (1810–49)

Like Schumann and Chopin, Berlioz is regarded as an archetypal "Romantic" artist, both for the nature of his work and for the colourful events of his life, which are documented in his entertaining *Memoirs*.

The son of a provincial French doctor, he intended to pursue a medical career, but the grisly scenes of carnage he encountered at medical school in Paris put him off. Instead he began music lessons, first privately and then at the Paris Conservatoire.

ABOVE: Hector Berlioz composing his opera Les Troyens *(The Trojans).*

Sensitive, passionate and impulsive by nature, Berlioz was prone to violent emotions. In 1827 he saw an English theatre company performing *Hamlet* at the Odéon Theatre, and was immediately stricken with wild admiration, both for Shakespeare and for Harriet Smithson, the attractive Irish actress who played Ophelia. His unrequited passion found an outlet in 1830 in the extraordinary, programmatic *Symphonie fantastique*, subtitled "Episodes in the life of an artist". In the first three of its five movements, "the beloved" appears in various transformations as a melodic motif (which Berlioz called the *idée fixe*), whether in "passions and dreams", at a ball, or during a pastoral idyll (which owes much to Beethoven). In the fourth movement, "March to the Scaffold", the artist dreams that he has murdered his beloved and is being led to the guillotine; in the last, a grotesque witches' sabbath, the beloved has been transformed into a hag, her theme obscenely distorted.

In 1832 Berlioz finally persuaded Harriet Smithson to marry him. But proximity to the Beloved proved less appealing than worship from afar. Although he never divorced Harriet (who died of alcoholism in 1854), he formed a liaison from 1841 onwards with the

ABOVE: A cartoon of Berlioz conducting, surrounded by some of the bizarre instruments he deployed – including a cannon!

ABOVE: Harriet Smithson as Ophelia. Berlioz became obsessed with her and eventually married her, with disastrous consequences.

Life and works

Nationality: French

Born: La-Côte-Saint-André, near Grenoble, 1803; **died:** Paris, 1869

Specialist genres: Romantic orchestral and choral works, large-scale opera.

Major works: *Symphonie fantastique* (1830); *Harold en Italie* (1834); *Grande messe des morts* (1837); *Roméo et Juliette* (1838–9); overtures *Le corsaire* (1831) and *Le carnaval romain* (1844); *La damnation de Faust* (1846); Te Deum (1849); *Les Troyens* (1856–8).

singer Marie Recio, who later became his second wife.

During the 1830s Berlioz produced some of his finest works, including the symphony with obbligato viola, *Harold en Italie*. This work was commissioned by Paganini, who paid the struggling composer 20,000 francs for the piece, although he never played the solo part because he said it did not adequately display his talents as a virtuoso.

Large-scale works

Berlioz's predilection for the monumental led him to compose enormous scores for huge orchestral forces (although he himself played only the guitar, he was a master of orchestration and wrote an influential treatise on the subject). His colossal works for chorus and orchestra included a Requiem (1837), the dramatic symphony *Roméo et Juliette* (1838–9), the *Grande symphonie funèbre et triomphale* (1840), and the operas *Benvenuto Cellini* (1834–7), and *Les Troyens* (*The Trojans*, 1856–8).

Berlioz never had enough money. He was forced to supplement his income by working as a music critic, and by touring Europe as a conductor. In 1846 *La damnation de Faust*, a "dramatic cantata" based on the play by Goethe – whom Berlioz declared, together with Shakespeare, the guiding influence of his life – failed to attract attention in Paris, though it scored a great success in Russia. But his oratorio *L'enfance du Christ* (*The Childhood of Christ*) achieved a modest success in 1854, and the exquisite "Shepherds' Farewell" scene has always remained a popular favourite.

Les Troyens finally reached the stage in 1863, when the second part only, *Les Troyens à Carthage*, was performed in Paris. Its failure broke Berlioz's heart, and his last years were clouded by depression and ill-health. (The opera was not staged in its entirety in French until 1969.) In the early 1860s he completed his last work, the sparkling Shakespearean opera *Béatrice et Bénédict*, but thereafter wrote little until his death.

Re-evaluation

While his large-scale works are still performed relatively infrequently because they are so expensive to mount, the *Symphonie fantastique* and the concert overtures (especially *Les francs-juges*, the Byronic *Le corsaire* and *Le carnaval romain*) have remained popular, as has the delicately scored orchestral song-cycle, *Les nuits d'été* (*Summer Nights*, 1841), based on a series of poems by Théophile Gautier.

Berlioz is still perceived as an "oddball" composer, and his originality has been derided as incompetence. But the persuasive advocacy of writers such as David Cairns and conductors such as Colin Davis and Roger Norrington have restored some previously neglected masterpieces, such as *Les Troyens*, to the repertoire, and affirmed Berlioz's importance as one of the foremost 19th-century composers.

Above: Caricature of Berlioz conducting, by Georges Tiret-Bognet (born 1855).

Felix Mendelssohn

A romantic who felt at ease within the mould of classicism.

PABLO CASALS (1876–1973)

Felix Mendelssohn was born into a wealthy and cultured Jewish family. His grandfather Moses was a liberal philosopher, and his father, Abraham, a prominent banker who fled from Hamburg (where Felix and his sister Fanny were born) to Berlin, to escape Napoleon's marauding troops. The Mendelssohn family enjoyed a privileged middle-class existence in Berlin, where the children (two girls and two boys) were baptized as Christians, and their father became a town councillor.

At the family home, the young Felix encountered many well-known philosophers, actors, artists, writers and musicians, and showed precocious talent in music, drawing and poetry. By the age of 13 he was already an accomplished composer, and in 1821 he was introduced by his teacher Karl Zelter to Goethe. A strong friendship based on shared interests developed between the literary giant (then aged 70) and the talented boy. Mendelssohn dedicated his Third Piano Quartet to Goethe, who greatly appreciated the young man's frequent visits to his home in Weimar.

ABOVE: Felix Mendelssohn (1809–47), painted by Gustav Zerner.

Musical impressions

Mendelssohn travelled a great deal as a young man, visiting Switzerland, Italy and Britain. He responded passionately both to literature and to impressions of people and landscapes encountered on his travels, both of which influenced his essays in the Classical musical forms of his day – symphony, overture, concerto, sonata and quartet. At the age of 16 he composed the brilliant Octet for strings, whose scherzo was inspired by the "Witches' Sabbath" scene in Goethe's *Faust*; two early overtures were inspired

LEFT: The Leipzig Conservatory of Music, founded by Mendelssohn in 1843.

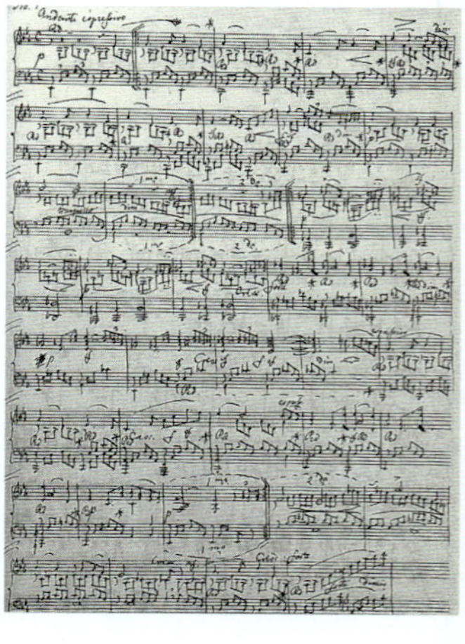

RIGHT: The autograph score of the first of Mendelssohn's six Songs Without Words *for piano (1829).*

Life and works

NATIONALITY: German

BORN: Hamburg, 1809;
DIED: Leipzig, 1847

SPECIALIST GENRES: Symphonies, overtures, concertos, piano pieces, songs.

MAJOR WORKS: Five symphonies; incidental music to *A Midsummer Night's Dream* (1826–42); Octet for strings (1825); *Hebrides* overture (1830); Violin Concerto (1844); two piano concertos; eight books of *Lieder ohne Worte* (*Songs Without Words*) for piano (1829–45); *Elijah* (1846).

respectively by Shakespeare (*A Midsummer Night's Dream*) and Goethe (*Calm Sea and Prosperous Voyage*). Two of his five mature symphonies – the *Scottish* (No. 3, dedicated to Queen Victoria) and the *Italian* (No. 4) – reflect his impressions of landscapes. His 1829 tour of Scotland also inspired the famous *Hebrides* overture, written after a visit to Fingal's Cave on the Isle of Staffa.

Classical style

In Mendelssohn's two piano concertos, the much-loved Violin Concerto and the *Scottish* Symphony, he made original experiments in form, such as the recycling of thematic material and the linking of movements, which later became a feature of much Romantic music. Yet, for all his Romantic traits, he was a worthy successor to Beethoven and Schubert in his fluent handling of musical material. Schumann called him "the Mozart of the 19th century – the one who sees most clearly through the contradictions of the period and for the first time reconciles them".

Mendelssohn's musical legacy

Through his tireless work as adminstrator and conductor, especially of the Lower Rhine Music Festival in Düsseldorf and the Leipzig Gewandhaus Orchestra, Mendelssohn was responsible for resurrecting buried treasures such as Bach's Passions and B minor Mass, and Handel's oratorios (on which he modelled his own *St Paul* and *Elijah*). He also helped to establish the role of the conductor, and raise standards of choral and orchestral performance.

In addition, Mendelssohn promoted the careers of other composers and performers, including Robert and Clara Schumann, Berlioz, the violinists Joseph Joachim, Ferdinand David (1810–73) and Henri Vieuxtemps (1820–81), and the pianist and composer Anton Rubinstein (1829–94). Many of his protégés were invited by Mendelssohn to join the staff of the newly opened Leipzig Conservatory (inaugurated in 1843), which under his direction became one of the most respected musical institutions in Europe.

ABOVE: An Art Deco programme cover for a dramatized pageant performance in London in 1936 of the oratorio Elijah *by Mendelssohn.*

In 1837 he married Cécile Jeanrenaud, daughter of a Lutheran pastor. They had five children and their marriage was happy but all too short: Mendelssohn died of overwork and grief in November 1847, aged only 38, shortly after hearing of the death of his beloved sister Fanny.

ABOVE: An annotated drawing made by Mendelssohn during his 1829 tour of Scotland.

Frédéric Chopin

After playing Chopin, I feel as if I had been weeping over sins that I had never committed, and mourning over tragedies that were not my own.

OSCAR WILDE (1854–1900), "THE CRITIC AS ARTIST"

Chopin epitomizes the figure of the "Romantic artist": withdrawn, temperamental, talented and doomed to a premature death from tuberculosis. Like Paganini, he was both composer and performer (although his concert-giving was actually very limited), but his music established the piano as the 19th century's most popular instrument. He was also an important figure in the early nationalist movement, drawing inspiration from the folk idioms of his native Poland.

Born of mixed French and Polish parentage, Chopin began to compose before he was seven, and made his first public appearances as a pianist. On leaving school at 16 he enrolled at the Warsaw Conservatory, where he began to compose in earnest, and on graduating three years later he decided to seek his fortune abroad. In August 1829 he made his debut in Vienna, playing two of his own piano works, including the set of Variations, Op. 2, whose publication Robert Schumann greeted with the immortal words, "Hats off, gentlemen, a genius!"

ABOVE: Frédéric Chopin (1810–49), painted by Albert Graefle.

Polish themes

Chopin then returned to Warsaw, intending to leave soon afterwards on a European concert tour, but the tour was postponed owing to the volatile political situation and, meanwhile, Chopin fell in love. While he dallied in Warsaw, unwilling to leave, he worked simultaneously on two piano concertos. From his early youth he had been fascinated by the rhythms and melodic vitality of Polish folk music, and the finales of both concertos are strongly influenced by Polish dances – particularly the mazurka. After giving their premières with great success,

LEFT: An artist's impression of Chopin at the piano, composing his Preludes.

RIGHT: The monastery of Valldemosa on the island of Majorca, where Chopin and George Sand took refuge in 1838.

Chopin left Poland for Paris. On the way, he composed the great *Revolutionary* Study, in response to the devastating news that the Russians had captured Warsaw.

Paris

Chopin gave his first concert in Paris in February 1832. Although he was not a great success with the public, he was introduced to Parisian *salon* society, where his music was a triumph. From then onwards – although he rarely played in public – he became an instant celebrity. He was a sought-after teacher, consorted with the wealthy and powerful, and enjoyed the friendship of fellow composers (Liszt, Berlioz, Bellini and Meyerbeer), writers such as Heinrich Heine and Honoré de Balzac, and artists such as Eugène Delacroix.

Chopin also found lovers in this talented milieu – first the aristocratic singer Delfina Potocka, and then the writer Aurore Dudevant (George Sand), whom he met in 1836 at the home of Liszt's mistress. Their intense relationship lasted for nine years. They spent the winter of 1838 in Majorca, hoping to reap the benefits of peace and a warm climate; but inclement weather and local hostility forced them to take refuge in the derelict monastery of Valldemosa. There Chopin finished his Twenty-four Preludes and other works, including the C sharp minor Scherzo. From then on he spent the winters in Paris and the summers at George Sand's country estate, but the affair finally fizzled out in 1847. By this time Chopin was seriously ill with consumption.

In 1848, Chopin was persuaded to visit England, where he played privately for fashionable social occasions. His last public appearance was at a charity concert for the benefit of Polish refugees. He died at his Paris home on 17 October 1849.

ABOVE: Chopin playing the piano in Prince Radziwill's salon in Paris, painted in 1887 by Hendrik Siemiradzki.

ABOVE: The writer Aurore Dudevant, alias George Sand (1804–76), Chopin's lover during the 1840s.

Chopin's music

Apart from the concertos and a handful of pieces for cello and flute, Chopin's output is all for solo piano. He borrowed the Irish composer John Field's new form, the nocturne, and raised it to fresh heights of subtle expression. His *études*, preludes, waltzes, impromptus and mazurkas were written to exploit and develop piano technique; while the later polonaises, the *fantaisies*, the scherzos, ballades, the Barcarolle and the two sonatas, were all virtuoso works.

Contemporaries praised the "exquisite delicacy and liquid mellowness" of his tone, and the "pearly roundness of his passages of rapid articulation". These are still the hallmarks of great Chopin interpretation.

Life and works

NATIONALITY: Polish

BORN: Zelazowa Wola, near Warsaw, 1810; **DIED:** Paris, 1849

SPECIALIST GENRES: Solo piano music.

MAJOR WORKS: Two piano concertos; three sonatas; four scherzos; 25 preludes; 27 *études*; 19 nocturnes; 44 waltzes; ten polonaises; 56 mazurkas; four ballades.

Robert Schumann

To me, Schumann's memory is holy.
The noble, pure artist forever remains my ideal.

JOHANNES BRAHMS (1833–97)

Just as Mozart and Beethoven dominated the musical scene in the late 18th and early 19th centuries, Mendelssohn and Schumann were the standard-bearers until 1850. Schumann's personality and career exemplify musical Romanticism: his moody nature, fluctuating between exuberance and deep depression; his prolonged struggle to win the hand of his adored Clara; his receptiveness to literary stimuli, his obsession with numerology and secret ciphers, and finally his collapse into madness and early death, possibly as a result of syphilis (which, together with tuberculosis, put a premature end to many a flourishing Romantic talent).

ABOVE: Robert Schumann (1810–56), painted by Gustav Zerner.

Literary influences

Schumann was the youngest child of a bookseller, whose interest in literature he clearly inherited. While still a schoolboy he began to compose music, and also to write articles and drama. He formed a society for the study of German literature, and in the novels of Jean Paul (pseudonym of Johann Paul Richter, 1763–1825) he found a role model for the two conflicting sides of his own personality, which he later characterized as Florestan (extrovert and impetuous) and Eusebius (dreamy, melancholic, introverted).

While studying law in Leipzig he began to take piano lessons with Friedrich Wieck, whose nine-year-old daughter Clara was showing extraordinarily precocious talent as a pianist. By now Schumann had decided to follow a career in music, but a hand injury (possibly a result of muscular weakness caused by mercury treatment

ABOVE: The market-place at Zwickau, where Schumann was born.

ABOVE: Schumann's study at his home in Zwickau.

for syphilis) put paid to his hopes of becoming a concert pianist. Instead, he decided to concentrate on composition and criticism.

Early works

By 1832 Schumann had published two major piano pieces: the *Abegg* Variations, based on a waltz theme derived from the name of a girl who had taken his fancy, and *Papillons (Butterflies)*, a set of pieces linked by events at a masked ball described in a novel by Jean Paul. He also began work on a symphony.

In 1834 he founded the influential music periodical *Neue Leipziger Zeitschrift für Musik*, which he used to promote new musical talent, including Brahms and Chopin. He also used its pages to fight artistic philistinism by way of an imaginary society, the Davidsbund, or "League of David" (named after the vanquisher of Goliath), whose members were given fanciful names: Schumann himself was either Florestan or Eusebius; Clara Wieck was Chiara or Chiarina; her father was Master Raro, and Mendelssohn was Felix Meritis. These names appeared in Schumann's set of 18 "characteristic pieces" for piano, *Davidsbündlertanze (Dances of the League of David*, 1837).

ABOVE: A romantic lithograph of Schumann composing his song-cycle Dichterliebe *(*A Poet's Love*).*

Life and works

Nationality: German

Born: Zwickau, Saxony, 1810; **died:** Endenich, near Bonn, 1856

Specialist genres: Songs, piano and orchestral works inspired by extra-musical impulses.

Major works: Piano music including *Carnaval* (1835), *Kinderszenen*, Fantasie in C and *Kreisleriana* (all 1838); about 250 songs, including song-cycles *Dichterliebe, Frauenliebe und -leben* (1840); four symphonies (No. 1 *Spring*, 1841, No. 3 *Rhenish*, 1850); Piano Concerto (1841–5).

Marriage to Clara

In 1834 Schumann fell in love with Ernestine von Fricken, to whom he became secretly engaged (and for whom he wrote the set of piano pieces later titled *Carnaval*). When he discovered that she was only the illegitimate daughter of a Baron, he broke off the engagement and

RIGHT: Schumann composing at his piano. He had hoped to be a pianist, but was overshadowed by his more accomplished wife, Clara.

ABOVE: Clara and Robert Schumann. Their marriage in 1840 marked the beginning of a partnership that was rare for its time.

transferred his affections to Clara Wieck, by now a delicate, dark-haired beauty of 15. Clara's father, who guarded his daughter jealously, was furious, and forbade Schumann to contact Clara. Then began an acrimonious six-year battle between Wieck – who made outrageous allegations against Schumann's character – and the lovers. Finally, in 1840, a court ruling paved the way for Schumann's marriage to Clara, which took place on 12 September.

Thus began one of the most remarkable musical marriages – a partnership far ahead of its time – in which both husband and wife tried to combine family life with successful, independent careers. Clara Schumann (1819–96) was one of the most extraordinary women of her time. Her fragile appearance belied a steely inner strength, which enabled her to continue her demanding schedule of concert appearances all over Europe (she was one of the finest pianists of her age) while also coping with repeated pregnancies and child-rearing. While the marriage was not without its strains (Schumann resented his wife's success, which overshadowed his own reputation as a composer), Clara stimulated her husband's creative imagination, acting as muse, confidant and critic.

Productive years

From 1840 onwards, almost in regular annual cycles, Schumann poured out song-cycles – including *Myrthen (Bridal Wreath)*, his wedding present to Clara, *Liederkreis* ("song-cycle"), *Frauenliebe und -leben* (*Woman's Love and Life*), and *Dichterliebe* (*A Poet's Love*) – chamber music (including a piano quartet and quintet, and three piano trios), and a body of piano music unsurpassed by any other contemporary composer. It was Clara who encouraged Robert to try his hand at larger-scale works. These included concertos for piano (the popular A minor Concerto was written for her), violin and cello; four symphonies, and other symphonic works including the exuberant *Konzertstück* for four horns and orchestra and the *Manfred* overture, inspired by Byron.

Schumann's orchestral music has been criticized for heavy-handed orchestration (partly the result of his

ABOVE: Clara Schumann (1819–96), photographed in middle age. She outlived her husband by 40 years.

ABOVE: An illustration to "Du bist wie eine Blume" ("You are Like a Flower") from Myrthen, *Schumann's wedding present to Clara.*

own ineptitude as a conductor), but any defects are amply compensated for by its melodic charm and ingenious construction. Schumann's innovations include the recurring use of motto themes and other cyclical devices: in the D minor Symphony (No. 4), he directed that the thematically linked movements should be played without a break.

His large-scale vocal works include the secular oratorio *Das Paradies und die Peri* (1843), one opera, *Genoveva* (1850) and choral music including *Scenes from Goethe's "Faust"* (1853). As a composer of songs and piano music, he proved himself a worthy successor to Schubert. His piano music encapsulates an enigmatic private world, full of literary and musical allusions, autobiographical references and cryptograms: many of the piano pieces are built around references to Clara, such as the musical equivalents of the letters of her name. His songs include settings of Goethe, Adelbert von Chamisso (1781–1838), Eduard Mörike (1804–75) and Joseph von Eichendorff (1788–1857), but his settings of Heinrich Heine (1797–1856), particularly the *Dichterliebe* cycle and some of the *Romanzen und Balladen*, are unsurpassed for their subtlety and lyricism.

Final years

In 1843 the Schumanns were reconciled with Friedrich Wieck, no doubt anxious to see his first grandchild. After a concert tour of Russia the following year they moved from Leipzig to Dresden. Schumann had always been prone to fits of deep depression and ill-health, and in 1846 he was so beset by nerves and chronic illness that he composed very little. By 1849 (when a revolutionary insurrection forced the family temporarily to flee Dresden), Schumann was becoming disillusioned by his failure to find a real job, and in 1850 he accepted an offer to become municipal music director in Düsseldorf.

His years in Düsseldorf were marked by failing health and mental instability, which adversely affected his abilities as a conductor and caused increasing problems with his employers. He became obsessed with phenomena such as table-turning, and suffered aural and cerebral disturbances. Among the highlights of his later years were his meetings with the young Johannes Brahms, whom Schumann hailed in his magazine as a musician of the future, and the violinist Joachim, for whom Schumann wrote his Fantaisie for violin and orchestra and the Violin Concerto. Among his last compositions were the charming *Phantasiestücke* (*Fairy-tales*, 1849) for clarinet, viola and piano, and five Romances (1853) for cello and piano.

Schumann's mental faculties finally gave way completely in February 1854, and he began to experience hallucinations. After a failed suicide attempt, he was committed to an asylum. During the two and a half years in which he was incarcerated there, he was not allowed to see Clara. She was finally summoned to his bedside two days before his death on 29 July 1856.

ABOVE: A page from the autograph manuscript of Schumann's Piano Sonata No. 3 in F minor, Op. 14, signed by the composer.

ABOVE: An illustration to Schumann's song "Der Nussbaum" ("The Walnut Tree"), No. 3 in the song-cycle Myrthen.

Franz Liszt

I have not seen any musician in whom musical feeling ran, as in Liszt, into the very tips of the fingers and there streamed out immediately.

FELIX MENDELSSOHN (1809–47)

As a composer, Liszt tends to stand on the sidelines of music history, partly because he does not fall neatly into the German symphonic tradition, stretching from Beethoven and Schubert, through Schumann and Mendelssohn, to Brahms and Bruckner. But his influence on 19th-century music was enormous: he was a superlative performer (the pianistic equivalent of Paganini), an outstanding teacher, and a dedicated champion of the "music of the future", expressed both in his own innovative and highly individual work, and in his promotion of Wagner.

Liszt was the son of an official at the Hungarian court of Haydn's employer, Prince Nikolaus Esterházy. He showed prodigious talent as a pianist, giving his first piano recital at the age of nine, and Prince Nikolaus funded his education in Vienna, where he moved from an early age in aristocratic circles.

ABOVE: A portrait of Franz Liszt in old age, when he styled himself the "abbé Liszt" (Liszt the abbot).

Paris

In the 1820s the flamboyant young virtuoso began to cause a sensation in Paris (where his family moved) and London, where he played for King George IV. Back in Paris in the early 1830s he met Berlioz and Paganini, and made piano transcriptions of some of their works, including Paganini's Caprices, which in Liszt's version became the *Grandes études de Paganini*. He was also greatly influenced by Chopin's Romantic style.

In 1834 he began a liaison with the Countess Marie d'Agoult, which produced three children (their second daughter Cosima later married Wagner). They began a peripatetic existence in Switzerland and Italy, during which time Liszt compiled his *Années de pèlerinage* (*Years of Pilgrimage*) for piano, and the *Album d'un voyageur*.

LEFT: Liszt's summer residence on the corner of the Ilm Park in Weimar.

RIGHT: Title page of the score of Liszt's Hungarian Rhapsody *No. 11.*

By 1839 the relationship was under strain, and Liszt resumed his touring career as a virtuoso. He and the countess finally separated in 1844, and Liszt began a period of wild womanizing, which contrasted oddly with his secret desire to become a priest. In 1848 he became music director to the ducal court at Weimar, where he eventually settled with his new companion, Princess Carolyne Sayn-Wittgenstein (who was trying to obtain a divorce from her husband). She shared Liszt's interest in religion and mysticism, and encouraged him to write his most ambitious works.

ABOVE: Liszt playing at a Parisian salon in 1840, painted by Joseph Danhauser. Listening (from left to right) are Alexandre Dumas, Victor Hugo, George Sand, Niccolò Paganini, Gioacchino Rossini and Countess Marie d'Agoult, Liszt's mistress.

Weimar

The Weimar years (1848–59) represent the zenith of Liszt's composing career. Most of his major works date from this period. They include two pieces inspired by the Faust legend – the *Faust* Symphony (based on Goethe) and *Episodes from Lenau's "Faust"* – the *Dante* Symphony; over a dozen symphonic poems inspired by literary or pictorial models, including *Tasso*, *Les préludes* (after a poem by Alphonse de Lamartine), *Mazeppa, Hamlet* and *Hunnenschlacht* (*The Battle of the Huns*); the E flat Piano Concerto, the *Totentanz* (*Dance of Death*) for piano and orchestra, and piano works including the Transcendental Studies, the B minor Sonata, many of the Hungarian Rhapsodies, and the *Harmonies poétiques et religieuses*. In addition, Liszt championed works by other up-and-coming composers, giving the premières of operas by Wagner, Schumann, Berlioz, Verdi and Donizetti, among others. During his tenure, Weimar became known as the haven of the "New German School".

Life and works

NATIONALITY: Hungarian

BORN: Raiding, 1811; **DIED:** Bayreuth, 1886

SPECIALIST GENRES: Tone-poems, programme symphonies, piano works.

MAJOR WORKS: *Années de pèlerinage* (1836–77); 19 *Hungarian Rhapsodies* (1846–85); piano concertos; *Funérailles* for solo piano (1849); tone-poems *Mazeppa, Tasso, Les préludes* and *Orpheus* (1851–4); Piano Sonata in B minor (1853); *Dante* Symphony (1856); *Faust* Symphony (1857); *Mephisto Waltz* No. 1 (1861).

Holy orders

By 1860, however, Liszt had fallen out with conservative Weimar society (which disapproved of his open affair with Carolyne Sayn-Wittgenstein, and his promotion of "avant-garde" music). He spent most of his later life in Rome, separated from the princess (who was never granted her divorce), and in 1865 he took minor holy orders.

A historian who saw him at the time described him as "Mephistopheles disguised as an abbé": his "diabolical" qualities, like Paganini's, were enhanced by his excessively tall, thin appearance, with long hair, originally blond, now white. He was still much sought-after as a teacher.

Liszt's later compositions are mostly sacred, and include the oratorios *Die Legende von der heilige Elisabeth* (*Legend of St Elisabeth*, 1857–62) and *Christus* (1862–7). However, they also include the Second and Third *Mephisto Waltzes*, one for orchestra (1880) and one for piano (1883). Among his last works – which became increasingly impressionistic in style – was *La lugubre gondola*, inspired by a premonition of his son-in-law Richard Wagner's death in Venice in 1882. Liszt himself died of pneumonia four years later in Bayreuth, having travelled there to attend the music festival.

Charles Gounod

A man has only a certain number of virtues, and all of Gounod's are concentrated on his art.

GEORGES BIZET (1838–75)

Gounod is remembered today chiefly for his opera *Faust*, based on Goethe's drama; and for the song "Ave Maria", an arrangement of his Meditation for violin on Bach's Prelude No. 1 in C. In fact, he was a prolific composer whose music was influential in both France and England.

Gounod's father was a painter and his mother a pianist. Like Berlioz, he studied at the Paris Conservatoire, winning the Prix de Rome in 1839. In Italy he fell under the spell of 16th-century polyphonic music, and began to write sacred music of his own (he also seriously considered becoming a priest). But he also met two influential women – the singer Pauline Viardot-Garcia (1821–1910), who introduced Gounod to the theatrical world, and Fanny Hensel (1805–47), who introduced him to her brother Felix Mendelssohn.

ABOVE: A scene from Goethe's Faust *– Faust tempted by Mephistopheles, painted in the mid 1820s by Eugène Delacroix.*

ABOVE: Charles Gounod (1818–93). His operas influenced Bizet and Tchaikovsky.

In 1843 Gounod visited the Mendelssohns in Leipzig, where he heard the famous Gewandhaus Orchestra, and music by Bach (then rarely performed).

Opera

On returning to Paris Gounod began to write grand operas in the currently fashionable style of Meyerbeer, together with elaborate masses and other church music. His opera *Faust* was performed at the Théâtre-Lyrique in 1859, and was an instant success: Gounod's gift for memorable tunes (such as the "Soldier's Chorus" and Marguerite's "Jewel Song"), and his subtle musical characterization of the doomed lovers, appealed to a Parisian audience growing weary of Meyerbeerian bombast. None of his other operas (even *Roméo et Juliette*, 1867) was ever quite as successful.

England

Between 1870 and 1875 Gounod took refuge from the Franco-Prussian War in England, where his music appealed to Victorian sentimentality. Here, he acquired a ferocious English mistress, Georgina Weldon (he was chronically unfaithful), and founded the Gounod Choir, which eventually became the Royal Choral Society. In the 1880s he was preoccupied with composing oratorios (two of which were written for the Birmingham and Norwich festivals). Apart from the popular *Petite symphonie* for 10 wind instruments (1885), few of his later works have survived the test of time.

Life and works

NATIONALITY: French

BORN: Paris, 1818; **DIED:** Paris, 1893

SPECIALIST GENRES: French grand opera, oratorios.

MAJOR WORKS: *Faust* (1859); *Roméo et Juliette* (1867); *La rédemption* (1881); *Mors et vita* (1884).

Georges Bizet

I am not made for the symphony; I need the theatre,
I can do nothing without it.

BIZET

Bizet's fame rests largely on just one work – the opera *Carmen* – but although his output was primarily operatic, several of his instrumental works, particularly the early Symphony in C, the suite *Jeux d'enfants* (*Children's Games*) and the incidental music to Alphonse Daudet's play *L'Arlésienne* (*The Girl from Arles*), have found a regular place in the repertoire.

Bizet studied at the Paris Conservatoire, winning many prizes, including the coveted Prix de Rome in 1857. Among his teachers was the opera composer Jacques Halévy, whose daughter he later married. The coolly classical Symphony in C was written at the age of 17, and in 1857 Bizet's one-act opera *Le docteur miracle* won joint first prize in a composition competition. He spent the years 1858–60 in Rome, where he picked up the chronic throat complaint which eventually killed him.

ABOVE: Georges Bizet (1838–75), composer of the highly popular opera Carmen, *the tragic story of the life, loves and death of a gypsy. Bizet wrote* Carmen *towards the end of his short life.*

Life and works

NATIONALITY: French

BORN: Paris, 1838; **DIED:** Bougival, 1875

SPECIALIST GENRES: Opera.

MAJOR WORKS: Symphony in C (1855); *Les pêcheurs de perles* (1863); *Jeux d'enfants* (1871); *Carmen* (1874).

Early set-backs

In 1863 Bizet's first important opera, *Les pêcheurs de perles* (*The Pearl-fishers*), was put on at the Théâtre-Lyrique in Paris. It failed, although the famous duet from Act 1, "Au fond du temple saint", has always been a popular favourite. Afterwards Bizet was obliged to take up hack work from publishers in order to survive financially. Meanwhile he worked on several more operatic projects, none of which achieved success. The colourful Provençal background of Daudet's play *L'Arlésienne*, for which Bizet provided incidental music in 1872, inspired him to find his true métier, and it was the similarly exotic setting and tragic story of Prosper Mérimée's *Carmen* which finally fired his imagination.

Carmen

Bizet's great opera was produced at the Opéra-Comique on 3 March 1875. It met with initial hostility, but within the next four years critics and audiences had come to appreciate the subtlety, power and originality of this vibrant score, and it was being performed all over Europe and in America. Bizet did not live to see its success. He died of a heart attack brought on by rheumatic fever on the night of its 33rd performance, just after the singer playing Carmen had fainted during the famous card-scene in which the gypsy heroine foretells her own death.

ABOVE: Célestine Galli-Marié, the first Carmen, who fainted on stage in the fortune-telling scene on the night Bizet died.

Other Composers of the Era

Sounds overflow the listener's brain
So sweet, that joy is almost pain.
PERCY BYSSHE SHELLEY (1792–1822)

ABOVE: Luigi Cherubini (1760–1842), in front of an Italian painting. This portrait was done in the year of his death by Ingres.

ABOVE: Daniel-François-Esprit Auber (1782–1871), a pupil of Cherubini and a successful opera composer.

Although the main focus of early Romantic opera lay in Italy, France did not lag far behind. One of the most influential figures was Luigi Cherubini (1760–1842), who straddled the transitional period between Classicism and Romanticism. He began his career in his native Italy, where several of his early operas were produced, and then settled in Paris just before the Revolution. During the early Napoleonic era, Cherubini produced his most influential operas in Paris, including *Médée* (*Medea*, 1797), *Les deux journées* (*The Two Days*, also known as *The Water-carrier*, 1800) and *Anacréon* (1803). He then fell out with Napoleon, and in 1805 went to Vienna, where he met Haydn and Beethoven (whose *Fidelio* owes much to *The Water-carrier*). In 1816 Cherubini became a professor (later, from 1822, director) of the Paris Conservatoire, where his influence as a teacher was far-reaching.

ABOVE: Costume designs for an 1827 German production of Daniel Auber's opera Le maçon *(*The Mason*), a musical drama written in the style of French* opéra comique.

Among Cherubini's pupils was Daniel Auber (1782–1871), who in 1842 succeeded his teacher as director of the Paris Conservatoire. He wrote nearly 50 operas, many in collaboration with the dramatist Eugène Scribe, of which the most famous are *La muette de Portici* (*The Dumb Girl of Portici*, 1828, which ends with a dramatic earthquake), *Fra diavolo* (*Brother Devil*, 1830), *Le domino noir* (*The Black Mask*, 1837) and *Manon Lescaut* (1856, a subject later tackled by Massenet and Puccini).

Bizet's teacher, Jacques Halévy (1799–1862), was another pupil of

ABOVE: The Irish composer John Field (1782–1837), who invented the nocturne.

Cherubini and also taught at the Paris Conservatoire from 1827 onwards. He was the principal singing coach at the Paris Opéra, 1829–45. Of his 30 or so operas, only *La Juive* (*The Jewess*, 1835) is occasionally revived.

Opera in Germany

Several German contemporaries of Weber advanced the cause of German Romantic opera, including Albert Lortzing (1801–51), one of the few composers who actually starved to death (he needed money so badly that he sold the valuable copyrights in his successful operas for a pittance). These included *Zar und Zimmermann* (*Tsar and Carpenter*, 1837), *Der Wildschütz* (*The Poacher*, 1842) and *Undine* (1845), based on Friedrich la Motte Fouqué's Romantic fairy-tale of 1811. This story had previously been adapted by the composer and writer Ernst Theodore Amadeus Hoffmann (1776–1822) for his 1816 opera of the same name.

Heinrich August Marschner (1795–1861), Weber's co-conductor at Dresden in the 1820s, was also influenced by the Romanticism of Hoffmann. He fared better than Lortzing, although his earlier operas – including the Gothic horror opera *Der Vampyr* (Leipzig, 1828), *Der Templar und die Jüdin* (*The Templar and the Jewess*, based on Scott's *Ivanhoe*, 1828) and *Hans Heiling* (Berlin, 1833) – achieved far greater success than his later works. He stands midway between Weber and Wagner as a pioneer of German Romantic opera.

Instrumental music

In the instrumental field, the violinist, conductor and composer Louis Spohr (1784–1859) scored great success in Germany, Vienna (where he led the orchestra at the Theater an der Wien) and London, where there was a considerable vogue for his work. From 1822 he was court conductor and later music director at the German court of Hesse-Kassel. He was one of the first conductors to use a baton. Spohr's operas have not survived, but his instrumental pieces are still played. They include 10 symphonies, 18 violin concertos, 4 clarinet concertos, and a quantity of chamber music, including string quartets and quintets, an octet for strings and wind, a fine nonet for strings and wind, and a quintet for piano and wind.

ABOVE: The Frenchman Jacques Fromenthal Halévy (1799–1862) taught Bizet.

ABOVE: The Swedish violinist and composer Franz Berwald (1796–1868).

His Swedish contemporary Franz Berwald (1796–1868) was an amateur composer. He ran an orthopaedic institute in Berlin, and then managed a glassworks in Sweden, before being appointed Professor of Composition at the Swedish Royal Academy of Music shortly before his death. Berwald is now remembered for his *Symphonie singulière* (No. 3, 1845), and for his charming *Grand septet* in B flat for wind and strings.

The Irish composer John Field (1782–1837) studied with Clementi in London, and went on to enjoy a successful European career as a virtuoso pianist, from his base in St Petersburg. He invented the short piano piece known as the "nocturne", a form and style borrowed by Chopin. Field's 19 examples are still in the solo piano repertoire.

The Rise of Nationalism

A traditional Catalan festival held on Ash Wednesday to celebrate the beginning of Lent, painted in 1907 by Xavier Nogues (1873–1940).

The Nationalist Movement

The art of music above all other arts is the expression of the soul of a nation.

RALPH VAUGHAN WILLIAMS (1872–1958)

Up to the 19th century, music had been perceived as a common international language. Italian opera held sway in all European countries, as popular in Vienna, Stockholm, Madrid or London as in Venice or Rome; while the German symphonic style of Haydn, Mozart and Beethoven was adopted and copied by all European composers of their time. Only towards the middle of the 19th century did composers start to become aware of cultural differences between nations, an awareness prompted partly by political events, and partly through the Romantic cult of individualism, celebrating the unique qualities of both individuals and nations.

ABOVE: A Bohemian Landscape with Shepherds, *painted in 1841 by Ludwig Richter.*

Revolutions of 1848

The nationalist movement took root in central Europe, where in the 1830s a wave of nationalist sentiment swept through Germany, Poland, Belgium and northern Italy (at that time ruled by Austria). Over the next decade, the desire of autonomous states for political independence from the mighty empires that ruled them coincided with the democratic urge to replace monarchies with republican governments more in tune with the needs of ordinary citizens. This unstoppable force flared into violence in the year 1848, when patriotic sentiment and revolutionary fervour spread across France, Italy, Germany and central Europe. Although the revolutions failed, and autocratic rule tottered on in some countries until World War I, a new spirit of

LEFT: The Old Market-place in Prague, painted in 1865.

RIGHT: Mlle Eglantine's Dancing Girls – *a poster of the Belle Epoque in Paris, by Henri de Toulouse-Lautrec (1864–1901).*

nationalistic patriotism informed European politics from this time onwards, spreading into culture and the arts.

Folk music

In music, this patriotic fervour encouraged composers to seek inspiration in their national roots, particularly folk culture (often viciously suppressed by the ruling authorities). In beleaguered Poland, carved up by neighbouring powers after the Congress of Vienna, Chopin indicated his revolutionary sympathies by his use of Polish folk dances, especially the polonaise and the mazurka.

The nationalist movement was particularly strong in Russia (where Italian music – and Italian composers – had long reigned supreme at the cosmopolitan court in St Petersburg). Glinka was the first composer to draw inspiration from the distinctive melodic patterns and rhythms of Russian folk songs and dances, and his example was taken up with proselytizing zeal by Balakirev and his disciples, known as "The Mighty Handful", or "The Five". They in turn influenced Tchaikovsky, whose music, while not consciously "nationalistic", is still recognizably Russian in inspiration, drawing on folk legends and idioms, and epic tales from Russian history.

Landscape and people

The central European areas of Bohemia, Slovakia and Hungary, whose native culture had been suppressed by centuries of foreign domination, were particularly receptive to the new spirit of nationalism. The Bohemian composer Smetana was the first to celebrate the rich history and characteristic landscape of his native land in a series of tone-poems entitled *Má vlast* (*My Homeland*), and in a series of operas based on Czech subjects, from historical or mythical figures such as Libuše, to contemporary peasant life in *The Bartered Bride*. He in turn influenced his pupil Dvořák, who effortlessly incorporated Czech song and dance idioms into European symphonic structures.

ABOVE: Spanish gypsy flamenco dancers, painted in 1898 by Ricardo Canals y Llambi (1876–1931).

ABOVE: The colourful costumes of 19th-century Russian ballet dancers.

Nationalism was by no means confined to central Europe. Edvard Grieg, Norway's greatest composer, was trained in the German musical tradition, but his music draws plentifully on the folk idioms which he picked up on walking excursions into the Norwegian mountains.

In Spain, Albéniz and Granados exploited the colourful characteristics of Moorish-derived flamenco in their piano and orchestral works; in Austria, the talented Strauss family turned Vienna into the waltz capital of the world, and in England, then languishing under a dearth of native talent, the quintessentially "English" Savoy Operas of W. S. Gilbert and Arthur Sullivan exploited a rich vein of satirical English humour.

Mikhail Glinka

I should like to unite in legitimate bonds the Russian popular song with the good old Western fugue.

GLINKA

Mikhail Glinka is regarded as the founding father of Russian nationalism in music. A contemporary of the Romantic poet Alexander Pushkin (1799–1837), he spent his early childhood with his grandmother, in whose care he first came into contact with the real music of Russia – the folk songs, pealing bells and ecclesiastical chants which would later inform his own music.

Glinka encountered Western music for the first time in his early teens, after he was sent to school in St Petersburg, where he studied violin and piano (including some lessons with John Field). On leaving school he became a minor civil servant, a job which left him plenty of time to indulge his passion for music as an enthusiastic amateur singer and pianist.

ABOVE: Mikhail Glinka (1804–57) working on his opera Ruslan and Lyudmila, *painted by Ilya Repin.*

Opera

He began to compose songs and chamber music in the 1820s, but a prolonged trip to Italy in the early 1830s left him with a passionate interest in opera. His own first opera, *A Life for the Tsar* – based on the patriotic story of a heroic Russian peasant who saves the tsar's life at the cost of his own – was written after his return to Russia, and proved hugely successful on its première in 1836.

Glinka found himself acclaimed as Russia's leading composer (although, to be fair, there was little competition), and encouraged by his success he immediately embarked on his next opera, *Ruslan and Lyudmila*. Unlike his earlier work, *Ruslan* was not well received. Its plot, based on Pushkin's fairy-tale (and involving such staging nightmares as a gigantic talking head), was cumbersome and ill-suited to the stage, and Glinka composed the score piecemeal. But its musical content – an appealing blend of elements drawn from Russian folk music, exotic orientalism and touches of "grotesquerie" – proved a rich legacy for all later Russian composers, as did his enthusiasm for the music of Spain (evinced in his two Spanish Overtures). Although Glinka died relatively young, his influence stretched far into the 20th century.

ABOVE: A cartoon of Mikhail Glinka by V. Samoilov (1853).

Life and works

NATIONALITY: Russian

BORN: Smolensk, 1804; **DIED:** Berlin, 1857

SPECIALIST GENRES: Opera and orchestral works in Russian nationalist style.

MAJOR WORKS: *Ivan Susanin (A Life for the Tsar*, 1836); *Ruslan and Lyudmila* (1842); Spanish overtures *Jota Aragonesa* (1845) and *Night in Madrid* (1848).

"The Mighty Handful"

Show me a people who have more songs!
NIKOLAY GOGOL (1809–52), 'THE CONTEMPORARY"

This curious crowd of dedicated drinkers, who were largely amateur composers, was given its nickname ("moguchaya kuchka") by the critic Vladimir Stasov in 1867. Their self-styled leader was Balakirev, while Borodin worked as a chemist, Rimsky-Korsakov was a naval officer and César Cui was a military engineer, and the most gifted, Mussorgsky, was a civil servant whom the rest regarded with a certain contempt. Nevertheless, their influence on Russian music in the late 19th century was immense.

Mily Balakirev

Balakirev began piano lessons with his mother as a young child and became a proficient pianist. While still quite young he came into contact with the music of Mikhail Glinka – one of his own earliest compositions was a piano fantasy on Glinka's opera *A Life for the Tsar*. Glinka imbued Balakirev with a strong sense of the importance of Russian nationalism, especially in music.

In the early 1860s Balakirev began to assemble a small band of like-minded disciples around him, and also played a major role in founding the Free School of Music in St Petersburg (he became its director in 1868). From this period date the beginnings of Balakirev's twin obsessions – collecting Russian folk music from far-flung regions and editing the works of other composers.

Balakirev was prone to fits of chronic illness and depression, and he was never a prolific composer. His single most frequently performed work is the ferociously difficult "oriental fantasy" for piano, *Islamey*. His main reputation was as an uncompromising critic of other composers' works. Tchaikovsky, among others, fell victim to Balakirev's stinging criticisms.

Of Balakirev's disciples, César Cui (1835–1918) was the least important. He wrote some 15 operas and other stage works, all of which have now disappeared from the repertoire.

Life and works

NATIONALITY: Russian

BORN: Nizny-Novgorod, 1837; **DIED:** St Petersburg, 1910

SPECIALIST GENRES: Romantic orchestral and piano works using Russian idioms.

MAJOR WORKS: *Overtures on Russian Themes* (1858, 1864); two symphonies; *Islamey* (1869); many other works for piano; symphonic poem *Tamara* (1882).

ABOVE: Mily Balakirev (1837–1910), the driving force behind Russian musical nationalism.

RIGHT: The statue of Peter the Great in front of the Cathedral in St Petersburg (1844).

Alexander Borodin

Borodin wrote only one opera, but music from it is still a concert favourite. The illegitimate son of an elderly Russian prince, Borodin was brought up by his gentle, cultured mother, and showed an early interest in music. But his chief love was science, and he became a distinguished professor of chemistry, founding a School of Medicine for Women.

In 1862 Borodin met Balakirev, and immediately began work on a symphony. It was performed in 1867 with great success, and he started work on his second. Shortly afterwards, in 1870, he began work on the opera *Prince Igor*, whose composition dragged on over the next 17 years, and remained unfinished at his death. Although it was subsequently completed by Rimsky-Korsakov, it is rarely performed, but the exotic "Polovtsian Dances" which end Act II (in Rimsky-Korsakov's orchestration) have always been highly popular, as have the Second Symphony in B minor and the languorous Nocturne from the Second String Quartet. Many of Borodin's most famous tunes formed the basis of the 1953 musical *Kismet*.

ABOVE: Alexander Borodin (1833–87), the composer of Prince Igor*, one of the most colourful Russian nationalist operas.*

Modest Mussorgsky

Arguably the most original composer of "The Five", Mussorgsky was bedevilled by mental instability, exacerbated by his heavy drinking. He showed an early talent for music, becoming a proficient pianist, but was destined for an army career. He completed his training and enlisted in the élite Preobrazhensky Regiment, but resigned his commission within two years. By then he had met Balakirev, with whom he began to study music seriously.

Financial difficulties then forced him to take a job in the civil service, while he continued to struggle with his first opera, *Salammbô*, based on Flaubert's novel. Although he started various projects with great enthusiasm, he finished few of them, and his three great operas – *Boris Godunov*, *Khovanshchina* (*The Khovansky Affair*) and *Sorochintskaya yarmarka* (*Sorochintsy Fair*) – were all left incomplete at his death (from alcoholic epilepsy), just after his 42nd birthday. He is also remembered

Life and works

NATIONALITY: Russian

BORN: St Petersburg, 1833; **DIED:** St Petersburg, 1887

SPECIALIST GENRES: Opera and orchestral works influenced by Russian and oriental idioms.

MAJOR WORKS: Symphony No. 2 in B minor (1877); *V srednei Azii* (*In the Steppes of Central Asia*, 1880); String Quartet No. 2 (1885); *Kniaz Igor* (*Prince Igor*, 1887).

ABOVE: Russian folk dancers. All five composers in "The Mighty Handful" drew inspiration from their native folk music.

Life and works

NATIONALITY: Russian

BORN: Karevo, 1839; **DIED:** St Petersburg, 1881

SPECIALIST GENRES: Opera in nationalistic idiom, piano works, songs.

MAJOR WORKS: *Boris Godunov* (1872); *Khovanshchina* (1872–5); *Kartinki s vistavki* (*Pictures at an Exhibition*) for piano (1874); *Night on the Bare Mountain* (1877); songs; song-cycles.

ABOVE: Modest Petrovich Mussorgsky (1839–81), painted in the year of his death by Ilya Repin.

for his orchestral piece *Ivanova noch na Lisoi gore* (*Night on the Bare Mountain*), inspired by a witches' sabbath, the famous *Kartinki s vistavki* (*Pictures at an Exhibition*) for piano, later orchestrated by Ravel, and his affecting song-cycles *Detskaya* (*The Nursery*, 1870), *Bez solntsa* (*Sunless*, 1874) and *Piesni i plyaski smerti* (*Songs and Dances of Death*, 1875–7).

Nikolay Rimsky-Korsakov

The most active and prominent of "The Mighty Handful" (and the youngest), Rimsky-Korsakov was born into a well-to-do naval and military family. He managed to combine a career as a naval officer with a productive sideline in composition. In 1871 he became professor of composition and instrumentation at the St Petersburg Conservatory.

Like his musical colleagues, he was deeply influenced by the nationalist work of Glinka, and he too fell under Balakirev's spell. Orchestration was Rimsky-Korsakov's great strength, and his talent for orchestral colour, combined with exotic, oriental-sounding harmonies, produced many rich and glowing works including the *Capriccio espagnol* (*Spanish Caprice*), the symphonic suite *Sheherazade*, inspired by tales from the *Thousand and One Nights*, and the *Voskresenaya* (*Russian Easter Festival Overture*). This heady blend of Russian folk material and orientalism also informed the scores of many of his 15 operas.

Rimsky-Korsakov devoted as much time to his friends' work as to his own. He was responsible for orchestrating and completing, among others, Borodin's *Prince Igor*, and several works by Mussorgsky, including *Night on the Bare Mountain* and the operas *Boris Godunov* and *Khovanshchina*. Naturally he applied his own ripe orchestral palette to these works, and the modern trend in performance is to return as far as possible to the originals.

ABOVE: Sheherazade and the Sultan – a scene from the Russian Ballet version of Rimsky-Korsakov's Sheherazade.

ABOVE: Nikolay Rimsky-Korsakov (1844–1908), one of the most popular Russian composers of his day.

Life and works

NATIONALITY: Russian

BORN: Tikhvin, near Novgorod, 1844; **DIED:** Liubensk, near St Petersburg, 1908

SPECIALIST GENRES: Operas based on Russian fairy-tales.

MAJOR WORKS: *Snegurochka* (*The Snow Maiden*, 1881); *Capriccio espagnol* (1887); *Sheherazade* Suite (1888); *Voskresenaya* Overture (1888); *Sadko* (1898); *Tsar Saltan* (1900); *Skazkanie o nevidimom gradie Kitezhe* (*The Tale of the Invisible City of Kitezh*, 1903–4); *Zolotoy Petushok* (*The Golden Cockerel*, 1906–7).

Pyotr Ilyich Tchaikovsky

Music is not illusion, but revelation.

TCHAIKOVSKY (ATTRIB.)

Tchaikovsky could claim to be the world's most popular "classical" composer. His music has always held a special appeal, for its passion, lyricism, extravagant emotionalism, and glowing orchestral colour. It reflects the extremes of temperament of its composer – a moody, melancholy character, prone to fits of depression, but also of heightened optimism.

Throughout his life, Tchaikovsky was torn between his desire for a "normal" family life, and his homosexual nature. This constant, unhappy struggle was reflected in his music, particularly the later symphonies. Although associated with "The Mighty Handful", Tchaikovsky was never a member of that nationalist group. Much of his own work, however, draws on a rich vein of Russian folk culture, which he successfully fused with the Western symphonic tradition. He wrote: "As far as the Russian element in my music is concerned, this is because I grew up in the provinces, imbued from earliest childhood with the indescribable beauty of the characteristic features of Russian folk music."

ABOVE: Pyotr Ilyich Tchaikovsky (1840–93), arguably the greatest and most popular Russian composer of the 19th century.

Early life

Tchaikovsky was the son of a mining engineer, and was born near the Urals. From his delicate, epileptic, French mother he inherited his hypersensitive nature and a tendency to hypochondria. When he was eight, the family moved to St Petersburg, where Tchaikovsky enrolled in the junior department of the School of Jurisprudence, a training-ground for the civil service. By this time, he had acquired twin younger brothers, Anatoly and Modest. He was exceptionally close to his mother, and her shocking death in a cholera epidemic when Tchaikovsky was 14 was a trauma from which he never really recovered.

LEFT: Tchaikovsky's father, Ilya Petrovich, with his twin sons Anatoly and Modest.

RIGHT: The square in front of the Mariinsky Theatre in St Petersburg in 1812.

Tchaikovsky graduated from the School of Jurisprudence in 1859, but found life in the civil service uncongenial. When a new music conservatory opened in St Petersburg in 1862, he enrolled as a student. He graduated in 1866, and found a job as a harmony teacher at the Moscow Conservatory, which had just been established by his mentor, the pianist and composer Nikolay Rubinstein (1835–81). The successful performance of an early overture in March 1866 encouraged him to start work on a symphony, entitled *Winter Daydreams*, which was performed under Rubinstein's baton in 1868. Modelled on Mendelssohn's *Italian* and *Scottish* Symphonies, it uses melodies influenced by Russian folk tunes.

ABOVE: A page from the autograph piano reduction of Tchaikovsky's ballet Swan Lake *(1877). The score is a masterpiece and the ballet is a major part of the dance repertoire.*

Music for the stage

Meanwhile Tchaikovsky was working on his first opera, *Voyevoda*, which was performed at the Bolshoy Theatre in Moscow in February 1869. Shortly afterwards Tchaikovsky met Balakirev, who recognized a major new talent and encouraged Tchaikovsky to tackle the tone-poem *Romeo and Juliet*. Its subject-matter, dealing with the favourite Russian themes of love and death, fired the composer's imagination, and it quickly became one of his most popular works.

ABOVE: The Swan Princess *by M. A. Vrubel (1867–1910), inspired by the heroine of* Swan Lake.

In May 1872, while staying at the country estate of his beloved sister Alexandra and her family, Tchaikovsky wrote his Second Symphony, known as the *Little Russian*, which incorporates genuine Ukrainian folk tunes into its musical fabric. It was well received, but he still wanted to achieve operatic success. This eluded him until after his first venture into the world of ballet, with *Lebedino ozero* (*Swan Lake*), written for the Imperial Ballet in Moscow. Though its first production in 1877 was a disaster, it was the first of his three great ballet scores – the others are *Spyashchaya krasavitsa* (*The Sleeping Beauty*) and *Shchelkunchik* (*The Nutcracker*) – which are still the cornerstones of the classical ballet repertoire.

In 1874 Tchaikovsky's confidence received another severe dent when Nikolay Rubinstein contemptuously rejected his First Piano Concerto as "worthless and unplayable". Tchaikovsky rightly ignored the criticism, and refused to alter the score. After Hans von Bülow gave its première in Boston, USA, the following year with great success, Rubinstein was forced to admit his

Life and works

NATIONALITY: Russian

BORN: Kamsko-Votkinsk, 1840; **DIED:** St Petersburg, 1893

SPECIALIST GENRES: Symphonies, ballets, opera.

MAJOR WORKS: Symphonies No. 1–6; Piano Concerto No. 1; *Swan Lake* (1877); Violin Concerto (1878); *Eugene Onegin* (1879); *Manfred* Symphony (1886); *The Sleeping Beauty* (1889); *The Queen of Spades* (1890); *The Nutcracker* (1891–2).

ABOVE: A scene from the 1993 Royal Ballet production of The Nutcracker.

mistake. Meanwhile Tchaikovsky – who spent as much time as possible travelling outside Russia – saw Bizet's *Carmen* in Paris, and Wagner's *Ring* at the opening of the Bayreuth Festival Opera. Under these twin influences he composed his tone-poem *Francesca da Rimini* (1876), based on the famous episode in Dante's *Inferno*, and, in complete contrast, the classically poised *Rococo Variations* for cello and orchestra.

Marriage

Around the same time, he began his long association with the multi-millionairess Nadezhda von Meck, the widow of a railway tycoon, who befriended the composer, commissioned his works and supported him financially, on condition they should never meet. Her patronage enabled Tchaikovsky to concentrate on composition, and rescued him from the emotional chaos caused by his hasty and imprudent marriage in 1877 to a mentally unbalanced music student, Antonina Milyukova, who had pestered him with love-letters.

Tchaikovsky had evidently hoped that marriage would bring "normality" to his life, but found himself unable to reconcile his wife's physical demands with his homosexuality. An attempt at reconciliation brought him to the brink of suicide, and within weeks of the wedding he fled to the safety of his brother's house in St Petersburg. Tchaikovsky never saw his wife again, though they were never divorced. In 1896, three years after his death, she was declared insane and spent the rest of her life in an asylum.

Fatalism

In the immediate aftermath of his disastrous marriage, Tchaikovsky composed his Fourth Symphony, dedicated to Madame von Meck. He told her, "There is a programme to our symphony…the introduction is the seed of the whole work…this is Fate, the fatal force which prevents the realization of our hopes of happiness."

From then onwards, his work became increasingly dominated by the idea of Fate. It pervades his opera *Eugene Onegin*, based on Pushkin's verse novel, a powerful emotional drama set against the colourful background of Russian country life. The opera had uncanny parallels with Tchaikovsky's own situation, particularly in the ardent letter written by the heroine, Tatyana, to the insensitive Onegin, who fails to appreciate her true worth until many years later.

The same sense of predestination dominates the Fifth Symphony (1888), whose famous opening theme represents "complete resignation before Fate", while the second

ABOVE: The Mariinsky Theatre in St Petersburg. Many operas and ballets by Tchaikovsky, including The Sleeping Beauty *and* The Nutcracker, *were first performed there.*

ABOVE: Tchaikovsky with his favourite nephew, "Bob" Davidov, son of the composer's beloved sister Alexandra.

movement, with its exquisite opening horn solo, is a radiant love-song. Both Fate and Pushkin provided the scenario for Tchaikovsky's last successful opera *Pikovaya dama* (*The Queen of Spades*), a chilling supernatural tale of the death and destruction wrought by a gambler's obsession.

In 1878 Tchaikovsky resigned his teaching job at the Moscow Conservatory. From then onwards he spent much time abroad, in Switzerland, where he completed the Violin Concerto (another work strongly influenced by Russian folk themes), and in Italy (the inspiration of the *Capriccio italien* and the *Souvenir de Florence*). In 1880 he commemorated the historic defeat of Napoleon's army with the brash but ever-popular *1812* Overture, which he described as "loud and noisy…and probably artistically worthless".

By 1884 Tchaikovsky felt the need to settle down, and found himself a country house near Klin, outside Moscow. He renewed one acquaintance, with Balakirev (who prompted him to compose the Byronic *Manfred* Symphony), but lost another when, in October 1890, his substitute mother-figure Madame von Meck abruptly discontinued their 14-year relationship.

Last years

The death of his sister in 1891 overshadowed an otherwise triumphant visit to the USA, and by the end of 1892 Tchaikovsky was beset by morbid fears. His last symphony, dubbed the *Pathétique* by his brother Modest, represents his final confrontation with the Fate that had dogged him. Tchaikovsky said that the symphony's "ultimate essence is Life", but that the anguished finale (marked *Adagio lamentoso*) represented Death. A week after its first performance on 28 October 1893, Tchaikovsky was dead, at 53.

The circumstances of his death remain a mystery. He is said to have died (like his mother) of cholera, after drinking a glass of unboiled water. Some scholars believe that he committed suicide, either by drinking contaminated water deliberately or by taking arsenic, to avoid becoming embroiled in a homosexual scandal over a relationship with a public figure.

ABOVE: A scene from the English National Ballet's 1999 production of Swan Lake, *with Tamara Rojo and Patrick Armand.*

ABOVE: The Retreat from Moscow *by the Polish artist Jan van Chelminski (1851–1925). Napoleon's rout by the Russian army inspired Tchaikovsky's* 1812 *Overture.*

Bedřich Smetana

Here is a composer with a genuine Czech heart,
an artist by the Grace of God!
FRANZ LISZT (1811–86)

Nationalist feeling was particularly strong in 19th-century Bohemia, where Czech customs, culture, and even language were suppressed by its German-speaking Austrian rulers. Smetana was the first Czech composer openly to draw inspiration from national legends, history and landscape, and to incorporate the melodic patterns and rhythms of folk music into his work.

The son of a German-speaking master brewer, Smetana showed early promise as a pianist, and having studied in Prague and Plzen despite parental opposition, he decided to make music his career. He began by making a precarious living as a concert pianist and teacher, during which time he met the Schumanns and Liszt. In 1848 he took an active role in the unsuccessful Prague Revolution, helping to man the street barricades, and the following year he married a fellow pianist, Kateřina Kolářová.

ABOVE: Bedřich Smetana, influential in the central European nationalist movement.

Of their four daughters, three died in childhood, followed by the consumptive Kateřina herself in 1858. The family had spent much of the previous two years in Göteborg, Sweden, where Smetana had opened a music school, and where he had begun to compose symphonic tone-poems modelled on the works of Liszt, including *Richard III* and *Wallensteins Lager*, based on Schiller's play.

Czech nationalism

A few months after his wife's death, Smetana became engaged to his brother's sister-in-law, whom he married in 1860. He returned to Sweden that year, but events in his homeland were changing fast. The Austrians had suffered heavy defeats at the hands of Napoleon III's armies, and the time was ripe for a resurgence of Czech national feeling.

Smetana returned home early in 1861, hoping to become conductor

ABOVE: The Bohemian town of Litomyšl, where Smetana was born in 1824. Bohemia was part of the Austrian Empire at this time.

ABOVE: A view of Prague, showing the banks of the river Vltava, the inspiration for one of the movements in Má vlast *(My Homeland).*

of the new Prague Provisional Theatre, which had just opened for the performance of opera and drama, but having been raised as a German-speaker it took time to convince the authorities of his ambitions for Czech music. His first opera, *Braniboři v Čechách* (*The Brandenburgers in Bohemia*), with a libretto by the nationalist poet Karel Sabina, was produced there in January 1866 to great enthusiasm. It was quickly followed by *Prodaná nevěsta* (*The Bartered Bride*), which, with its appealing blend of rustic lyricism and the skilful incorporation of Czech dances, became Smetana's most popular opera.

Prague Provisional Theatre

In the autumn of 1866 Smetana was finally appointed conductor to the Provisional Theatre, where he introduced many major works to the repertoire, among them his own *Dalibor* (1868), based on a legendary Czech hero, and *Dvě vdovy* (*The Two Widows*, 1874). His most overtly patriotic work, *Libuše* (dealing with the legendary founder of the Czech ruling dynasty), was composed between 1869 and 1872, but had to wait until June 1881 for its première, at the triumphant opening of the National Theatre.

During the composition of *Libuše*, Smetana also worked on his great cycle of symphonic poems celebrating Czech history, legend and topography, entitled *Má vlast* (*My Homeland*). The most popular individual item has always been *Vltava*, a portrait of the river that runs through Prague.

Deafness and disability

In the early 1870s Smetana became aware that his health was deteriorating: he complained of giddiness and hearing problems (the result of syphilis). In October 1874 he went completely deaf in one ear. He was also suffering from financial problems, but nevertheless managed to complete a new opera, *Hubička* (*The Kiss*), in 1876. At the same time he wrote his E minor String Quartet, subtitled "From My Life", whose last movement is dominated in the coda by a sustained high note representing the shrill whistling sound which Smetana suffered permanently as a result of his deafness.

Like Beethoven, Smetana continued to compose in spite of his disability. A seventh opera, *Tajemství* (*The Secret*, 1878), was followed by two new patriotic symphonic poems, *Tábor* (1878) and *Blaník* (1879), both inspired by episodes from Czech history. (*Tábor* is built around an early 15th-century Hussite chorale, effectively the Czech national anthem.)

Smetana's last opera, *Čertova stěna* (*The Devil's Wall*, 1882), took three years to write, during which time he complained of feeling as if he were standing "under a huge waterfall". He completed his Second String Quartet in March 1883, but his condition deteriorated and a year later he was taken to the Prague lunatic asylum, where he died on 12 May 1884.

ABOVE: *Smetana at his piano, composing the opera* The Bartered Bride *(1866).*

Life and works

NATIONALITY: Czech

BORN: Litomyšl, 1824; **DIED:** Prague, 1884

SPECIALIST GENRES: Nationalistic Czech operatic and orchestral music.

MAJOR WORKS: *The Bartered Bride* (1866); *Má vlast* (1872–9); String Quartet No. 1 in E minor *From My Life* (1876); *The Kiss* (1876).

Antonín Dvořák

I should be glad if something occurred to me as a main idea that occurs to Dvořák only by the way.

JOHANNES BRAHMS (1833–97)

Dvořák stands at the heart of the Czech nationalist musical movement. Like his contemporary Tchaikovsky, he succeeded in fusing folk idioms (the inflections of folk melodies and the characteristic rhythms of Czech dances such as the "furiant") with the symphonic techniques of his predecessors Beethoven and Brahms. His symphonies (particularly the three later ones), tone-poems, chamber and piano music are all part of the mainstream repertoire, and his operas (especially *Rusalka*, 1900) are becoming more widely known through frequent revivals.

Dvořák's father was the village butcher, and wanted his son to follow the same trade, but Antonín began to learn the violin at an early age and was eventually allowed to study music. He attended the Prague Organ School, and began his career as principal viola in the orchestra of the Provisional Theatre. He also began to compose and teach. He fell in love with a pupil, Josefina Čermáková, but when she rejected him he married her younger sister, Anna, in 1873.

By 1874 Dvořák had already completed four symphonies and two operas. That year he achieved his first real breakthrough when he entered several compositions in a competition intended to help struggling young artists. The jury included Brahms, who recognized Dvořák's talent, awarded him first prize, and took a fatherly interest in promoting his career.

ABOVE: Antonín Dvořák, the most famous Czech composer of his time. He was equally popular in England and the USA.

Brahms recommended Dvořák to his own publisher, who in 1878 commissioned a set of eight orchestral *Slavonic Dances* and within a year had published them, together with three *Slavonic Rhapsodies*, a Serenade for wind instruments, a String Sextet and Quartet, songs and piano duets. The infectiously tuneful *Slavonic Dances* in particular were a huge success, and assured Dvořák's international reputation.

England

From then on, Dvořák's works were performed as far afield as London and New York. In 1882 August Manns conducted the Sixth Symphony at the Crystal Palace in London, and the Stabat Mater was performed with great success in London the following year.

In 1884 Dvořák visited England for the first time, conducting some of his own works, including the Sixth Symphony and the *Scherzo capriccioso* for orchestra. He was immediately invited to write a new symphony (the Seventh, in D minor) for the Royal Philharmonic Society, and two large-scale choral works for the Birmingham and Leeds Festivals: the dramatic cantata *The Spectre's Bride* for Birmingham, and the oratorio *St Ludmila* for Leeds.

Life and works

NATIONALITY: Czech

BORN: Nelahozeves, 1841; **DIED:** Prague, 1904

SPECIALIST GENRES: Opera, symphonies, tone-poems, chamber music.

MAJOR WORKS: Nine symphonies, including No. 9 *From the New World* (1893); Serenade for strings (1875); Stabat Mater (1877); *Slavonic Dances* (1878 and 1886); Requiem (1890); Cello Concerto in B minor (1895); operas; chamber music; piano music; songs.

London also saw the performance in 1887 of the *Symphonic Variations*, conducted by Hans Richter, and, in 1890, of the Eighth Symphony – often known as the *English*, although it is a thoroughly "Bohemian" work. The next year Dvořák received an honorary doctorate from Cambridge University.

America

In 1891 he was invited to become director of the new National Conservatory of Music in New York, at a very attractive salary. Dvořák spent five months touring Bohemia with several new works – including the Dumky Piano Trio and a cycle of three overtures, *V přírodě (In Nature's Realm)*, *Carnaval* and *Othello* – before sailing for New York in spring 1892.

He spent three years there, teaching, conducting and composing. The Ninth Symphony (*From the New World*), the *American* String Quartet and Quintet, the Cello Concerto (whose coda reflects Dvořák's grief at hearing of the death of his sister-in-law Josefina), and the charming Violin Sonatina (dedicated to his six children) were all composed there. Several of these works show the influence of American folk music, especially the negro spiritual.

ABOVE: The National Theatre in Prague, opened on 18 November 1883. Dvořák's opera The Jacobin *was premièred there six years later.*

Return to Prague

The lure of his native Bohemia eventually proved too strong, and after 1895 Dvořák decided not to return to America. Instead he resumed teaching at the Prague Conservatory, and spent time with his family. The last decade of his life produced many new works, including two string quartets, four symphonic poems based on Czech folk tales – *Vodník* (*The Water Goblin*), *Zlatý kolovrat* (*The Golden Spinning-wheel*), *Polednice* (*The Noonday Witch*) and *Holoubek* (*The Wild Dove*), 1896–7 – and his two best-known operas, *Čert a Káča* (*Kate and the Devil*, 1899) and *Rusalka* (1900), both based on fairy-tales. He died on 1 May 1904, and had a state funeral.

LEFT: Dvořák with his wife and children, photographed shortly after their arrival in New York, 1892.

RIGHT: Dvořák conducting at the Chicago World Fair in 1893. The programme included the Eighth Symphony and three of the Slavonic Dances.

Edvard Grieg

I am sure my music has a taste of codfish in it.

GRIEG

Grieg was Dvořák's Scandinavian equivalent: a composer working outside the mainstream European symphonic tradition, though trained within it, who brought to his music a warmth and natural melodic facility that owed much to the folk music of his native land.

Grieg's father, Alexander, was a prosperous merchant of Scottish descent (the family name was originally Greig), who held the post of British Consul to the Norwegian port of Bergen. His mother, Gesine Hagerup, was an excellent pianist who undertook the musical education of her fourth child, Edvard, instilling in him a love for the music of Mozart, Weber and Chopin.

In 1858 the Grieg family was visited by the charismatic violinist Ole Bull, one of the pioneers of the fledgling Norwegian nationalist movement. Bull persuaded Grieg's parents to send him to the Leipzig Conservatory, where he studied piano with the composer and pianist Ignaz Moscheles (1794–1870) and composition with Carl Reinecke (1824–1910). He also heard Clara Schumann play her husband's Piano Concerto, which had an enormous influence on his own future concerto.

ABOVE: A portrait of Edvard Grieg (1843–1907), whose music epitomizes the scenic beauty of Norway.

Norwegian music

Grieg began his career in Bergen, then went to Copenhagen. There he met his cousin and future wife, the singer Nina Hagerup, for whom he wrote many of his songs. His growing sympathy with the Norwegian nationalist movement dates from this period, when he met the young nationalist composer Rikard Nordraak. The two of them planned to found a society for the promotion of Norwegian music, but Nordraak died of tuberculosis. During the winter of

ABOVE: Grieg with his wife Nina – the chief interpreter of his songs – photographed in 1906, not long before his death.

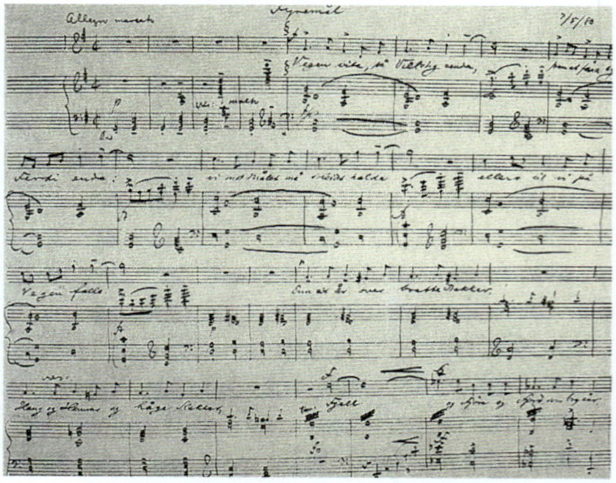

ABOVE: The autograph manuscript of Grieg's song Fyremaal *(1880). Grieg often drew on Norwegian folk music for inspiration.*

1865–6 Grieg also visited Rome, where he met the playwright Henrik Ibsen. He married Nina in June 1867: their long partnership survived the death in infancy of their only child, Alexandra, and Grieg's later infidelities.

Grieg had already begun to write piano pieces with a national tinge (including the first of many sets of *Lyric Pieces*), but in 1868 his enthusiasm was aroused by his discovery of a volume of Norwegian folk songs. The influence of these mountain melodies spilled over into the Piano Concerto, which Liszt played through at sight when the Griegs visited him in Italy in 1869. On returning to Norway, and with Liszt's encouragement, Grieg determined to make a name for himself. He gave a concert of his own works (songs, piano pieces, and sonatas for piano and violin), and established an Academy of Music in the Norwegian capital, Christiania (now Oslo).

Peer Gynt

Grieg also began to collaborate with the playwright and poet Bjørnstjerne Bjørnson, director of the Christiania Theatre, on incidental music for his play *Sigurd Jorsalfar* (1872) and a potential opera. But it was Ibsen's request for incidental music to his play *Peer Gynt* in 1874 which fired Grieg's creative imagination. The resulting music, which includes "Morning", "In the Hall of the Mountain King" and "Solveig's Song", is well known from two orchestral suites, and rivals the Piano Concerto in popularity.

ABOVE: A Norwegian folk dance. The distinctive idioms of these dances, and the sounds made by Norwegian folk instruments, permeated all of Grieg's music.

Life and works

NATIONALITY: Norwegian

BORN: Bergen, 1843; **DIED:** Bergen, 1907

SPECIALIST GENRES: Songs, piano music.

MAJOR WORKS: Piano Concerto in A minor (1868); *Peer Gynt* Suites (1874–5); *Holberg* Suite (1884); 66 *Lyric Pieces* for piano (1867–1901); 140 songs.

Troldhaugen

From the mid 1870s Grieg combined long European concert tours as a conductor and pianist with increasing periods of time spent in reflection and composition amid the beauty of the Norwegian mountains. He was particularly fond of the Hardanger district, where he composed in a small wooden hut by a lake. On frequent walking expeditions into the mountains he heard and collected folk songs and dances, whose idioms infuse his own piano pieces and songs, including the cycle *Haugtussa* (*The Mountain Maid*).

In 1884, the year he completed the anachronistic *Holberg* Suite for strings, based on 17th-century dances, he had a house built at Troldhaugen, above the Hardanger fjord near Bergen, where he entertained friends such as Percy Grainger. His much-loved home is celebrated in "Wedding Day at Troldhaugen", included in the eighth book of *Lyric Pieces*, 1896.

By 1900 Grieg was suffering increasingly from lung disease. He was still much in demand internationally, and retained his life-long interest in his national folk music (his last works include a piano arrangement of Norwegian peasant fiddle tunes, called *Slåtter*). He died on the point of leaving for England on another concert tour, and his ashes were buried at Troldhaugen, in the side of the cliff overlooking the fjord.

ABOVE: The great Norwegian playwright Henrik Ibsen (1828–1906). At Ibsen's request, Grieg wrote incidental music for his play Peer Gynt *(1874).*

Isaac Albéniz

Everything is possible on the piano.
FERRUCCIO BUSONI (1866–1924)

While French and Russian composers such as Bizet, Lalo and Rimsky-Korsakov were flirting with Spanish idioms, Albéniz was the first genuinely Spanish composer of international reputation. Born in Catalonia, he was a child prodigy, making his public debut as a pianist at the age of four. He made his first concert tour at eight, and then enrolled as a student at the Madrid Conservatory, but a year later, still aged only ten, he ran away to Castile, where he went round various cities earning enough to live on by playing the piano as a vaudeville act.

ABOVE: An Andalucian folk dance. The bell-tower of Seville Cathedral is in the distance.

ABOVE: The Spanish composer Isaac Albéniz (1860–1909), one of the masters of atmospheric piano music.

From then onwards, he suffered from incurable wanderlust. In 1872 he took off once more, this time as a stowaway on a boat bound for South America. He returned to Spain in 1873, but then left for England and then Leipzig, where he continued his studies. A scholarship enabled him to study composition and piano in Brussels, after which he spent several years trailing around Europe in the wake of Liszt.

In 1883 Albéniz settled briefly in Barcelona, where he married and had three children. Around 1890 he finally gave up his concert career, but still flitted between London (where he was commissioned to write three operas based on librettos written by a wealthy patron) and Paris, where he taught piano and made friends with other notable composers. From 1903 onwards he lived near Nice, moving to Cambo-les-Bains in the Pyrenees shortly before his death. His last years were spent working on the four books of piano pieces collectively called *Iberia*, tonal portraits of Spain which were orchestrated by Fernandez Arbós (1863–1939) and other composers after Albéniz's death.

Albéniz's most important works are for solo piano. All are underpinned by the rhythms and timbres of Spanish folk music. The 12 pieces that make up the *Iberia* Suite are extraordinarily forward-looking, almost impressionistic in style: they influenced both Debussy and Ravel.

Life and works

NATIONALITY: Spanish

BORN: Camprodón, 1860; **DIED:** Cambo-les-Bains, 1909

SPECIALIST GENRES: Virtuoso piano music.

MAJOR WORKS: *Iberia* (1906–9); Piano Concerto (c.1887); *Rapsodia española* for piano and orchestra (1887).

Enrique Granados

I am not a musician but an artist.

GRANADOS

Albéniz's compatriot Enrique Granados was also from Catalonia. He was born seven years after Albéniz, and also became known as a brilliant pianist. In 1887 he went to Paris to study the piano, returning to Barcelona two years later, and making his debut there in 1890. In 1898 his comic opera *Maria del Carmen* was produced in Madrid, winning its composer a royal commendation. From then onwards Granados divided his time between composing, teaching and performing, either as a solo pianist, or in company with musicians such as the French violinist Jacques Thibaud (1880–1953) and the Spanish cellist Pablo Casals (1876–1973).

Granados went on to write several more stage works inspired by Spanish themes, but his greatest success lay in his solo piano music. This included a set of 12 Spanish dances, and the piano suite *Goyescas*, a set of six highly original pieces each inspired by a painting by Goya (the most famous is "Quejas, o la Maja y el ruiseñor" – "The Maiden and the Nightingale").

The huge success of *Goyescas*, both in Spain and France, led indirectly to his death. Before leaving Paris, he had proposed to turn the suite into an opera. But the Paris Opéra prevaricated over the commission, partly as a result of the outbreak of war, and instead, Granados offered the work to the Metropolitan Opera in New York. In January 1916 he and his wife crossed the Atlantic to attend the opera's première. They returned in March, via Liverpool, from where they embarked on the liner *Sussex*, bound for Dieppe. The ship was torpedoed in the English Channel by a German submarine, and Granados drowned trying in vain to save his wife.

ABOVE: Enrique Granados (1867–1916). Like Albéniz, his works were influenced by Spanish folk idioms.

Life and works

NATIONALITY: Spanish

BORN: Lérida, 1867;
DIED: English Channel, 1916

SPECIALIST GENRES:
Piano music incorporating Spanish idioms.

MAJOR WORKS: 12 *Danzas españolas* for piano (1892–1900); *Goyescas* Suite for piano (1911).

ABOVE: The Clothed Maja, *a typical painting by Francisco Goya (1746–1828), now in the Prado in Madrid. Goya's paintings inspired several works by Granados.*

Arthur Sullivan

You ought to write a grand opera, Sir Arthur, you would do it so well.

QUEEN VICTORIA (1819–1901)

Arthur Sullivan was one of the most talented English composers of the 19th century, but he can only be described as a "nationalist" by default. In fact, he was impeccably trained in the German tradition. The son of a bandmaster, he won the first Mendelssohn Scholarship to the Royal Academy of Music in London, and went on to study at the Leipzig Conservatory, where he met Liszt and Grieg, before returning to England in 1861 to become a church organist. He was appointed Professor of Composition at the Royal Academy in 1866.

ABOVE: Sir Arthur Sullivan (1842–1900). He could never take his brilliantly successful "Savoy Operas" seriously.

Savoy Operas

Sullivan was determined to succeed as a composer of serious and worthy music, particularly oratorio. But it was his meeting in 1871 with the playwright William Schwenk Gilbert (1836–1911) that ensured his lasting fame. Their first collaboration, *Thespis*, was a failure. But their second, *Trial by Jury* (1875), written at the instigation of the theatrical impresario Richard D'Oyly Carte, was a triumphant success. It was the first of a brilliant sequence known as the "Savoy Operas", operettas produced mostly at the Savoy Theatre in the Strand, London (which D'Oyly Carte – scenting huge profits – leased specially). Nearly all Gilbert and Sullivan's collaborations were resounding successes, *HMS Pinafore* running for 700 nights.

ABOVE: The cover of a piano arrangement by Bucalossi of songs from The Mikado*, inspired by the vogue for Orientalism.*

Composer and librettist were perfectly suited. Gilbert's hilariously witty librettos, parodying eminent British institutions such as the law, the House of Commons, the police, the women's movement, the "Aesthetic" movement led by Oscar Wilde, and recognizable figures in public life, were perfectly matched by Sullivan's incomparable gift for musical parody (of Handel, Donizetti, Wagner, Verdi and others), allied with a gift for fluent melody and apt orchestration.

The partnership came under strain during *The Gondoliers*, and their last two operas, *Utopia Limited* (1893) and *The Grand Duke* (1896), were less successful. Sadly, Sullivan disparaged his own talents, rating his serious music, such as the grand opera *Ivanhoe*, much more highly. His assessment proved mistaken: the Savoy Operas have never lost their immense popularity, while the "serious" works have sunk without trace.

Life and works

NATIONALITY: British

BORN: London, 1842; **DIED:** London, 1900

SPECIALIST GENRES: Operetta.

MAJOR WORKS: *The Sorcerer* (1877); *HMS Pinafore* (1878); *The Pirates of Penzance* (1879); *Patience* (1881); *Iolanthe* (1882); *Princess Ida* (1884); *The Mikado* (1885); *Ruddigore* (1887); *The Yeomen of the Guard* (1888); *The Gondoliers* (1889).

Jacques Offenbach

The opéra-bouffe is simply the sexual instinct expressed in melody.

New York Times, 1876

While the "Savoy Operas" of Gilbert and Sullivan took a wry look at Victorian England, France found its equivalent in the sparkling operettas of Jacques Offenbach.

Offenbach's German-Jewish family took their name from their home town of Offenbach-am-Main. His father Isaac was a cantor at a Cologne synagogue, who in 1833 took two of his sons, Julius and Jacques (by then a promising cellist), to Paris. Jacques was enrolled at the Conservatoire, but left after a year, and found a job in the orchestra at the Opéra-Comique. He also began to play in Paris salons, for which he wrote many pieces for cello and piano. During the 1840s he earned a living chiefly as a performer, and in 1850 he was appointed conductor at the Théâtre Français. In 1855 he rented the small Marigny theatre in the Champs-Elysées, where he put on a summer programme of short comic pieces. The success of this venture encouraged him to move to a more permanent venue at the Théâtre Comte, which he renamed the Bouffes-Parisiens.

ABOVE: Jacques Offenbach (1819–80). His operettas took Paris by storm in the late 1800s.

Life and works

NATIONALITY: German

BORN: Cologne, 1819; **DIED:** Paris, 1880

SPECIALIST GENRES: French operetta and opéra-bouffe.

MAJOR WORKS: *Orphée aux enfers* (*Orpheus in the Underworld*, 1858); *Geneviève de Brabant* (1859); *La belle Hélène* (1864); *La vie parisienne* (1866); *La grande duchesse de Gérolstein* (1867); *La périchole* (1868); *Les contes d'Hoffmann* (1881).

Burlesque opera

Over the next 25 years Offenbach turned out over 90 stage works. His witty, light-hearted operettas satirized composers such as Wagner and Meyerbeer and captured the prevailing hedonistic spirit of Second Empire Paris, with its passion for music-hall dances and its relentless debunking of the Establishment.

In the mid 1870s his audiences began to tire of his productions and a run of expensive failures left him bankrupt, just at the time that Johann Strauss, whom Offenbach had encouraged to write operetta, was enjoying his greatest success with *Die Fledermaus*. Offenbach turned to a different kind of opera.

The Tales of Hoffmann

Offenbach's reputation also rests on his one more serious work, *Les contes d'Hoffmann*, which was left unfinished at his death. His supreme lyrical gift informs this tale of thwarted love, based on three stories by the Romantic author E. T. A. Hoffmann which are treated as episodes from his life. The "Giulietta" act, set in Venice, contains the "Barcarolle" which, together with the "Can-can" from *Orpheus*, ranks among the world's most famous melodies.

ABOVE: A can-can dance from Offenbach's La vie parisienne, *1866. Rossini called Offenbach "the Mozart of the Champs-Elysées".*

"The Waltz Kings"

Where he fiddles, all dance – dance they must...

IGNAZ MOSCHELES (1794–1870)

If Sullivan personified Victorian England and Offenbach Second Empire Paris, 19th-century Vienna belonged to the Strauss family. Johann Strauss and his sons took the Austrian capital by storm with a torrent of light music – polkas, galops, quadrilles, marches, and particularly waltzes. In their hands the waltz, a sophisticated form of the Austrian *Ländler,* superseded its humble peasant origins to become the favoured dance of working-class dance halls and aristocratic ballrooms alike.

ABOVE: Johann Strauss II, painted at the height of his fame in 1888 by August Eisenmenger (1830–1907).

Johann Strauss the elder

The composer, conductor and violinist Johann Strauss (1804–49) was the son of an innkeeper of Hungarian-Jewish origin. A talented violinist, he started out as the friend and partner of Josef Lanner, director of a popular dance orchestra. In 1825 they parted company and Strauss formed his own ensemble, which soon began playing at popular Viennese taverns. Within a few years the Strauss orchestra had been engaged to play in the dance hall at the fashionable Sperl Inn in the suburb of Leopoldstadt, a popular venue which attracted distinguished foreign visitors including Chopin, the young Richard Wagner, and the writer Hans Christian Andersen.

ABOVE: Johann Strauss I (1804–49) with his colleagues playing at a ball in Vienna.

The repertoire of the Strauss orchestra ranged from dances, such as Strauss's own *Champagne Waltz* and *Sperl Festival Waltz*, to fantasies on popular operatic airs of the time by Bellini, Auber, Rossini, Meyerbeer and others. Of Strauss's vast output, perhaps the best-known piece is the *Radetsky March* (1848).

From 1833 onwards the Strauss orchestra began to travel abroad, not only throughout Austria and Germany, but also to Paris and London, where it took part in Queen Victoria's coronation celebrations. Back in Vienna, Strauss was created Imperial Director of Court Dance Music. He had six children with his wife Anna (three of their

ABOVE: The cover of a piano reduction of Strauss II's Promenade Quadrille.

ABOVE: Josef Strauss (1827–80), one of Johann II's younger brothers, also a talented musician.

sons carried on the family tradition), before leaving her to live with a mistress who bore him another seven offspring. He died, aged 45, of scarlet fever caught from one of his children.

Johann Strauss II

NATIONALITY: Austrian

BORN: Vienna, 1825; **DIED:** Vienna, 1899

SPECIALIST GENRES: Viennese dance music and operetta.

MAJOR WORKS: *Die Fledermaus* (1874); *Der Zigeunerbaron* (1885); waltzes, including *Morgenblätter* (*Morning Newspapers*, 1864), *An der schönen blauen Donau* (*The Blue Danube*, 1867), *Geschichten aus dem Wienerwald* (*Tales from the Vienna Woods*, 1868) and *Wein, Weib und Gesang* (*Wine, Woman and Song*, 1869); polkas, including *Tritsch-Tratsch* (1858) and *Unter Donner und Blitzen* (*Thunder and Lightning*, 1868).

Johann Strauss the younger

Strauss's eldest son, Johann, was known as "The Waltz King". He learnt the violin against his father's wishes, and in 1844 set up a rival orchestra that merged with the original Strauss band after the death of Johann I. Between 1856 and 1886 Strauss and his orchestra toured Europe, finding particular favour in St Petersburg, and also visited America.

His own compositions – waltzes, polkas, quadrilles and marches – were even more wildly acclaimed than his father's, and many of his waltzes are almost symphonic in scope. His works captured the hedonistic spirit of the Austro-Hungarian Empire at the height of its glory before World War I.

Strauss was also a talented composer for the theatre. Of his 18 light operas and ballets, the two outstanding works are *Die Fledermaus* (*The Bat*), an irresistible blend of Offenbachian wit and Viennese suavity; and *Der Zigeunerbaron* (*The Gypsy Baron*), in which Viennese Romanticism is spiced with Hungarian gypsy idioms. Both are still often performed.

Johann's younger brothers Josef (1827–80) and Eduard (1835–1916) both shared in the direction of the Strauss family orchestra, and both wrote dance music of a similar kind, though neither achieved the same immense popularity as their father and elder brother.

ABOVE: Eduard Strauss (1835–1916), the youngest of the Strauss brothers, pictured by a Vanity Fair cartoonist in 1895.

ABOVE: The Viennese Ball *by Wilhelm Gause (1853–1916). The dance music of the Strauss family was the staple musical fare for such occasions.*

Other Nationalistic Composers

Art must be parochial in the beginning to be cosmopolitan in the end.

George Moore (1852–1933), "Hail and Farewell"

Many minor French composers flourished during the 19th century, among them Léo Delibes (1836–91), a composer and organist who, like Offenbach, became noted for his operettas. His posthumous fame rests on two ballet scores for the Paris Opéra – *Coppélia* (1870, based on a story by E. T. A. Hoffmann) and *Sylvia* (1876) – and three operas. These include *Lakmé* (1883), based on a popular oriental subject. It contains the challenging coloratura "Bell Song" and the seductive "Flower Duet" for women's voices, "Dôme épais de jasmin".

ABOVE: Emmanuel Chabrier (1841–94), painted in 1881 by Edouard Manet.

Delibes's younger contemporary Jules Massenet (1842–1912) specialized in opera and oratorio: he excelled at erotic suggestion (particularly if it involved a penitent prostitute), whether in a biblical or secular context. His most famous operas include *Hérodiade* (1881, based on the story of Salome), *Manon* (1884, based on the story by Abbé Prévost later tackled by Puccini), *Werther* (1892, based on Goethe's famous early novel), *Thaïs* (1894, which contains the famous "Meditation" for solo violin), *Cendrillon* (*Cinderella*, 1899), and *Don Quichotte* (1910, based on Cervantes's *Don Quixote*). Massenet's operas were enormously popular in his day; audiences today find them rather sickly and over-sentimental, but *Manon* and *Werther* are still in the repertoire.

ABOVE: A painting entitled Norwegian Landscape: Evening *(c.1904) by Walter Leistikow. Many composers took inspiration from the wild Norwegian scenery.*

Emmanuel Chabrier (1841–94) was a civil servant who decided to turn to music after hearing Wagner's *Tristan und Isolde*. His operas include *L'étoile* (1877), *Gwendoline* (1886) and *Le roi malgré lui* (*King despite himself*, 1887), all of which have had occasional revivals, but his most famous piece is the sparkling, Iberian-sounding orchestral rhapsody *España* (1883).

Edouard Lalo (1823–92) also drew inspiration from south of the Pyrenees, in his *Symphonie espagnole* (1874) for violin and orchestra, which he followed with a *Fantaisie norvégienne* (1880) for the same combination. He wrote several operas and ballets, of which *Le roi d'Ys* (*The King of Ys*, 1888) was the only success.

Apart from Grieg, Norway produced two more composers of note. Johan Svendsen (1840–1911) spent some

ABOVE: The French composer Edouard Lalo (1823–92), who drew inspiration from the landscapes of Spain and Norway.

ABOVE: Johan Svendsen (1840–1911), a fellow countryman of Grieg, whose works include a set of Norwegian Rhapsodies.

ABOVE: Christian Sinding (1856–1941), a Norwegian composer chiefly remembered for the piano piece Rustle of Spring.

time in Paris, and became a close friend of Wagner before returning to Norway as a teacher and conductor. His works include two symphonies, concertos for cello and violin, a Romance for violin and orchestra, and a set of *Norwegian Rhapsodies*.

Christian Sinding (1856–1941) spent most of his life in Oslo. Like Svendsen, he was principally noted for instrumental works, which included four symphonies, three violin concertos and a piano concerto, chamber music, songs, and many piano pieces, of which *Rustle of Spring* (1909) is still much played.

In Bohemia, Dvořák's pupil and son-in-law Josef Suk (1874–1935) carried on the tradition of Smetana and Dvořák, but without the overt use of Czech national idioms. He was also a brilliant violinist, who from 1892–1933 played in the Bohemian String Quartet. His grandson, the violinist also called Josef Suk (born 1929), carries on the family tradition. Suk's most important works were for orchestra. They include an early Serenade for strings (1892), *Pohádka* (*Fairy-tales*, 1900), and the huge *Asrael* Symphony (1905–6), written after Suk lost both his father-in-law and his young wife. This work marked the first phase of a vast symphonic cycle, whose other components were *Pohádka léta* (*A Summer's Tale*, 1907–9), *Zrání* (*The Ripening*, 1912–17), and *Epilog* (1920–9). All represent Suk's personal attempt to come to terms with the central tragedy of his life. Although much of Suk's music is not directly inspired by Czech folk music, his last work was a Czech dance (*Sousedska*, 1935) for chamber ensemble.

ABOVE: The violinist Josef Suk (born 1929), Dvořák's great-grandson, who carries on the family musical tradition. In 1961 he became leader of the Czech Philharmonic Orchestra.

The Later Romantics

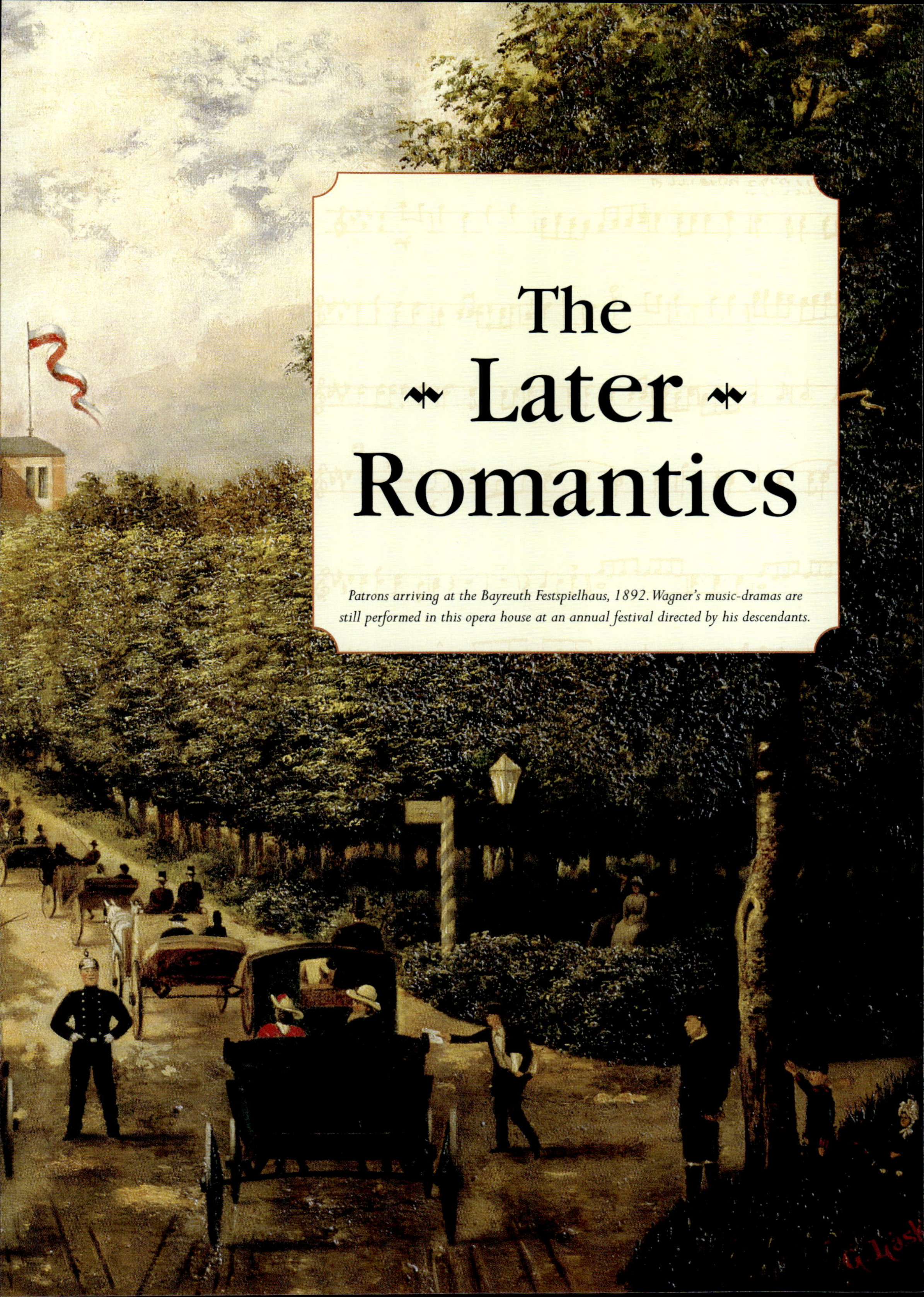

Patrons arriving at the Bayreuth Festspielhaus, 1892. Wagner's music-dramas are still performed in this opera house at an annual festival directed by his descendants.

Music on the Grand Scale

We are the music makers,
We are the dreamers of dreams.
ARTHUR O'SHAUGHNESSY (1844–81)

Two musical giants dominated the second half of the 19th century, each with a very different approach to composition. Johannes Brahms saw himself as belonging to the mainstream German symphonic tradition. Although overawed by the legacy of Beethoven, he – even more than Schumann or Mendelssohn – continued and expanded the Beethovenian principle of motivic construction. Brahms's four symphonies represent "pure", abstract music: unusually for a Romantic composer, they are unaffected by external influences such as literature or landscape. Brahms was primarily an instrumental composer. He wrote no opera, and his preferred media were orchestral, chamber and solo piano music. Yet, as his choral music and his many superb songs demonstrate, he was by no means indifferent to the power of words.

At the opposite pole stood the extraordinary figure of Richard Wagner, whose works are almost entirely operatic. One of the most forceful and influential characters in music history, Wagner was highly receptive to influences of all descriptions – literature, myth, drama, poetry, painting, politics and philosophy. These combined to produce his "music of the future" – a vision of *Gesamtkunstwerk*, a "total art work", which would unite music, drama, poetry and the visual arts, and which he strove to achieve in his gigantic later operas, particularly the four constituents of the *Ring* cycle, *Tristan und Isolde*, *Parsifal* and *Die Meistersinger von Nürnberg*.

ABOVE: The interior of the Teatro alla Scala, Milan; an aquatint from 1819. La Scala is one of the world's greatest opera houses.

LEFT: A snowy Finnish landscape – the inspiration for symphonies by Sibelius.

The operas and tone-poems of Richard Strauss owe an enormous debt to Wagner, as do the symphonies of Bruckner and Mahler (although both were equally influenced by Brahms). Wagner's influence was inescapable, and his genius so persuasive that the more unpleasant aspects of his personality – particularly the virulent anti-Semitism expressed in his polemical writings, which certainly contributed to the climate of opinion in Germany that led to Hitler's National Socialism – tend to have been overlooked.

ABOVE: The Leipzig Opera House in the Augustusplatz, built between 1864 and 1867 (destroyed in World War II).

Italian opera

Meanwhile, as in the early part of the century, Italian music continued to be dominated by opera, but in a very un-Wagnerian style. Giuseppe Verdi took on the mantle of Rossini, producing a sequence of 26 operas over some 57 years which have since remained the backbone of the international repertoire. Verdi was Wagner's only real rival in the operatic field, but his works are firmly based in the Italian *bel canto* tradition.

His successor, Giacomo Puccini, wrote far fewer works but almost all have held their place in the operatic canon. Puccini owed his success to an unerring sense of theatre and a persuasive melodic gift, allied to a taste for sentimental plots which still reduce audiences to tears. In the hands of less talented composers, this taste for melodrama degenerated into the *verismo* school of sex and violence, which nonetheless produced two isolated masterpieces: the one-act *Cavalleria rusticana* (*Rustic Chivalry*, 1890) by Pietro Mascagni (1863–1945) and *I pagliacci* (*The Clowns*, 1892) by Ruggero Leoncavallo (1858–1919), which are usually performed together in a double-bill.

Nationalism

By the second half of the 19th century nationalism was in full swing and few composers remained untouched by an awareness of their national culture. Mahler in Austria, Sibelius in Finland, Fauré and Saint-Saëns in France, Elgar in England and Rachmaninov in Russia all made original contributions to the musical literature of their respective countries, broadly working with the language of late Romanticism.

All except Fauré were important symphonic writers, particularly Mahler and Sibelius. Elgar occupies a special place in British music as the most gifted English composer since Purcell. His music distilled the essence of Edwardian England, while Rachmaninov inherited Tchaikovsky's ability to write superb tunes, expressed with a passion that seems essentially "Russian".

ABOVE: The cover of The International Quadrille *by Charles d'Albert, showing the opening of the Crystal Palace in London in 1862. It became a favourite concert venue.*

ABOVE: Outside the Bayreuth Festspielhaus, 1892. The theatre was built in the 1870s specifically for performances of Wagner's music-dramas.

Johannes Brahms

I believe Johannes to be the true Apostle, who will also write Revelations.

ROBERT SCHUMANN (1810–56), IN A LETTER TO JOACHIM

One of the greatest symphonic composers of the 19th century, Brahms came from a relatively humble background. His father, Johann Jakob, played the double bass in the Hamburg city orchestra. His mother, who was 17 years older than her husband, came from a middle-class family who had fallen upon hard times: she had been Johann Brahms's housekeeper. Their second child Johannes was born on 7 May 1833.

Early years

Brahms learnt the piano from the age of seven, and from 1846 onwards he also studied composition. In 1848 he gave his first public recital, and that year he also met the Hungarian violinist Eduard Reményi (1830–98), a refugee from Austrian oppression in his homeland. Five years later Reményi and Brahms set off on a concert tour, during which they met another Hungarian violinist, Joseph Joachim, and stayed at Weimar with Liszt. Brahms also travelled to Düsseldorf to visit Robert and Clara Schumann, who were both deeply impressed with the pianistic and compositional talents of this "young eagle", as Schumann described him.

ABOVE: Johannes Brahms (1833–97), painted by N. Piontkovsky.

Shortly after their meeting, Schumann suffered a complete breakdown, and in 1854 Brahms returned to Düsseldorf to help Clara, with whom he fell deeply in love. Their relationship – whether physically consummated or not – was central to Brahms's life, and may have affected his attitude to other women: though he had close female friends, he never married. During her long widowhood, Clara acted as mentor to the young composer, encouraging him – as she had done with Schumann – to push his art to the limits.

In 1857 Brahms spent some months in Detmold, where he tried out his first orchestral works (two serenades) with the court orchestra. Two years later he settled back in

ABOVE: The influential Hungarian violinist Joseph Joachim (1831–1907), the dedicatee of Brahms's Violin Concerto.

ABOVE: A drawing of Brahms (aged 20) done at the request of Robert Schumann by Laurens, 1853.

Life and works

NATIONALITY: German

BORN: Hamburg, 1833; **DIED:** Vienna, 1897

SPECIALIST GENRES: German Romantic symphonies, concertos, chamber music, piano music, songs.

MAJOR WORKS: Four symphonies; two piano concertos; *Ein Deutsches Requiem* (1868); *Alto Rhapsody* (1869); Violin Concerto (1878); chamber and piano works; about 200 songs.

Hamburg, where he founded a women's choir and began to write choral music. In the meantime he had completed his First Piano Concerto, begun at the time he met the Schumanns. Brahms himself gave the première of this huge work in Hanover, where it met with success; but five days later, in Leipzig, the audience greeted it coolly. By this time Brahms was making himself unpopular by publicly dissociating himself from Liszt and the "New German School". His uncompromising stance probably caused the Leipzig publisher Breitkopf & Härtel to reject his manuscripts, including the Piano Concerto.

Vienna

In 1862, with several more compositions completed (including the Sextet in B flat, and sets of piano variations on themes by Handel and Schumann), Brahms left Hamburg for Vienna. Six months later he was appointed director of the Vienna Singakademie, where he indulged his awakening interest in early music, but he soon found the administrative burden of the new job tiresome, and resigned after a few months.

ABOVE: Brahms in 1867, shortly before he decided to move to Vienna, and one year before he wrote the German Requiem*.*

In 1864 he returned home on hearing that his parents' marriage was in trouble – his mother was ill and his father resented having to look after her. Their separation, followed by his

ABOVE: A Viennese street scene during the time of Brahms: the Fruit Market on the quayside near the Maria Theresa Bridge, 1895.

mother's death in January 1865, was a bitter blow (Brahms commemorated her death in the slow movement of his powerful Horn Trio).

In 1868 Brahms decided to settle permanently in Vienna, but continued playing his own works on frequent concert tours. In 1872 he became conductor of the Vienna Gesellschaftskonzerte, but held the post for only three years. A new breed of professional virtuoso conductors such as Hans Richter (1843–1916), Hans von Bülow (1830–94), and Hermann Levi (1839–1900) had arrived on the scene, and Brahms wisely realized his own limitations. In 1869 he had already had a taste of critical vitriol when Wagner (fearing a new and talented rival) had viciously attacked him in an article entitled "On Conducting". From then onwards, Brahms devoted himself to composition.

ABOVE: The Town Hall in Hamburg, the city where Brahms was born in 1833.

After many years of work, in 1868, Brahms had completed *Ein Deutsches Requiem (A German Requiem)* for soloists, chorus and orchestra – a deeply felt response to biblical passages on the subject of death, mourning and consolation – and during the Franco-Prussian War he was hailed as a "patriot", having used material from the Lutheran Bible rather than the traditional Latin text of the Catholic liturgy. He responded by composing the *Triumphlied (Song of Triumph)* in the summer of 1871 to celebrate Germany's victory. By 1873, when he finished his popular *St Anthony Variations (Variations on a Theme of Haydn)* for orchestra, he was earning enough to be able to live on the income from his concerts and publications, and felt sufficiently secure to turn down a lifelong contract offered by the publisher Fritz Simrock (he also rejected an honorary doctorate offered by Cambridge University).

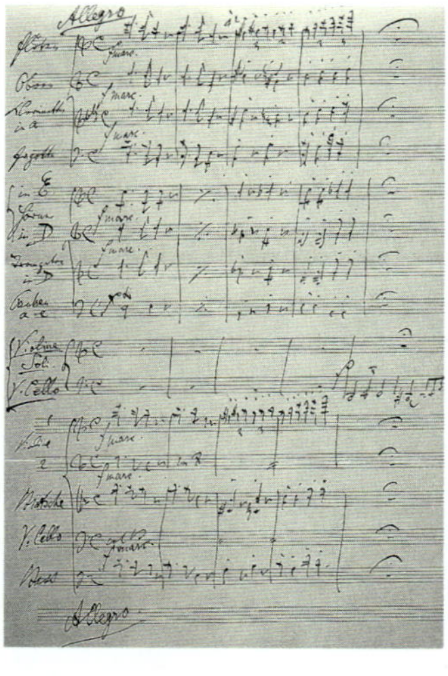

ABOVE: The opening page of the autograph score of Brahms's Double Concerto for violin and cello (1887).

Symphonic success

Three years later, with Clara Schumann's constant encouragement, Brahms finally completed his First Symphony in C minor, begun over 20 years earlier. Its long gestation had been haunted by the ghost of Beethoven, and by Brahms's fear that the work would be rejected because it was not "programmatic". But the Viennese public received it with enthusiasm, and

ABOVE: Brahms (centre) on the day of Clara Schumann's funeral, 20 May 1896. He had loved her ever since their first meeting.

Brahms immediately began work on a second symphony.

In the late 1870s he adopted the habit of spending the summers in the Austrian countryside, at Pörtschach on Lake Wörther in Carinthia. There he completed the Second Symphony in D, the brilliant Violin Concerto (whose gypsy finale pays homage to Joachim, its Hungarian dedicatee), the G major Violin Sonata, the two Rhapsodies, Op. 79, and the eight Piano Pieces, Op. 76. From 1880 onwards he found another summer refuge at Bad Ischl, where he wrote the Piano Trio in C, the Quintets in F and G, the Three Motets, Op. 110, and many of his late chamber and vocal works.

ABOVE: Brahms at the piano – a posthumous sketch by Beckerath, 1899. Brahms had always been a fine pianist, having played since the age of seven.

In 1881 Brahms conducted his satirical *Akademische Festouvertüre (Academic Festival Overture)*, based on students' songs, in Breslau, where the University had awarded him a doctorate. He did not care for honours, and failed to attend the degree ceremony. That year he completed the Second Piano Concerto in B flat – a *tour de force* of power and vitality, and a milestone of pianistic virtuosity. He also had a major disagreement with Joachim, who was intending to divorce his wife. Brahms took Frau Joachim's side, and the violinist broke off all relations with Brahms. (They were eventually reconciled in 1887, when Brahms wrote the Double Concerto for Joachim and the cellist Robert Hausmann.)

Also from 1881, the conductor Hans von Bülow – a great admirer of Brahms – offered the composer the use of the Meiningen court orchestra to try out his new works. These included the Third and Fourth Symphonies. The Third, in F, was written in Wiesbaden in 1883, and the Fourth, in E minor, during two summer holidays in southern Austria, and performed on a European tour with the Meiningen Orchestra in the autumn of 1885. In its *passacaglia* finale, Brahms paid homage to another lifelong influence, that of J. S. Bach.

ABOVE: The sixth book of Brahms's Collected Songs.

Last works

Brahms spent the following three summers at Hofstetten on Lake Thun, where he wrote his Second Cello Sonata in F major, two more violin sonatas, and the C minor Trio. By 1890 he had resolved to stop composing, but broke his resolution to write four clarinet works inspired by the brilliant playing of Richard Mühlfeld (1856–1907), principal clarinettist with the Meiningen Orchestra: the Clarinet Trio and Quintet and two clarinet sonatas. Clara Schumann's death in May 1896 prompted one final work – the *Vier ernste Gesänge (Four Serious Songs)* – but by then Brahms himself was mortally ill from liver cancer. He died on 3 April 1897, and was buried in Vienna's central cemetery.

Anton Bruckner

Bruckner! He is my man!

RICHARD WAGNER (1813–83)

Bruckner's name is often coupled with Mahler's – but for no other reason than that both were Austrian and both wrote important, large-scale symphonies. In all other respects they were very different.

Bruckner's father was the village schoolmaster and organist at Ansfelden in central Austria. Anton, the eldest of five surviving children, was taught by his father, and by the age of ten was already a proficient organist. He also came into contact with the Catholic musical tradition at the nearby monastery of St Florian, where he enrolled as a chorister at the age of 13, after his father's death. St Florian was to remain the focus of Bruckner's life, and he chose to be buried there, beneath the organ.

Bruckner began his career as an ordinary schoolmaster in two provincial villages. Eventually, in 1845, he returned as a teacher and then as organist to St Florian. His first important compositions, including a Requiem Mass and the *Missa solemnis* in B flat, date from his early years there.

ABOVE: The Austrian composer Anton Bruckner – a portrait by H. Kaulback.

By 1855 Bruckner had decided he wanted to become a professional musician. While working as organist at Linz Cathedral, he enrolled on a correspondence course in harmony and counterpoint at the Vienna Conservatory. He graduated in 1861 at the advanced age of 37, with glowing references. But he still felt he lacked musical knowledge, and sought further tuition in symphonic form and orchestration with the principal cellist and conductor at the Linz municipal theatre, who engaged him in a thorough study of Beethoven and Mendelssohn.

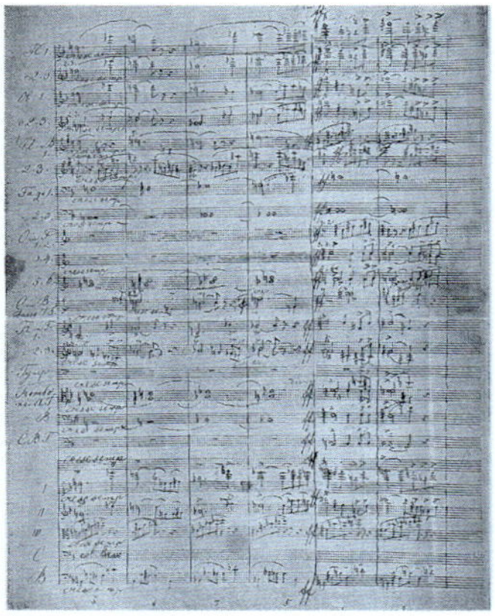

LEFT: A page from Bruckner's Ninth Symphony, left unfinished at his death.

RIGHT: The organ at the Abbey Church of St Florian. Bruckner was a chorister and then organist there, and is buried beneath the organ.

Life and works

NATIONALITY: Austrian

BORN: Ansfelden, 1824; **DIED:** Vienna, 1896

SPECIALIST GENRES: Symphonies, church music.

MAJOR WORKS: Nine symphonies, including No. 4 (*The Romantic*, 1874–81), No. 7 (1883), No. 8 (1885–90) and No. 9 (unfinished, 1896); Te Deum (1884).

ABOVE: The Graben, one of the principal streets in Vienna, in Bruckner's time. Bruckner lived in Vienna from 1868 until his death.

The impact of Wagner

Up to this point, Bruckner had been competent but characterless as a composer. Then, in 1863, he heard Wagner's *Tannhäuser*, and the experience changed his life. Overwhelmed by Wagner's genius, Bruckner immediately began to try his own hand at symphonic composition. During the mid 1860s he attended many performances of Wagner's music, and even met the great man, while his budding confidence led to the composition of three masses and the Symphony No. 1 in C minor (1865–6).

After suffering a nervous breakdown brought on by intense overwork, Bruckner was eventually persuaded to apply for a professorship at the Vienna Conservatory, to which he was appointed in 1868. He also became organist at the Imperial Chapel in Vienna, and received a government grant to allow him to compose. He lived in Vienna until his death, leaving for occasional visits to Paris and London, where his organ recitals were greeted with huge acclaim.

In Vienna (where he was appointed a lecturer at the University in 1875) he devoted much of his energy to composing symphonies. Between 1871 and his death, he turned out eight more (No. 9 remained unfinished).

Despite Bruckner's growing fame, he encountered enormous opposition and hostility from two anti-Wagnerite sources. The Vienna Philharmonic Orchestra either rejected his symphonies as "unplayable" or deliberately sabotaged their performances, and the influential critic Eduard Hanslick – a supporter of Brahms – took every opportunity to denounce Bruckner's symphonies, especially the Third (which Bruckner, in an enthusiastic fit of hero-worship, had unwisely dubbed his *Wagner* Symphony). Diffident by nature and fatally lacking in self-esteem, Bruckner also suffered from the interference of well-meaning but misguided "friends" who persuaded him to make cuts and alterations to the scores of his symphonies, in the interests of "accessibility". Many still exist in various hybrid versions.

ABOVE: The beginning of the Gloria from Bruckner's Mass in D minor (1864), a page from the autograph score.

Bruckner's first real success came at the age of 60, with the Leipzig première of his Seventh Symphony in 1884. He had finally found critical acceptance, although he continued to revise his scores obsessively. Official honours came his way during the last decade of his life. A simple, pious, old-fashioned man, he never married, although he proposed to a succession of astonished young women. He had a morbid obsession with dead bodies, and left instructions that his own should be embalmed.

Giuseppe Verdi

It may be a good thing to copy reality;
but to invent reality is much, much better.

VERDI, 1876

Verdi was the greatest Italian opera composer of the 19th century. Unlike Wagner, who strove to create a new type of music-drama, Verdi worked within the Italian tradition of his predecessors, but throughout his long career his technique became ever more fluent, his characterizations more rounded and expressive, and his response to the text increasingly refined.

His masterpieces are the Shakespearean operas *Otello* (1887) and *Falstaff* (1893), written when he was in his 70s, but works from all periods of his life form the backbone of the present-day operatic repertoire.

ABOVE: Giuseppe Verdi (1813–1901), the greatest Italian opera composer of the 19th century.

Early years

Verdi was born in Lombardy, at a small village in the vicinity of Parma. He began to play the keyboard when he was three, and at ten he was sent to study in Busseto. In 1831 he became the protégé of a music-loving merchant, Antonio Barezzi, who financed his further musical education privately in Milan, Verdi having been rejected by the Milan Conservatory. Verdi then returned to Busseto as the town's music director. In 1836, aged 22, he married Barezzi's daughter Margherita. They had two children, who both died in infancy.

In 1838 Verdi began work on his first opera, *Oberto*. He, his wife and baby son moved to Milan, where the opera had been accepted for production at La Scala. It was premièred in November 1839, a few weeks after his son's death, and in June 1840 Verdi's wife also died. During this sad period, Verdi was working on a new opera, the comedy *Un giorno di regno* (*King for a Day*), which failed utterly at its première at La Scala in September 1840.

Verdi was so discouraged that he almost gave up composing, but a friend persuaded him to begin work on *Nabucco*, based on the biblical story of Nebuchadnezzar. This – his earliest well-known work, famous for its chorus of Hebrew slaves "Va, pensiero" – was a triumphant

ABOVE: The French dramatic soprano Rose Caron as Desdemona in Verdi's Otello. *She created the role in 1894.*

ABOVE: Arturo Toscanini, one of the great Verdi interpreters, conducting the orchestra of La Scala Opera House in May 1946.

ABOVE: A set design (c.1862) by Carlo Ferrario for Verdi's grand opera La forza del destino *(*The Force of Destiny*).*

ABOVE: A scene from a performance of Verdi's Aida *at the 1991 Savonlinna Opera Festival in Finland.*

success, and was soon being performed all over Europe. Before long, Verdi's name was being linked with the emerging nationalist movement in Italy, as choruses such as "Va, pensiero" and the Scottish exiles' lament from *Macbeth* (1847) were interpreted as coded rallying-cries for the oppressed Italian nation.

Galley years

With *Ernani* (1844), Verdi entered on a period he later called his "galley years", producing a string of operas for Rome, Milan, Naples, Venice, Florence, Trieste, and even London (*I masnadieri – The Brigands*, 1847). His early operas, up to *La battaglia di Legnano* (*The Battle of Legnano*, 1849), were still influenced by Rossini, and generally dealt with historical subjects (including the Shakespearean opera *Macbeth*).

Luisa Miller (1849) was the first of a series of works in which the subject-matter became more personal and intimate. The finest operas of this period are *Rigoletto* – the tragic tale of a hunchbacked court jester who seeks to avenge his daughter's seduction but inadvertently causes her death; *Il trovatore* (*The Troubadour*), another tragedy with the motif of revenge at its heart; and *La traviata* (*The Woman Gone Astray*), Verdi's version of *La dame aux camélias* by Alexandre Dumas. The story of the courtesan who finds true love, sacrifices it for her lover's honour, and dies of consumption, is one of the most popular operas ever written.

Grand opera

Verdi's third period began with *Les vêpres siciliennes* (*The Sicilian Vespers*, Paris, 1855), and includes *Simon Boccanegra*, *Un ballo in maschera* (*A Masked Ball*), *La forza del destino* (*The Force of Destiny*, produced in St Petersburg in 1862), *Don Carlos* (Paris) and *Aida* (Cairo). During this period he spent much time on the country estate he had bought near his birthplace, with his second wife, the soprano Giuseppina Strepponi (1815–97).

In 1861, after the Italian War of Independence, Verdi was elected to the new Italian parliament, and for the next four years mixed politics with composition. After *Aida*, he wrote little except his dramatic Requiem commemorating the death of the Italian nationalist poet Alessandro Manzoni (1785–1873).

Life and works

NATIONALITY: Italian

BORN: La Roncola, near Busseto, 1813;
DIED: Milan, 1901

SPECIALIST GENRES: Italian grand opera.

MAJOR WORKS: *Nabucco* (1842); *Rigoletto* (1851); *Il trovatore* (1853); *La traviata* (1853); *Simon Boccanegra* (1857); *Un ballo in maschera* (1859); *La forza del destino* (1862); *Don Carlos* (1867); *Aida* (1871); Requiem (1874); *Otello* (1887); *Falstaff* (1893).

Last works

The huge success of the Requiem prompted Verdi's publisher, Ricordi, to suggest a collaboration with the composer-librettist Arrigo Boito (1842–1918), on an opera based on Shakespeare's *Othello*. It took Verdi another decade to begin work on *Otello*, which with *Falstaff* marked the culmination of his career. His last work, in 1898, was a set of *Quatro pezzi sacri* (*Four Sacred Pieces*), including a Te Deum and Stabat Mater. By then Verdi had lost his beloved second wife, he was over 80 and worn out. He died in Milan in January 1901, leaving his fortune to a home for aged musicians which he had built in Milan, and which he regarded as "his greatest work".

Richard Wagner

Wagner's opera style recognizes only superlatives.

EDUARD HANSLICK (1825–1904)

The figure of Richard Wagner straddles the 19th century like a colossus. Composer, critic, polemicist, his abundant energy allowed him to a pursue a vision with a ruthless single-mindedness beyond the comprehension of ordinary mortals.

His operas, rooted in the German Romantic tradition, remain (like Verdi's) the cornerstones of the modern repertoire, but they require performers of extraordinary power and stamina. There are still few sopranos and tenors able to do justice to roles such as Siegfried, Brünnhilde, Tristan and Isolde, and many singers have burnt out their voices in the attempt.

ABOVE: An evocative portrait of Richard Wagner (1813–83), by Lenbach. Wagner was much given to striking romantic poses.

interested in the theatre, and in 1832 he began work on his first, abortive, opera. He realized from the start that he would only ever be able to work with his own librettos.

He began his theatrical career as a chorus-master in Würzburg, where he completed his first opera *Die Feen* (*The Fairies*). It remained unperformed, but already Wagner was showing a dogged determination to succeed. He began work on a third opera, *Das Liebesverbot* (*Love's Interdict*), based on Shakespeare's *Measure for Measure*, and joined a travelling theatre company as music director. *Das Liebesverbot* had a single performance in Magdeburg in 1836, before the company went bankrupt.

ABOVE: A costume design by Franz Gaul for the 1873 production of Wagner's early opera Rienzi *at the State Theatre in Brunswick.*

Early years

Friedrich Wagner died of typhus soon after his son Richard was born, and his mother Johanna married Ludwig Meyer, who introduced his stepson to the world of the theatre and music. The family moved to Dresden, where the young Wagner came into contact with Weber, then conductor at the Royal Theatre. According to Wagner, it was Weber who instilled in him "a passion for music". After his stepfather's death the family returned to Wagner's birthplace, Leipzig, where he completed his education at school and university. By now he was passionately

ABOVE: Senta leaps to her death – an Art Nouveau illustration of the final scene of The Flying Dutchman.

ABOVE: A domestic vision of Wagner at home with his second wife Cosima, daughter of Franz Liszt.

ABOVE: A scene from the last act of Rienzi, *premièred at the Dresden Hoftheater on 20 October 1842.*

By this time Wagner had fallen in love with the actress Minna Planer, whom he married on 24 November. Six months later Minna ran off with another man, but was reconciled with her husband in October 1837. Their relationship remained stormy.

Paris

Wagner was working at Riga (now in Latvia) when he began *Rienzi*. By March 1839, when his contract ended, he was heavily in debt (a *Leitmotif* of his career). He, Minna and their huge dog were obliged to flee from his creditors by ship to London.

In September they arrived in Paris, where Wagner hoped to establish himself as a composer. Instead he found himself trying to make ends meet from journalism, while financial problems landed him in a debtors' prison. He did, however, come into contact with a great deal of new music, and with literature, especially the Germanic legends of Tannhäuser and Lohengrin. His Paris period thus laid the foundations of several future operas, including *Der fliegende Holländer* (*The Flying Dutchman*), which he finished in 1841. The famous, storm-tossed overture to this dramatic tale, of a restless ghost who is finally redeemed by faithful love, was inspired by Wagner's own experiences on the ship from Riga.

Dresden

In 1842 *Rienzi* was finally performed, with considerable success, at the Dresden court theatre, which agreed to mount *The Flying Dutchman* in January 1843. Although Wagner was disappointed with the latter's reception, his career was finally launched, and he was offered the post of conductor in Dresden. In April 1843 he completed *Tannhäuser*, based on the legend of the knight – seduced from his duties by the pleasures of Venus – who is redeemed by a divine miracle. *Tannhäuser* was premièred in Dresden in October 1845.

Wagner began work on *Lohengrin*, which was finished in 1848, the year of revolution in Europe. Wagner's pro-revolutionary sympathies implicated him (by default) in the Dresden uprising of May 1849, and in fear of his life he escaped to Switzerland. He settled in Zurich, where he worked on his creative manifesto, *Opera and Drama*, and also began work on the texts of a new project, based on the ancient Nordic saga of the Nibelungs. *Lohengrin* could not now be produced in Dresden, so Wagner sent the score to Liszt, who had sufficient confidence in it to risk censure by mounting a production in Weimar in August 1850. It eventually became an outstanding success, although Wagner himself was unable to attend a performance until 1861.

Life and works

NATIONALITY: German

BORN: Leipzig, 1813; **DIED:** Venice, 1883

SPECIALIST GENRES: German Romantic opera and music-dramas.

MAJOR WORKS: *Der fliegende Holländer* (1841); *Tannhäuser* (1843); *Lohengrin* (1848); *Tristan und Isolde* (1859); *Die Meistersinger von Nürnberg* (1867); *Der Ring des Nibelungen* (1853–74); *Parsifal* (1882).

ABOVE: A Romantic impression of Wagner composing his epic saga Der Ring des Nibelungen, *a cycle of four operas completed in 1874.*

Music of the future

Lohengrin – another legendary tale of knightly chivalry with a strong magical element – marked the end of Wagner's involvement with conventional German Romantic opera. In *Opera and Drama* he set out his visionary ideal of the "music of the future", in which music and drama became indivisible. The last 30 years of his life were dedicated to realizing this ideal.

By 1852 Wagner was again chronically in debt. He was helped by the merchant Otto Wesendonk, with whose wife, Mathilde, he fell in love. Their affair inspired the opera *Tristan und Isolde*, which Wagner began in 1857. This passionate portrayal of an adulterous love which can find fulfilment only in death is one of the supreme achievements of Western art. In it, Wagner pushed chromatic harmony to its limits, from the unresolved, "yearning" motif of the Prelude to the ecstatic dignity of Isolde's "Liebestod" ("love-death") in which she is finally united with Tristan as the strained "Tristan chord" achieves its radiant resolution.

Munich

Wagner's personal troubles continued. His wife discovered his liaison with Mathilde Wesendonk, and Wagner fled to Venice. With the police at his heels he moved on to Lucerne (where he finished *Tristan*) and then to Paris, where performances of *Tannhäuser* in 1861 were disrupted by an organized and noisy claque.

A political amnesty of 1860 allowed Wagner to return to Germany, but he spent the next three years travelling from city to city dodging his creditors, until a knight in shining armour appeared in the person of the "mad" King Ludwig II of Bavaria. Ludwig paid off Wagner's debts and offered him sanctuary in Munich, where *Tristan und Isolde* was first performed on 10 June 1865, under the baton of Hans von Bülow. Wagner repaid Bülow by beginning an affair with his wife Cosima (daughter of Liszt and the Countess Marie d'Agoult), who bore him two daughters, Isolde and Eva.

Wagner now had to leave Germany again in the face of Bavarian opposition to his powerful influence over the king and the vast sums of money that were being lavished on him from the public purse. Minna Wagner having died in 1866, Cosima von Bülow moved in with Wagner at his new home – financed by Ludwig – at Tribschen, outside Lucerne, where their son Siegfried was born in 1869. (This event inspired Wagner to compose the *Siegfried Idyll*, rehearsed in secret and played as a surprise for Cosima on Christmas morning.) After Cosima's divorce from Bülow, she and Wagner were married in 1870.

ABOVE: The Festspielhaus at Bayreuth, built to Wagner's specifications by Gottfried Semper between 1871 and 1876 for the performance of Wagnerian music-dramas.

Cosima – a formidable woman – kept Wagner on a short leash throughout their marriage, but protected his interests, and enabled him to compose in peace.

ABOVE: A 1914 stage set for the "Garden of Enchantment" in Parsifal, *designed by Thomas Edwin Mostyn (1864–1930).*

Bayreuth

In June 1868 *Die Meistersinger von Nürnberg* – a blend of comedy, philosophy, radiant young love and wisdom as embodied in the person of Hans Sachs the cobbler – had been premièred in Munich. At the same time, Wagner continued working on his *Ring* cycle, but realized that no existing theatre was suitable for such a large project. With King Ludwig's help, he raised the money to build a dedicated "Festival Theatre" at Bayreuth, where his operas are still performed at an annual festival directed by members of the Wagner family. The new theatre was inaugurated in August 1876 with three complete performances of the *Ring* cycle of four works – *Das Rheingold, Die Walküre, Siegfried* and *Götterdämmerung* (*The Twilight of the Gods*).

Der Ring des Nibelungen – which contains over 12 hours of music – is held together by a complex system of musical references called *Leitmotifs*, in which characters and situations are identified by individual musical motifs, such as the joyous horn call associated with the hero Siegfried. By now Wagner's musical language had succeeded in merging voices and orchestra into one continuous texture, at the opposite end of the spectrum from the Italianate concept of opera as separate arias, ensembles and choruses. This complex, endlessly evolving web of sound proved an ideal vehicle for the grandiose Nibelung drama, which reaches its shattering conclusion as Valhalla burns and the world ends.

In 1882 Wagner finished his last opera, *Parsifal*, based on the quasi-religious myth of the quest for the Holy Grail, with its miraculous powers of healing. It was performed at Bayreuth in the summer of 1882, conducted by Hermann Levi. Wagner himself conducted the last scene of the final performance. Two weeks later, suffering from a heart condition, he took his family to Venice, where he died of a heart attack on 13 February 1883.

LEFT: Brünnhilde, from Arthur Rackham's 1910 watercolour illustrations to The Rhinegold *and the Valkyrie.*

RIGHT: The "Good Friday" scene from a 1950s Bayreuth production of Parsifal, *produced by Wagner's grandson Wieland.*

Gustav Mahler

To write a symphony is, for me, to construct a world.

MAHLER

Mahler was a transitional figure. A contemporary of Sigmund Freud and the painter Gustav Klimt, his massive orchestral works are rooted in the 19th-century Austro-German symphonic tradition and speak in a rich, late-Romantic idiom inflected with folk idioms, yet look forward to 20th-century preoccupations such as neurosis and mysticism. His most important works are his ten symphonies and his songs with orchestral accompaniment, which influenced them. Four of the symphonies – Nos. 2, 3, 4 and 8 – have substantial vocal and choral parts, which has tended to limit their performance potential, and for almost five decades after Mahler's death his works were largely neglected, admired only by a small band of devotees, until the advocacy of conductors such as Bruno Walter, Georg Solti and Rafael Kubelík in Europe, Leonard Bernstein in America and Norman del Mar in Britain, restored them to the repertoire.

ABOVE: Gustav Mahler in the loggia of the Vienna Court Opera House, where he was conductor from 1897 until 1907.

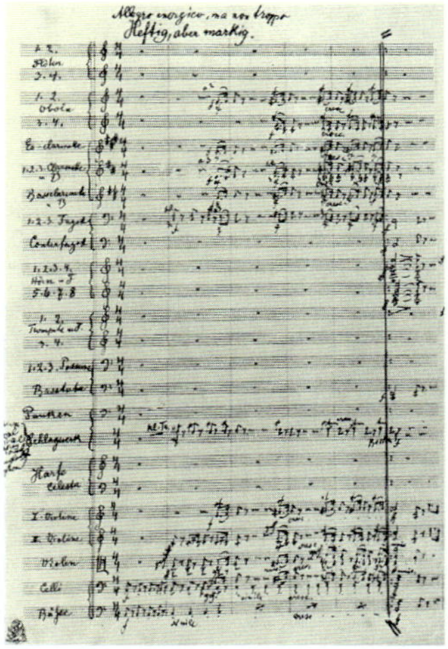

ABOVE: A page from the autograph score of Mahler's Sixth Symphony (1903–6).

Conducting

Mahler was born into a Jewish family and, although he later converted to Catholicism, his career was to some extent blighted by the anti-Semitic attitude of the Austrian establishment. He showed musical promise as a child, and studied at the Vienna Conservatory from 1875–8, where he wrote the cantata *Das klagende Lied* (*The Song of Sorrow*). From 1880 onwards he made his living as a conductor at provincial theatres in Upper Austria, Slovenia, Bohemia, and then at Kassel in Germany, where he composed the song-cycle *Lieder eines fahrenden Gesellen* (*Songs of a Wayfarer*), and started his First Symphony.

In 1885 Mahler spent a year in Prague, and then moved to Leipzig. There he met the Weber family, who introduced him to the folk poetry collection *Des Knaben Wunderhorn* (*The Youth's Magic Horn*, published in 1805–8). From 1887 onwards he began to set some of the

ABOVE: Mahler's wife Alma with their daughters Maria and Anna, c.1906–7.

Life and works

NATIONALITY: Austrian

BORN: Kaliste, 1860; **DIED:** Vienna, 1911

SPECIALIST GENRES: Symphonies, song-cycles.

MAJOR WORKS: Ten symphonies; *Lieder eines fahrenden Gesellen* (1883); *Kindertotenlieder* (1903); *Das Lied von der Erde* (1909).

*ABOVE: Mahler rehearsing his Eighth Symphony (*Symphony of a Thousand*). The huge choir extends all around the auditorium.*

Wunderhorn poems, which were reworked in his earlier symphonies. Between 1888 and 1891 he worked as conductor of the Royal Opera in Budapest, before moving to the Stadttheater in Hamburg, where he conducted Wagner's *Tristan* in May 1891. By 1892 he had completed his First Symphony (first performed at Weimar in 1894), and had begun work on a second (the *Resurrection*). By then he had established a working pattern of conducting during the winter seasons, and retreating to the mountains to compose in the summer. The Third Symphony was finished in this way at Steinbach in the Salzkammergut.

Vienna

In 1897 Mahler was appointed conductor at the Vienna State Opera (one of his first productions there was Wagner's *Ring* cycle). He remained at Vienna for ten years, as one of the Opera's most distinguished music directors. In 1901 he found a new lakeside retreat at Maiernigg in Carinthia, where over the next few summers he composed the Fourth, Fifth, Sixth and Seventh Symphonies, the *Rückert-Lieder*, the *Kindertotenlieder* (*Songs on the Death of Children*) and other works. The glorious *Adagietto* of the Fifth Symphony was an expression of his love for Alma Schindler, stepdaughter of the Viennese artist Carl Moll, whom Mahler married in 1902. Contrary to popular belief, the deeply affecting *Kindertotenlieder* predated the death from scarlet fever of the couple's elder daughter Maria in 1907, although Alma believed that the cycle had "tempted providence".

ABOVE: The Metropolitan Opera House, New York, in the early 20th century. Mahler was appointed conductor there in 1908.

Mahler's Eighth Symphony (*Symphony of a Thousand*) dates from 1906–7. It was based on the text of a medieval hymn and the closing scene of Goethe's *Faust*, Part II. Mahler thought it "the greatest work I have yet composed". At the end of 1907, the victim of a vicious press campaign, he was obliged to resign his Vienna post, and also discovered that he had a potentially fatal heart condition. He was appointed conductor at the Metropolitan Opera House, New York, from January 1908, but continued to spend the summers in Europe, where he composed *Das Lied von der Erde* (*The Song of the Earth*), based on Chinese poems about the transience of life. He also completed his Ninth Symphony and began a Tenth.

In February 1911 Mahler became seriously ill, and died in Austria, aged 50. *Das Lied von der Erde* and the Ninth Symphony were given posthumous performances; the Tenth was completed in the 1960s by the British scholar Deryck Cooke.

Edward Elgar

Look out for this man's music;
he has something to say and knows how to say it.
HUBERT PARRY (1848–1918)

Like Arthur Sullivan (another composer knighted for his services to British music), Edward Elgar transcended the class barriers of his age, rising from humble origins to epitomize – in musical terms – Britain at the height of her Imperial glory.

ABOVE: Edward Elgar revived British music almost single-handedly.

Early life

He was born within sight of the Malvern Hills near Worcester, where his father ran a music shop and was organist at St George's Catholic Church. Edward's first job on leaving school was to help his father in both capacities, and he also began to play the violin in local orchestras and chamber groups. In the early 1880s he began to make a living as a freelance player, teacher, conductor and self-taught composer with instrumental groups in the Malvern area. His composing ambitions were stimulated by his marriage in 1889 to his piano pupil Alice Roberts, daughter of a retired major-general. Alice, who was 40 when she married the 31-year-old Elgar, had social pretensions, and she persuaded her husband to move to London, where their only daughter, Carice, was born in September 1890.

ABOVE: Elgar conducting in the studio in 1919, the year he wrote his Cello Concerto.

Success as a composer at first eluded Elgar, and the following year the family moved back to Malvern, where he resumed his teaching activities and strove to overcome a sense of social inferiority. His persistence paid off when his overture *Froissart* was published.

Creative period

By the mid 1890s Elgar was becoming known for the cantatas he had composed for provincial festivals, including *The Black Knight* (1893) and *King Olaf* (1896), and in 1897 he finally achieved a breakthrough in London with the *Imperial March* for Queen Victoria's Diamond Jubilee.

In 1899 his first truly original composition, the orchestral *Enigma Variations*, was performed at St James's Hall in London. The Variations – each a

Life and works

NATIONALITY: English

BORN: Broadheath, near Worcester, 1857; **DIED:** Worcester, 1934

SPECIALIST GENRES: Orchestral music, oratorios.

MAJOR WORKS: Symphonies No. 1 and 2; *Enigma Variations* (1899); *Sea Pictures* (1899); *Pomp and Circumstance* Marches (1901–30); *The Dream of Gerontius* (1900); Introduction and Allegro for string orchestra (1905); Violin Concerto (1910); *Falstaff* (1913); Cello Concerto (1919).

thinly disguised character portrait of a friend (including Elgar himself and his wife) – were recognized as a work of genius, while the underlying "enigma" – an unnamed tune which Elgar said "goes through and over the whole set" – has never been positively identified. The Variations encapsulate Elgar's musical style: noble, expansive, but tinged with plangent nostalgia for the English countryside.

In the autumn of 1899 the contralto Clara Butt sang Elgar's orchestral song-cycle *Sea Pictures* at the Norwich Festival, and he was commissioned to write an oratorio for the 1900 Birmingham Festival. The result was *The Dream of Gerontius*, based on a metaphysical Catholic text by Cardinal Henry Newman. Elgar was bitterly disappointed by the initial failure of this great work (which has since been recognized as a masterpiece), but the same year he was awarded an honorary doctorate by Cambridge University. His orchestral works were becoming popular, including the overture *Cockaigne*, inspired by London, and the first two *Pomp and Circumstance* Marches, of which the trio section from the first was later allied to the words of the verse "Land of Hope and Glory" written by A. C. Benson for the coronation of Edward VII. In 1904 Elgar was knighted.

The same year, the Elgars moved to a large house in Hereford, where over the next few years he wrote another oratorio (*The Kingdom*), the Introduction and Allegro for string orchestra (1905), and two symphonies. In 1910 Fritz Kreisler gave the première of Elgar's Violin Concerto, an eloquent work which bears an enigmatic dedication in Spanish: "Herein is enshrined the soul of..." This soul may have been that of John Everett Millais's daughter, Alice Stuart-Wortley, to whom Elgar seems to have been deeply attached.

ABOVE: The programme for a gala performance at the Royal Opera House, 1902, in the presence of the new King Edward VII and Queen Alexandra, at which Elgar's Coronation Ode *was performed.*

In 1912 Elgar returned to London, to a grand house in Hampstead, where he wrote the cantata *The Music Makers* (1912) and the symphonic poem *Falstaff* (1913). He was greatly distressed by World War I, which he saw destroying the society in which his works were rooted, and his personal response was the elegiac Cello Concerto and three chamber works – a violin sonata, a string quartet and a piano quintet (all 1919). These were to be his last major works.

Post-war years

After Lady Elgar's death in 1920, Elgar wrote little more. He was created Master of the King's Music in 1924, and in 1932, the year the young Yehudi Menuhin made his historic recording of the Violin Concerto, the BBC commissioned a third symphony. Elgar was still working on it when he died of cancer on 23 February 1934. His wish that no one should "tinker" with it was respected for over 60 years, until it was completed by Anthony Payne (born 1936) and performed in 1997.

ABOVE: Yehudi Menuhin (aged 16) recording Elgar's Violin Concerto in 1932, with the composer conducting.

Jean Sibelius

Give me the loneliness either of the Finnish forest or of a big city.

SIBELIUS

The careers of Jean Sibelius and Edward Elgar have many parallels, although Sibelius, eight years Elgar's junior, outlived the English composer by more than 20 years. Each was responsible for a musical renaissance in his native land, and each developed a highly distinctive idiom, inspired to a certain extent by the musical characteristics of his native culture. Both composers lapsed into creative silence after middle age.

Sibelius was born into a Swedish-speaking family. His father, a doctor, died of cholera when Jean – who gallicized his given name, Johan – was still an infant, and the boy was brought up by his mother and grandmother. He was a promising violinist (he hoped to become a soloist), and was composing by the age of ten. From an early age he was much influenced by the *Kalevala*, the Finnish national epic, which – allied to an intense response to landscape and nature – was to provide the impetus for his own work.

ABOVE: A coloured drawing from 1904 of the Finnish composer Jean Sibelius (1865–1957) by Albert Edelfelt.

After leaving school Sibelius originally intended to study law, but gave it up in favour of music. In the 1880s he studied first in Helsinki, and then in Berlin and Vienna, where he made many influential contacts, but also began the heavy drinking and financial irresponsibility which were to mar his later life.

Nationalism

Sibelius returned to Finland in 1891, where he worked on *Kullervo*, a symphonic poem for soprano, baritone, chorus and orchestra based on the *Kalevala*. Its immediate success established him as Finland's leading composer. In June 1892 he married the daughter of a Finnish nationalist general, thereby cementing his own identification with the nationalist movement (Finland was at that time part of the Russian Empire).

Although Sibelius never used actual folk tunes, his works of the 1890s are all distinctively Finnish. They include the four tone-poems based on the exploits of the legendary hero Lemminkäinen, of which the third is *Tuonelan joutsen* (*The Swan of Tuonela*); two more tone-poems –

ABOVE: A panoramic photograph of Helsinki, the capital of Finland, c.1910. Sibelius studied music at Helsinki's Conservatoire from 1886–8, where he became friends with the Italian/German composer Ferruccio Busoni (1866–1924) who was a member of the teaching staff.

ABOVE: A photograph of Sibelius taken when he was a student in Vienna in his early 20s.

En saga and *Skogsrået* (*The Wood-nymph*) – and the incidental music to *Karelia* (from which Sibelius made an orchestral suite). All these show the characteristic features of Sibelius's musical style, especially his liking for short motifs which are spun out symphonically, his use of *ostinato* patterns, and his effective handling of orchestration, with woodwind highlighted against an atmospheric string background, giving the impression of wind-blown open spaces.

Symphonies

In 1897 Sibelius – who was constantly in debt – was awarded a state pension which allowed him to concentrate on composing. Two years later he completed the tone-poem *Finlandia* and his First Symphony, clearly influenced by Tchaikovsky. It was followed by six more symphonies, written between 1902 and 1924, each of which is highly individual. The Second (1902) and the Fifth (1915) are perhaps the most popular (like Beethoven's, the Fifth is a "heroic" work); while the Fourth (1911) is compact and austere in tone, the Sixth more pastoral, and the short Seventh (originally called *Fantasia sinfonica*) is in a single movement. An Eighth Symphony was written, but immediately destroyed.

During the early years of the 20th century, Sibelius travelled extensively, visiting England, Bohemia and Italy. The Violin Concerto dates from 1903, a period in which Sibelius's drinking and debt put his marriage under strain. In 1904 he built himself a villa outside Helsinki, where he lived for the rest of his life. The tone-poems *Pohjolan tytär* (*Pohjola's Daughter*) and *Oinen ratsastus ja auringonnousu* (*Night-ride and Sunrise*) date from this period, as does the incidental music to Maurice Maeterlinck's *Pelléas et Mélisande* (a play which Debussy used as the basis for his opera) and *Belsazars gästabud* (*Belshazzar's Feast*, a Biblical episode later set by William Walton).

Life and works

NATIONALITY: Finnish

BORN: Hämeenlinna, 1865; **DIED:** Järvanpää, 1957

SPECIALIST GENRES: Symphonies.

MAJOR WORKS: Seven symphonies; *En saga* (1892–1902); *Lemminkäinen Legends* (1893–7); *Karelia* Suite (1893); *Finlandia* (1899); Violin Concerto (1903–5).

ABOVE: An impressionistic illustration of Sibelius's tone-poem The Swan of Tuonela *(1893–7) by I. J. Belmont.*

Silence

In 1908 Sibelius underwent an operation for suspected throat cancer, and his later works have an intensified bleakness. He continued to travel throughout Europe and to America to conduct his works until the outbreak of World War I, an event which virtually ended his creative life. After the war he wrote only four more major pieces, including incidental music for Shakespeare's *The Tempest* (1925), and his last symphonic poem, *Tapiola* (1926). For the remaining 31 years of his life, he composed nothing, disliked talking about his music and became increasingly reclusive.

Camille Saint-Saëns

There is nothing more difficult than talking about music.

SAINT-SAËNS

The French composer Camille Saint-Saëns was, like Mozart and Mendelssohn, a child prodigy. His father died just after he was born, and he was brought up by his mother and an aunt who began to teach him the piano when he was two. He was composing by the age of three, and played concertos by Mozart and Beethoven when he was ten. He also showed a keen interest in other intellectual pursuits, particularly archaeology, geology, astronomy and philosophy.

Saint-Saëns studied at the Paris Conservatoire, and was organist at the Madeleine church in Paris from 1857–76. After hearing him improvise, Liszt declared him the greatest organist in the world. In return, Saint-Saëns acknowledged Liszt's influence on his own symphonic poems of the 1870s: *Le rouet d'Omphale* (*Omphale's Spinning Wheel*), *Phaëton*, the enormously popular *Danse macabre*, and *La jeunesse d'Hercule* (*Hercules' Youth*). In 1871 he was a founder-member of the Société Nationale de Musique, set up to promote performances of works by younger French composers.

Saint-Saëns was much attached to his mother but, much to her disapproval, when he was 40 he married a girl half his age. Their two young sons died tragically within six weeks of each other, and after just six years of marriage, Saint-Saëns walked out on his wife. After his mother's death in 1888 he spent much time abroad, especially in North Africa, and many of his works, such as the Fifth Piano Concerto, make use of exotic harmonies.

His most famous and enduring works include the opera *Samson et Dalila*, the First Cello Concerto, the Introduction and Rondo Capriccioso for violin and orchestra, the five piano concertos, the Organ Symphony (No. 3), and *Le carnaval des animaux* (*The Carnival of the Animals*), written as a private joke for performance by friends.

ABOVE: Camille Saint-Saëns (1835–1921). He was an amazingly prolific composer – "I compose music as a tree produces apples", he said.

LEFT: The entrance to the Paris Conservatoire de Musique et de Déclamation in the rue Bergère, where Saint-Saëns studied.

Life and works

NATIONALITY: French

BORN: Paris, 1835; **DIED:** Algiers, 1921

SPECIALIST GENRES: Tone-poems, piano concertos.

MAJOR WORKS: Piano Concerto No. 2 (1868); Cello Concerto No. 1 (1873); *Danse macabre* (1874); *Samson et Dalila* (1877); Symphony No. 3 (1886); *Le carnaval des animaux* (1886).

Gabriel Fauré

For me...music exists to elevate us as far as possible above everyday existence.

FAURÉ, IN A LETTER TO HIS SON PHILIPPE, 1908

Fauré was Saint-Saëns' favourite pupil at the Ecole Niedermeyer in Paris. Like his teacher, he was a gifted pianist and organist, and began his career as an organist in Rennes. In 1871 he became organist at Ste Sulpice in Paris, and was also active in the foundation of the Société Nationale de Musique, where many of his own works were given their premières.

Fauré's engagement to Marianne Viardot (the daughter of a famous singer) produced three fine chamber works: the First Violin Sonata, the First Piano Quartet, and the Ballade for piano. In 1882, five years after Marianne broke off the engagement, he married Marie Fremiet, the daughter of a sculptor. The marriage, which produced two sons, was unhappy, and Fauré found consolation with other women, including Emma Bardac (the second Mme Debussy), for whom he wrote the tender song-cycle *La bonne chanson*, and for whose daughter Hélène (nicknamed Dolly) he wrote the *Dolly* Suite for piano duet.

ABOVE: Gabriel Fauré (1845–1924), aged 18. He studied with Saint-Saëns, and later taught at the Paris Conservatoire.

Fauré continued to earn a living as organist, choir-master and teacher, and was able to compose only in his spare time. He was happiest with small-scale genres such as songs, piano and chamber music: many of his delicate, elusive songs are settings of texts by the Symbolist poet Paul Verlaine. His famous Requiem – probably his best-known work – took over 20 years to finish. In the late 1890s he was appointed principal organist of the Madeleine church in Paris, and also became a professor of composition at the Paris Conservatoire, where his pupils included Ravel. He became director of the Conservatoire in 1905.

By the age of 50 Fauré was well-known in Parisian society (his friends included Marcel Proust). By this time he was attempting larger-scale works, including the incidental music to Maeterlinck's play *Pelléas et Mélisande* (which also inspired Debussy and Sibelius), the orchestral suite in 18th-century style *Masques et bergamasques* (1919) and the stage works *Prométhée* and *Pénélope*.

He retired from the Conservatoire in 1920, and was finally able to devote himself to composition, although by this time he was losing his hearing. His late works were mostly for chamber combinations, including a Piano Trio and Piano Quintet.

ABOVE: Fauré playing the organ at the Church of the Madeleine in Paris, where he was principal organist for many years.

Life and works

NATIONALITY: French

BORN: Pamiers, Ariège, 1845; **DIED:** Paris, 1924

SPECIALIST GENRES: Songs, piano and chamber music.

MAJOR WORKS: Songs and song-cycles; piano music, including *Dolly* Suite (1897); *Pavane* (1887); Requiem (1888); *Pelléas et Mélisande* (1892); *Pénélope* (1913).

Giacomo Puccini

*I shall feel it [the story of Manon] as an Italian,
with desperate passion.*

PUCCINI

Puccini was the last great exponent of Italian Romantic opera. His operas have always held a special place in the affections of audiences, and rival Verdi's in popularity. He was born into a dynasty of musicians who since the 18th century had been organists at the church of San Martino in Lucca. It had been intended that Puccini should follow the family tradition, but seeing a performance of Verdi's *Aida* at Pisa made him decide to become an opera composer.

ABOVE: *A portrait of Giacomo Puccini (1858–1924) painted in Paris in 1899, three years after he wrote his highly popular opera* La Bohème.

Milan

In 1880 a scholarship enabled Puccini to enrol at the Milan Conservatory. He graduated in the summer of 1883, having entered a one-act opera, *Le villi* (*The Witches*), in a competition sponsored by a music publisher. It came nowhere, but the next year Puccini played it through at a party attended by Verdi's publisher Ricordi. *Le villi* was staged in 1884, and Ricordi immediately commissioned another opera, *Edgar*, from the young composer, and signed him up.

Edgar was performed at La Scala in Milan in 1889, but was not well received (the composer himself described it as a "mistake"). But his next opera, *Manon Lescaut* (based, like Massenet's opera *Manon*, on the novel by Abbé Prévost), was a huge success at its Turin première in 1893. Puccini had found a winning formula: that of the young, doomed heroine whose flawed character leads to an affecting early death. He repeated it with *La Bohème* (*The Bohemian Girl*), first performed at Turin in 1896 under Toscanini; but it took some time for this romantic drama of love and death in a Montmartre garret – now one of the world's most popular operas – to catch the public's imagination.

Puccini's next opera, *Tosca*, performed in Rome in 1900, was an excursion into the brutal world of *verismo*. Its

ABOVE: *Puccini at home in the music-room of his villa at Torre del Lago, near Lucca.*

ABOVE: *A stage set for Act I of Puccini's* Tosca, *set in the Roman church of S Andrea delle Valle.*

"body count" – an attempted rape, a murder, a faked execution by firing squad which turns out to be real, and a final, dramatic suicide – has rarely been surpassed. Critics have always been snooty about *Tosca* (one described it memorably as "a shabby little shocker"), but Puccini's marvellous melodic gift and innate sense of drama save it from mere sensationalism.

ABOVE: A poster for the original 1904 production of Madama Butterfly. *Butterfly is shown bidding farewell to her child before killing herself.*

Based on a real-life incident, as related in David Belasco's play, *Madama Butterfly* (La Scala, 1904) returned to the "weepie" genre. The tragic tale of a Japanese geisha, betrayed and abandoned by the American naval lieutenant she believes to be her husband, took the operatic world by storm after Puccini revised it into three acts. Another Belasco play, *The Girl of the Golden West*, provided the subject-matter for Puccini's next opera, *La fanciulla del West*, premièred at the New York Metropolitan Opera in December 1910 with Enrico Caruso and Emmy Destinn in the leading roles.

Puccini made a political mistake with his next opera, accepting a commission from the directors of a Viennese theatre instead of an Italian one, drawing accusations of treachery. The little-known *La rondine* (*The Swallow*) was first performed during World War I, though in Monte Carlo rather than Vienna. Puccini worked simultaneously on a "Grand Guignol" triptych of one-act operas: the horrific *Il tabarro* (*The Cloak*), the sentimental tragedy *Suor Angelica* and his one comedy, *Gianni Schicchi*, the most successful of the three. The triptych was premièred in New York in December 1918.

"Nessun dorma"

Puccini had lived since 1891 at his villa at Torre del Lago outside Lucca, with his wife Elvira (his married mistress until 1904). In 1909 their servant girl committed suicide when unjustly accused by the jealous Elvira of having an affair with Puccini. This tragedy may have inspired the character of Liù, the gentle, lovable slave girl in Puccini's last opera *Turandot*, based on an oriental fairy-tale. The work includes the aria "Nessun dorma", popularized by the "Three Tenors" at a concert staged in conjunction with the 1990 football World Cup in Italy. *Turandot* was destined to have a happy ending, when the cruel princess Turandot is outwitted by Prince Calaf and finally succumbs to love. But Puccini died of a heart attack during treatment for throat cancer in November 1924, leaving the final love duet unfinished.

ABOVE: A page from the manuscript score of La Bohème *(1896). Puccini has indicated Mimi's death with a skull and crossbones in the margin.*

Life and works

NATIONALITY: Italian

BORN: Lucca, 1858;
DIED: Brussels, 1924

SPECIALIST GENRES:
Italian opera.

MAJOR WORKS:
Manon Lescaut (1893);
La Bohème (1896);
Tosca (1900);
Madama Butterfly (1904);
Turandot (1926).

Richard Strauss

From time to time the cruellest discords are succeeded by exquisite suavities, that caress the ear with delight.

CAMILLE SAINT-SAËNS (1835–1921), OF "SALOME"

Richard Strauss, like Rachmaninov, was a composer who outlived his era. Elgar and Sibelius stopped composing shortly after World War I, perhaps realizing that the spirit of the age contradicted their personal artistic visions; but their contemporaries Strauss and Rachmaninov enjoyed a late Romantic Indian summer, oblivious to stylistic change.

Strauss was born in 1864, the son of the principal horn player in the Munich court orchestra. His father Franz played horn solos in the premières of Wagner's *Tristan und Isolde* (1865) and *Die Meistersinger von Nürnberg* (1868), but the young Richard first encountered Wagner's operas a few years later. A precociously gifted child, he had learnt the piano from the age of four and the violin from eight.

Strauss's first important work, the *Serenade* for wind instruments, was performed in Berlin in 1882 by members of the famous Meiningen Orchestra, whose conductor Hans von Bülow commissioned the young composer's Suite in B flat. During this period Strauss also wrote his First Horn Concerto, a cello sonata, a symphony (No. 2, premièred in New York), and several song settings. In the summer of 1885 Strauss became von Bülow's assistant at Meiningen, and took over from von Bülow a month later. From then on, his career was divided between conducting and composing.

ABOVE: A portrait of the young Richard Strauss (1864–1949), probably dating from the 1890s.

Tone-poems

In 1886 Strauss moved on to the Munich court opera, where he became interested in the theories of Wagner and Arthur Schopenhauer, and in Liszt's tone-poems. His own first venture into this genre, *Aus Italien*, dates from 1886. Between 1889,

LEFT: Strauss directing an opera from the pit, 1929, by Wilhelm Viktor Krausz.

RIGHT: The frontispiece to the original piano score of Elektra *(1909), designed by Louis Corinth.*

when he moved to Weimar as assistant conductor to the court opera, and 1898, when he became chief conductor of the Royal Opera in Berlin, he wrote a sequence of seven magnificent tone-poems: *Don Juan*, *Macbeth*, *Tod und Verklärung* (*Death and Transfiguration*), *Till Eulenspiegels lustige Streiche* (*Till Eulenspiegel's Merry Pranks*), *Also sprach Zarathustra* (*Thus Spake Zarathustra*), *Don Quixote* and *Ein Heldenleben* (*A Hero's Life*). Together with the *Symphonia domestica* (1902–4) and *Ein Alpensinfonie* (1911–15), they represent Strauss's most important orchestral works.

ABOVE: *The Dresden Court Opera House, where many of Strauss's operas were performed.*

Opera

However, it was in the field of opera that Strauss achieved fame. Inspired by his marriage in 1893 to the soprano Pauline de Ahna, he began his long love affair with the voice – especially the female voice. His first opera, *Guntram* (1894), was a failure, and his second, *Feuersnot* (*Fire Famine*, 1901), is rarely performed; but from *Salome* (1905) onwards he created a series of magnificent and individual works which are rarely out of the repertoire. *Salome* (based on Oscar Wilde's scandalous play) and *Elektra* (based on Sophocles' drama) caused international sensations owing to Strauss's explicit treatment of their subjects. Musically, both owe much to Wagner; *Salome* in particular is a masterpiece of sensuous, overblown late Romanticism. The royalties from *Salome* alone enabled Strauss to build himself a luxurious villa at Garmisch.

The librettist of *Elektra*, Hugo von Hofmannsthal (1874–1929), worked with Strauss over the next two decades: their most successful collaboration was the Mozartian comedy *Der Rosenkavalier*. With Hofmannsthal, Strauss went on to create *Ariadne auf Naxos*, *Die Frau ohne Schatten* (*The Woman without a Shadow*, 1914–17), *Die ägyptische Helena* (*The Egyptian Helen*, 1923–7) and *Arabella* (1929–32), completed after Hofmannsthal's death. Strauss's librettist for his next opera, *Die schweigsame Frau* (*The Silent Woman*, 1933–4) was the Jewish Stefan Zweig, but the prevailing political climate in Germany required Strauss to choose an Austrian librettist, Joseph Gregor, for his subsequent operas: *Friedenstag* (*Peace Day*, 1935–6), *Daphne* (1936–7) and *Die Liebe der Danaë* (*Danaë's Love*, 1938–40).

Strauss's political naivety led to his exploitation by the Nazi Reichsmusik-kammer, which appointed him its president in 1933 but removed him two years later (his daughter-in-law was Jewish). He spent the war years in Vienna (where he wrote his last opera, *Capriccio,* in 1940–1), but afterwards moved to Switzerland while he was investigated – and eventually cleared of Nazi affiliations – by the denazification tribunal.

Strauss's last works are mainly instrumental: they include *Metamorphosen* for 23 solo strings (1945, a lament for the devastation of Germany), the Second Horn Concerto, the Oboe Concerto, sonatinas for wind instruments, and the radiant *Vier letzte Lieder* (*Four Last Songs*, 1948) for voice and orchestra. He died at his home in Garmisch, aged 85.

Life and works

NATIONALITY: German

BORN: Munich, 1864; **DIED:** Garmisch, 1949

SPECIALIST GENRES: Late Romantic tone-poems, Wagnerian-style opera.

MAJOR WORKS: Tone-poems *Macbeth* (1886–8), *Don Juan* (1888–9), *Tod und Verklärung* (1888–9), *Till Eulenspiegels lustige Streiche* (1894–5), *Also sprach Zarathustra* (1895–6), *Don Quixote* (1896–7) and *Ein Heldenleben* (1897–8); operas *Salome* (1905), *Elektra* (1909), *Der Rosenkavalier* (1911) and *Ariadne auf Naxos* (1911–12); *Capriccio* (1940–1); *Four Last Songs* (1948).

Sergei Rachmaninov

I feel like a ghost wandering in a world grown alien.
I cannot cast out the old way of writing and I cannot acquire the new.

RACHMANINOV

Rachmaninov was the last of a tradition of great pianist-composers, and the last of the Russian Romantics. The dramatic sweep of his music, combined with a haunting Russian melancholy, holds a powerful appeal. His three symphonies and four piano concertos are much loved.

He had his earliest piano lessons from his mother, a trained pianist. In 1882 his family moved to St Petersburg, where Rachmaninov entered the Conservatory. But when his parents separated, he transferred to Moscow, where he studied with the strict teacher Nikolay Zverev, and from 1888 onwards, with Alexander Ziloti (1863–1945) for piano and Anton Arensky (1861–1906) for composition. He graduated from the piano class of the Moscow Conservatory in the summer of 1891, completing his First Piano Concerto at the same time. The next year, his one-act opera *Aleko* won him the Conservatory's highest award for composition and, shortly after graduating, he wrote one of his most popular pieces, the Prelude in C sharp minor for piano.

ABOVE: Sergei Rachmaninov, painted in 1925 while he was living in the USA, by Konstantin Andreyevich Somov.

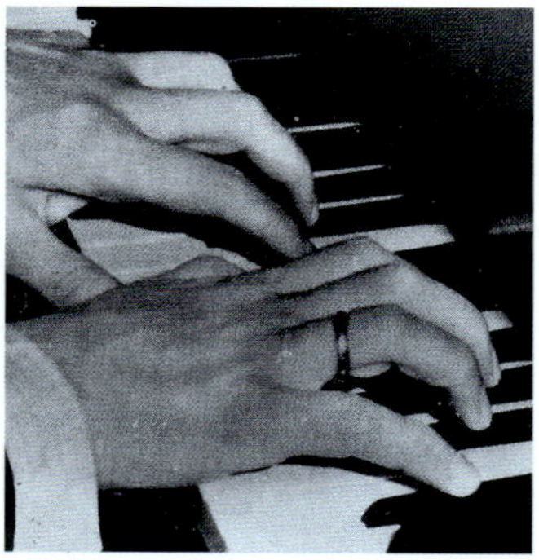

ABOVE: Rachmaninov had unusually large hands, able to cope with big stretches – an advantage for a virtuoso pianist.

In 1897, Rachmaninov's good luck changed when his First Symphony, in D minor, was performed at a Russian Symphony Concert, conducted by Alexander Glazunov. The performance was a disaster (Glazunov was rumoured to be drunk), and the critic César Cui described the piece as "a programme symphony on the Seven Plagues of Egypt". It was not performed again until 1945. Rachmaninov suffered a nervous breakdown, and could not compose anything for three years. In due course he underwent a successful course of hypnotic treatment with a Dr Nikolay Dahl, which restored his confidence and enabled him to start work on the Second Piano Concerto, the theme of whose slow movement was used to memorable effect in David Lean's 1945 film *Brief Encounter*.

Rachmaninov gave the première of his new concerto, dedicated to Dr Dahl, on 9 November 1901, and a few months later, after finishing his cantata *Spring*, he married his cousin Natalya Satina. Over the next few years he occupied himself with opera composition, until the illness of his daughter Irina obliged the family to move to Dresden in 1906. There he completed his Second Symphony (the

ABOVE: Alexander Glazunov is reputed to have ruined the première of Rachmaninov's First Symphony by conducting while drunk.

ABOVE: Red Square in Moscow, with St Basil's Cathedral illuminated. Rachmaninov drew inspiration from the Russian Orthodox liturgy, and wrote some fine sacred vocal music.

slow movement with its long-breathed clarinet solo is a masterly piece of writing), the First Piano Sonata, and the symphonic poem *The Isle of the Dead*, inspired by a painting by the Swiss artist Arnold Böcklin.

In 1909 Rachmaninov made his first visit to America, where he toured with a new work, the Third Piano Concerto. Over the next few years he spent the summers on his country estate, where he wrote the 13 Preludes for piano, Op. 13 (1910), the Liturgy of St John Chrysostom (1910), the *Etudes-tableaux* for piano, Op. 33 (1911), the 14 Songs, Op. 34, and the Second Piano Sonata (1913). During the winters he toured as a pianist, a routine that continued until the outbreak of World War I. His other major compositions of this period include the choral symphony *The Bells* (1913) and the *All-night Vigil* for unaccompanied choir (1915).

America

In 1917, the dangerous political situation in Russia forced Rachmaninov and his family into exile, first in Sweden, and then in America, where he remained for the rest of his life. From 1918 onwards he wrote little, spending most of his time performing. The Fourth Piano Concerto was written in 1926, but when it failed to achieve the success of its predecessors Rachmaninov was forced to revise and shorten it.

In 1931 he composed his last solo piano work, the *Variations on a Theme of Corelli*, followed by the brilliant *Rhapsody on a Theme of Paganini* for piano and orchestra (1934), the Third Symphony (1935–8), and the Symphonic Dances, his last work (1940). By early 1943 he was exhausted and ill, but he continued to tour. He died of cancer at his home in Beverly Hills on 28 March 1943, four days before his 70th birthday.

Life and works

NATIONALITY: Russian

BORN: Semyonovo, 1873; **DIED:** Beverly Hills, 1943

SPECIALIST GENRES: Piano concertos, solo piano music.

MAJOR WORKS: Four piano concertos; three symphonies; 24 Preludes for piano (1892–1910); *Rhapsody on a Theme of Paganini* (1934).

Other Composers of the Era

. . . some world far from ours
Where music and moonlight and feeling
Are one.

PERCY BYSSHE SHELLEY (1792–1822)

Like Rachmaninov, Alexander Glazunov (1865–1936) was among the late Russian Romantic composers. A pupil of Rimsky-Korsakov, he wrote his First Symphony at the age of only 16, and became a protégé of Balakirev. From the 1880s onwards he travelled widely, meeting Liszt in Weimar, and conducting in Paris and London. In 1905 he became director of the St Petersburg Conservatory. He suffered great hardship during the Russian Revolution, and in 1928 left Russia altogether, eventually settling in Paris. His works, which are more cosmopolitan than nationalist, include nine symphonies, two piano concertos, a popular Violin Concerto, a late Saxophone Concerto (1931), seven string quartets, and a ballet, *The Seasons* (1899).

ABOVE: Alexander Glazunov (1865–1936). Like Rachmaninov, Stravinsky and Prokofiev he left Russia after the Revolution.

ABOVE: The Polish composer Karol Szymanowski (1882–1937), director of the Warsaw Conservatory.

The Polish composer Karol Szymanowski (1882–1937) spent much of his early life in the Ukraine, but between 1905 and 1908 he lived in Berlin, where he wrote his first symphony. His Russian home was destroyed during the Revolution, and in 1920 he moved to Warsaw, where he became director of the Conservatory (later the Academy). He died of tuberculosis. His piano music was championed by Polish pianists including Artur Rubinstein, while his two violin concertos were premièred by the Polish violinist Paul Kochansky. His Stabat Mater (1925–6) is highly regarded.

Mahler's exact contemporary Hugo Wolf (1860–1903) was also his fellow pupil at the Vienna Conservatory. An enthusiastic Wagnerite, he antagonized many people with his critical attacks on Brahms. He is remembered for his exquisite songs – the worthy successors of Schubert and Schumann. They include 53 settings of poems by Mörike, 20 by Eichendorff, 51 by Goethe, 44 songs in the *Spanisches Liederbuch* (*Spanish Songbook*, 1891), a total of 46 in the two volumes of the *Italienisches Liederbuch* (*Italian Songbook*, 1892–6) and three poems by Michelangelo (1898). Apart from songs, his best-known work is the *Italian Serenade* (1892) for string orchestra (originally for quartet). In 1897, a victim of syphilis, he went mad and was confined to an asylum.

The German composer Max Bruch (1838–1920) worked as a conductor in Berlin, Bonn, Liverpool, Breslau and Scotland, and became a professor of composition at the Berlin Hochschule. An enormously prolific composer, he is remembered today chiefly for three

ABOVE: The Austrian composer Hugo Wolf (1860–1903). A brilliant composer of Lieder, he contracted syphilis and died insane.

ABOVE: Max Bruch (1838–1920) never quite lived up to his early promise, but his Violin Concerto in G minor is much played.

works, the G minor Violin Concerto (1868), the *Scottish Fantasy* for violin and orchestra (1880), and *Kol Nidrei* (1881), an *adagio* on a Hebrew melody for cello and orchestra.

France

The Belgian-born César Franck (1822–90) became organ professor at the Paris Conservatoire in 1872. An outstanding organist, he wrote a great deal of sacred music, but is chiefly

ABOVE: Sir Hubert Parry (1848–1918), chiefly remembered for his setting of Blake's Jerusalem *and for the six* Songs of Farewell.

ABOVE: Vincent d'Indy (1851–1931), who founded the Schola Cantorum in Paris in the 1890s.

remembered for his Organ Symphony in D minor (1886–8), the Symphonic Variations for piano and orchestra (1885), the Piano Quintet (1878–9), the Violin Sonata (1886) and *Panis angelicus* (1872, for tenor, organ, harp, cello and double bass).

His pupil Vincent D'Indy (1851–1931), an admirer of Wagner like his teacher, was a founder of the Schola Cantorum in Paris in 1894, originally for the study of church music but, from 1900 onwards, a general music school. He wrote several operas, but his best-known work is probably the *Symphonie sur un chant montagnard français (Symphony on a French Mountaineer's Song*, 1886).

Wagner also influenced the works of Paul Dukas (1865–1935), whose first major success, *L'apprenti sorcier (The Sorcerer's Apprentice*, 1897, based on a story by Goethe), is still much performed. Dukas wrote a fine opera based on a play by Maeterlinck, *Ariane et Barbe-bleue (Ariadne and Bluebeard*, 1907), similar in atmosphere to Debussy's *Pelléas et Mélisande*, but his strict self-criticism meant that he published only a few of his compositions and destroyed much of his work before he died.

ABOVE: Paul Dukas (1865–1935). A contemporary of Debussy, he is remembered chiefly for The Sorcerer's Apprentice.

Britain

In late Victorian England, Hubert Parry (1848–1918) and Charles Villiers Stanford (1852–1924) – both professors at the Royal College of Music, London – had enormous influence on a younger generation of British composers, whom they numbered among their many pupils. Parry taught at Oxford University; Stanford, the composer of seven symphonies, taught at Cambridge.

ABOVE: Sir Charles Villiers Stanford (1852–1924) portrayed in a 1905 Vanity Fair cartoon.

The Early Twentieth Century

An example of post-impressionist art – Woman with a Yellow Jacket *(1913) by the German artist August Macke (1887–1914).*

Music in a New Framework

Musical innovation is full of danger to the state, for when modes of music change, the laws of the state always change with them.

PLATO (C.428–347 BC)

By the closing years of the 19th century, it was clear that Romanticism had run its course. New trends were apparent in literature and art: in the Symbolist poems of Paul Verlaine, Charles Baudelaire and Stéphane Mallarmé and the plays of Maurice Maeterlinck; in the impressionist paintings of Claude Monet, Camille Pissarro and Edouard Manet, in which representational art gave way to blurred outlines and emphasis on the shifting play of light.

As the 20th century dawned, Impressionism was succeeded by post-Impressionism, and by a bewildering array of new artistic movements: the Fauves, with their bold outlines and brash colours, the Expressionist art of Edvard Munch and Wasily Kandinsky, the cubism of Pablo Picasso, the stark lines of Bauhaus art and architecture. Music, as ever, followed behind, when the focus of new trends moved decisively from central Europe to Paris.

ABOVE: Around the Piano *(1885) by Henri Fantin-Latour (1836–1904).*

ABOVE: An Allegory of Happiness *by Julio Romero de Torres (1880–1930).*

Impressionism in music

In musical terms, composers realized that they need no longer be subject to the tyranny of traditional tonality – a system which had lasted for 400 years. One of the pioneers of the "music of the future" was the Frenchman Claude Debussy, whose fluid structures, built out of the repetition of tiny motifs with colouristic instrumental effects, were likened to impressionist techniques in painting. Little of Debussy's mature music could be said to be in a "key"; instead, its gravitational centre constantly shifts as a result of his use of chromatic harmony.

Atonality

Meanwhile, the Austrian composer Arnold Schoenberg began writing in a lush, late-Romantic style, but in the first decade of the 20th century he pushed chromatic harmony to its limits, experimenting first with atonality, in which the 12 notes of the chromatic scale are treated equally, and then with an original method of musical organization called the "12-note system". This method – in which musical building-blocks are created from "tone-rows" consisting of all 12 notes of the scale – influenced many succeeding composers, including Berg and Webern (who were Schoenberg's pupils), Stravinsky, Messaien, Boulez and Stockhausen. They used it in various ingenious ways and adapted it to their own particular ends.

Nationalism

Meanwhile, musical nationalism continued to flourish: in England in the works of Ralph Vaughan Williams, Frederick Delius and Gustav Holst; in Denmark in the works of Carl Nielsen; in central Europe in the works of the Hungarians Béla Bartók and Zoltán Kodály and the Czech composer Leoš Janáček, the spiritual descendant of Dvořák. All these composers were ardent collectors of their national folk songs, first by transcribing them manually, and then, when phonographic equipment became available, recording them.

The USA – still a relatively young nation – acquired its first major composer in the form of the highly original Charles Ives, quickly followed

ABOVE: L'homme au violon *(*The Man with the Violin*), painted in 1918 by the Spanish artist Juan Gris (1887–1927).*

ABOVE: Dancing in Vienna shown in a post-World War I painting entitled Once upon a Time.

by others: Samuel Barber, George Gershwin (a populist master), and Aaron Copland, who deliberately set out to create distinctively "American" music.

Music and politics

The political upheavals of the 20th century, particularly the two world wars, had a profound effect on music, as on other art forms. During the economic depression which followed World War I, composers were forced to pare down their musical resources. Works that had required huge and expensive symphony orchestras gave way to small chamber ensembles, evident in the post-war works of Igor Stravinsky and the eclectic group of mainly French composers known as "Les Six".

Another noticeable influence during the 1920s and '30s was that of jazz, exported to Europe from the USA, and taken up with enthusiasm in England, France and Germany (especially in the works of Kurt Weill).

The rise of Nazi Germany in the 1930s struck a grievous blow. The works of "decadent" composers such as Weill were banned, and central Europe was emptied of Jewish musicians, both composers and performers, and of "non-conformist" Aryans. Some – including Schoenberg, Hindemith and Weill – fled to Britain and the USA (where they greatly enriched the musical lives of their adopted nations), while others were murdered. Apart from the aged Richard Strauss, Germany lost most of its finest composers: perhaps the best-known composer who stayed was Carl Orff, remembered only for his popular cantata *Carmina burana*, and for an influential teaching method.

Similarly, in Soviet Russia, Stalin's purges struck fear into all serious composers. The two finest Russian composers of the 20th century, Prokofiev and Shostakovich, both survived, but suffered severely under a tyrannical regime driven by political dogma and opposed to artistic innovation.

This drawing on the cover of The Theatre World *review journal shows Spanish dancers in the 1920s.*

Claude Debussy

It's music on the points of needles.

CÉSAR FRANCK (1822–90)

From the late Baroque period to around 1890, mainstream Western music was firmly rooted in Germany and Austria. Not until the late 19th and early 20th centuries did the line of succession stretching from Bach to Mahler begin to branch out, with major composers emerging from Russia, Bohemia, England, Scandinavia and the USA. It was a Frenchman, Claude Debussy, who broke the German monopoly, revitalizing French music with his uniquely subtle art, and opening up a new sound-world for the 20th century. His music explored "the mysterious relationship between Nature and Imagination".

Debussy's life centred on Paris, which was fast becoming the hub of European culture. He was born on 22 August 1862 in the suburb of St Germain-en-Laye, where his parents ran a china shop. The young Claude

ABOVE: Claude Achille Debussy (1862–1918). His unique sound-world opened the door to a new century.

Achille and his siblings were often packed off to their Aunt Clémentine in Cannes, where Debussy began to learn the piano with a former pupil of Chopin. At the age of ten he entered the Paris Conservatoire, where he unnerved his teachers with experimental harmonic improvisations at the keyboard.

Despite his unorthodox tendencies, he won the coveted Prix de Rome in 1884 with his cantata *L'enfant prodigue*, but his sojourn in Rome was not a happy one, and he returned to Paris – where he had been conducting a love affair with a married woman – in the spring of 1887. The same year he became intoxicated with Wagner's music and in 1888 visited Bayreuth. Although Debussy later described Wagner's music as "a beautiful sunset that was mistaken for a dawn", it held a life-long fascination for him. He even began work on a Wagnerian opera, but

LEFT: Entrance to the Exposition Universelle (1889) by Jean Beraud (1849–1936).

RIGHT: Debussy with his daughter Chou-Chou. He was already gravely ill with cancer when this photograph was taken in 1916.

ABOVE: A drawing by René Bull illustrating Debussy's Prélude à "L'après-midi d'un faune" *dating from 1913, the year after Nijinsky's scandalous choreographic version for the Ballets Russes.*

abandoned it when he realized that his own music needed to be "flexible and adaptable to fantasies and dreams".

Impressionism

Debussy had already found inspiration in the elusive works of the Symbolist poets, including Verlaine, whose verses he had begun to match with delicate, ethereal settings. At the same time he began to experiment with new piano sonorities, and with a scale based on whole tones, without a firm key centre. Among his early piano works are a pair of Arabesques and the *Petite suite* for piano duet.

The Javanese gamelan music Debussy heard at the 1889 Paris Exposition left a lasting impression, when he realized that economy of means – a single, shrill clarinet or a gong – could

Life and works

NATIONALITY: French

BORN: St Germain-en-Laye, 1862; **DIED:** Paris, 1918

SPECIALIST GENRES: Orchestral and piano music.

MAJOR WORKS: *Prélude à "L'après-midi d'un faune"* (1892–4); *Pelléas et Mélisande* (1893–1902); *Nocturnes* (1899); *La mer* (1905); *Images* (1905–7); Preludes for piano (1910, 1913); *Jeux* (1913).

ABOVE: The Great Wave of Kanagawa *(1831) by the Japanese artist Katsushika Hokusai (1760–1849). This print inspired Debussy's symphonic seascape* La mer.

ABOVE: A piece of 17th-century Chinese embroidery. Debussy loved Oriental art, and drew inspiration from it for some of his piano pieces.

be just as effective as a full-blown symphony orchestra. The influence of Art Nouveau, then all the rage in Paris, resulted in his cantata *La damoiselle élue* (*The Blessed Damozel*, 1888), based on a poem by the Pre-Raphaelite artist and writer Dante Gabriel Rossetti.

In the early 1890s Debussy found a tiny apartment in Montmartre, then the centre of artistic "bohemian" life. Surrounded by the artists, writers, fellow musicians, laundresses and prostitutes who constituted the district's lively residents, he set up house with his girlfriend Gabrielle Dupont and embarked on a period of penniless squalor but artistic creativity. During this period he developed his characteristic style, capturing in subtle, shifting harmonies and fragments of melody the essence of a breath of wind, the rustle of leaves, or a shaft of moonlight.

Sometimes his inspiration came from an antique dream-world peopled by masked Harlequins and Columbines playing mandolins and dancing sarabands. These visions sprang to life in the *Suite bergamasque* (1890) for piano, of which the third piece is the haunting "Clair de lune", the suite *Pour le piano* (1894–1901), and in the Verlaine settings called *Fêtes galantes* (1891 and 1904). From the same period dates the String Quartet (1893), and his most famous orchestral piece, the *Prélude à "L'après-midi d'un faune"* (*Prelude to "The Afternoon of a Faun"*, 1894). Based on an erotic monologue by Mallarmé about a faun lying in the grass one hot summer's afternoon in ancient Greece, dreaming of making love to two beautiful but elusive nymphs, the piece – turned into a scandalous ballet in 1912 by the dancer Nijinsky – was a triumphant success. According to the conductor and composer Pierre Boulez, from the first languid notes of the faun's flute, "music began to beat with a new pulse".

ABOVE: The Scottish soprano Mary Garden (1874–1967) as Mélisande, the heroine of Debussy's Pelléas et Mélisande. *She created the role at the Paris Opera in 1902.*

In the mid 1890s Debussy worked on the opera *Pelléas et Mélisande*, based on a Symbolist drama by the Belgian writer Maurice Maeterlinck. His infinitely subtle music, economically scored, and using silence as "perhaps the only way of throwing the emotional weight of a phrase into relief", perfectly complemented Maeterlinck's perplexing play, in which the characters seem to lack normal motivation. It took nine years for *Pelléas* to reach the stage, when it was greeted with incomprehension and hostility. It is now recognized as a masterpiece.

During this period, Debussy had lived off a small annual allowance from a publisher. Constant lack of money caused friction between him and Gaby, and the couple finally separated in 1898, just as Debussy finished another orchestral work, the three *Nocturnes*. These poetic evocations of a cloudy day over the river Seine, a Parisian carnival complete with brass band, and a delicate seascape with mermaids singing, are among his most "impressionistic" pieces, as are the contemporary set of *Estampes* (*Prints*) for piano, consisting of the pseudo-oriental *Pagodes*, *Soirée dans Grenade* (*Evening in Granada*, a languid Spanish habanera), and the virtuosic *Jardins sous la pluie* (*Gardens in the rain*).

ABOVE: A page from the autograph score of Act I of Pelléas et Mélisande.

Marriage

In 1899 Debussy – whose dark, Mephistophelean looks made him immensely attractive to women – replaced Gaby with a pretty bottle-blonde model called Lilly Texier. Ill-educated and tubercular, Lilly proved an entirely unsuitable wife. In 1903 Debussy met Emma Bardac, Fauré's ex-mistress, now the wife of a banker. They fell passionately in love and eloped to Jersey (where he wrote the piano piece *L'île joyeuse*). Lilly Debussy tried to shoot herself and Debussy was ostracized by his friends, but he and Emma set up house together in the fashionable Avenue du Bois de Boulogne, where their adored daughter Claude-Emma (Chou-Chou) was born in 1905. For the rest of his life Debussy attempted to keep Emma in the style to which she had become accustomed, often with great difficulty, and their ten-year marriage was frequently under strain, especially when he was obliged to leave on long conducting tours.

In 1905 Debussy completed his symphonic seascape *La mer*, a vivid example of his ability to create, through a mosaic of melody and delicate touches of instrumentation, an impression of the interplay between light and water. Over the next few years he also completed two sets of *Images* for piano, the delightful *Children's Corner* (1906–8) for his daughter, two books of piano Preludes, and a set of orchestral *Images*: *Rondes de printemps* (*Dances of Spring*), *Iberia* and *Gigues*. In 1911 he tried his hand at ballet music in *Khamma*, written for the Canadian dancer Maud Allan, and in 1913, in the masterly score *Jeux* (*Games*), written for Diaghilev's Ballets Russes and choreographed by Nijinsky.

Last works

By 1914 Debussy knew that he was mortally ill with cancer of the colon. Deeply distressed by the carnage of World War I, he worked feverishly to finish two sets of piano studies, inspired by Chopin's, and three pieces for two pianos, *En blanc et noir* (1915), each dedicated to a friend killed in action. His last works were three out of a projected set of six sonatas – abstract music in a new, austere style

ABOVE: The Russian impresario Sergei Diaghilev, the driving force behind the Ballets Russes. He commissioned Debussy's Jeux.

– for cello and piano, violin and piano, and flute, viola and harp. He did not live to write the other three, dying during a German bombardment on 25 March 1918. His sonatas were published with the simple inscription: "Claude Debussy: musicien français".

ABOVE: An impressionist seascape – Storm at Agay, *1895, by Jean Baptiste Guillaumin (1841–1927).*

Maurice Ravel

All the same, he had talent, that Ravel.

RAVEL

Debussy and his younger contemporary Ravel are often classed together as "impressionist" composers, and in life they sometimes found themselves in unintentional rivalry. In fact, the music of each was quite individual.

Ravel was the son of an engineer of Swiss origin and his Basque wife. When he was a baby the family moved to Paris, where Ravel spent the rest of his life. Like Debussy, he showed early promise as a pianist, and when he was 14 he entered the Paris Conservatoire. During his student days he came into contact with Javanese gamelan music (at the 1889 Paris Exposition), Russian music and Wagner, all of which indirectly influenced his own work.

Having graduated from the piano class in 1895, Ravel returned two years later to study composition with Fauré. An interest in Renaissance literature encouraged him to set poems by Clément Marot (c.1497–1544), and to write the *Menuet antique* (1895) and the *Pavane pour une infante défunte* (*Pavan for a Dead Infanta*, 1899) for piano; the latter became one of his most popular works. However, his outstandingly original talent disconcerted the Conservatoire's staid establishment, and he failed to win the Prix de Rome five times. Indeed, when he was eliminated in the first round in 1905, having already composed the virtuoso piano piece *Jeux d'eau* (1901), the String Quartet (1902–3), and the ravishing orchestral song-cycle *Shéhérazade* (1903), a huge public row forced the resignation of the Conservatoire's director.

ABOVE: The French composer Maurice Ravel (1875–1937), painted as a young man by Henri-Charles Manguin.

LEFT: Ravel at the piano. He was a brilliant pianist, and often performed his own music.

RIGHT: Ravel's villa, Le Belvedere, at Montfort-l'Amaury, near Paris.

Les Apaches

By now Ravel was a member of the artistic circle of poets, musicians, critics and painters known as "Les Apaches". His tiny stature, his addiction to elegant clothes and his impeccable toilette ensured his social popularity. His sexual proclivities are still unclear, but he never married and remained deeply attached to his mother. With the "*affaire* Ravel" at the Conservatoire behind him, he concentrated on composition, including the *Sonatine* (1903–5) and *Miroirs* (1904–5) for piano, the Introduction and Allegro for harp and chamber ensemble, the song-cycle *Histoires naturelles* (1906), and the evocative orchestral *Rapsodie espagnole* (1907–8). He also began work on his first opera, *L'heure espagnole* (1907–9), influenced by his Basque origins, and in 1911 turned his piano suite *Ma mère l'oye* (*Mother Goose*), originally written for two children, into a ballet score. From the same period dates his most famous ballet, *Daphnis et Chloé* (1909–12), which was commissioned by Diaghilev.

ABOVE: A design by Leon Bakst (1866–1924) for Act I of the Russian Ballet production of Ravel's Daphnis et Chloé *in Paris, 1912.*

ABOVE: Spanish flamenco dancing. Ravel's Boléro *pays homage to his lifelong love of Spain.*

War years

At the outbreak of World War I, Ravel was working on his Piano Trio. Turned down for military service on the grounds of his size, he became an ambulance driver on the Western Front until his health broke down. The death of his mother in 1916 was a cruel blow. His creative response to tragedy was *Le tombeau de Couperin* (1917), an anachronistic keyboard suite commemorating fallen friends, and the post-war *La valse*, a savage vision of a ghostly waltz to destruction. In 1921 Ravel moved to a small villa at Montfort-l'Amaury near Paris, which he filled with cats, toys and delicate *objets d'art*. His love of children was reflected in his next opera, *L'enfant et les sortilèges* (*The Child and the Magic Spells*, 1925), in which he used a libretto by Colette (1873–1954) to recreate an enchanted childhood world peopled by talking toys and animals. He commemorated Debussy's early death with his Duo for violin and cello, composed the song-cycle *Chansons madécasses* (1925–6) for the American patroness Elizabeth Sprague Coolidge, and began work on two violin works, *Tzigane* (1924) and the Sonata (1923–7).

Last works

In 1928, the year he visited America, Ravel composed the ballet *Boléro*, whose success came to haunt him. His two brilliant piano concertos (one for the left hand, in F, for the pianist Paul Wittgenstein, who had lost his right arm during World War I) appeared soon after this. His last work was the set of songs *Don Quichotte à Dulcinée* (1932–3), written for a film based on Cervantes' novel.

For the last five years of his life Ravel suffered from Pick's disease, an illness accelerated by brain damage sustained in a car crash. He died in 1937.

Life and works

NATIONALITY: French

BORN: Ciboure, Basses-Pyrénées, 1875; **DIED:** Paris, 1937

SPECIALIST GENRES: Virtuoso piano music, orchestral works.

MAJOR WORKS: *Pavane pour une infante défunte* (1899); *Jeux d'eau* (1901); *Miroirs* (1904–5); *Gaspard de la nuit* (1908); *Daphnis et Chloé* (1909–12); *Le tombeau de Couperin* (1917); *L'enfant et les sortilèges* (1925); *Boléro* (1928); two piano concertos (1929–31).

Erik Satie

My brother was always difficult to understand.
He doesn't seem to have been quite normal.

OLGA SATIE

A contemporary of Debussy and Ravel, Erik Satie was a pioneer of the avant-garde. His satirical, anti-bourgeois attitudes and eccentric demeanour anticipated Dadaism and Surrealism, while his spare, whimsical musical style was the antithesis of late Romanticism. He had enormous influence on the group of composers known as "Les Six", as well as on later figures such as John Cage.

The son of a French father and a Scottish mother, he was born in Honfleur on the Normandy coast, and moved to Paris in 1878. He studied at the Paris Conservatoire, but achieved little success. His early works for piano include *Sarabandes* (1887), the hypnotic *Gymnopédies* (1888) and the exotic-sounding *Gnossiennes* (1890). For several years he earned a meagre living playing the piano in Montmartre bars and cabarets, and also became involved with the occult Rosicrucian sect, "founding" the Metropolitan Church of the Art of Jesus the Conductor.

ABOVE: An anonymous drawing of Satie in chalk, dated 1890 and inscribed "A mon ami Erik Satie" ("To my friend Erik Satie").

ABOVE: Erik Satie (1866–1925), one of the great eccentrics.

Around 1890 Satie met Debussy, beginning a 25-year friendship in which Debussy was very much the superior partner, with Satie as his court jester. During this period Satie had a tempestuous love affair with the painter Suzanne Valadon (the mother of Utrillo), and became known for eccentric gestures, such as buying 12 identical grey velvet suits. In 1898 he left Montmartre for the grim suburb of Arcueil-Cachan, where he lived in one small, bare room.

Satie's later compositions often have deliberately obscure titles, such as *Trois véritables préludes flasques (pour un chien) (Three flabby preludes for a dog)*, *Choses vues à droite et à gauche (sans lunettes) (Things seen from the right and left without spectacles)* and *Trois morceaux en forme de poire (Three pear-shaped pieces)*, though there are actually seven.

During World War I Satie collaborated with the writer Jean Cocteau (1889–1963), the choreographer Leonid Massine and the painter Pablo Picasso on the 1917 ballet *Parade* for Diaghilev's Ballets Russes. The work set out to introduce the principles of Cubism to the stage, and Satie's jazz-influenced score – including parts for typewriter, whistle and siren – caused a scandal. In complete contrast was the cantata *Socrate* (1919), which he wanted to be "white and pure like antiquity". Subsequent collaborations with Massine and Picasso, and with Francis Picabia and Réné Clair, produced the ballets *Mercure* and *Relâche (No Show,* 1924). By then Satie had become a recluse. A heavy drinker, he died of sclerosis of the liver in July 1925.

Life and works

NATIONALITY: French

BORN: Honfleur, 1866; **DIED:** Paris, 1925

SPECIALIST GENRES: Minimalist piano music.

MAJOR WORKS: Many piano works, including *Trois gymnopédies* (1888) and *Trois gnossiennes* (1890); ballet *Parade* (1917); cantata *Socrate* (1919).

Alexander Scriabin

It was like a bath of ice; cocaine and rainbows.
HENRY MILLER (1891–1980), "NEXUS"

Alexander Scriabin's early career has many parallels with Rachmaninov's. Like Rachmaninov, he was equally gifted as a composer and as a pianist. His mother (who died just over a year after he was born) had been a fine pianist, and he was brought up by female relatives.

Scriabin began his piano studies in Moscow with Nikolay Zverev – who also taught Rachmaninov – before entering the Conservatory in 1888, the same year as Rachmaninov. Shortly after graduating in 1892 with the second gold medal (Rachmaninov won the first), Scriabin came to the attention of the Russian millionaire publisher and philanthropist Belyayev, who began to publish his early works (including a set of 12 Studies), and sent him off on a European tour, playing his own music. From this period date several sets of piano Preludes, the Second Piano Sonata, and the Piano Concerto, which Scriabin composed on his return to Moscow.

In 1897 he married the young pianist Vera Isaakovich, with whom he had four children. But his intensely egotistical nature caused him to abandon her seven years later for another young admirer, his former pupil Tatiana Schloezer. At the same time, Scriabin gave up his teaching post at the Moscow Conservatory, and settled in Switzerland.

By 1903 he had already begun to compose orchestral music, including two symphonies, and was becoming increasingly involved in mysticism, dabbling in Nietzschean theories and

ABOVE: The Russian pianist and composer Alexander Scriabin (1872–1915), a portrait in oils by A.Y. Golovin.

the occult teachings of Madame Blavatsky, the founder of the Theosophical Society. Philosophical and mystical ideas began to influence his work from the Third Symphony (*Le divin poème*) onwards, particularly the sensuous *Poème de l'extase* (*Poem of Ecstasy*), and *Prométhée*, subtitled *Le poème du feu* (*The Poem of Fire*), in which Scriabin developed the theory of synaesthesia, according to which art that appealed to all the senses would trigger a cataclysmic effect. To this end, different keys were associated with specific colours, demonstrated in performance by the use of coloured lighting. His Seventh and Ninth Piano Sonatas (1911 and 1912–13) are subtitled respectively *Messe blanche* and *Messe noire*.

In 1908 Scriabin returned to Russia, where his works were received with enormous enthusiasm. His later music, mostly for piano, is highly chromatic. In 1914 he visited London for a concert of his works conducted by Henry Wood, and during his stay he developed an ulcer on his lip which would not heal. He died of septicaemia on 27 April 1915.

Life and works

NATIONALITY: Russian

BORN: Moscow, 1872; **DIED:** Moscow, 1915

SPECIALIST GENRES: Piano and orchestral music influenced by mysticism.

MAJOR WORKS: Ten sonatas and 85 preludes for piano; Piano Concerto (1896); *Le poème de l'extase* (1905–8); *Prométhée* (1910).

Ferruccio Busoni

I want to attain the unknown!

BUSONI, 1905

Like Scriabin, the pianist and composer Ferruccio Busoni was a maverick, important in his own right, but not profoundly influential. Italian by birth, he spent much of his career in Germany and Austria. His father was an Italian clarinettist, and his mother, a pianist of German origin. Busoni's parents began his musical education, and he gave his first public piano recital at the age of eight.

In 1876 the family moved to Graz, where Busoni conducted a performance of his own Stabat Mater (now lost), at the age of 12. He then moved to Vienna, where he met Brahms and dedicated to him the set of six Studies for piano, and an *Etude en forme de variation*. Brahms recommended that Busoni should move to Leipzig, where he met many eminent musicians, and wrote his Second String Quartet. He also began to make arrangements of organ works by Bach, re-composing them in contemporary style.

In 1890 Busoni married the daughter of a Swedish sculptor, whom he had met in Helsinki (one of their sons became a painter). He taught briefly in Moscow, but then decided to resume his career as a concert pianist in the USA. In 1894 he settled in Berlin, where he promoted orchestral concerts of the most avant-garde music, including works by Debussy, Bartók, Delius and Fauré.

Busoni also began to make daring harmonic experiments – similar to Schoenberg's although with a different approach – in his own music, especially in the set of Six Sonatinas for piano (1910–20). His orchestral music includes an extraordinary five-movement Piano Concerto which incorporates a male-voice chorus, and a more conventional Concertino for clarinet and chamber orchestra. Towards the end of his life he was preoccupied with stage works, including the operas *Die Brautwahl* (*The Bridal Choice*, after E. T. A. Hoffmann, 1912), and *Doktor Faust* (after Marlowe), which was left unfinished at his death.

ABOVE: The Italian/German composer Ferruccio Busoni (1866–1924).

LEFT: A scene from the 1999 Salzburg Festival production of Doktor Faust, *Busoni's last opera, with Thomas Hampson as Faust and Chris Merritt as Mephistopheles.*

Life and works

NATIONALITY: Italian

BORN: Empoli, near Florence, 1866; **DIED:** Berlin, 1924

SPECIALIST GENRES: Virtuoso piano works, opera.

MAJOR WORKS: Piano Concerto (1904); *Arlecchino* (1914–16); *Doktor Faust* (1916–24).

Ralph Vaughan Williams

What we want in England is real music, even if it be only a music-hall song.

VAUGHAN WILLIAMS, "THE VOCALIST" (1902)

Vaughan Williams was one of a group of composers who contributed to the renaissance of English music in the 20th century. Born in Gloucestershire, he studied music at Cambridge University and the Royal College of Music, London, where his teachers included Parry and Stanford. (In later years, he also studied with Bruch and Ravel.) He began his career as a church organist in London and, with his friend Gustav Holst, initiated a systematic study and collection of English folk songs, which – together with his interest in Tudor music – profoundly influenced his own compositions.

In 1906 Vaughan Williams was appointed musical editor of *The English Hymnal*, for which he wrote some famous hymn tunes, such as "For All the Saints" (*Sine nomine*). He also became director of the amateur Leith Hill Music Festival in Dorking, Surrey, from 1905 until his death. From 1919 until 1939 he was a professor of composition at the Royal College of Music. He married twice, the first time in 1897; after his wife's death in 1951 he married the poet and librettist Ursula Wood.

Vaughan Williams' musical style has a distinctively "English" quality, derived from his use of the modality of folk song, tinged with an elusive mysticism. He was drawn to the mystical poetry of Walt Whitman, whose verses he set in *A Sea Symphony* (1903–9) and *Toward the Unknown Region* (1905–6). Other early works included the *Fantasia on a Theme of Thomas Tallis* for double string orchestra and the settings of poems by A. E. Housman, *On Wenlock Edge* (1908), for voice and string quartet, as well as the ever-popular part-song "Linden Lea" (1901) and the *Songs of Travel* (1901–4), based on Robert Louis Stevenson's poems.

Altogether Vaughan Williams wrote nine symphonies, including No. 2 (*A London Symphony*, 1912–13), No. 3 (*Pastoral*, 1916–21), No. 5 (1938–43, which with the gritty No. 6 of 1944–7 was perceived as the composer's response to war), and the *Sinfonia antarctica* (1949–52, based on his score for the 1948 film *Scott of the Antarctic*). His orchestral music also includes *The Lark Ascending* (a rhapsody for violin and orchestra), concertos for violin, oboe and tuba, *A Norfolk Rhapsody*, the Fantasia on "Greensleeves" (1934) and the overture *The Wasps* (1909).

Vaughan Williams wrote in many genres, including stage and film music. His six operas are relatively infrequently revived, but his ballet score *Job: A Masque for Dancing* has remained in the orchestral repertoire.

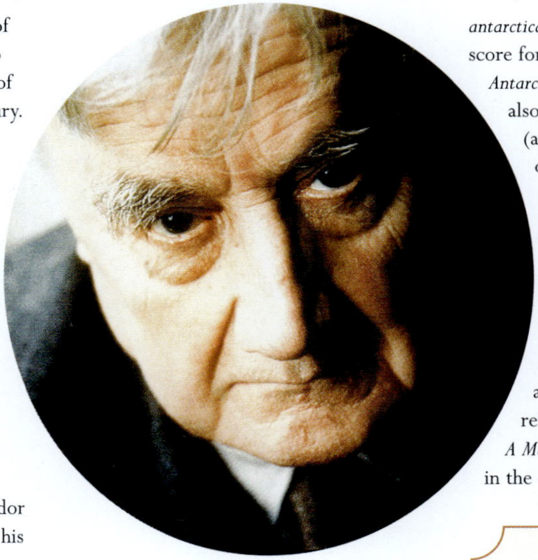

ABOVE: A photograph of Ralph Vaughan Williams (1872–1958), taken in 1952 – the year of his 80th birthday.

Life and works

NATIONALITY: English

BORN: Down Ampney, 1872; **DIED:** London, 1958

SPECIALIST GENRES: Symphonies, stage works influenced by English folk song.

MAJOR WORKS: Nine symphonies; *Fantasia on a Theme of Thomas Tallis* (1910); *The Lark Ascending* (1914); *Serenade to Music* (1938); operas *Hugh the Drover* (1910–14), *Sir John in Love* (1924–8), *Riders to the Sea* (1925–32) and *The Pilgrim's Progress* (1949); ballet *Job* (1927–30).

Gustav Holst

Never compose anything unless the not composing of it becomes a positive nuisance to you.

HOLST, 1921

Holst was born into a less privileged background than his friend Vaughan Williams, whom he met as a fellow student at the Royal College of Music in London in the 1890s. His family was of Swedish descent, and his father was an organist and piano teacher in Cheltenham.

Holst earned a living first as a trombonist, and then as a teacher in London. From 1903–20 he taught music at a girls' school in Dulwich and in 1905 he was appointed director of music at St Paul's School for Girls in Hammersmith, where he remained until his death. He was also music director at Morley College, South London, from 1907–24, professor of music at Reading University, and a teacher at the Royal College of Music.

ABOVE: The British composer of Swedish origin Gustav Holst (1874–1934), photographed in 1925.

ABOVE: The planets inspired Holst's most famous orchestral work.

He lived in Richmond (where his daughter Imogen, who also became a composer, was born in 1907) and then had a riverside house in Barnes, but composed in his room in St Paul's School at weekends and during school holidays.

Like Vaughan Williams, Holst was strongly influenced by English folk song, which informed many of his works, including *A Somerset Rhapsody* (1906–7), the Suites for military band (1909–11), the *St Paul's* and *Brook Green* suites for strings (1913 and 1933), *A Moorside Suite* for brass band (1928) and the scherzo *Hammersmith* for military band or orchestra (1930–1).

Holst's interest in mysticism and Eastern religion also permeated his music. He learned Sanskrit in order to translate hymns from the Rig Veda, which he set for chorus and orchestra in 1908; his first major work, *The Mystic Trumpeter*, was performed at the Queen's Hall in 1905, and oriental philosophy underpins his opera *Sāvitri*. His most popular work is undoubtedly the orchestral suite *The Planets*, of which "Mars" is a terrifying vision of approaching war. The lyrical central section of "Jupiter" was later used to set the patriotic hymn "I Vow to Thee, My Country".

Towards the end of his life, Holst's style became more austere. His later works included the Hardy-inspired tone-poem *Egdon Heath* (1927), the Concerto for two violins (1929), the operas *At the Boar's Head* and *The Wandering Scholar* and the Choral Fantasia (1931). He died in 1934, following surgery for haemorrhagic gastritis.

Life and works

NATIONALITY: English

BORN: Cheltenham, 1874; **DIED:** London, 1934

SPECIALIST GENRES: Orchestral and stage works influenced by mysticism and native folk song.

MAJOR WORKS: *The Planets* (1914–16); operas *Sāvitri* (1908), *The Perfect Fool* (1922), *At the Boar's Head* (1924) and *The Wandering Scholar* (1929–30).

Frederick Delius

It is only that which cannot be expressed otherwise that is worth expressing in music.

DELIUS, "AT THE CROSSROADS" (1920)

A contemporary of Debussy, Delius was born in northern England but lived in France for much of his life. His musical style was an amalgam of English lyrical nostalgia, the Impressionism of Debussy, and Mahlerian post-Romanticism.

The son of a German-born wool merchant, Delius was brought up in Bradford, Yorkshire. His father attempted to dissuade him from considering a musical career and packed him off to Florida to manage an orange plantation, but while in America he studied music theory with an organist, Thomas Ward, and his father relented. In 1886 he was allowed to study music in Leipzig, where he befriended Grieg, but soon left to settle in Paris, where he became friends with the painters Paul Gauguin and Edvard Munch. From his Paris years date the operas *Irmelin* (1890) and *Koanga* (1895–7), the Piano Concerto (1897) and the tone-poem *Paris, the Song of a Great City* (1899).

In 1897 Delius married the Norwegian artist Jelka Rosen and settled in Grez-sur-Loing near Fontainebleau. However, his bohemian lifestyle in Paris had left him with the grim legacy of syphilis, which eventually killed him. His most famous opera, *A Village Romeo and Juliet* – a tragic *Tristan and Isolde*-like tale of young love doomed by parental emnity – was written between 1899 and 1901. From this period also date the distinctive works of his maturity, including *Brigg Fair* (1907, a set of variations on an English folk song), the cantata *Sea Drift* (a setting

ABOVE: Frederick Delius was born in Yorkshire but spent most of his life in France.

of Walt Whitman's poem), *A Mass of Life* (not a religious mass, but a setting of text from Nietzsche's *Also sprach Zarathustra*), the *Songs of Sunset* (1906–8), the First Dance Rhapsody for orchestra (1908) and the opera *Fennimore and Gerda* (1908–10).

Delius continued to compose prolifically through the second decade of the 20th century. The quintessentially "English"-sounding orchestral mood pictures *On Hearing the First Cuckoo in Spring* and *Summer Night on the River*, together with the *Song of the High Hills* for chorus and orchestra, date from 1911. During World War I he returned temporarily to England, where he wrote the Second Dance Rhapsody, sonatas for violin and cello, two concertos and his secular Requiem commemorating the war dead.

Although he spent very little of his life in England, his music still has a very "English", pastoral feel, enhanced by his fondness for triplet rhythmic patterns.

From 1922 onwards, as he became increasingly paralysed and his sight began to fail, he ceased to compose, but in 1928 he enlisted the help of the young Yorkshire musician Eric Fenby as his amanuensis. Among his later works are the *Songs of Farewell*, *A Song of Summer* for orchestra (1930), a third violin sonata, and the *Idyll* for soprano, baritone and orchestra (1930–2). He died at Grez in 1934, but was re-interred in Surrey a year later.

Life and works

NATIONALITY: English

BORN: Bradford, 1862; **DIED:** Grez-sur-Loing, near Fontainebleau, 1934

SPECIALIST GENRES: Orchestral and choral music.

MAJOR WORKS: *A Village Romeo and Juliet* (1899–1901); *Appalachia* (1898–1903); *Sea Drift* (1903–4); *A Mass of Life* (1904–5); *Brigg Fair* (1907); Requiem (1914–16); Double Concerto (1915–16); Violin Concerto (1916); Cello Concerto (1921); *Songs of Farewell* (1930).

Leoš Janáček

I want to gather the sun's rays into my hands, I want to plunge myself in shadow, I want to pour out my longings to the full: all directly.

JANÁČEK, 1927

Born in 1854, the Czech composer Leoš Janáček might have belonged to the late 19th-century nationalist tradition, the successor to Smetana, Dvořák and Suk. But in fact, most of his music dates from the last 30 years of his long life, and he is therefore regarded as a 20th-century composer. His reputation rests largely on the extraordinary series of late operas which, until the 1960s, were largely unknown outside Europe. The efforts of conductors such as Charles Mackerras brought them to the attention of British and American audiences, and they are now regarded as masterpieces.

Born in rural Moravia, the son of a schoolmaster, Janáček studied music in Brno, the capital of Moravia, and Prague. He then returned to Brno as a music teacher, founding an organ school there in 1881. The same year he married his pretty 15-year-old pupil, Zdenka Schulzová. Although the marriage was never formally dissolved, it was deeply unhappy almost from the start. The patriotic Janáček resented the fact that his wife was German-speaking, and they appear to have been sexually incompatible. Two children were born: their son Vladimir died at the age of two, and their daughter Olga at the age of 20, in 1903.

ABOVE: Leoš Janáček's work embodied the spirit of Czech nationalism, expressed in a moving and distinctive musical language.

Folk songs

Janáček's early compositions include many choral pieces, for both mixed and male-voice choirs. While working on his first opera, *Šárka* (1887–8), he began to collect and edit Moravian folk songs, whose characteristic idioms – based on the flexible rhythms of speech – influenced his own compositions, giving them an entirely distinctive sound. His first important opera, *Jenůfa*, has a Moravian folk setting. This powerful tale of a young peasant girl's betrayal by her faithless lover, resulting in the murder of her newborn baby by her distraught foster-mother, was completed in 1903. It was first performed in Brno in January 1904, just before Janáček's 50th birthday.

LEFT: Janáček with his young wife Zdenka Schulzová, photographed around the time of their ill-fated marriage.

RIGHT: Janáček's cottage at his birthplace, Hukvaldy. He was there with his great love Kamila Stösslová when he was taken fatally ill.

Neither of his next two operas, *Osud* (*Fate*, 1903–7) and *Výlety páně Broučkovy* (*The Adventures of Mr Brouček*, 1908–18), based on a satirical novel by Svatopluk Čech, were notably successful. For the first two decades of the 20th century Janáček concentrated on piano music, notably the Sonata (1905), *Po zarostlém Chodníčku* (*On an Overgrown Path*, 1901–8) and *V mlhách* (*In the Mists*, 1912), chamber music and male-voice choruses. Up to this point he had written little orchestral music, but the tone-poem *Šumařovo dítě* (*The Fiddler's Child*) dates from 1912. *Taras Bulba*, an orchestral piece inspired by the heroic exploits of a Cossack leader, was written during World War I, and after the Czech Republic declared its independence in 1918, Janáček commemorated the event with *The Ballad of Blaník* (1920).

Life and works

NATIONALITY: Czech

BORN: Hukvaldy, Moravia, 1854; **DIED:** Ostava, 1928

SPECIALIST GENRES: Czech opera, orchestral works, part-songs.

MAJOR WORKS: Operas *Jenůfa* (1894–1903), *Katya Kabanová* (1919–21), *The Cunning Little Vixen* (1921–3), *The Makropoulos Case* (1923–5) and *From the House of the Dead* (1927–8); *Taras Bulba* (1915–18); Sinfonietta (1926); Glagolitic Mass (1926).

ABOVE: Costume design for the Vixen Bystrouška by Josef Capek (1887–1945) for the Prague première of The Cunning Little Vixen *on 18 May 1925.*

Late flowering

In May 1916 *Jenůfa* finally received its Prague première. Around the same time, the 62-year-old composer met Kamila Stösslová, the young wife of a Jewish antique-dealer. Despite the 38-year age gap between them, Janáček became infatuated with Kamila, and his passion for her inspired the radiant, life-affirming works of his old age. The first of these was *Zápisník zmizelého* (*The Diary of One who Disappeared*, 1917–19), a song-cycle dealing with a young man's love for a gypsy girl (Janáček constantly likened the dark-haired Kamila to a gypsy). This was followed by a stream of operas: the tragic *Katya Kabanová*, the life-enhancing *Příhody lišky bystroušky* (*The Cunning Little Vixen*), *Věc Makropulos* (*The Makropulos Case*), with its icy but fatally attractive heroine, and *Z mrtvého domu* (*From the House of the Dead*), based on Dostoyevsky's grim novel about life in a Siberian prison camp. Kamila appears in various guises in all these, and she also inspired his two string quartets, *Kreutzer Sonata* (1923), based on Tolstoy's tale of adultery and revenge, and *Listy důvěrné* (*Intimate Letters*, 1928), as well as the wind sextet *Mládí* (*Youth*, 1924).

By now, Janáček was famous both at home and abroad. He visited England in 1926, shortly after writing the extrovert Sinfonietta, his best-known orchestral work. The same year he also completed the Glagolitic Mass, to an Orthodox text, and the Capriccio for piano (left hand) and chamber ensemble.

During the last seven years of his life, he worked mainly at his cottage at Hukvaldy, to which he often invited Kamila and her children. He was taken ill there in August 1928, and died in hospital of pneumonia. Kamila died seven years later; Janáček's wife, Zdenka, died in 1938.

ABOVE: A woman dressed in Moravian national costume, from the Brno area. Janáček loved to see Kamila wearing national dress.

Béla Bartók

Bartók's name...stands for the principle and the demand for regeneration stemming from the people, both in art and in politics.

ZOLTÁN KODÁLY (1882–1967)

Bartók was the greatest Hungarian composer since Liszt. He and Kodály put Hungary on the international musical map.

Both Bartók's parents were musical, and he was taught the piano by his mother. He began to compose at the age of nine, and made his pianistic debut at 11. In 1903 he emerged from his studies at the Budapest Academy as a virtuoso pianist and a promising composer.

From the start, Bartók immersed himself in the idioms of Hungarian folk music. His first folk song collection was published in 1906, and in 1907 he became a piano professor at the Budapest Academy, a post which enabled him to pursue systematic research into folk music from Hungary, Romania, Slovakia and Transylvania. From this time onwards he began to publish folk song anthologies for voice and piano, and arrangements of folk songs, such as *For Children* (1908–9). The Ten Easy Pieces, the 14 Bagatelles (both 1908) and the ferocious *Allegro barbaro* for piano (1911) are also strongly Hungarian in idiom. Another new influence, the atmospheric music of Debussy, informed Bartók's works from the First String Quartet (1908).

ABOVE: An evocative portrait by Roboz of the Hungarian pianist and composer Béla Bartók (1881–1945).

Works for the stage

In 1909 Bartók married his pupil Márta Ziegler, who gave birth to a son in 1910. The next year Bartók completed his one-act opera *A kékszakállú herceg vára* (*Duke Bluebeard's Castle*). This masterly score, based on a psychological interpretation of the Bluebeard legend, was not performed until 1918, after his ballet *A fából faragott királyfi* (*The Wooden Prince*) had been successfully staged in Budapest. Up to that point, Bartók's compositions had been largely neglected in his own country, but growing recognition of his talent prompted a second ballet, *A csodálatos mandarin* (*The Miraculous Mandarin*, 1918–19), whose sordid subject-matter caused outrage at its Cologne première in 1926. (The mandarin is lured into a robbers' den by a prostitute, but though stabbed and hanged by the men he refuses to die until he has had sex with her.)

During the post-war years Bartók began to tour widely as a pianist. In 1923 – when his Dance Suite, celebrating the 50th anniversary of the union of Buda and Pest, was premièred – he divorced Márta and married another young piano pupil, Ditta

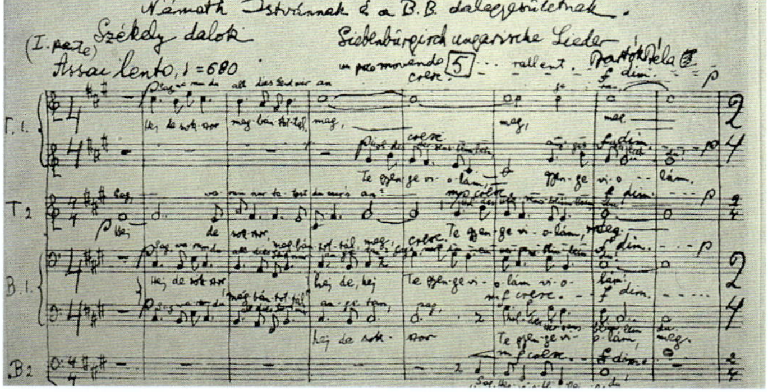

ABOVE: The opening manuscript page of Bartók's Hungarian folk song arrangements Székely dalok *(*Székely Songs*) for six male voices (1932).*

ABOVE: Bartók listening to his folk song recordings on a phonogram in 1915. He was one of the major folk song collectors.

ABOVE: Bartók giving a piano concerto performance in Budapest in 1938. His second wife, Ditta Pásztory, is sitting behind him.

Pásztory. A second son was born in 1924.

Meanwhile, Bartók continued his dual career as pianist and composer. Many of his piano works – such as the First and Second Concertos (1926 and 1930–1), the Sonata, the Suite *Out of Doors*, and the Nine Little Pieces (all 1926) – were written for himself to play. His Third and Fourth String Quartets date from the late 1920s, as do the two Rhapsodies for violin and piano, both written for Hungarian virtuosi. The *Cantata profana* (1930) – a paean to the brotherhood of nations – was premièred in London in 1934, the year Bartók finally relinquished his teaching duties at the Budapest Academy to concentrate on his ethnomusicological work.

Life and works

NATIONALITY: Hungarian

BORN: Nagyszentmiklos (now in Romania), 1881;
DIED: New York, 1945

SPECIALIST GENRES: Orchestral and piano music influenced by central European folk idioms.

MAJOR WORKS: Six string quartets (1908–39); *Duke Bluebeard's Castle* (1911–18); *The Miraculous Mandarin* (1919); *Microkosmos* (1926–39); three piano concertos (1926–45); *Music for Strings, Percussion and Celesta* (1936); *Contrasts* (1938); Concerto for Orchestra (1943).

New musical structures

The late '30s – a period during which Bartók was preoccupied with musical structure, especially arch forms and constructions based on mathematical rules – produced some of his finest compositions, including the Fifth and Sixth String Quartets. He was equally concerned with timbre, exploiting the innovative sounds produced on conventional instruments, in works such as the *Music for Strings, Percussion and Celesta* and the 1939 Divertimento for strings. The Sonata for two pianos and percussion (1937) was premièred by Bartók and his wife; the Second Violin Concerto (1937–8) was written for Zoltán Székely and *Contrasts* for the violinist Joseph Szigeti and the clarinettist Benny Goodman. During the 1930s Bartók also published *Microkosmos*, six books of piano teaching pieces.

America

In 1940, alarmed by the threat of fascism, the Bartóks left for America, where they settled in New York. The last five years of Bartók's life were clouded by public neglect, financial worries and declining health. In 1943 he was diagnosed as suffering from a rare form of cancer. He completed his most popular work, the Concerto for Orchestra (premièred by Serge Koussevitsky and the Boston Symphony Orchestra), in the summer of 1943, and the solo Violin Sonata, written for Yehudi Menuhin, the following March. His last works were the Third Piano Concerto (1945), written for his wife, and the Viola Concerto for the Scottish-born player William Primrose, which was left unfinished at his death in September 1945.

ABOVE: The anti-hero of Duke Bluebeard's Castle, *portrayed by Janos Kass.*

Zoltán Kodály

Some day the ringing tower of Hungarian music is going to stand.

Kodály, 1932

Like his friend and collaborator Bartók, Kodály raised the international profile of Hungarian music by fertilizing Western styles with Magyar folk idioms. An authority on folk music, he was also an important teacher, producing a vast body of musical educational material.

The son of a stationmaster, he spent his childhood and youth in the countryside, before enrolling at Budapest University to read languages. He simultaneously began to study composition at the Budapest Academy, where he was awarded a doctorate for his study of Hungarian folk song. From 1905 onwards he began to collect and record folk songs, often collaborating with Bartók, with whom he shared a vision of "an educated Hungary, reborn from the people". Like Bartók, Kodály devoted much of his life to the publication of folk song anthologies and arrangements.

ABOVE: Zoltán Kodály, photographed towards the end of his long life.

ABOVE: The Liszt Academy of Music in Budapest, where Kodály studied composition, and where he later became deputy director.

In 1906 he received a travelling scholarship to study in Berlin and Paris, where he came into contact with Debussy's music. On his return he was appointed a professor at the Budapest Academy, becoming its deputy director in 1919. But his tenure of that post was abruptly curtailed by political intrigue, and his career was only rescued after the triumphant 1923 première of his oratorio *Psalmus hungaricus*, written – like Bartók's Dance Suite – to celebrate the 50th anniversary of the union of Buda and Pest. A performance in Zurich in 1926 marked the beginning of his international fame.

The same year (1926), Kodály's opera *Háry János* was performed in Budapest, and world-famous conductors such as Arturo Toscanini, Rudolf Mengelberg and Wilhelm Furtwängler began to include the orchestral suite taken from it (which includes a prominent part for the cimbalom, a Hungarian dulcimer) in their repertoires. It was followed by other major orchestral works: the *Dances of Marosszek* (1930), the *Dances of Galánta* (1933), the *Peacock* Variations, based on a Hungarian folk tune (1939, written for the Amsterdam Concertgebouw Orchestra), and the Concerto for Orchestra (1939–40, for the Chicago Symphony). Like Bartók, Kodály opposed fascism, but he remained in Hungary when it came under Nazi rule. After the war he supervised the publication of the folk material he had collected, and continued to write educational works. In later life he was showered with honours.

Life and works

NATIONALITY: Hungarian

BORN: Kecskemét, 1882; **DIED:** Budapest, 1967

SPECIALIST GENRES: Orchestral and choral music influenced by folk music.

MAJOR WORKS: *Psalmus hungaricus* (1923); *Háry János* (1925–6); *Dances of Galánta* (1933); Concerto for Orchestra (1939–40).

Carl Nielsen

Music is life, and, like it, inextinguishable.
NIELSEN, MOTTO OF THE FOURTH SYMPHONY (1916)

Nielsen was the Danish equivalent of Grieg or Sibelius. Born into an impoverished family (his father was a painter), he began to scrape out melodies as a child on an instrument made from firewood. He started learning the violin at six and began playing in his father's folk band. In the mid 1880s he studied at the Copenhagen Conservatory, and first achieved success with his Little Suite for strings, performed at Tivoli in 1888.

The next year Nielsen became a violinist in the royal chapel, where he was able to broaden his musical outlook. During a trip to Paris in 1891 he met and married a sculptress, and on his return finished the first of a sequence of six symphonies, on which his reputation largely rests. No. 1 is an early example of "progressive tonality", beginning in one key and ending in another, while No. 2 (*The Four Temperaments*, 1901–2) uses the technique of thematic variation.

At much the same time Nielsen completed his first opera, *Saul og David*, followed a few years later by the comic opera *Maskarade*.

From 1908 until 1914 Nielsen combined composing with a position at the Royal Theatre, and then with teaching at the Copenhagen Conservatory, whose director he became in 1931, just before his death. He consolidated his foremost position in Danish musical life with three more symphonies (No. 3, *Sinfonia espansiva*, 1910–11; No. 4, *The Inextinguishable*, 1914–16; and No. 5, 1921–2), the Violin Concerto (1911), piano works including the Chaconne and the Theme and Variations, the tone-poem *Pan and Syrinx* (1917–18) and the exotic, colourfully scored incidental music to the play *Aladdin* (1918–19). His Fourth and Fifth Symphonies are imaginatively constructed, with innovative use of percussion (in a passage in the Fifth, the side-drum is instructed to improvise "in order to try to destroy the music").

Between 1914 and 1925 Nielsen published many volumes of Danish folk song arrangements, and his later works are mostly for chamber combinations or smaller orchestra. He died of heart disease in 1931.

Life and works

NATIONALITY: Danish

BORN: Nørre-Lyndelse, near Odense, 1865; **DIED:** Copenhagen, 1931

SPECIALIST GENRES: Symphonies.

MAJOR WORKS: Six symphonies; *Saul og David* (1898– 1901); *Maskarade* (1904–6).

ABOVE: The Danish composer Carl Nielsen (1865–1931), photographed as a young man.

RIGHT: The Royal Theatre in Copenhagen, where Nielsen's operas were performed, and where he worked from 1908–14.

Percy Grainger

I object to jazz and vaudeville having all the best instruments.

GRAINGER, 1930

The Australian composer and pianist Percy Grainger was brought up by his mother (to whom he was devoted) in Melbourne. In 1895 he left Australia for Europe, where he entered the Conservatory in Frankfurt; and in 1901 he settled in London to begin his career as a concert pianist, using it as a base for concert tours throughout Europe. He often visited Scandinavia, where he became a close friend of Grieg and a notable interpreter of his Piano Concerto; he was also a friend of Delius from 1907 onwards (Delius's orchestral rhapsody *Brigg Fair* is based on a Lincolnshire folk tune collected by Grainger).

In 1905 Grainger joined the English Folk Song Society, becoming an ardent folk song collector in company with Cecil Sharp, Holst and Vaughan Williams. Folk song infused much of his work, from piano arrangements such as the ever-popular *Country Gardens*, *Green Bushes*, *Molly on the Shore* and *Shepherds' Hey*, to arrangements for wind band, and original orchestral works such as *Mock Morris*. Much of his vocal music is now out of fashion, since he often set jingoistic verses by Kipling and other colonial writers. His original large-scale works, which include *The Warriors* for three pianos, orchestra and tuned percussion, have also fallen out of favour, with the exception of *Handel in the Strand* (1932) for strings, based on Handel's *Harmonious Blacksmith* Variations treated in music-hall style.

In 1914 Grainger moved to the USA, where he became a US citizen, and settled in White Plains, New York State. His mother committed suicide in 1922, and over the next six years Grainger spent much time in Denmark, collecting Danish folk songs, and returned twice to Australia. In 1928 he married a Swedish artist, who was presumably willing to put up with his sado-masochistic sexual practices and other eccentricities – their wedding took place before a huge audience in the Hollywood Bowl. The rest of his life was a long creative decline, although he spent his last years experimenting with "free music", dispensing with the conventions of harmony, form and instrumentation.

ABOVE: The Australian-born pianist and composer Percy Grainger (1882–1961).

ABOVE: Grainger at the piano with his adored (and domineering) mother, Rose, in the music room of their American home in 1921.

Life and works

NATIONALITY: Australian

BORN: Melbourne, 1882; **DIED:** White Plains, New York, 1961

SPECIALIST GENRES: Folk song settings and original works using ingenious instrumental combinations.

MAJOR WORKS: *The Warriors* (1912–16); *Handel in the Strand* (1932); Suite *A Lincolnshire Posy* (1940).

Charles Ives

This fascinating composer...was exploring the 1960s during the heyday of Strauss and Debussy.

IGOR STRAVINSKY (1882–1971)

Charles Ives, one of the most innovative figures in music history, was America's first major composer. His father was a town bandmaster with a most original musical mind. His experiments with acoustics and pitch, using quarter-tones, polytonality, tone clusters and simultaneously playing pieces in different keys, intrigued his young son. Ives later incorporated the unusual sounds of his childhood experiences into his own music.

In 1894 Charles went to Yale University, where he studied composition and wrote the first of his four symphonies. After graduating he moved to New York, where he worked in insurance, and by 1906 he and his partner, Julian Myrick, had set up their own very successful insurance agency which made them millionaires. Ives married Harmony Twichell in a union of lasting happiness, but long hours of work combined with spare-time composing undermined his health, and in 1918 he had a heart attack. During a year's convalescence he embarked on the publication of his music. He retired from the insurance business in 1930.

ABOVE: Charles Ives (1874–1954), an essentially amateur composer who gave American music an individual identity.

Life and works

NATIONALITY: American

BORN: Danbury, Connecticut, 1874; **DIED:** New York, 1954

SPECIALIST GENRES: Orchestral and piano music, often on American themes.

MAJOR WORKS: Five symphonies; *Variations on "America"* (1891); *Three Places in New England* (1904); Piano Sonata No. 2 *Concord* (1910–15); 114 songs.

Most of Ives's major compositions were written before 1920. Many were inspired by "American" landscapes, festivals, traditions, or historical events. They include four numbered symphonies (the Fourth introduces a chorus into the finale); the *Holidays Symphony* (1904–13), in which the movements are "Washington's Birthday", "Decoration Day", "Fourth of July" and "Thanksgiving Day"; *Central Park in the Dark* (1906); and three Sets for orchestra, of which No. 1 is entitled *Three Places in New England*. He also wrote several psalm settings for various vocal combinations and organ or orchestra; over 20 Studies for piano, of which several describe stages of a baseball game; the huge *Concord* Sonata for piano, with optional parts for viola and flute; the epigrammatic three-page Sonata (1905) and the early *Variations on "America"* for organ.

Ives was a Satie-like figure, who often used punning titles (such as *Five Take-offs* or *Six Protests*). In *The Unanswered Question* (1906) for chamber ensemble, a solo trumpet asks "the question", to which a woodwind choir frantically attempts to find an answer. His innovative musical style had enormous influence on later American composers.

ABOVE: Yale University in New Haven, USA, where Ives studied in the 1890s. He was an enthusiastic member of the baseball team.

Arnold Schoenberg

I am a conservative who was forced to become a revolutionary.

SCHOENBERG

Schoenberg was one of the seminal figures of 20th-century music. He loosened the grip of traditional tonality and explored new ways of working with the 12 notes of the chromatic scale. Although his own music is still generally misunderstood and has never achieved great popularity with audiences, his influence on other composers was immense.

He was born in Vienna, into an orthodox Jewish family, and began to learn the violin at eight. His father died when he was 15, and he was forced to leave school and take a job as a bank clerk. In the evenings he studied music, philosophy and literature, and taught himself to play the cello. His first composition lessons came from Alexander Zemlinsky, whose sister Mathilde he married in 1901. By that time he had written a string quartet, the string sextet *Verklärte Nacht* (*Transfigured Night*), and *Gurrelieder* (*Songs of Gurra*), for five voices, narrator, choir and orchestra. At that time Schoenberg was writing in a post-Romantic, Mahlerian style, but his works met with incomprehension from the start.

ABOVE: The Austrian composer Arnold Schoenberg (1874–1951), painted by Richard Gerstl (1883–1908).

Berlin

At the end of 1901 Schoenberg moved to Berlin, where he supported his family (including his daughter Gertrud, born in 1902) first by providing and arranging music for a cabaret, and then by teaching at the Stern Conservatory. He spent the next 30 years see-sawing between Berlin and Vienna, where he moved back in 1903 as a private teacher (his most notable pupils were Alban Berg and Anton Webern). His son Georg was born in Vienna in 1906.

By 1907–8 Schoenberg was experimenting with atonality and free dissonance, in works such as the First and Second Quartets, the song anthology *Das Buch der hängenden Gärten* (*The Book of the Hanging Gardens*), and the Three Piano Pieces, Op. 11, and in his major works of 1909 – the dramatic monologue *Erwartung* (*Awaiting*) and the Five Orchestral

ABOVE: The Reichstag (Parliament) building in Berlin in Schoenberg's time. He moved to Berlin in 1901and taught at the Stern Conservatory.

ABOVE: A drawing by B. F. Dolbin of Schoenberg directing a performance of his Pierrot lunaire *on 17 November 1940.*

ABOVE: A view of modern-day Los Angeles. In 1936 Schoenberg was appointed Professor of Music at the University of Southern California, Los Angeles. He became an American citizen in 1941 and remained on the West Coast of the United States until his death in 1951, aged 76.

Pieces, Op. 16. They were greeted with outright hostility by the conservative Viennese, and when Schoenberg applied for a professorship at the Vienna Academy of Music and Dramatic Art, he encountered virulent anti-Semitism.

As a result, in 1911 he moved back to Berlin, where his *Pierrot lunaire* (*Moonstruck Pierrot*, 1912) for voice and chamber ensemble was well received. The work represents the first use of a technique Schoenberg called *Sprechstimme* ("speaking voice"), also known as *Sprechgesang* ("speech song"), in which the singer "speaks" rather than sings each note, starting on the pitch indicated but immediately leaving it in a rise or fall. Meanwhile, in 1912, the long-delayed orchestral version of *Gurrelieder* was applauded in Vienna, much to Schoenberg's disgust. Nonetheless he moved back to Vienna in 1915, when he briefly enlisted in the army but was discharged owing to poor health.

Life and works

NATIONALITY: Austrian

BORN: Vienna, 1874; **DIED:** Los Angeles, 1951

SPECIALIST GENRES: Orchestral, chamber and piano music in styles varying from late Romantic to serialism.

MAJOR WORKS: *Verklärte Nacht* (1899); *Gurrelieder* (1900–11); Chamber Symphony No. 1 (1906); Three Piano Pieces, Op. 11 (1909); Five Orchestral Pieces, Op. 16 (1909); *Pierrot lunaire* (1912); Five Piano Pieces (1923); *Moses und Aron* (1930–51).

New tonality

After the war Schoenberg founded the Society for Private Musical Performances, which until 1921 gave some 350 performances of new music by himself, his pupils and colleagues. His works of the early 1920s laid the foundation of his revolutionary "12-note" style in the Five Piano Pieces, Op. 23, the Serenade and the Piano Suite. His wife died in 1923, but less than a year later he married Gertrud, sister of the violinist Rudolf Kolisch. He had three more children, including two sons born after he emigrated to the USA.

From 1925 until 1933 Schoenberg taught at the Prussian Academy of Arts in Berlin, where he wrote several major works including the Variations for Orchestra, and the operas *Von heute auf morgen* (*From One Day to the Next*, 1928–9) and *Moses und Aron* (1930–2; the title was deliberately spelt this way by Schoenberg to avoid the unlucky number of 13 letters). In 1933 Hitler's anti-Semitic legislation robbed him of his job and forced him to leave Germany for good, despite the fact that he had been baptized a Christian in 1898.

America

The family spent the summer in France, where Schoenberg re-converted to Judaism, and then sailed for America, where he began teaching in New York and Boston. A lifelong sufferer from asthma, he moved for the sake of his health to the West Coast, where he taught at the University of Southern California. His late works include concertos for violin and piano, the Fourth String Quartet (1936) and the String Trio (1946), the *Ode to Napoleon Buonaparte* (1942) and several pieces inspired by his faith, including *Kol nidre* (*All Vows*, 1938), his setting of the prayer for Yom Kippur, and *A Survivor from Warsaw* (1947). A deeply superstitious man, Schoenberg foretold his own death from heart failure on 13 July 1951.

Alban Berg

The best music always results from ecstasies of logic.

BERG, IN "NEW YORK TIMES"

While Schoenberg's music is still an acquired taste, that of his pupil Alban Berg has always been more accessible to a wider audience. His two operas and his Violin Concerto are among the finest 20th-century works.

Like Webern, Berg spent most of his working life in Vienna, taking summer holidays in the Carinthian mountains where his family had an estate, and where he later bought a villa on the shores of Lake Wörther. He grew up surrounded by creative people – artists such as Gustav Klimt and Oskar Kokoschka, writers such as Peter Altenberg and Stefan Zweig – who formed a close-knit circle rather like the Schubertians of a century earlier. Around 1904 Berg began to study with Schoenberg: his first works include the beautiful Seven Early Songs (1905–8), which are clearly in the German Romantic tradition. But within a few years, by the time he wrote the Four Songs, Op. 2, Berg was already beginning to push traditional tonality to its limits, and the String Quartet, Op. 3 (1910), is a strikingly original piece, based around the whole-tone scale. The highly compressed *Altenberg-Lieder* of 1912 drew criticism from Schoenberg, who perhaps found them too original for his liking.

ABOVE: Alban Berg, the most accessible composer of the "Second Viennese School".

In 1911 Berg married Helene Nahowski after a four-year courtship. Until the 1970s their marriage was carefully portrayed (especially by the widowed Helene) as idyllically happy. But in 1977 a copy of the score of Berg's *Lyrische Suite* for string quartet (1925–6) came to light, heavily annotated by the composer, which left no doubt that this major work owed its existence to Berg's clandestine love-affair with a married woman, Hanna Fuchs-Robettin. The musical equivalents of her initials are interwoven with Berg's own to produce the underlying motif of the work.

LEFT: Adele Bloch-Bauer *by Gustav Klimt (1862–1918), an exponent of decadent, Symbolist art featuring* femmes fatales *like Berg's Lulu.*

ABOVE: A stage design by Vladislav Hofman for the last act of Berg's Wozzeck, *for the Prague première in 1926, one year after the opera's debut in Berlin.*

Life and works

NATIONALITY: Austrian

BORN: Vienna, 1885; **DIED:** Vienna, 1935

SPECIALIST GENRES: Opera, orchestral and chamber music in atonal style with serial elements.

MAJOR WORKS: String Quartet (1910); *Lyric Suite* (1925–6); *Wozzeck* (1917–22); *Lulu* (1929–35); Violin Concerto (1935).

ABOVE: Wozzeck murders Marie in the last act of the 1990 English National Opera production of Wozzeck.

In September 1914 Berg sent Schoenberg two of his Three Orchestral Pieces, Op. 6, evidently hoping to heal the rift between them. Among Berg's most accessible orchestral works, the Three Pieces revert to a Mahlerian style, using traditional forms – "Prelude", "Round Dance" (with elements of Viennese dances, the waltz and the *Ländler*) and "March".

Operas

At the same time, Berg began work on the first of his two operas. He had seen the Viennese première of the 19th-century play *Wozzeck* by Georg Büchner (1813–37), and "at once decided to set it to music". But the war (during which he served in the Austrian army) intervened, and *Wozzeck* the opera was not completed until 1922, by which time Berg had had ample experience of the privations of a soldier's life at first hand.

Wozzeck is a masterpiece, both for its sympathetic portrayal of the main protagonists – the downtrodden, exploited soldier, and the faithless mistress whom he eventually murders – and for its complex, innovative structure. A carefully constructed sequence of scenes is grouped into three acts, with Acts I and III framing the pivotal central act; the five scenes in Act I are described as "character pieces", each relating Wozzeck to another character in the drama. Berg described Act II as a "symphony in five movements", focusing on Wozzeck's disintegrating relationship with Marie.

ABOVE: Manon Gropius, the daughter of Mahler's widow Alma and her second husband Walter Gropius.

Act III consists of five inventions, each based on an *ostinato* rhythmic pattern or theme. But Berg's genius ensured that the audience's attention is focused not on such compositional wizardry, but on the drama itself.

Similar structural complexities underpin his last opera, *Lulu*, based on Frank Wedekind's two plays *Erdgeist* (*Earth Spirit*) and *Die Büchse der Pandora* (*Pandora's Box*). Again, the drama pivots around the large-scale rondo structure of Act II, with Lulu's Act III clients (after her descent into prostitution) paralleling – dramatically and musically – her lovers in Act I. Her last, fatal, encounter is with Jack the Ripper.

Lulu remained incomplete at Berg's death, and there is evidence that his widow obstructed its completion and performance during her lifetime. Berg's work on the opera had been interrupted by the composition of his last completed work, the elegiac Violin Concerto, written as a Requiem for Manon Gropius (daughter of Mahler's widow Alma and her second husband, the architect Walter Gropius), who died at 18 from polio. Shortly after completing it in August 1935 Berg suffered an insect sting which turned septic. He died of septicaemia four months later, aged 50.

Anton Webern

He shook the foundation of sound as discourse in favour of sound as sound.

JOHN CAGE (1912–92)

Webern produced perhaps the most compressed output of any composer in history: his complete works – some of which last only a few seconds in performance – have been recorded on to three CDs. He adopted the serial (12-note) technique of his teacher Schoenberg, and pursued it with ruthless concentration, paring it down to its essence.

Webern grew up in Vienna, Graz and Klagenfurt (his aristocratic family had a summer estate in Carinthia, where he developed a life-long love of walking, botany and geology). He was taught the piano by his mother, and after leaving school in 1902 he went to the University of Vienna, where he studied musicology, composition, cello and piano. His early works, including the Piano Quintet (1907) and the Op. 1 Passacaglia for orchestra (1908), are in the Brahmsian tradition.

ABOVE: Anton Webern (1883–1945), a composer of extreme intellectual rigour.

ABOVE: Anton Webern at the keyboard.

Between 1904 and 1908 Webern studied privately with Schoenberg. From 1908 onwards he held various conducting posts, and played a leading role in the Society for Private Musical Performances, for which he made many chamber arrangements of pieces by himself and others. In the 1920s and early '30s he conducted many workers' choral societies and symphony concerts, at which he introduced works by Mahler, his fellow pupil Berg, Max Reger and even Charles Ives. From 1927 he was employed as music adviser to Austrian Radio, but he lost all these jobs under the Nazi regime, when his music was banned. From 1938 onwards he worked as a freelance for his publisher, Universal Edition. He was accidentally shot dead by an American soldier during the last weeks of World War II, while visiting his daughter.

Webern's works up to the late 1920s were atonal in style. From 1928 onwards he adopted serial technique, often using *Klangfarbenmelodie* (timbre melody), in which changes of timbre rather than pitch define the melody. Many of his works are scored for chamber ensembles and use complex structural forms such as canon, palindrome and variation form.

Life and works

NATIONALITY: Austrian

BORN: Vienna, 1883; **DIED:** Mittersill, near Salzburg, 1945

SPECIALIST GENRES: Chamber and orchestral works.

MAJOR WORKS: Symphony, Op. 21 (1928); Concerto for nine instruments, Op. 24 (1931–4); three cantatas; String Quartet, Op. 28 (1936–8); piano Variations (1935–6); orchestral Variations (1940).

Kurt Weill

I write for today. I don't care about posterity.

WEILL

Kurt Weill was the musical personification of the Weimar Republic. His acidic blend of social realism and jazz reflected the decadent Germany of the 1920s, a time of economic depression, political upheaval and desperate hedonism. Together with his principal collaborator Bertolt Brecht (1898–1956), Weill created a new genre of music theatre, which he later developed on Broadway after his emigration to the USA.

The son of a Jewish cantor in Dessau, Weill studied briefly at the Berlin Hochschule and took masterclasses with Busoni. His first major work, the opera *Der Protagonist*, was performed in Dresden in 1926, and shortly afterwards he was introduced to the left-wing playwright Bertolt Brecht. Among the first fruits of the Brecht/Weill collaboration was *Die Dreigroschenoper* (*The Threepenny Opera*), a modern reworking of John Gay's *The Beggar's Opera* (1728), an English ballad opera set in the Soho underworld of thieves and pimps. It was premièred in Berlin in 1928 (with Weill's wife, Lotte Lenya, as Jenny), and scored a huge success with its bitter-sweet jazz idioms and savagely ironic subject. Its central song, "The Ballad of Mack the Knife", became an international hit.

ABOVE: Kurt Weill (1900–50), photographed after his move to the USA.

In 1930 the partnership's second opera – *Aufstieg und Fall der Stadt Mahagonny* (*The Rise and Fall of the City of Mahagonny*) – was premièred in Leipzig. By now Weill's music had been targeted by the emerging forces of fascism, and after the Nazi seizure of power in 1933 Weill fled to France, where his ballet *Die sieben Todesünden* (*The Seven Deadly Sins*), to a scenario by Brecht, was produced in Paris without much success.

In 1935 Weill left France for the USA, where he settled permanently. In 1938 he achieved his first Broadway success with *Knickerbocker Holiday*, which contains the evocative "September Song". He went on to write another ten Broadway shows, of which the best known are *Lady in the Dark* (with Ira Gershwin, 1940), *One Touch of Venus* (1943), *Street Scene* (1946), and *Lost in the Stars* (1949). He also wrote film and radio scores, but all his concert music, which includes a Violin Concerto (1924) and two symphonies, belongs to his "German" period.

Life and works

NATIONALITY: German

BORN: Dessau, 1900; **DIED:** New York, 1950

SPECIALIST GENRES: Theatre music using jazz and cabaret idioms.

MAJOR WORKS: *Die Dreigroschenoper* (1928); *Aufstieg und Fall der Stadt Mahagonny* (1930).

ABOVE: An album of songs from Weill's famous work, The Threepenny Opera *(1928).*

Francis Poulenc and "Les Six"

Above all do not analyse my music – love it!

POULENC

"Les Six" was the appellation given in 1920 by the French critic Henri Collet to a group of promising young avant-garde composers, who specialized in "shocking the bourgeoisie" along the lines of their mentor, Erik Satie. As a homogeneous group, Les Six – who drew their inspiration from Parisian streetlife, music halls and circus bands – lasted only a few years before going their separate ways.

The most important member was Francis Poulenc, who first attracted attention with his *Rapsodie nègre* for baritone and chamber ensemble (1917). Born into the family of pharmaceutical manufacturers which is now the multinational Rhône-Poulenc company, Poulenc never had to earn a living. He began learning the piano at five, and later studied with the Spanish pianist Ricardo Viñes (1875–1943). In the early 1920s he took private composition lessons, his first major work being settings of Cocteau's *Cocardes*

(1919). Stravinsky recommended Poulenc to the impresario Sergei Diaghilev, who commissioned the ballet with chorus *Les biches* (1923). A sophisticated blend of lyricism with 1920s jazz idioms, the ballet was a great success, but during the 1920s and early '30s Poulenc concentrated on songs – many written for his recital partner, the baritone Pierre Bernac (1899–1979) – and piano music, including two chamber concertos.

He might have remained an essentially frivolous composer, had not the death of a close friend in a car crash prompted his re-conversion to Catholicism. Poulenc visited the shrine of the Black Virgin at Rocamadour, and the musical result – *Litanies à la vierge noire* (1936) – was the first of a series of fine sacred works. These included the Mass in G (1937), two motets for unaccompanied choir (1941), the Stabat Mater (1950) and the exultant Gloria (1959).

Other important late works include the Sextet and sonatas for cello, violin, flute, clarinet and oboe; the operas *Les mamelles de Tirésias* (*The Breasts of Tirésias*), *Les dialogues des Carmélites*

ABOVE: Francis Poulenc (1899–1963), photographed in 1949.

LEFT: Parisians enjoying themselves in the 1920s – Dancing at the Moulin Rouge *by Marcel Leprin (1891–1933).*

Life and works

NATIONALITY: French

BORN: Paris, 1899; **DIED:** Paris, 1963

SPECIALIST GENRES: Stage works, concertos, piano music, sacred vocal music.

MAJOR WORKS: Concerto in D minor for two pianos (1932); Organ Concerto (1938); *Les mamelles de Tirésias* (1944); Stabat Mater (1950); *Les dialogues des Carmélites* (1953–6); *La voix humaine* (1958); Gloria (1959).

(the story of a group of nuns during the French Revolution) and *La voix humaine* (*The Human Voice*), the cantata *Figure humaine* (1943), and concertos for organ and piano. All these works allowed Poulenc to develop a naturally lyrical style leavened with wit and irony.

ABOVE: Five of "Les Six" with the poet Jean Cocteau, on the viewing platform of the Eiffel Tower in 1921. From left to right: Tailleferre, Poulenc, Honegger, Milhaud, Cocteau and Auric.

Arthur Honegger

The Swiss composer Honegger (1892–1955) came to fame first with his "dramatic psalm" *Le roi David* (1921), and again three years later with *Pacific 231*, a musical representation of a steam locomotive. A great admirer of Bach, whose influence is evident in his music, Honegger's best-known works are his five symphonies, particularly No. 3, *Liturgique* (1945–6), No. 4, *Deliciae basilienses* (1946), and No. 5, *Di tre re* (*Of the three Ds*, 1950); the *Pastorale d'été* (*Summer Pastoral*, 1920); and the staged oratorio *Jeanne d'Arc au bûcher* (*Joan of Arc at the Stake*, 1934–5), based on a text by Paul Claudel.

Darius Milhaud

Milhaud (1892–1974) studied at the Paris Conservatoire, where he later taught after World War II. The only Jewish member of Les Six, he was forced to leave France in 1940 and settled in the USA, where he taught in California and Colorado. Milhaud (who spent much of his life in a wheelchair due to rheumatoid arthritis) experimented with polytonality. An enormously prolific composer, he is best known for his 1919 jazz and Latin American-influenced ballet score *Le boeuf sur le toit* (*The Ox on the Roof*); the ballet *La création du monde* (1923); and for the two-piano suite *Scaramouche* (1939). Many of his stage works were based on his friend the poet Paul Claudel's adaptations of Greek myths.

Other members of Les Six

Of the three less well-known members of Les Six, Georges Auric (1899–1983) began as a composer for Diaghilev's Ballets Russes in the 1920s and went on to specialize in film music, writing the scores for the films of Jean Cocteau.

Louis Durey (1888–1979) was only briefly a member of the group. In 1936 he joined the French Communist Party, and after 1945 wrote "music for the masses" in accordance with communist doctrine, setting texts by Mao Zedong and Ho Chi-Minh.

Germaine Tailleferre (1892–1983) was a fine pianist, who wrote over a dozen operas, two ballets, orchestral music including concertos for piano and harp, chamber music including a Pastorale for flute and piano and two violin sonatas, songs, and a few piano pieces. However, her two husbands apparently both discouraged her from composing.

ABOVE: Arthur Honegger (1892–1955).

The French composer Darius Milhaud (1892–1974) conducting.

Aaron Copland

Music that is born complex is not inherently better or worse than music that is born simple.

COPLAND

Copland was the most influential American composer of his time. He strove to create a recognizable "American" idiom, and came to represent the "Establishment" in American music, even though he himself was an outsider, by virtue both of his immigrant background and his homosexuality. Although his life spanned almost the whole of the 20th century, many of his most important works date from the first half of the century.

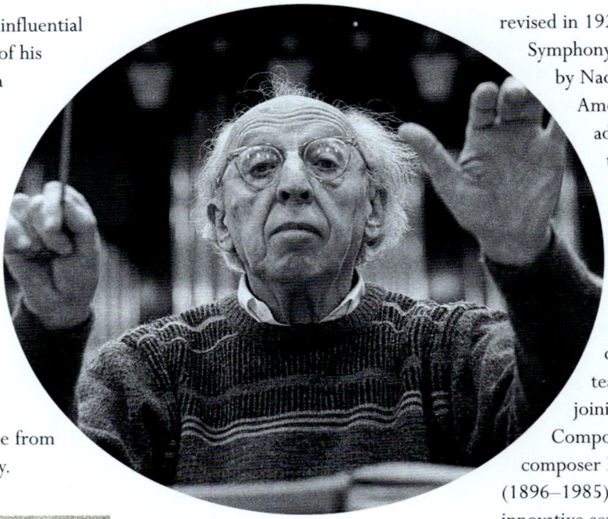

ABOVE: Aaron Copland (1900–90), the most prominent American composer of the 20th century, still conducting at the age of 81.

ABOVE: Eugene Loring as Billy in the original Ballet Caravan production of Copland's Billy the Kid *at the Chicago Opera House, 16 October 1938.*

Copland's parents were Lithuanian/Russian Jews who had become prosperous Brooklyn storekeepers, and he grew up with a keen interest in music. From 1917 he took composition lessons with the conservative Rubin Goldmark in New York, but when he was 20 he decided to seek more creative stimulation in Paris.

He studied for four years with Nadia Boulanger (1887–1979), one of the most dynamic teachers of her age, and threw himself into the frenzied creative melting-pot of 1920s Paris, absorbing influences from all directions, including Stravinsky and Les Six. In 1925 his Organ Symphony (which he revised in 1928, without organ, as Symphony No. 1) was performed by Nadia Boulanger on an American tour, eliciting the admiring comment from the conductor Walter Damrosch (1862–1950): "If he can write like that at 23, in five years he'll be ready to commit murder." On his return to New York, Copland divided his time between teaching and composing, joining the League of Composers and – with his fellow composer Roger Sessions (1896–1985) – sponsoring an innovative series of new music concerts in New York.

Life and works

NATIONALITY: American

BORN: New York, 1900;
DIED: New York, 1990

SPECIALIST GENRES:
"American" ballet scores, orchestral music.

MAJOR WORKS:
Piano Concerto (1926); *Billy the Kid* (1938); *Fanfare for the Common Man* (1942); *Rodeo* (1942); *Appalachian Spring* (1944); Symphony No. 3 (1944–6).

Popular music

Copland had firm convictions about the role of music in society, and was determined to show that the arts and industry could co-exist on equal terms. His ideas were honed by the Depression and the looming war: he decided that his own music must be, above all, accessible, and he gave it a specifically American sound by incorporating elements of jazz and folk music. Copland's first major hit was the ballet *El salón México* (1936), and from 1938 onwards he produced a series of influential ballets on "American" subjects: *Billy the Kid*, *Rodeo* (for Agnes de Mille) and *Appalachian Spring*. This last, written for Martha Graham's dance company, is a tender portrait of a close-knit pioneering community in the Appalachian mountains, whose aspirations are embodied in the Shaker hymn-tune "Simple Gifts". At the same time he began to write film scores, of which the best-known were for *Of Mice and Men* (1939), *Our Town* (1940), *The Red Pony* (1948) and the Oscar-winning *The Heiress* (1949).

Several other notable works date from this specifically "American" period, including the urban landscape *Quiet City* (1939), *A Lincoln Portrait* for speaker and orchestra (1942), based on Lincoln's speeches; and *Fanfare for the Common Man*, written as an antidote to the usual pompous VIP fanfares. His Piano Variations of 1930 remains his best-known solo work (a Piano Sonata dates from 1939–41, and a Violin Sonata from 1943).

ABOVE: A steer wrestler in action at a rodeo in Idaho. Copland's "cowboy ballet" Rodeo *celebrates this American tradition.*

Serialism

Copland's post-war works were more abstract and notably less successful: by then fashions were changing and the fast-paced modern idioms of Leonard Bernstein had overtaken Copland's in the popularity stakes. Among his later works, the beautiful *Twelve Poems of Emily Dickinson* for voice and piano (1950), the Piano Quartet (1950, which uses 12-note technique), the orchestral *Music for a Great City* (1964), and the *Threnody in memoriam Stravinsky* for flute quartet (1971) are the most memorable. His opera *The Tender Land* (1952–4) was not well received.

From 1940–65 Copland was head of the composition faculty at the Berkshire Music Center at Tanglewood, and also taught at Harvard, where his lectures were published as *Music and Imagination* (1952). He was showered with honours, including a Pulitzer Prize.

ABOVE: A pastoral landscape in the Appalachians, such as inspired Copland's ballet Appalachian Spring *(1944).*

ABOVE: Martha Graham in Appalachian Spring, *seen here with her dance company in 1954.*

George Gershwin

I don't think there has been such an inspired melodist on this earth since Tchaikovsky... but if you want to speak of a composer, that's another matter.

LEONARD BERNSTEIN (1918–90)

Gershwin was one of the most popular composers of the 20th century, and one of history's greatest songwriters. From 1916 until his untimely death from a brain tumour at the age of only 39, he turned out a stream of great melodies which became instant classics. Songs such as "Swanee", "'S Wonderful", "Someone to Watch Over Me", "Embraceable You", "He Loves and She Loves", "I Got Rhythm" (and dozens more) rank with the best of Irving Berlin, Cole Porter and Jerome Kern, but were also much admired by "serious" musicians.

The son of a Russian Jewish immigrant family, Gershwin studied piano, theory and harmony as a child with several distinguished musicians, although he was never good at reading music. In 1914 he went to work for a Tin Pan Alley music publisher and began to write songs for other people's shows. From 1919 onwards he wrote his own Broadway musicals, many in collaboration with his brother Ira

(1896–1983). They included *Lady be Good* (1924), *Oh, Kay!* (1926), *Strike Up the Band* (1927), *Funny Face* (1927), *Girl Crazy* (1930) and *Of Thee I Sing* (1931). From 1931 onwards he also wrote film scores (the songs "Let's Call the Whole Thing Off", "Shall We Dance?" and "They Can't Take That Away From Me" were written for the 1937 film *Shall We Dance?*).

In 1924 the bandleader Paul Whiteman commissioned Gershwin's famous *Rhapsody in Blue* for piano and jazz ensemble. The story goes that Gershwin did not know he was supposed to write it until he saw an advertisement for Whiteman's forthcoming "Experiment in Modern Music" concert in a newspaper. Ira Gershwin suggested the title, after a painting by Whistler. Its triumphant success led to commissions for the Piano Concerto, the orchestral tone-poem *An American in Paris*, and ultimately to the opera *Porgy and Bess*, set among the black community of the Deep South and using its folk music and rhythms. It is still the only American opera to be performed internationally on a regular basis.

ABOVE: George Gershwin, painted by himself a year before his death from a brain tumour.

LEFT: A poster advertising the 1959 film version of Porgy and Bess.

Life and works

NATIONALITY: American

BORN: Brooklyn, 1898; **DIED:** Beverly Hills, 1937

SPECIALIST GENRES: Popular songs.

MAJOR WORKS: *Rhapsody in Blue* (1924); Piano Concerto in F (1925); Preludes for piano (1926); *An American in Paris* (1928); *Porgy and Bess* (1935).

Samuel Barber

As to what happens when I compose,
I really haven't the faintest idea.
BARBER

Samuel Barber's style eschewed the idiomatic "Americanisms" of Copland and looked back to the late-Romantic European tradition. He began to learn the piano at the age of six, and began composing at seven. At 14 he became one of the first students at the Curtis Institute in Philadelphia, where he studied piano, composition, conducting and singing. He nearly became a professional baritone.

Barber's student years at the Curtis Institute produced his first mature compositions, including the popular *Dover Beach* (a setting of a poem by Matthew Arnold for baritone voice and string quartet which Barber himself recorded in 1935), the Serenade for string quartet, and the Cello Sonata, all of which gave him scope to develop his characteristic lyrical, expressive style. In 1928 he won a travelling scholarship with his Violin Sonata, and another in 1933 for his overture *The School for Scandal*. In the mid 1930s further scholarships, including the American Prix de Rome, enabled him to spend time in Italy. His compositions there included the First Symphony and a String Quartet, the slow movement of which, transcribed for orchestra, became the famous Adagio for strings (first recorded by Toscanini).

From 1939 until 1942 Barber taught at the Curtis Institute, and from 1943 until 1974 he lived in New York State with the Italian composer Gian Carlo Menotti (born 1911), who wrote the libretto for Barber's first opera, *Vanessa*. His Second Symphony (later withdrawn) was written during war service. His post-war works included a fine Cello Concerto (1945), the ballet *Medea* (1946), the Piano Sonata, *Summer Music* for wind quintet (1955), the vocal works *Knoxville: Summer of 1915* (1947), *Hermit Songs* (1952–3), and *Prayers of Kierkegaard* (1954), and three operas, of which *Antony and Cleopatra* (1965–6), based on Franco Zeffirelli's reworking of Shakespeare, was an expensive failure. A post-Romantic, Barber shunned innovation, and continued, as he said, to "go on doing his thing" until the end of his life.

ABOVE: The American composer Samuel Barber (1910–81).

Life and works

NATIONALITY: American

BORN: West Chester, Pennsylvania, 1910; **DIED:** New York, 1981

SPECIALIST GENRES: Orchestral, chamber and operatic works, in neo-Romantic idiom.

MAJOR WORKS: *Dover Beach* (1931); *The School for Scandal* Overture (1933); Adagio for strings (1938); Piano Sonata (1949); opera *Vanessa* (1958); Piano Concerto (1962).

ABOVE: Philadelphia, Pennsylvania, at dusk. Barber studied there at the world-famous Curtis Institute.

Igor Stravinsky

Bach on the wrong notes.
SERGEI PROKOFIEV (1891–1953)

Stravinsky was arguably the greatest – and certainly the most versatile – composer of the 20th century. He was keenly receptive to new trends – from neo-classicism to 12-note music – and perceived the advantages of a protean approach to composition. He also shed his personal skin several times throughout his long life, acquiring two wives and three changes of nationality.

ABOVE: Igor Stravinsky, photographed by Tappe in 1965, while he was writing the Requiem Canticles, *his last major work.*

Russian period

The son of an opera singer, Stravinsky went to school in St Petersburg, and began piano lessons when he was nine. On a summer vacation in the country he met Rimsky-Korsakov, who became his teacher and mentor. His early Piano Sonata in F sharp minor was performed at Rimsky-Korsakov's house, and a Symphony in E flat and the orchestral fantasy *Feu d'artifice* (*Fireworks*, strongly influenced by Debussy) were largely written under the elder composer's tuition. Stravinsky had no other formal musical education; during this time he spent a couple of years reading law at university, but found it uncongenial. He left in 1905 and the following year he married his cousin Katerina Nossenko, who bore him four children.

ABOVE: A portrait of Stravinsky conducting, by the artist Milein Cosman. Stravinsky conducted recordings of his entire output.

Diaghilev's Ballets Russes

In 1909 the *Scherzo fantastique* and *Feu d'artifice* were performed in St Petersburg. In the audience was the impresario Sergei Diaghilev (1872–1929), whose celebrated Ballets Russes employed the dancer Mikhail Fokine and the designers Léon Bakst and Alexandre Benois. Diaghilev lacked a composer for his 1910 Paris season, and he decided to try out the young Stravinsky with a commission for *L'oiseau de feu* (*The Firebird*), based on a Russian folk legend. Stravinsky's brilliant and colourful score – strongly influenced by his Russian forebears including Balakirev, Tchaikovsky and Rimsky-Korsakov – was a huge success.

His next score for Diaghilev began life as a concert piece for piano and orchestra, but then turned into *Petrushka*, based on a grotesque tale of lust and murder in a Russian puppeteer's booth. Another huge success at its Paris première in June 1911, *Petrushka* conjures up a vanishing world of Russian peasant life, complete with exotic and exhilarating dances for Cossacks, coachmen, wet-nurses and a host of other characters.

During 1912 Stravinsky worked on his third Diaghilev ballet, *Le sacre du printemps* (*The Rite of Spring*). Its première at the Théâtre des Champs-Elysées on 29 May 1913 caused a riot among its outraged audience. Even now, the primitive violence of Stravinsky's score – especially when coupled with Nijinsky's explicit choreography (the ballet concerns an ancient fertility rite in which a young virgin is selected for ritual sacrifice) – still packs an electrifying punch.

In 1914 Stravinsky's first opera, *Le rossignol* (*The Nightingale*, based on Hans Christian Andersen's fairy-story), was produced under the aegis of the Ballets Russes at the Paris Opéra. (Five years later Stravinsky arranged the music as a symphonic poem, *Le chant du rossignol*, which was choreographed as a ballet by Leonid Massine with designs by Henri Matisse.)

When war broke out the composer and his family took refuge in Switzerland, where he worked on a new ballet score, *Les noces* (*The Wedding*), scored for four-part chorus, four soloists, four pianos and percussion ensemble. Stravinsky's researches into Russian folk music for this project also inspired several secondary works, including the burlesque *Renard* (1915–16).

By 1918 Stravinsky had already abandoned the lush orchestral resources of his pre-war ballets in favour of more sparsely scored, chamber-orientated works. These included *L'histoire du soldat* (*The Soldier's Tale*, for three actors, dancer, and small instrumental ensemble) and the ballet *Pulcinella*, based on a *commedia dell'arte* theme with music "arranged" from fragments attributed to Pergolesi, at the suggestion of Diaghilev. *Pulcinella* – which ushered in Stravinsky's absorption in neo-classicism – was first performed at the Paris Opéra on 15 May 1920, with décor and costumes by Picasso. Stravinsky later arranged the music as suites for cello and piano and for violin and piano.

ABOVE: Stravinsky in his study in later life – a photographic portrait by Karsh of Ottawa.

Life and works

NATIONALITY: Russian

BORN: Oranienbaum, near St Petersburg, 1882; **DIED:** New York, 1971

SPECIALIST GENRES: Stage works (ballet, opera, oratorios), sacred music.

MAJOR WORKS: *L'oiseau de feu* (1910); *Petrushka* (1911); *Le sacre du printemps* (1912); *L'histoire du soldat* (1918); *Les noces* (1914–23); *Oedipus rex* (1926–7); *Symphony of Psalms* (1930); *Dumbarton Oaks* (1938); Symphony in Three Movements (1942–5); *The Rake's Progress* (1948–51).

ABOVE: The Moor, the Ballerina and Petrushka – a 1913 illustration by René Bull of the three main characters in Stravinsky's ballet Petrushka.

ABOVE: Cynthia Harvey and Anthony Dowell as the Firebird and the Prince in the Royal Ballet's production of The Firebird, *Stravinsky's first ballet score for Diaghilev.*

ABOVE: *A scene from Stravinsky's third Diaghilev ballet,* The Rite of Spring.

Paris season with the opera-oratorio *Oedipus rex*, based on a Latin version of the tragic myth by the poet Jean Cocteau. Neither Diaghilev nor the audience really appreciated this strange hybrid, which is now recognized as a masterpiece. Stravinsky had already begun to cut loose from Diaghilev. His next ballet score, *Apollon musagète* (a title later abbreviated to *Apollo*), was written to a commission from the American patroness Elizabeth Sprague Coolidge, and was the first of Stravinsky's ballets to be choreographed by George Balanchine (1904–83). It was followed by *Le baiser de la fée* (*The Fairy's Kiss*), a Tchaikovskian pastiche, for Ida Rubinstein's rival troupe. Diaghilev had little time to complain: he died in Venice in August 1929. The following year, Stravinsky was commissioned by Serge Koussevitzky (1876–1951) to celebrate the 50th anniversary of the Boston Symphony Orchestra with the *Symphony of Psalms*; and in 1931 he began an association with the violinist Samuel Dushkin, for whom he wrote the Violin Concerto and the Duo Concertante for violin and piano.

In 1934 Stravinsky became a naturalized French citizen. The same year he collaborated with André Gide

French period

After the war, Stravinsky decided to make France his home, settling in Paris and Biarritz. The early 1920s saw the composition of several purely instrumental works, including the *Symphonies of Wind Instruments* (1921), dedicated to Debussy's memory, and the Concerto for Piano and Wind (1923–4). He also worked on *Mavra*: a one-act *opera buffa* based on Pushkin, and completed the orchestration of *Les noces*. These two works marked the end of his "Russian" period. At the same time, he began an affair with a married actress, Vera Soudeikine, to whom he dedicated the Octet for wind instruments (1922–3). To his wife Katarina he dedicated the Serenade in A (1925), one of many piano works written in the 1920s which also included the Capriccio for piano and orchestra (1928–9) and the Sonata (1924).

In 1927 Stravinsky celebrated the 20th anniversary of Diaghilev's first

ABOVE: *Stravinsky (right), photographed in 1921 with the impressario Sergei Diaghilev, founder of the Ballets Russes.*

ABOVE: *Stravinsky conducting in later life. He moved to the USA in 1939 and remained there for the rest of his life.*

ABOVE: Stravinsky rehearsing the orchestra of La Scala, Milan, in preparation for the première of his opera The Rake's Progress.

(1869–1951) on the musical melodrama *Perséphone*, again for Rubinstein, which was coolly received. But by the mid 1930s his main commissions were coming from the other side of the Atlantic. They included the ballet *Jeu de cartes* (*The Card Game*, choreographed by Balanchine in 1937 for the American Ballet), the pseudo-Baroque chamber concerto *Dumbarton Oaks*, and the Symphony in C for the Chicago Symphony Orchestra (1940).

American period

The imminent outbreak of World War II, combined with the deaths of his elder daughter, his wife and his mother, drove Stravinsky to seek sanctuary in the USA. On 9 March 1940 he married Vera Soudeikine, then settled in Hollywood and applied for US citizenship. The early works of his American years include the Symphony in Three Movements, the *Circus Polka* (1942) for dancing elephants in the Barnum and Bailey Circus, *Scènes de ballet* (1944) for a Broadway revue, the *Danses concertantes* (1941–2), and the *Ebony Concerto* for the jazz clarinettist Woody Herman (1913–87). Stravinsky's last neo-classical work was the opera *The Rake's Progress* (1948–51), inspired by William Hogarth's famous series of etchings, to a libretto by W. H. Auden (1907–73) and Chester Kallman (1921–75). It was premièred in Venice in September 1951.

Last works

After *The Rake's Progress* Stravinsky's style underwent a major change. His meeting in 1948 with the conductor Robert Craft (born 1923), an admirer of Schoenberg, introduced Stravinsky to the music of the Second Viennese School. The first fruit of his own experiments with serial technique was the *Canticum sacrum* (1955), designed for performance in St Mark's, Venice. Two further stage works date from his later years: the ballet *Agon* (1953–4), and the musical play *The Flood* (1961–2), based on the York and Chester mystery plays and first produced on American television.

Many of Stravinsky's later works, from the 1948 Mass onwards, sprang from religious impulses. They include *Threni* (*Lamentations of the Prophet Jeremiah*) for solo voices, chorus and orchestra (1957–8), the cantata *A Sermon, a Narrative and a Prayer* (1960–1), the "sacred ballad" *Abraham and Isaac* for baritone and chamber orchestra (1962–3), *Introitus* for men's voices and ensemble (1965), and his last major work, the *Requiem Canticles* for soloists, chorus and orchestra (1965–6). One of his last works was the charming setting for voice and piano of Edward Lear's poem "The Owl and the Pussy-Cat" (1966).

In 1969 Stravinsky and his wife moved to New York, where he died two years later. He was buried near Diaghilev in Venice.

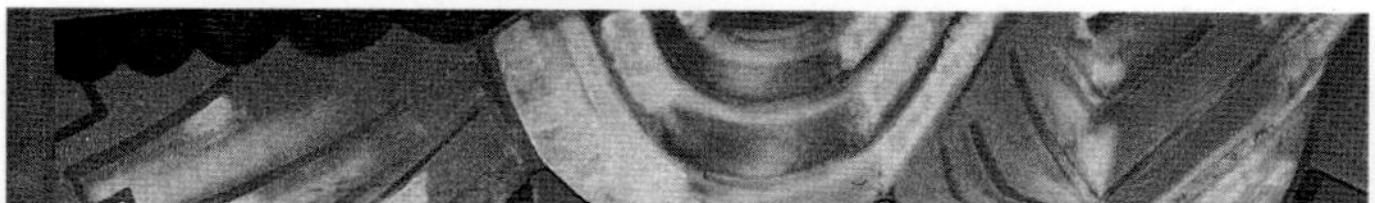

ABOVE: The Rake's Progress *is a quasi-Mozartian full-length opera based on an English libretto. This photograh shows a 1952 performance at the Berlin State Opera.*

Sergei Prokofiev

I abhor imitation and I abhor the familiar.

PROKOFIEV

Prokofiev, together with Stravinsky and Shostakovich, belongs to the trio of great Russian composers of the 20th century. Like Stravinsky, he left Russia after the Revolution, settling in America and Paris, but unlike him, Prokofiev then returned in the 1930s, with mixed fortunes. He was a noted composer of stage music, but also – like Shostakovich – made significant contributions to both the symphonic and concerto repertoires.

Prokofiev was the only child of a wealthy and cultured family. He began to compose at five, and studied privately with Reinhold Glière (1875–1956). In September 1904 he entered the St Petersburg Conservatory, where he spent ten years. By the time of his public debut as a composer and pianist on New Year's Eve 1908, he was already an accomplished composer with a reputation for writing astringent, avant-garde music with a tendency to shock.

Prokofiev's life changed dramatically after his father's death in 1910, when he had to start earning a living. His response was to write the first of his five piano concertos, which caused uproar among critics. It was followed by a second (1913), which apparently left its listeners "frozen with fright, hair standing on end". Nevertheless, Prokofiev graduated from the Conservatory in June 1914 with the prestigious Rubinstein Prize.

ABOVE: Sergei Prokofiev, painted in 1934 by Pyotr Konchalovsky (1876–1956).

As a reward, his mother took him to London. There he met Diaghilev, who commissioned a ballet from him. Prokofiev's first attempt was a failure, and his second, *Chout* (*The Buffoon*), remained unperformed until 1921. Meanwhile Prokofiev had returned to a Russia torn by internal political strife and suffering from the deprivations of war. He spent the war years working on his opera *Igrok* (*The Gambler*, 1917, based on Dostoyevsky), the luminous First Violin Concerto (1916–17), and the ebullient, Haydnesque *Classical Symphony*, one of his most popular works. When the political situation deteriorated after Lenin seized power, Prokofiev emigrated to the USA.

America and France

At first, his sensational piano-playing excited the American public, and the Chicago Opera commissioned the opera *The Love for Three Oranges* (which, after initial production problems, eventually became the only one of his ten or so operatic projects to achieve international success in his lifetime). But Prokofiev's performing career had stalled, and in 1922 he left for Paris, where he spent the next 14 years. His works of those years include three ballets, the Third, Fourth and Fifth Piano Concertos (the Fourth, written for Paul Wittgenstein in 1931, for left hand only), the Second Violin Concerto and the First Cello Concerto, and the Second, Third and Fourth Symphonies, as well as piano pieces and songs.

Return to Russia

By 1933 Prokofiev had received many invitations from his homeland, which he revisited several times. His decision to return permanently in 1936 was influenced by the increasing number of Russian commissions he was receiving, including the film music for *Lieutenant Kijé* (1934), and *Romeo and Juliet* for the Bolshoy Ballet (although

ABOVE, FROM LEFT TO RIGHT: The conductor Ernst Ansermet, Diaghilev, Stravinsky and Prokofiev, c.1921.

the company initially rejected the score), but he chose an inopportune time to return, just as the Soviet authorities were beginning to interfere in artistic matters.

His first "Russian" works therefore included innocuous pieces, such as the much-loved *Peter and the Wolf* for children; and over the next decade Prokofiev made a determined attempt to provide "Soviet realist" works which would satisfy Stalinist criteria. But these did not save him from oppression. During World War II his Spanish-born wife Lina was arrested on trumped-up charges of spying and sent to a labour camp under dubious circumstances; by then Prokofiev had formed a liaison with a Communist Party member, Mira Mendelson, with whom he lived until his death. In 1948 Prokofiev was among the composers denounced in the Stalinist press for "formalist perversions".

However, the best works of Prokofiev's "Soviet" period – the film score for Eisenstein's *Alexander Nevsky* (1938), the operas *Obrucheniye v Monastyre* (*The Duenna*, 1940–1, based on Sheridan), and *Voyna i mir* (*War and Peace*, 1941–3, based on Tolstoy), the Second String Quartet (1941), and the Fifth Symphony (1944) – remained true to his own artistic ideals. His last works included another Eisenstein film score, *Ivan the Terrible* (1945–7), the Sixth and Seventh Symphonies (1945–7), the ballets *Cinderella* (1940–4) and *Kamenniy tsvetok* (*The Tale of the Stone Flower*, 1948–53), and the Symphony-Concerto for cello and orchestra (1950–2), written for Mstislav Rostropovich (born 1927). Prokofiev died of a brain haemorrhage on the same day as Stalin.

ABOVE: Prokofiev at work in the 1930s. He finally returned to Russia in 1936, having been enticed back by promising commissions.

Life and works

NATIONALITY: Russian

BORN: Soutzovka, Ukraine, 1891; **DIED:** Moscow, 1953

SPECIALIST GENRES: Symphonies, concertos, stage works.

MAJOR WORKS: Seven symphonies, including *Classical Symphony* (1917); five piano concertos; two violin concertos; *The Love for Three Oranges* (1919); *Romeo and Juliet* (1935–6); *Peter and the Wolf* (1936); *War and Peace* (1941–3).

ABOVE: The pas de deux *from Prokofiev's ballet* Romeo and Juliet *(1935–6), written for the Bolshoy Ballet in Moscow. This performance took place at the Savonlinna Opera Festival in Finland.*

Paul Hindemith

Tell Hindemith that I am extremely pleased with him.
ARNOLD SCHOENBERG (1874–1951), 1924

The German-born composer, conductor, string player and teacher Paul Hindemith spent the early part of his career in Frankfurt, where he was a violinist in the Opera orchestra from 1915 until 1923, and where he studied composition at the Hoch Conservatory until 1917.

In 1921 two one-act operas, *Mörder, Hoffnung der Frauen* (*Murder, Hope of Women*), and *Das Nusch-Nuschi* (based on a play for Burmese marionettes), were performed in Stuttgart, where their scandalous subjects aroused controversy and gained notoriety for Hindemith. At the same time, the Amar Quartet (in which he played viola) was formed by the composer and Licco Amar to première his second String Quartet at the first Donaueschingen Festival, because the ensemble booked to play it had found it too difficult.

Two years later Hindemith was invited to join the festival's committee, and under his guidance it became Germany's leading festival for the promotion of new music. Meanwhile, Hindemith adopted an entirely different style: his series of seven works entitled *Kammermusik* ("chamber music") looked back to Baroque forms and polyphony. During the 1920s he taught at the Berlin Hochschule für Musik, and continued to play viola in the Amar Quartet. In 1929 he appeared at a London Promenade Concert as soloist in William Walton's Viola Concerto.

Although Hindemith was not Jewish, his wife was, and he was attacked by the Nazi party for the unacceptable atonality of his music, and the fact that he openly associated with Jewish musicians. Despite the support of the conductor Wilhelm Furtwängler, who conducted the première of his *Mathis der Maler* Symphony in March 1934, Hindemith found himself on a list of proscribed composers. His opera *Mathis der Maler* (*Mathis the Painter*, based on the life of the 16th-century artist Grünewald), from which he had taken themes for the symphony, was banned by the Nazis and first performed in Switzerland in 1938.

ABOVE: The German composer Paul Hindemith (1895–1963).

As life in Nazi Germany became impossible, Hindemith joined the general exodus of talent. After some years teaching in Turkey, in 1939 he settled in New York, where he held several university lectureships and was head of the school of music at Yale. In 1953 he settled in Switzerland. He died of pancreatitis in Frankfurt.

Hindemith was a prolific composer – almost too prolific for his own good. Concerned about the widening gap between the serious composer and the public, he was anxious that his music should be accessible to amateur players as well as professional performers. His works include a great deal of instrumental and educational music written with this in mind, and quantities of chamber music. His best-known works include the ballet *Nobilissima visione* (*Most Exalted Vision*) and the Rilke song-cycle *Das Marienleben* (*Scenes from the Life of Mary*). Many of his works are still neglected.

Life and works

NATIONALITY: German

BORN: Hanau, near Frankfurt, 1895; **DIED:** Frankfurt, 1963

SPECIALIST GENRES: Orchestral, chamber and piano music in German neo-classical idiom.

MAJOR WORKS: *Das Marienleben* (*Scenes from the Life of Mary*, 1922–3); operas *Cardillac* (1926) and *Mathis der Maler* (1933–4); *Nobilissima visione* (1938); *Symphonic Metamorphosis on Themes of Carl Maria von Weber* (1943).

William Walton

As a musical joker he is a jewel of the first water.

Ernest Newman (1868–1959), reviewing "Façade"

The son of a Lancashire choirmaster and singing teacher, William Walton became a chorister at Christ Church, Oxford, when he was ten. At the age of 16 he entered Oxford University to read music, leaving two years later without a degree but having acquired a taste for high living. For the next decade he lived as the "adopted brother" of the eccentric Sitwell family in Chelsea and Italy, also spending lengthy periods at the homes of other wealthy admirers – which freed him to compose without the burden of having to earn a living. In 1920s London he associated with the "Fitzrovian" artistic community immortalized in Anthony Powell's series of novels *A Dance to the Music of Time*, which included the composers Lord Berners, Constant Lambert and Peter Warlock. During these bohemian years Walton became keenly interested in jazz, and made his name with the satirical entertainment *Façade*, based on a number of witty poems by Edith Sitwell (1887–1964) and composed when he was only 19. It is still his most popular work.

ABOVE: William Walton, photographed towards the end of his life, in 1978. He was knighted in 1951.

Larger-scale works followed: the overture *Portsmouth Point* (1925), the Sinfonia Concertante (1926–7), and the Prokofiev-influenced Viola Concerto. In 1931 the oratorio *Belshazzar's Feast* burst upon the English choral scene at the Leeds Festival. Overnight Walton found himself acclaimed as Elgar's successor, a position he consolidated with his First Symphony, the Violin Concerto and the patriotic coronation march *Crown Imperial* (1937).

During the 1940s Walton concentrated on film music, a genre crowned by his three masterly Shakespearean collaborations with Laurence Olivier (*Henry V* in 1944, *Hamlet* in 1947, and *Richard III* in 1955). In 1948 he and his young Argentinian wife Susana Gil abandoned England for the idyllic Mediterranean island of Ischia. The early 1950s were chiefly occupied with his opera *Troilus and Cressida*, but its Covent Garden reception was disappointing. Later works included the Cello Concerto (1956), a Second Symphony (1959–60), and the *Missa brevis* (1966) written for Coventry Cathedral, but few recaptured the sparkle of Walton's earlier years. Knighted in 1951, he died aged 81, a pillar of the musical Establishment.

Life and works

NATIONALITY: English

BORN: Oldham, 1902; **DIED:** Ischia, 1983

SPECIALIST GENRES: Orchestral music, film scores, stage music.

MAJOR WORKS: *Façade* (1921–2); *Belshazzar's Feast* (1929–31); Symphony No. 1 (1935); Viola Concerto (1929); Violin Concerto (1938–9); *Troilus and Cressida* (1954).

ABOVE: A poster for Laurence Olivier's film version of Shakespeare's Henry V *(1944), for which Walton provided a stirring score.*

Other Composers of the Era

Tonality is a natural force, like gravity.

Paul Hindemith, "The Craft of Musical Composition" (1937)

Spain produced its share of important 20th-century composers. Manuel de Falla (1876–1946) was much influenced by Spanish musical traditions, from Andalucian folk song to 16th-century Spanish polyphony. His one-act opera *La vida breve* (*Life is Short*) won a prize in Madrid in 1905, but was not produced until 1913 (in Nice), by which time Falla had been living in France for six years. In 1915 he wrote the ballet-pantomime *El amor brujo* (*Love the Magician*), but his fame was established in 1919 when Diaghilev produced the ballet *El sombrero de tres picos* (*The Three-cornered Hat*) in London. Falla's other major works include *Noches en los jardines de España* (*Nights in the Gardens of Spain*) for piano and orchestra (1916), the *Fantasia bética* for solo piano (1919), a Harpsichord

ABOVE: The Spanish composer Manuel de Falla (1876–1946) in 1924 in his studio in Granada, Andalucia.

ABOVE: Ottorino Respighi (1879–1936), an Italian composer in the Romantic tradition.

Concerto (1926) and the chamber opera *El retablo de Maese Pedro* (*Master Peter's Puppet Show*, 1919–22). After the Spanish Civil War he moved to Argentina.

The blind Spanish composer Joaquín Rodrigo (1901–99), who taught music history at Madrid University from 1947 onwards, is chiefly known for two works for guitar and orchestra: the *Concierto de Aranjuez* (1939) and the *Fantasia para un gentilhombre* (1954). His other works, which include concertos for cello, piano, violin, flute, and multiple guitars, are less often performed.

Another popular, middle-of-the-road composer was the Italian Ottorino Respighi (1879–1936), who studied with Rimsky-Korsakov and ended up teaching at the Liceo di Santa Cecilia in Rome, where he died. His richly scored tone-poems in the Straussian mould have always been popular, especially *Fontane di Roma* (*Fountains of Rome*, 1914–16), *Pini di Roma* (*Pines of Rome*, 1923–4), the *Trittico botticelliano* (*Three Botticelli Pictures*, 1927), *Gli uccelli* (*The Birds*, 1927), and *Feste romane* (*Roman Festivals*, 1928). His ballet *La boutique fantasque* (*The Marvellous Toyshop*, 1919) is based on Rossini transcriptions.

Britain

Walton's English contemporaries included a group of composers based in the Bloomsbury area of London – the "Fitzrovia" of Anthony Powell's novels. Powell's character Morland was based on the composer and conductor Constant Lambert (1905–51), who began his short but brilliant career

ABOVE: The blind Spanish composer Joaquín Rodrigo (1901–99) playing the piano at his Madrid home, c.1975.

ABOVE: The British composer and conductor Constant Lambert (1905–51) in the 1930s.

with panache when his ballet *Romeo and Juliet* was commissioned by Diaghilev and performed in Monte Carlo in 1926. The next year, Lambert took London by storm with his irresistible, jazz-influenced cantata *The Rio Grande* for piano, chorus and orchestra, based on a poem by Sacheverell Sitwell (1897–1988). From 1941–7 he was music director of Sadler's Wells Ballet, and a one-time lover of the dancer Margot Fonteyn. His second wife

ABOVE: Aram Khachaturian (1903–78), composer of Spartacus *(used as theme music for the TV series "The Onedin Line").*

Isabel was a renowned artist and sculptress. Lambert's heavy drinking contributed to his early death. (His son Kit, who also died young, was the manager of the rock group The Who.)

One of Lambert's closest friends was the eccentric composer Philip Heseltine (1894–1930). Heseltine used his own name as an editor of early music, and the pseudonym "Peter Warlock" for performances and publication of his own compositions, which included many folk-song-influenced vocal settings, and the Renaissance-style *Capriol Suite* for string orchestra (1926). Warlock is presumed to have committed suicide.

Another eccentric English composer of the period was Gerald, Lord Berners (1883–1950), an aristocratic painter, author, diplomat and composer with a Satie-esque sense of humour. His best-known work is the ballet *The Triumph of Neptune* (1926), another Diaghilev commission.

Central Europe

The majority of German and Austrian Jewish composers managed to flee Nazism, but a notable group of Czech composers failed to survive the war. Among them was Ervín Schulhoff (1894–1942), who was interned at the Theresienstadt detention camp and then deported to Wülzbourg concentration camp, where he died. His works, which include eight symphonies, two string quartets, a sextet and four piano sonatas, show the influence of jazz and of other new developments.

While composers such as Prokofiev and Shostakovich managed to survive the Stalinist regime but still retain a strong individual voice, others bowed to the political pressure to produce music that the authorities would consider accessible to the masses. The Armenian composer Aram Khachaturian (1903–78) attracted Prokofiev's attention with his Trio for

ABOVE: Peter Warlock, the pen-name of Philip Heseltine (1894–1930).

piano, clarinet and violin, and achieved wide success with his First Symphony, his Piano Concerto and the 1942 ballet *Gayané* (which includes the popular "Sabre Dance"). His Second Violin Concerto, however, incurred official displeasure, and he abandoned serious composition in favour of neutral film scores. After Stalin's death he resumed his former career with the ballet *Spartacus*, premièred by the Kirov in 1956.

ABOVE: The Czech composer Ervín Schulhoff (1894–1942), one of the most prominent musical victims of the Nazis.

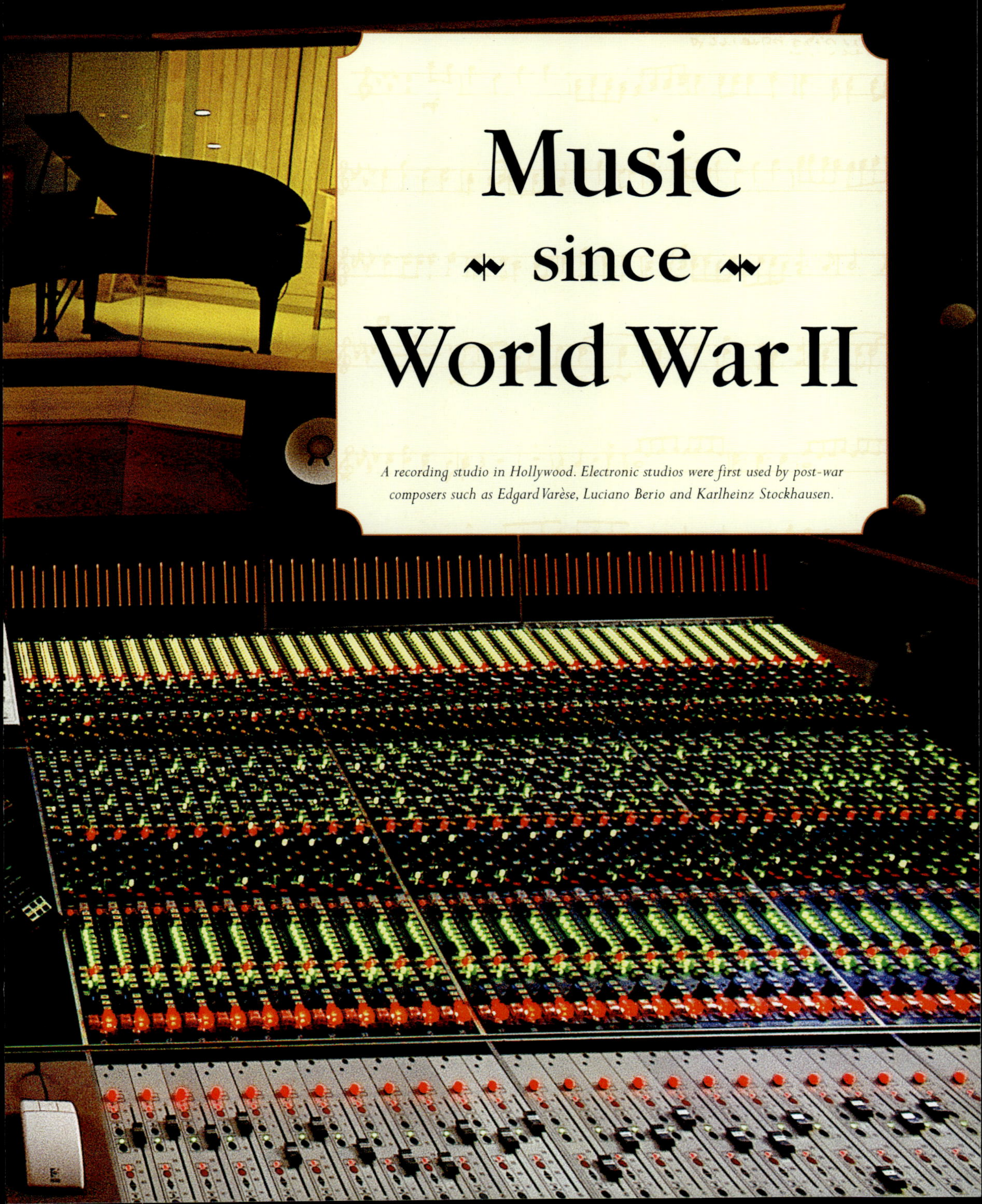

Music since World War II

A recording studio in Hollywood. Electronic studios were first used by post-war composers such as Edgard Varèse, Luciano Berio and Karlheinz Stockhausen.

Modern Music

The serial idea is based on a universe that finds itself in perpetual expansion.

PIERRE BOULEZ (BORN 1925)

From the late 20th century, music has become more fragmentary than at any previous historical period. There are no longer "schools" of composition: each composer now strives to find an original and entirely individual voice. If they draw inspiration from other music, it is from the works of individual predecessors rather than from general trends.

Both Shostakovich and Benjamin Britten came into their own after 1945, the year that Britten revitalized British opera with *Peter Grimes*. While Britten's principal importance lies in vocal music, especially his fine sequence of operas, Shostakovich was primarily an instrumental composer. Both were inspired by the playing of the Russian cellist Mstislav Rostropovich, for whom Shostakovich wrote his cello concertos and Britten his Cello Symphony and three solo suites. Both composers worked in an essentially tonal medium, unaffected by avant-garde developments.

Britain has maintained a strong operatic tradition since 1945, in the works of Britten, Michael Tippett, Harrison Birtwistle, Peter Maxwell Davies, and now a younger generation of composers, including Mark-Anthony Turnage and Thomas Adès. In America, Leonard Bernstein revitalized the American musical, especially with his brilliant *West Side Story* (1957), but has proved perhaps more influential as a conductor than as a composer. Meanwhile, Copland (though active up until his death) ceded the mantle of senior American composer to Elliott Carter, whose orchestral and chamber music is characterized by the most rigorous intellectual discipline and formal perfection.

ABOVE: VE Day, 8 May 1945. Crowds in Whitehall, London, cheering Prime Minister Winston Churchill and members of the Cabinet after the announcement of Germany's surrender.

ABOVE: The first landing on the Moon – the Apollo 11 mission, 1969.

Minimalism

The experiments of John Cage proved a blind alley in themselves (the notorious *4' 33"* took music to its furthest extreme – complete silence), but Cage's ideas have taken root, most obviously in the American minimalist school of Steve Reich, Terry Riley, Philip Glass and John Adams, whose music relies on repetitive rhythmic and melodic *ostinati* for its hypnotic effect. The fact that such music has connections with the harmonic and rhythmic clichés of pop and rock music, as well as with Indian and African music (popular in the West since the 1960s), has contributed to its popularity. The British composer Michael Nyman (born 1944) uses similar techniques in his film scores.

Electronic music

Cage's use of aleatory, or chance, techniques (derived from the Chinese *I-Ching*, or *The Book of Changes*) has been independently adopted and developed to a limited extent by the Polish composer Witold Lutoslawski, and in a more intensely focused way by the Greek composer Iannis Xenakis, many of whose works use electronic tape. The use of electronic instruments, amplification and sampling has become widespread in "serious" music over the last 50 years. Composers who have

ABOVE: The American composer Philip Glass (born 1937) rehearsing with musicians in Los Angeles, March 1977.

ABOVE: Students using computers on the Electro-Acoustic Composition Course at Dartington, 1999.

made use of such techniques include the early Franco-American experimenter Edgard Varèse, the Italians Luciano Berio and Bruno Maderna, the British composer Jonathan Harvey, and the German Karlheinz Stockhausen, one of the leaders of the European avant-garde in the 1960s and '70s.

French music in the later 20th century was dominated by two composers. The idiosyncratic style of Olivier Messiaen was influenced by Eastern music, birdsong, the serial technique of Webern – which he refined still further – and his profound Catholic faith. His pupil Pierre Boulez, who founded the major European research centre into modern composing techniques, is a central figure in 20th–21st-century European music. Equally well-known as a conductor, he has helped to co-ordinate the work of composers from many different countries, as well as producing an important and highly original body of work rooted in the French tradition, but cross-fertilized by European avant-garde techniques.

Female composers

One encouraging feature of music in recent years has been the emergence of women composers, and the rediscovery, after centuries of neglect, of the music of talented women of the past, such as Fanny Mendelssohn (1805–47) and Amy Beach (1867–1944). Composers such as Judith Weir (born 1954), Sofia Gubaidulina (born 1931), Elena Firsova (born 1950) and Roxanna Panufnik (born 1968) are now beginning to challenge the traditional male hegemony in composition, as in many other fields, and are proving particularly adept in the developing fields of television and film music.

ABOVE: Kurt Masur conducting the New York Philharmonic in the Avery Fisher Hall, New York, 1998.

Dmitri Shostakovich

The music [Symphony No. 11] to me was self-evidently about Shostakovich's own experiences in the catastrophe of his life.

MICHAEL TIPPETT (1905–98)

Together with Stravinsky and Prokofiev, Shostakovich was one of the greatest Russian composers of the 20th century. His 15 symphonies and 15 string quartets are among the finest 20th-century works in those media.

Shostakovich began to learn the piano with his mother, a professional pianist. In 1919, aged only 13, he entered the St Petersburg Conservatory to study piano and composition: his teachers there included Glazunov. A phenomenally gifted student, his First Symphony (written as a diploma exercise) won international acclaim after its premières in Leningrad (1926), Berlin (under Bruno Walter), and Philadelphia (under Leopold Stokowski); a year later Shostakovich received an honourable mention as an entrant in the International Chopin Piano Competition.

During the 1920s Shostakovich – a firm adherent to Socialist ideals – concentrated on stage and film music. An opera, *Nos* (*The Nose*), and two ballets, *Zolotoy vek* (*The Golden Age*, 1927–30) and *Bolt* (1930–1), showed him developing a brittle, witty and satirical style which owed much to current European avant-garde influences, and for several years he was regarded as the "great white hope" of Soviet music.

ABOVE: Dmitri Shostakovich (1906–75), photographed at the Moscow Conservatory in the early 1960s.

Denunciation

Then came catastrophe. His opera *Lady Macbeth of the Mtsensk District*, a savage tale of adultery, murder and retribution, was produced in Moscow in 1934. At first it won critical acceptance both within Russia and abroad. But Stalin went to see it and was shocked by its graphic portrayal of sex and violence, and by its "advanced" musical idiom. On his orders, Shostakovich was savagely attacked in the press in 1936, in an article entitled "Chaos instead of Music".

Denounced also by his fellow composers, Shostakovich hurriedly withdrew the score of his Fourth Symphony, then in rehearsal, and responded with the more "accessible" Fifth Symphony (1937), which he described as "A Soviet artist's response to just criticism". For a while he

LEFT: Shostakovich composing at his Moscow flat.

RIGHT: A view of the Admiralty in St Petersburg, where Shostakovich was born and where he studied.

appeared to have been forgiven: the Fifth Symphony proved popular, his 1940 Piano Quintet received the Stalin Prize, and his Seventh Symphony, written during the German siege of Leningrad in 1941, became an international symbol of heroic resistance (even though its repetitive "invasion" theme was cruelly parodied by Bartók in his Concerto for Orchestra, written in America in 1943).

Shostakovich's next two symphonies were also inspired by the war: the Eighth (1943) by its savagery, and the Ninth (1945) in a spirit of rejoicing at its end. But in 1948 he was once again officially denounced (together with Prokofiev and others), accused of "formalist perversions" and "anti-democratic tendencies in music". Such denunciations, during the Stalinist purges of the late 1940s, were tantamount to a death sentence, and if Shostakovich's posthumously published *Memoirs* are to be believed, from then until Stalin's death in 1953 he lived in fear for his life. He kept his private artistic credo alive with intimate chamber works, while publicly he concentrated on "safe" works based on nationalistic themes.

Life and works

NATIONALITY: Russian

BORN: St Petersburg, 1906; **DIED:** Moscow, 1975

SPECIALIST GENRES: Symphonies, concertos, string quartets, operas.

MAJOR WORKS: 15 symphonies; concertos for piano, violin and cello; chamber music, including 15 string quartets; operas *The Nose* (1927–8) and *Lady Macbeth of the Mtsensk District* (1934).

ABOVE, FROM LEFT TO RIGHT: The great Russian cellist Mstislav Rostropovich (for whom Shostakovich wrote his cello concertos), Shostakovich, Rostropovich's wife – the soprano Galina Vishnevskaya – and the violinist David Oistrakh.

The post-Stalin era

After Stalin's death, Shostakovich returned to symphonic writing with the Tenth, Eleventh (*The Year 1905*) and Twelfth (*The Year 1917*) Symphonies. The late 1950s also produced the satirical musical comedy *Cheryomuschki* (*The Cherry Trees Estate*, 1958), a suite, *The Gadfly*, from his film score of 1955, the Second Piano Concerto (written in 1957 for his son Maxim, who became a well-known conductor), the First Cello Concerto (written in 1959 for Rostropovich), and the Seventh and Eighth String Quartets (1960).

In 1962 *Lady Macbeth* was restored to the Russian repertoire (under the new title *Katerina Ismailova*) and hailed as a masterpiece. Shostakovich then produced another controversial work, the Thirteenth Symphony (*Babi Yar*), based on poems by the Jewish writer Yevgeny Yevtushenko (born 1933). Its two successors, particularly the anguished Fourteenth Symphony of 1969 (settings of 11 poems by European writers), are preoccupied with death: the Fifteenth Symphony (1971), with its ironic references to other composers, seems to sum up Shostakovich's own career. The last decade of his life produced seven more string quartets, sonatas for violin and viola, and a further concerto each for violin and cello.

Towards the end of his life, Shostakovich was allowed to visit the West. He became a friend of Benjamin Britten, to whom the Fourteenth Symphony is dedicated. Like Britten, he died of heart failure in his 60s.

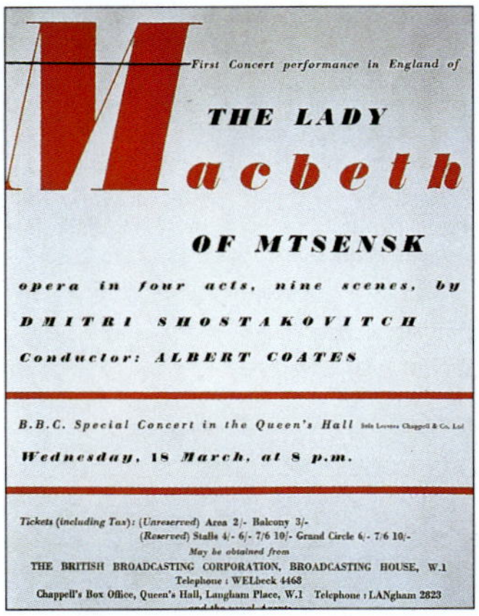

ABOVE: A programme for the first London concert performance of Shostakovich's opera Lady Macbeth of Mtsensk, *in 1935.*

Benjamin Britten

If wind and water could write music, it would sound like Ben's.

YEHUDI MENUHIN (1916–99)

Together with Michael Tippett, Britten dominated the British musical scene from the 1930s onwards. His roots lay in the music of Mozart and Verdi, and he never abandoned tonality, but he developed a distinctive style with wide appeal. Much of his music was inspired by specific performers, particularly the tenor voice of his lifelong companion, Peter Pears (1910–86).

Britten was born on St Cecilia's Day, 22 November 1913. He went to boarding school, but studied composition privately with Frank Bridge (1879–1941) in school holidays. In 1930 he entered the Royal College of Music in London, where he studied composition with John Ireland and honed his already formidable skills as a pianist. He wanted to continue his studies in Vienna with Alban Berg, having heard Berg's opera *Wozzeck* in 1934, but was discouraged by his parents and teachers.

ABOVE: Benjamin Britten, one of the major British composers of the 20th century.

ABOVE: Britten (left) with his lifelong companion Peter Pears in the garden of their house at Aldeburgh, Suffolk. This was one of the last photographs of Britten.

Early works

In 1935, by which time several early works including a Sinfonietta and an Oboe Quartet had already been performed, Britten began to work for the documentary film unit of the General Post Office, where he met the poet W. H. Auden. They shared left-wing political sympathies and collaborated on several works, including the orchestral song-cycle *Our Hunting Fathers* (1936) and the choral work *Ballad of Heroes* (1939). In that year Britten and Peter Pears followed Auden to the USA. By this time Britten's natural predilection for vocal music had already been confirmed with the Rimbaud song-cycle *Les illuminations* (1939), but the *Seven Sonnets of Michelangelo* of 1940 was the first of many works which Britten wrote expressly for Pears.

Instrumental works of the late 1930s and early '40s included the charming Rossini pastiche *Soirées musicales* (1936), the brilliant *Variations on a Theme of Frank Bridge* for strings (1937), concertos for piano (1938) and violin (1940), and the *Sinfonia da requiem* (1940). From then onwards, Britten wrote few specifically orchestral works. Exceptions were the *Young Person's Guide to the Orchestra* (1946) and the exquisite Serenade for tenor, horn and strings (1943, written

Life and works

NATIONALITY: English

BORN: Lowestoft, 1913; **DIED:** Aldeburgh, 1976

SPECIALIST GENRES: Opera and other stage works, vocal music.

MAJOR WORKS: Operas *Peter Grimes* (1944–5), *Billy Budd* (1951), *The Turn of the Screw* (1954), *A Midsummer Night's Dream* (1960) and *Death in Venice* (1973); *War Requiem* (1962); three "church parables"; chamber music and songs, including song-cycles and folk song arrangements.

for Pears and the horn player Dennis Brain), two of his most popular works; the Cello Symphony for Rostropovich (1963); and two "occasional" works written to celebrate the respective openings of the Snape Maltings concert hall and the Queen Elizabeth Hall in London.

Aldeburgh Festival

Britten decided to return home from America in 1942, having by chance read George Crabbe's 19th-century poem *The Borough*, an unflattering portrait of the Suffolk fishing village of Aldeburgh, which inspired his first major opera, *Peter Grimes*. Its première at Sadler's Wells on 7 June 1945 marked a milestone in British music, and in the history of opera. Britten and Pears settled first at Snape, a few miles inland, and then in Aldeburgh itself, where in 1947 they established the annual Aldeburgh Festival. Twenty years later, the festival's main venue moved from Aldeburgh's tiny Jubilee Hall to a converted malthouse at Snape.

Opera and choral works

Three original chamber operas followed *Peter Grimes*: *The Rape of Lucretia* (1946), the comedy *Albert Herring* (1947), both performed at Glyndebourne, and *The Little Sweep* (1949). In 1951, *Billy Budd* (based on Herman Melville's nautical tragedy) was performed at Covent Garden, followed two years later by Britten's one failure, *Gloriana* (intended to celebrate Elizabeth II's accession in 1953): later productions have led to its reassessment. *The Turn of the Screw*, based on Henry James's ghost story, was premièred in Venice, the city which inspired Britten's operatic swansong (and the most direct expression of his love for Pears), *Death in Venice*, based on Thomas Mann's novella. Many people

ABOVE: The Maltings at Snape, converted by Britten's efforts from an abandoned malthouse to a fine concert hall, the major venue for the Aldeburgh Festival.

consider his operatic masterpiece to be the Shakespearean *A Midsummer Night's Dream*.

During the 1960s Britten temporarily eschewed conventional operas in favour of three "church parables" written for performance in Orford Church in Suffolk: *Curlew River* (1964, inspired by Japanese Noh drama), *The Burning Fiery Furnace* (1966) and *The Prodigal Son* (1968). His next opera, *Owen Wingrave*, was written for television in 1970, though it subsequently transferred successfully to the stage. In 1962 his *War Requiem* was performed at the newly opened Coventry Cathedral, with an international cast of soloists, in a spirit of post-war reconciliation. The Requiem text is interwoven with the poetry of Wilfred Owen (1893–1918), and the work is a powerful expression of Britten's pacifism.

Besides composing, Britten was a fine conductor and pianist, and often toured in recital with Pears. In 1973 he had heart surgery, which curtailed his activities, and shortly before his death in 1976 he became the first British composer to be made a life peer.

ABOVE: A scene from the 1995 Covent Garden production of Peter Grimes*, with Bryn Terfel as Captain Balstrode, and Ben Heppner as the fisherman Grimes.*

Michael Tippett

I like to think of composing as a physical business. I compose at the piano and like to feel involved in my work with my hands.

TIPPETT

Like his younger contemporary Benjamin Britten, the English composer Michael Tippett grew up in Suffolk, and studied at the Royal College of Music in London. He left in 1928 and became a schoolteacher and part-time composer. His first mature works were the First String Quartet (1935), the First Piano Sonata (1936–7), and the Concerto for Double String Orchestra (1938–9), which belongs to the early 20th-century British tradition of works for string ensemble.

During the 1930s Tippett became involved in radical politics, organizing the "South London Orchestra of Unemployed Musicians". His passionate antipathy towards the horrors of war, initially aroused by the plight of European Jews, found expression in his deeply moving oratorio based on the true story of a Jewish boy who killed a Nazi diplomat, *A Child of Our Time* (1939–41), which articulates Tippett's lifelong belief in the opposing "dark" and "light" sides of human nature, present in everyone. The oratorio is influenced by Bach's Passions, with negro spirituals replacing Protestant chorales. Tippett was briefly imprisoned for his pacifist beliefs in 1943.

ABOVE: For the last two decades of Michael Tippett's life he was the undisputed "Grand Old Man" of British music.

ABOVE: Tippett composing at the piano in 1992. His sight failed in the last years of his life.

From 1940–51 Tippett was director of music at Morley College in South London. He subsequently became a full-time composer. His first opera, *The Midsummer Marriage*, was produced in 1952, and like each of its successors – *King Priam* (1961), *The Knot Garden* (1970), *The Ice Break* (1976), *New Year* (1989) – it spawned instrumental and vocal works, including an important series of five string quartets, four symphonies, four piano sonatas and the *Songs for Dov* (1969–70) for tenor and chamber orchestra.

In 1995, the year of his 90th birthday, a Tippett Festival at the Barbican in London included the première of his last major work, *The Rose Lake*, a "song without words for orchestra". His last work was "Caliban's Song", part of a *Tempest Suite* commissioned by the BBC to mark the tercentenary of Purcell's death. Renaissance and Baroque music had been a major influence on Tippett's earlier works, including the *Fantasia Concertante on a Theme of Corelli* for strings (1953).

Life and works

NATIONALITY: English

BORN: London, 1905; **DIED:** London, 1998

SPECIALIST GENRES: Opera, symphonies, string quartets.

MAJOR WORKS: Concerto for Double String Orchestra (1938–9); *A Child of Our Time* (1939–41); five operas, including *The Midsummer Marriage* (1952); Piano Concerto (1953–5); *The Vision of St Augustine* (1965); *The Mask of Time* (1980–2); four symphonies; five string quartets.

John Cage

It is better to make a piece of music than to perform one.

CAGE, "SILENCE" (1961)

The American composer John Cage was one of the most interesting experimental artists of his time. He studied with Henry Cowell (1897–1965, himself a noted pioneer of innovative techniques) and with Schoenberg, who called him "an inventor – of genius". From 1937 onwards he developed a strong interest in dance and percussion techniques, and in 1942 he moved from the West Coast to New York, where he began a long association with Merce Cunningham's dance company.

In 1938 he invented the "prepared piano" by inserting small domestic objects such as paperclips and rubber bands between the strings. This instrument, capable of producing extraordinary timbres, was used in Cage's early pieces such as *Sonatas and Interludes* (1946–8), and *Music for Marcel Duchamp* (1947). *The Wonderful Widow of Eighteen Springs* (1942) is a setting of a poem by James Joyce for voice and closed piano. A devotee of Zen Buddhism (before it became fashionable) and the *I-Ching*, Cage introduced aleatory (chance) techniques into his music, for instance in *Music of Changes* for piano (1951), in which the performance depends on the toss of a coin, and *Cheap Imitation* (1969), an alteration of Satie's *Socrate*, worked out using the *I-Ching*. With these works, he changed the nature of music by removing the necessity of intention from composition.

In 1952, with *Imaginary Landscape V*, Cage began to use electronic tape in his works. In the same year he "wrote" his notorious *4' 33"*, in which the performer sits at a silent piano and is required only to indicate the division of the work into three movements: the attention of the audience is directed to life (including the chance sounds of the environment) rather than art. Also from 1952 dates *Theater Piece* for Merce Cunningham, the first "musical happening", combining theatre, art and music. From then on Cage used a wide range of electronic media in his works, which are often scored for bizarre combinations. For example, *Imaginary Landscape IV* (1951) is for 12 radios and 24 players, *Speech* (1955) for five radios and newsreader, *HPSCHD* (1967–9) for seven harpsichord soloists and 51 tape machines, and *Postcard from Heaven* (1983) for between one and 20 harpsichords.

Cage was a musical philosopher. He believed that art was whatever the artist said it was: "I have nothing to say, I am saying it, and that is poetry." An avowed anarchist, he followed a strict macrobiotic diet, was a brilliant chess player and an expert on mushrooms.

ABOVE: Experimental composer John Cage, more a "musical philosopher" than a composer.

ABOVE: One of the "instruments" used in the performance by Ensemble Bash of The Art of Concealment *for percussion ensemble.*

Life and works

NATIONALITY: American

BORN: Los Angeles, 1912; **DIED:** New York, 1992

SPECIALIST GENRES: Experimental works for bizarre combinations.

MAJOR WORKS: Numerous works for percussion ensemble, prepared piano and various combinations of instruments and electronic media.

Leonard Bernstein

Any composer's writing is the sum of himself, of all his roots and influences.

BERNSTEIN, "THE JOY OF MUSIC" (1960)

Bernstein was one of the most flamboyant figures of 20th-century music. A talented pianist, composer of both "serious" works and extremely popular Broadway musicals and one of the finest conductors of his age, he excelled in every field he tackled (one of his fellow students remarked that he was "doomed to success").

He studied composition at Harvard University with Walter Piston (1894–1976), and conducting with Fritz Reiner (1888–1963) at the Curtis Institute in Philadelphia; in the early 1940s he attended summer schools at Tanglewood, Massachusetts, where he became Serge Koussevitzky's assistant. He was then invited to become assistant conductor of the New York Philharmonic Orchestra, and his big break came in November 1943, when he took over a concert at short notice from the indisposed Bruno Walter. This triumphant performance launched his career, helped by his striking good looks and charismatic personality.

From 1946 onwards Bernstein began to conduct opera, beginning with the US première of Britten's *Peter Grimes* at Tanglewood. In 1953 he became the first American to conduct at La Scala in Milan. He made his debut at the Metropolitan Opera House in 1964, and from 1958–69 he was principal conductor of the New York Philharmonic. He also guest-conducted many of the world's great orchestras.

Bernstein's parallel career as a composer began in 1944 with his ballet *Fancy Free* and his musical *On the Town*, which ran for 463 performances on Broadway. An adaptation of Voltaire's *Candide* (1954–6) had a disappointing reception and was later revised, but *West Side Story* (1957) made Bernstein's name. Written in collaboration with Stephen Sondheim (born 1930) and the choreographer Jerome Robbins (born 1918), this brilliant adaptation of the *Romeo and Juliet* story to a modern New York slum setting captured the spirit of the age.

The bisexual Bernstein was married to the Chilean actress Felicia Montealegre Cohn in 1951, and had three children.

ABOVE: Leonard Bernstein, photographed in the late 1960s.

LEFT: The ensemble song "America" from West Side Story*, as performed at the Prince Edward Theatre in London in 1998.*

Life and works

NATIONALITY: American

BORN: Lawrence, Massachusetts, 1918; **DIED:** New York, 1990

SPECIALIST GENRES: Populist stage works (ballets and musicals).

MAJOR WORKS: *On the Town* (1944); *Prelude, Fugue and Riffs* for clarinet and jazz ensemble (1949); *Candide* (1956); *West Side Story* (1957); *Chichester Psalms* (1965); *1600 Pennsylvania Avenue* (1976); three symphonies.

Elliott Carter

I am a radical, having a nature that leads me to perpetual revolt.

CARTER, C.1939

ABOVE: The American composer Elliott Carter (born 1908).

After Copland's death in 1990, Elliott Carter assumed the mantle of "Grand Old Man of American Music". But although he too studied with Nadia Boulanger in Paris in the early 1930s, his musical approach (apart from early works such as the First Symphony and the *Holiday Overture*) is very different from Copland's.

On returning to the USA after his Paris studies Carter became a musical director of Ballet Caravan (1936–40), and then began a long and distinguished teaching career in many major American universities and institutions. He has also spent long periods abroad, including fellowships of the American Academy in Rome, where he composed his Variations for Orchestra (1954–5). The Concerto for Orchestra and the Third String Quartet (1971) were also written in Italy.

Carter's output includes choral music, songs (including "Warble for Lilac Time", 1943, "A Mirror on Which to Dwell", 1975, and "In Sleep, In Thunder", 1981) and incidental music (including the 1937–9 ballet *Pocahontas*). But his most significant works are for orchestra or chamber groups, particularly the five string quartets, which are regarded as the most important since Bartók's. He is fascinated by the rhythmic and harmonic possibilities inherent in combining ensembles, as in the Symphony of Three Orchestras, the *Penthode* for five instrumental quartets (1984–5), and the Triple Duo (1982–3). The impact of experimental, radical influences on his underlying classical training has resulted in music of apparent complexity, underpinned by an inexorable musical logic of profound simplicity. The fusion of slow-moving formal structures with ebullient momentum gives Carter's work great dramatic power. His later works include an Oboe Concerto (1986–7) and Violin Concerto (1990), *Three Occasions* for orchestra (the third celebrated his own 50th wedding anniversary in 1989); and works for solo instruments, including *Changes* for guitar (1983), *Trilogy* (1992) for oboe and harp, and *Gra* (1993) for clarinet. A quintet for piano and wind, one of his finest later works, dates from 1992.

Life and works

NATIONALITY: American

BORN: New York, 1908

SPECIALIST GENRES: Complex polyrhythmic works.

MAJOR WORKS: Ballets *Pocahontas* (1937–9) and *The Minotaur* (1947); Piano Sonata (1946); Double Concerto for harpsichord and piano (1961); Concerto for Orchestra (1969); Symphony of Three Orchestras (1976–7); five string quartets.

RIGHT: Carter rehearsing his Triple Duo at the Royal Academy of Music in London.

Witold Lutoslawski

Dissonances are only the more remote consonances.

ARNOLD SCHOENBERG (1874–1951)

Lutoslawski was the major Polish composer of the 20th century. He began to compose at the age of nine, and also studied piano and violin. In 1932 he entered the Warsaw Conservatory, and two years later his Piano Sonata was broadcast on Polish Radio. His Symphonic Variations were performed at the 1939 Krakow Festival.

The war disrupted Lutoslawski's promising career. He was taken prisoner, but escaped and eked out a precarious living playing the piano in Warsaw cafés. Many of his manuscripts disappeared during the wartime devastation: one exception was the *Variations on a Theme of Paganini* for two pianos, which Lutoslawski adapted in 1978 for piano and orchestra. In post-war communist Poland he wrote music for radio, film and television, and folk-based music for children. His First Symphony (1949) was denounced as formalist, and banned for a decade, but his Little Suite for orchestra (1950) and the Concerto for Orchestra (1950–4) – a worthy successor to Bartók's – found acceptance.

In the post-Stalinist thaw, Lutoslawski began to enlarge his harmonic language, exploring different ways of using the notes of the scale. *Funeral Music* (1958), dedicated to Bartók, established his international reputation, and his works of the 1960s, such as *Jeux vénitiens* (*Venetian Games*, 1961), *Trois poèmes d'Henri Michaux* (1963) and the 1964 String Quartet began to experiment with chance elements. His most important works of the late 1970s include *Paroles tissées* (*Woven Words*, 1965, written for Peter Pears), the Second Symphony (1967), *Livre pour orchestre* (1968), the Cello Concerto (1970, for Rostropovich), Preludes and Fugue for 13 solo strings, *Les espaces du sommeil* (*Sleep's Spaces*, 1975) for baritone and orchestra, and *Mi-parti* (1976).

Many works were commissioned by major artists and ensembles, including the Third Symphony by the Chicago Symphony Orchestra, *Chain I* by the London Sinfonietta, *Chain II* by the violinist Anne-Sophie Mutter (born 1963), and *Chain III* for the San Francisco Symphony Orchestra.

Lutoslawski's last major works included a Piano Concerto (1988), *Interludium* for chamber orchestra (1989) and *Chantefables et chantefleurs* (1990) for soprano and orchestra.

ABOVE: Witold Lutoslawski, the most important Polish composer of his generation.

LEFT: Lutoslawski rehearsing at the Royal Academy of Music in London in 1980.

Life and works

NATIONALITY: Polish

BORN: Warsaw, 1913; **DIED:** Warsaw, 1994

SPECIALIST GENRES: Orchestral works.

MAJOR WORKS: Concerto for Orchestra (1954); *Funeral Music* (1958); Cello Concerto (1970); four symphonies; Piano Concerto (1988).

György Ligeti

It is precisely a dread of deep significance and ideology that makes any kind of engaged art out of the question for me.

LIGETI

One of Hungary's most important composers, Ligeti was born in Transylvania of Hungarian Jewish parents, and studied privately during the war in Budapest. After the war he went to the Budapest Academy of Music, where from 1950–6 he was a professor. He left Hungary in 1956, the year of the Soviet invasion, and took up residence in Vienna. He was invited to work at the West German Radio electronic studios in Cologne, and caused a sensation at the 1960 International Society for Contemporary Music Festival with *Apparitions* (1958–9). From 1959 onwards he taught annually on the summer courses for new music at Darmstadt. Ten years later he moved to West Berlin, and from 1973–89 he was professor of composition at the Hamburg Musikhochschule.

ABOVE: The Hungarian composer György Ligeti (born 1923), photographed in 1993.

Ligeti's early works were influenced by folk song and the music of Bartók. After a few experiments with electronic media in the late 1950s, he began to find an individual style in works such as *Apparitions* and *Atmosphères* for orchestra (1961), *Volumina* for organ (1961–2), and with the two works for solo voices and instruments called *Aventures* and *Nouvelles aventures* (1962–5). His works of the 1960s included a Requiem (1963–5), a Cello Concerto (1966), *Lux aeterna* for 16 solo voices (1966), the orchestral work *Lontano* (1967) and a chamber concerto for 13 instruments (1969–70). Some of his music was used – without his permission – in the score of Stanley Kubrick's 1968 film *2001: A Space Odyssey*.

Since the 1960s, Ligeti's most significant works have been *Clocks and Clouds* for 12-voice women's chorus and orchestra, *Melodien* (1971) and *San Francisco Polyphony* (1973–4), both for orchestra, a Double Concerto for flute and oboe (1972), a Piano Concerto (1985–8), a Violin Concerto (1992), a Horn Trio, subtitled "Homage to Brahms" (1982), a set of piano Etudes (1985), and the opera *Le grand macabre*. His individual style, which the composer describes as "micropolyphony", is derived from Webern.

ABOVE: "The Horse of the Apocalypse" being prepared in rehearsal for a performance of Ligeti's opera Le grand macabre *at the 1997 Salzburg Festival.*

Life and works

NATIONALITY: Hungarian

BORN: Kolozsvár (now Cluj in Romania), 1923

SPECIALIST GENRES: Orchestral and chamber music.

MAJOR WORKS: *Atmosphères* (1961); *Aventures* (1962); *Le grand macabre* (1972–6); *Clocks and Clouds* (1972).

Olivier Messiaen

Fantastic music of the stars.

KARLHEINZ STOCKHAUSEN (BORN 1928)

One of the most idiosyncratic composers of the 20th century, Messiaen was the son of an English teacher and a poet. He began to compose at the age of seven and, after discovering the music of Debussy, he decided at an early age to become a composer. He studied at the Paris Conservatoire from the age of 11, winning four first prizes in piano, history of music and composition, and during his last years there he wrote his Preludes for piano in the style of Debussy.

After graduating, Messiaen became organist at La Trinité in Paris, where he stayed for over 40 years. He also taught at the Ecole Normale de Musique, the Schola Cantorum, and the Paris Conservatoire (where he became professor of composition in 1966). He was a profoundly influential teacher: his pupils included Boulez, Stockhausen, Xenakis and Alexander Goehr (born 1932, who later taught at Cambridge University).

ABOVE: The French composer Olivier Messiaen, photographed in 1937.

ABOVE: Messiaen with the score of his Turangalîla-Symphonie *at the Oxford Festival in June 1967.*

Religious inspiration

Many of Messiaen's compositions celebrate love, both human and divine. The influence of his Catholic faith is omnipresent in his works, many of which take the form of religious "meditations", "homages" or acts of praise. Far from shying away from explicitly religious titles, as other composers in this predominantly secular age have done, Messiaen made his intention clear, in orchestral pieces such as *Les offrandes oubliées* (*Forgotten offerings*, 1930), *Hymne au Saint Sacrement* (1932), *Et exspecto resurrectionem mortuorum* (*And I Await the Resurrection of the Dead*, 1964) and *Eclairs sur l'au-delà* (*Illuminations of the Beyond*, 1988–92). His early *Quatuor pour la fin du temps* (*Quartet for the End of Time*) for clarinet, violin, cello and piano was written and first performed in a Silesian prison camp where Messiaen was interned by the Germans for two years during World War II. Vocal works on religious themes include the early Mass (1933), *Trois petites liturgies de la présence divine* (1944) and *La transfiguration de Notre Seigneur Jésus-Christ* (1965–9).

Messiaen's keyboard works have also been inspired by his faith, including *Vingt regards sur l'enfant Jésus-Christ* (1944) for piano; and a series of fine organ works including *L'ascension* (1934), *La nativité du Seigneur* (1935), *Méditation sur le mystère de la Sainte Trinité* (1969) and the *Livre du Saint Sacrement* (1984). His only opera, completed in 1983, was based on the life of St Francis of Assisi.

Other influences

While profoundly religious, Messiaen was equally alive to the force of human passion. *Poèmes pour Mi* (1936), for soprano and piano or orchestra, was written in celebration of his marriage to the violinist Claire Delbos. *Harawi* –

Life and works

Nationality: French

Born: Avignon, 1908; **died:** Paris, 1992

Specialist genres: Orchestral, piano and organ music.

Major works: *Quatuor pour la fin du temps* (1940); *Visions de l'amen* (1943); *Trois petites liturgies de la présence divine* (1943–4); *Harawi* (1945); *Turangalîla-Symphonie* (1946–8); *La transfiguration de Notre Seigneur Jésus-Christ* (1965–9); *Saint François d'Assise* (1983).

ABOVE: Messiaen rehearsing with students at the Royal Academy of Music in London, 1987.

songs of love and death with elements taken from Peruvian folk music – for soprano and piano, *Cinq rechants* (*Five Refrains*) for 12 solo voices, and the massive orchestral *Turangalîla-Symphonie* form a trilogy of works with a powerful erotic charge.

Another major influence was that of birdsong. Messiaen was an expert ornithologist and made a systematic, classified study of all French birds, recording and notating their songs. Their characteristic rhythmic and melodic patterns were transmuted into his own music in specific works such as *Réveil des oiseaux* (*Dawn Chorus*, 1953) and *Oiseaux exotiques* (1955–6) for orchestra, *Catalogue d'oiseaux* (1956–8) and *Petites esquisses d'oiseaux* (*Little Bird Sketches*, 1985) for piano, and *Le merle noir* (*The Blackbird*, 1951) for flute and piano. Elements of birdsong are found in most of his works.

Messiaen's music

Messiaen's musical language is immensely complex. He set out its principles in his book, *Technique de mon langage musical* (1944), which analyses the derivations of its rhythmic structures from Hindu and ancient Greek rhythms. His orchestral works are characterized by luscious harmonies and a vast range of timbres, some derived from exotic percussion instruments including the *ondes Martenot*, an electronic instrument played by Messiaen's second wife, the virtuoso pianist Yvonne Loriod. His fascination with colour and timbre is explored in many works, including *Chronochromie* (*Time-colour*) for orchestra (1960), *Couleurs de la cité céleste* (*Colours of the Celestial City*, 1963), and many of his organ works. His last orchestral work (1989) was entitled *Un sourire* (*A Smile*).

ABOVE: Much of Messiaen's music was influenced by birdsong.

Pierre Boulez

Music should be a collective magic and hysteria.

BOULEZ

Messiaen's most talented pupil was Pierre Boulez, who studied with him at the Paris Conservatoire after moving to Paris in 1942 from his native Montbrison in the Loire region. Boulez was originally destined for a career in engineering, but instead applied his exceptional mathematical brain to musical analysis and composition.

Twelve-note technique, which Boulez studied in the late 1940s with Schoenberg's pupil René Leibowitz (1913–72), influenced his own early works, the Sonatina for flute and piano (1946), the First Piano Sonata (1946), and *Le visage nuptial* (*The Nuptial Countenance*, 1946–7) for chamber ensemble, including two *ondes Martenot*. In 1948 his talent was recognized with the Beethovenian Second Piano Sonata and the cantata *Le soleil des eaux* (*The Sun of the Waters*), based on poems by René Char. The same year he began working on the "multiple choice" collection *Livre pour quatuor* for string quartet, to which he attempted to apply a technique of "total serialization". His most successful essay in this genre was *Structures I* (1952) for two pianos, but he quickly realized its limitations, and during the 1950s abandoned it in favour of freer techniques. He came to international attention in 1954 with *Le marteau sans maître* (*The Hammer without a Master*), settings of René Char poems for contralto and ensemble.

ABOVE: Pierre Boulez (born 1925), photographed in 1999.

ABOVE: Boulez conducting Stravinsky's The Rite of Spring *in 1963. Boulez never uses a baton to conduct.*

During the late 1950s and '60s Boulez taught at Darmstadt (an important centre of new music), Basle and Harvard. He also established a parallel career as a conductor. He was musical director of the BBC Symphony Orchestra (1971–5) and also of the New York Philharmonic (1971–8), and was a sought-after guest conductor (he conducted Wagner's *Ring* cycle at Bayreuth in 1976, and the first production of Berg's *Lulu* in Paris). From 1977–92 he was the founder-director of the Institut de Recherche et de Coordination Acoustique/Musique (IRCAM) in Paris, which provides computers and digital facilities for composition.

His most important later compositions – many of which are still being revised – include the Third Piano Sonata (1957), *Pli selon pli* (*Fold upon Fold*) for orchestra, *Eclat/Multiples* for ensemble, *Rituel in memoriam Bruno Maderna* (1974–5), two works called *Dérive* for small ensemble, *Domaines*, for clarinet and 22 instruments (1961–8); *...explosante-fixe...* (1971–89), and *Répons*, for ensemble including computers and live electronics.

Life and works

NATIONALITY: French

BORN: Montbrison, 1925

SPECIALIST GENRES: Music for various instrumental and vocal ensembles, piano works.

MAJOR WORKS: *Structures I* and *II* (1952–61); *Le marteau sans maître* (1954); *Pli selon pli* (1957–90); *Répons* (1981); three piano sonatas.

Karlheinz Stockhausen

In Stockhausen's good period I came to trust his music more than anything else.

PIERRE BOULEZ (BORN 1925)

When electronic music seemed to represent the future in the 1960s and '70s, Stockhausen was at its cutting edge. He studied at the Cologne Musikhochschule after the war, and then went to Cologne University, where his analytical skills impressed everyone. In 1951 he met Messiaen at the Darmstadt summer school, and went to Paris to study with him; at the same time he made his first experiments with *musique concrète* in the electronic music studios of French radio.

In 1953 Stockhausen went back to Cologne, where he worked in the electronic music studio of West German Radio (he became its director ten years later), and also studied acoustics at Bonn University. By the late 1950s he was himself a sought-after teacher: he has taught at Darmstadt, at various American universities, and at the Cologne Musikhochschule, where he has been a professor of composition since 1971.

Like many later 20th-century composers, Stockhausen's starting point was the music of Webern. In his own works he attempted a process of total serialization, of pitch, intensity, duration, timbre, and spatial position. He divided his compositions into "groups" or "moments" (as in *Momente*, 1961–4, for soprano, four chamber groups, and 13 instruments), and then experimented with varying the order of "groups" in performance (as in *Zyklus*, 1959, for percussion, and some of his *Klavierstücke* (*Piano Pieces*).

Since the 1970s Stockhausen has been working on a huge opera cycle called *Licht* (*Light*), one opera for each day of the week, which has spawned a series of related instrumental compositions.

ABOVE: Karlheinz Stockhausen (born 1928), one of the most influential German composers of the 20th century.

Life and works

NATIONALITY: German

BORN: Cologne, 1928

SPECIALIST GENRES: Serial and electronic music.

MAJOR WORKS: *Kontra-Punkte* (*Counter-points*, 1952–3); *Gruppen* (*Groups*) for three orchestras (1955–7); *Gesang der Jünglinge* (*Song of the Youths*, 1955–6); *Kontakte* (*Contacts*, 1959–60); *Stimmung* (*Mood*, 1968); *Ylem* (1972); *Aus dem sieben Tagen* (*From the Seven Days*, 1968).

ABOVE: Stockhausen in the recording studio. Many of his compositions use electronic media.

Iannis Xenakis

Mathematics is music for the mind; music is mathematics for the soul.

ANONYMOUS

Iannis Xenakis was born in Romania, but his parents moved back to their native Greece when he was ten. He began studying music from the age of 12, but was trained as an engineer. During the war Xenakis fought in the Greek Resistance, losing an eye and narrowly escaping death. In 1947 he went to Paris, where he studied with Arthur Honegger and Darius Milhaud, and then with Messiaen in the early 1950s.

Between 1947 and 1960 he worked with the French avant-garde architect Le Corbusier (1887–1965), designing the much-admired Philips Pavilion for the 1958 Brussels Exhibition, in which Varèse's specially commissioned *Poème électronique* was played. Xenakis subsequently began to make his name as a composer, and thereafter concentrated on music. He has taught at Indiana University in the USA and also in Paris, where he was professor of music at the Sorbonne from 1972–89.

Xenakis's strong interest in mathematics led him to introduce mathematical concepts and theories into his compositions, some of which are scored for traditional instruments, others for electronic media. He applied the term "stochastic" to music, relating to the theory of probability, which assumes that a chance sequence of events can reach a predetermined conclusion. In his own works (many of which have Greek titles), the elements of chance are not left to the performer (as in works by Cage or Lutoslawski), but are controlled by the composer, normally by using a computer. Some of his earlier pieces, such as *Nomos gamma* (1967–8) place an orchestra among the audience. His later pieces vary in size from *Okho* (1989) for three players, to *Dox-Orkh* and *Troorkh* (both 1991), respectively for violin and trombone with 89 other players.

ABOVE: The works of Iannis Xenakis (born 1922) are based on mathematical concepts and theories.

LEFT: Xenakis with one of his scores. He lost his sight in one eye while fighting in the Greek Resistance in 1947.

Life and works

NATIONALITY: Greek

BORN: Braïla, Romania, 1922

SPECIALIST GENRES: Compositions based on mathematical concepts and probability.

MAJOR WORKS: *Metastasis* (1953–4); *Oresteia* (1965–6); *Terretektorh* (1965–6); *Persephassa* (1969).

Luciano Berio

Abstract it may be, the human voice...

THOMAS MANN (1875–1955), "DR FAUSTUS"

Together with Bruno Maderna (1920–73), with whom he founded the Studio di Fonologia Musicale at Radiotelevisione Italiana in Milan in 1955, Luciano Berio is one of the most important Italian composers of his generation. He studied at the Milan Conservatory, and has been equally active as both teacher and composer. He has taught composition at Tanglewood, Mills College, California, Harvard University and the Juilliard School in the USA, at Dartington in Britain and at Darmstadt and Cologne in Germany. In the late 1970s he also worked with Boulez at IRCAM in Paris.

Berio's compositions reflect his fascination with the human voice, intensified by his marriage (1950–66) to the American singer/actress Cathy Berberian (1925–83). He draws inspiration from the juxtaposition of different musical processes, from Baroque vocal styles to modern techniques of serialism, indeterminacy and the use of electronics and computer technology. His idiomatic use of collage technique is demonstrated in his most popular work, *Sinfonia* for eight voices and orchestra, which quotes from a wide range of sources, including works by Mahler, Wagner, Ravel and Richard Strauss. He has also reworked music by Brahms and Schubert, most recently in *Rendering* (1989), attributed to "Schubert/Berio". Several of his pieces written for Cathy Berberian also use collage technique, in particular *Recital I (for Cathy)*, for mezzo-soprano and 17 instruments (1972).

Among Berio's best-known works are the *Quattro canzoni popolari* for voice and piano (1946–7); *Circles*, based on poems by e. e. cummings, for female voice, harp and percussion; *O King* (a homage to Martin Luther King), for mezzo and five players (1967); the series of solo works called *Sequenze I–XI* (*No. III*, for voice, was written for Berberian); and a related series called *Chemins* (*Paths*) for solo instrument(s) and ensemble or orchestra. He has written several theatre works, some in collaboration with distinguished writers such as Italo Calvino and Umberto Eco.

ABOVE: *Luciano Berio (born 1925), the major Italian composer of his generation.*

Life and works

NATIONALITY: Italian

BORN: Oneglia, 1925

SPECIALIST GENRES: Works for both conventional and electronic media.

MAJOR WORKS: *Epifanie* (1959–61); *Circles* (1960); *Sinfonia* (1968–9); *Coro* (1975–6); *Un re in ascolto* (*King in Waiting*, 1979–83); 11 *Sequenze* (1958–75); four *Chemins* (*Paths*, 1965–75).

ABOVE: *Berio rehearsing the BBC Symphony Orchestra in their Maida Vale recording studio in London, February 2000.*

Hans Werner Henze

My profession…consists of bringing truths nearer to the point where they explode.

HENZE, "MUSIC AND POLITICS" (1982)

Henze was the eldest of six children of a schoolmaster, who discouraged him from taking up music. He began composing at 12, but received no formal musical training until after the war (during which he had been attached to a unit making Nazi propaganda films). In 1946 he began to study harmony and counterpoint with Wolfgang Fortner (born 1907), and serial techniques with René Leibowitz. In 1953, after finishing his first opera, *Boulevard Solitude*, he settled in Italy.

During the 1960s Henze's music became associated with radical, left-wing politics. He shot to international fame in 1966 when his opera *The Bassarids*, with a libretto by W. H. Auden and Chester Kallman, was produced at the Salzburg Festival, and his 1968 oratorio *Das Floss der "Medusa"* (*The Raft of the "Medusa"*) – one of his best-known works – was written as a requiem for the guerrilla leader Che Guevara.

ABOVE: Hans Werner Henze (born 1926), considered the major German opera composer of his generation.

ABOVE: Hans Werner Henze at work in 1996.

Henze also began to work with young musicians, and in 1976 founded the Montepulciano Cantiere in Umbria for communal international music-making. Since 1980 he has taught composition at the Cologne Academy and at the Royal Academy of Music in London, and in 1988 he founded the Munich International Festival of New Music Theatre. He combines composing with conducting, and has been a guest conductor of the Berlin Philharmonic Orchestra.

During the 1970s and '80s Henze collaborated with the British playwright Edward Bond on works such as the "action for music" *We Come to the River*, the ballet *Orpheus* (1979) and the opera *The English Cat* (1980–2). His highly coloured, richly orchestrated works include several operas, of which the early works *Der Prinz vom Homburg* (1958), *Elegy for Young Lovers* (1959–61) and *Der junge Lord* (*The Young Lord*, 1964) are perhaps the best known: the latest is *Venus and Adonis* (1993–5) for singers and dancers. A prolific composer for both instruments and voices, he has also written nine symphonies, two violin concertos, two piano concertos and other concertante works, five string quartets, several ballets, and a great deal of vocal music.

Life and works

NATIONALITY: German

BORN: Gütersloh, Westphalia, 1926

SPECIALIST GENRES: Opera and theatre music.

MAJOR WORKS:
Boulevard Solitude (1951); *König Hirsch* (*King Stag*, 1956); *The Bassarids* (1966); *Das Floss der "Medusa"* (1968); *We Come to the River* (1976).

Other Composers of the Era

It is fortunate that to assert itself in music, a new generation does not need to destroy the works of its ancestors.

ERNST KŘENEK (1900–91), "HORIZONS CIRCLED" (1974)

Although the demand for contemporary music is relatively limited compared with that of earlier periods, many talented composers have achieved widespread popularity over the last 50 years.

America

In the USA, a group of so-called "minimalists" came to attention in the 1970s and '80s. Among them is Steve Reich (born 1936), who founded his own ensemble in 1966. He was much influenced by African and Asian drumming techniques, and all his works, which range from vocal and orchestral pieces such as *The Desert Music* (1982–4) for 27 amplified voices and orchestra, to the famous *Clapping Music* for two performers (1972), and *Different Trains* for string quartet and tape (1988), deal with *ostinato* patterns subtly altered by variations in time. Similar repetitive techniques govern the work of Terry Riley (born 1935), whose most famous piece is *In C* (1964).

Two other minimalists, Philip Glass (born 1937) and John Adams (born 1946) have developed the technique on a larger scale, including opera. Glass worked with Ravi Shankar (born 1920), and his style was influenced by Indian music. Of his many stage works, *Einstein on the Beach* (1974–5), *Akhnaten* (1980–3) and *The Making of the Representative for Planet 8* (1988) are the best known; while his orchestral works include *Glassworks* (1981) for chamber orchestra, and a Third Symphony (1994). Adams's style is more eclectic, and he has a substantial international following. The subject-matter of both his operas, *Nixon in China* (1984–7) and *The Death of Klinghoffer* (1990–1), had contemporary resonance; while his *Grand Pianola Music* (1981–2) for two sopranos, two pianos and small orchestra, *The Wound Dresser* (1988–9) for baritone and orchestra, and his 1993 Violin Concerto have become widely known.

ABOVE: The American composer Steve Reich (born 1936) introduced the "phasing" technique, whereby instruments play the same patterns at slightly different speeds.

ABOVE: Philip Glass (born 1937), another American minimalist, has been influenced by Indian music.

ABOVE: John Adams (born 1946) successfully applied minimalist techniques to opera, including Nixon in China *(1984–7).*

ABOVE: The Hungarian composer György Kurtág (born 1926) is a highly regarded teacher. His pupils have included the young British composer Thomas Adès.

Central Europe and Russia

The (Romanian-born) Hungarian composer György Kurtág (born 1926), reared in the Bartók-Kodály tradition, has achieved international acclaim for his subtly crafted orchestral and chamber music, often making use of voices and cimbalom. Among his best-known works are *Messages of the Late Miss R.V. Troussova* (1976–80) for soprano and chamber ensemble, *...quasi una fantasia...* for piano and instruments (1987–8), *The Sayings of Péter Bornemisza* (1963–8) for soprano and piano, *Hommage à R. Sch.* for clarinet, viola and piano (1990), and the four books of *Games* for piano (1973–6).

The Polish composer Henryk Górecki (born 1933) draws his inspiration from a wide variety of sources: medieval Polish music, Renaissance polyphony, Webernian serialism, and Romantic orchestration. His serenely meditative Third Symphony (*Symphony of Sorrowful Songs*, 1976) was one of the few "classical" pieces to reach the charts.

A similar serenity pervades the sacred choral music of the Estonian composer Arvo Pärt (born 1935), who settled in West Berlin in 1980. His techniques embrace serialism and minimalism, but within an accessible idiom. His works include a St John Passion (1982), and the popular *Cantus in Memory of Benjamin Britten* for strings and bell (1977).

In the former USSR, Alfred Schnittke (born 1934) is held in high regard. His early works were influenced by serialism, and by the avant-garde techniques of Stockhausen and Ligeti, but he has produced a substantial body of work in traditional genres, including symphonies, *concerti grossi*, sonatas, trios and quartets. Together with Schnittke, Sofia Gubaidulina (born 1931) is the most important Russian composer of the present day. Born in Tatar, her work has been influenced by the exotic timbres of Caucasian folk music, and by a sensitive response to words.

ABOVE: The recording of Polish composer Henryk Górecki's Third Symphony (1977) was a surprise "hit".

ABOVE: The Russian composer Sofia Gubaidulina (born 1931). Her work is influenced by Caucasian folk music.

Britain

The doyens of British music at the turn of the 21st century are Harrison Birtwistle and Peter Maxwell Davies (both born 1934), original members of the "Manchester School". Both have won wide acclaim, especially for their operas. Birtwistle has assumed the mantle of Britten and Tippett with an original series of theatre works, many inspired by myth. They include *Punch and Judy* (1966–7), *The Mask of Orpheus* (1973–84), *Gawain* (1987–94), *The Second Mrs Kong* (1993–4) and *The Last Supper* (2000), augmented by fine orchestral works including *The Triumph of Time* (1972), *Earth Dances* (1985–6) and *Endless Parade* for solo trumpet and strings (1986–7), written for the Swedish virtuoso Håkan Hardenberger (born 1961).

ABOVE: The doyen of contemporary British music – Harrison Birtwistle (born 1934), photographed in Los Angeles in 1994.

In the 1960s Maxwell Davies founded the contemporary music ensemble The Fires of London (originally The Pierrot Players), for which he wrote theatre pieces such as *Eight Songs for a Mad King* (1969), and vocal and instrumental works such as *Revelation and Fall* for soprano and instruments (1966). The landscape and culture of the Orkney Islands, where he has lived since the 1970s, have inspired many of his later works, including the operas *The Martyrdom of St Magnus* (1976–7), *The Lighthouse* (1979), and a series of *Strathclyde Concertos* for members of the Scottish Chamber Orchestra. He has written a great deal of music for children.

Many of Maxwell Davies' works spring from a religious impulse, as do all the later works of John Tavener (born 1944). Tavener derives his serene, meditative style from his Greek Orthodox faith, and has achieved fame with works such as *Ultimos ritos* (1972), *Resurrection* (1989), *Hymns of Paradise* (1992–3) and particularly *The Protecting Veil* for cello and strings (1987). He first attracted attention in the mid 1960s with his "crossover" cantata *The Whale*.

Several younger British composers promise exciting new developments in the 21st century. Among them are George Benjamin (born 1960), whose *Ringed by the Flat Horizon* (1979–80), *At First Light* (1982), and *A Mind of Winter* (1981) receive international performances. The Scottish composer James Macmillan (born 1959) came to prominence in 1990 with the orchestral work *The Confessions of Isobel Gowdie*, and has since produced an impressive body of work, largely inspired by his Catholicism.

ABOVE: Peter Maxwell Davies (born 1934). Like Birtwistle, he was a member of the "Manchester School".

Mark-Anthony Turnage (born 1960) draws inspiration from many sources including rock and jazz. His operas *Greek* (1986–8), *The Country of the Blind* (1997) and *The Silver Tassie* (2000) have received wide acclaim. Finally, Thomas Adès (born 1971), an extraordinarily talented prodigy, has won international awards for his fluent and characterful orchestral and chamber music. His first opera, *Powder Her Face* (1994–5), is being performed all over the world.

ABOVE: The British composer John Tavener (born 1944). His works are strongly influenced by the Greek Orthodox tradition.

ABOVE: Mark-Anthony Turnage (born 1960), one of the rising stars of the younger generation of British composers.

ABOVE: The extraordinarily gifted young British composer Thomas Adès (born 1971) has won international acclaim.

Glossary

Aleatoric music: music in which random or chance elements are allowed to determine the course of the piece.
Antiphonal singing: when two parts of a choir sing alternately.
Aria: an operatic solo.
Ars antiqua: (old art) style of medieval music based on plainsong and organum.
Ars nova: (new art) musical style of 14th-century France and Italy, less restrictive than *ars antiqua*, introducing new rhythms and more independent parts.
Atonal: not in any key.
Basso continuo: ("figured bass") an accompanying bass line for a keyboard instrument, with figures to indicate chords on which the player improvises.
Bel canto: (beautiful singing) Italian style of operatic singing, emphasizing beauty and evenness of tone and smooth phrasing.
Canon: a composition in which a melody begun in one part is repeated in another part, or parts, before the first has finished.
Cantata: an extended choral work (sometimes with solo parts), usually with orchestral accompaniment.
Cantus firmus: a melody borrowed from a religious or secular source, such as a folk song, as the basis for counterpoint from the 14th–17th centuries.
Chromatic scale: a scale ascending or descending by semitones.
Clef: the sign that fixes the position of a particular note on the staff.
Coda: concluding section of a movement or composition.
Concerto: a work for solo instrument(s) and orchestra, usually in three movements.
Concerto grosso: instrumental form contrasting a small group of instruments with a larger orchestral group.
Consort: a group of instruments, such as viols.
Counterpoint: the weaving together of two or more melodic lines to make musical sense, resulting in polyphony.
Development: in sonata form, the section of a movement following the initial statement of the themes, in which they are expanded or modified.
Exposition: the first part of sonata form, in which the main themes are stated.
Fugue: contrapuntal work in three or more parts of equal importance, which enter successively in imitation of each other.
Gradual: elaborate plainsong response to passages sung by the priest in a Mass.
Grand opera: 19th-century opera which is all sung, with no spoken dialogue.
Ground bass: a short bass theme persistently repeated.
Harmony: the simultaneous sounding of notes.
Homophony: music in which the parts move together, presenting a top melody with chords beneath.
Isorhythmic: Of motets, having a tenor line in which the rhythm, though not the pitch, is repeated many times.
Kapellmeister: the musical director of a private chapel, or of the musical staff at a German court.
Key: the classification of the notes of a scale, determined by the key-note.

Leitmotif: (leading motif) a short theme used repeatedly in a score – especially by Wagner – to denote an object, person or idea.
Libretto: the text of an opera or oratorio.
Madrigal: a contrapuntal setting in several parts of a secular verse.
Maestro di cappella: the musical director of a church, chapel or court in Italy.
Minimalism: term applied to works based on the repetition of very short figures.
Minuet: French rustic dance in triple time adapted to court use in the 17th century, and to symphonic use in the 18th century.
Mode: name for each of the ways of ordering the notes of a scale.
Monody: music on one line, without counterpoint or accompanying harmonies.
Motet: Ecclesiastical vocal musical form based on a given melody with other parts in counterpoint.
Motif, motive: a recognizable short group of notes in a work.
Motto theme: a theme that recurs during a piece of music, similar to a *Leitmotif*.
Musique concrète: music created on disc or tape by electronically modifying natural sounds.
Neume: a sign in medieval notation showing the pitch of a syllable of vocal music.
Nocturne: a short lyrical piece, usually for piano, in one movement.
Obbligato: a term used of an instrument having a compulsory or special role.
Opera buffa: comic opera.
Opera seria: serious and formal Italian opera, with heroic or mythological plot.
Oratorio: an extended musical setting of a religious text in semi-dramatic form.
Ostinato: a persistently repeated musical phrase or rhythm.
Overture: (1) a piece of orchestral music preceding an opera or play; (2) an orchestral work in one movement, usually with a title alluding to a literary or pictorial source.
Parody mass: a type of Mass common in the 16th century, based on a melody taken from another work.
Partita: an 18th-century term for a suite.
Plainsong: medieval church music consisting of a single line of unaccompanied music sung in "free" rhythm.
Polyphony: the simultaneous sounding of different notes, generally in counterpoint.
Polytonality: the simultaneous use of more than one key.
Prelude: a musical introduction, or a short self-contained piece.
Programme music: a piece of music interpreting a picture or story.
Recapitulation: in sonata form, the section of a movement which repeats the original themes after the development.
Recitative: speech-like singing in opera used for dialogue or to precede an aria.
Ricercare: contrapuntal instrumental work of 16th–18th centuries, often for keyboard.
Rondeau: a type of medieval French song with a refrain.
Scherzo: (a joke) a lively movement in a symphony developed by Beethoven to replace the minuet and trio.

Serialism: technique whereby a structural "series" of notes governs the total development of the composition. It led to the 12-note system of composition.
Sonata: an instrumental work in three or four movements and for one or two players.
Sonata form: a construction used in the first movement of a sonata or symphony, which is divided into three sections: exposition, development and recapitulation.
Song-cycle: a set of songs grouped by the composer in a particular order for performance, often based on a sequence of poems.
Stochastic: a term denoting a process of which the steps are governed by rules of probability.
Suite: an instrumental piece in several movements.
Symphony: a substantial orchestral work, usually in four movements.
Tablature: a system of writing music by indicating the position of the player's fingers, as used for the lute or organ.
Te Deum: a Latin hymn of thanksgiving to God.
Tenor: the highest normal male voice, so called because it held the melody in plainsong.
Tonality: the general key of a piece.
Tone cluster or note cluster: a group of adjacent notes played together.
Tone-poem: a substantial orchestral work intended to interpret a non-musical idea, picture or literary work.
Tone-row or note-row: a sequence of all 12 notes of the octave which forms the basis of a composition in 12-note music.
Trio: (1) a combination of three performers; (2) a work for three performers; (3) the centre section of a minuet, traditionally written in three parts.
Twelve-note system: the technique by which all 12 notes within an octave are treated as equal and placed in a particular order (note-row) to form the basis of the composition.
Virelai: medieval French song.

Acknowledgements

The publisher would like to thank the following picture libraries for the use of their pictures in the book (l=left, r=right, t=top, b=bottom, u=upper, m=middle). Every effort has been made to acknowledge the pictures properly; however, we apologize if there are any unintentional omissions, which will be corrected in future editions.

AKG, London: 1; 3; 6–7; 13t; 14t; 22t, bl; 24b; 30t; 40b; 42t; 46t; 47t; 48t; 50t; 52t; 55t; 56t, bl, br; 58t, bl, br; 59t, b; 60b; 61tl; 64t; 65t; 66bl; 70t; 72br; 73b; 74t; 75t; 77b; 78t, bl; 80tl, tr, b; 81bl; 82t; 83t; 84t, b; 86bl; 88t; 90t; 94bl, br; 105t; 110bl; 114bl; 126t, br; 129b; 130t; 148b; 149tl; 150–1; 152t; 153t, br; 164b; 165t, 170b; 172b; 185bl; 188t; 221b; 254; 256; *British Library* 8r; *Stefan Diller* 25t; *Marion Kalter* 194b; 241t; 246t, b; *Erich Lessing* 14b; 32b; 40t; 53b; 68–9; 70br; 71t; 77t; 79t; 81t; 87t; 88bl, br; 89b; 93b; 208bl; *Visioars* 86br.
Arena Images Ltd: *Ron Scherl* 43t; 249br; *Colin Willoughby* 238b.
Art Archive Ltd: 13b; 37t; 54b; 86t; 132br; 141t; 171b.
Bridgeman Art Library, London: 4; 5; 12; 15b; 16; 18–19; 20–1; 23b; 27t, b; 28t, b; 33b; 35b; 38–9; 41t, b; 42b; 48bl; 49b; 50b; 51tr, b; 62t; 63bl, br; 67tl, br; 70bl; 71b; 79b; 83b; 87bl; 91b; 92b; 93t; 95tl, br; 96–7; 98; 99b; 103t; 108t; 109; 110t; 113t, b; 114t; 115t; 116b; 118t; 119; 120b; 121t; 124–5; 126bl; 127t, b; 135b; 143b; 146t; 147b; 148t; 155b; 160br; 161l; 176t, bl, br; 182–3; 184t, b; 186t, bl, br; 187b; 189tl, b; 190t; 192t; 206t; 212b; 242t; © *Arthur Rackham Estate* 165bl; *Giraudon* 49b; 90b; 122tl; 191t; *David Lees* 42b; *Novosti* 178t.
Camera Press: 135tl; 149b; 154br; 171t; 220bl, br; 227bl; 230t, b; 234t; 250t; *Karsh* 211t; 212t; 217t; 219t; *Patraig O'Donnell* 240t.
Eye Ubiquitous: *James Davis* 152b; 232br.
Frank Lane Picture Agency Limited: *H. D. Brandl* 243b.
gettyone Stone: 45t; 156t; 177; 179; 196b; 206bl; 207; 215t, bl; 217b.
Hulton Getty: 215br; 226br; 242b.
Lebrecht Collection, London: 2; 8l; 9tr, b; 10; 11l, r; 15tl, tr; 22br; 23t; 26t, bl, br; 29t, b; 30b; 31t, b; 32t; 33t; 34t, b; 35t; 36t, b; 37bl, br; 43bl, br; 44t; 45b; 46br; 47b; 48br; 49t; 51tl; 52br; 53t; 54t; 55b; 57b; 60t; 61tr; 62bl, br; 66t, br; 67tr, bl; 72t, bl; 73t; 74bl; 76tl, tr, b; 78br; 85; 87br; 89t; 91t; 92tl, tr; 99tl; 100t, b; 101t, bl, br; 102t, b; 103b; 104t, b; 106t; 107; 108bl, br; 110br; 111t, b; 112t, bl, br; 114br; 115b; 116t; 117tl, tr, b; 118br; 120t; 121b; 122tr, b; 123tl, tr, b; 128t, b; 129t; 130b; 131tl, tr, b; 132t, bl; 133t, b; 136t, bl, br; 137; 138; 139bl, br; 140t, bl, br; 141b; 142t, b; 143t; 144t; 145t, b; 146bl; 147tl, tr; 149um, tr; 153bl; 154t, bl; 155t; 156bl, br; 157t, b; 158t, bl; 159b; 160t; 162t, bl, br; 163l, r; 164t; 166t, bl, br; 167t, b; 168t; 170t; 172t; 173t, b; 174t, bl, br; 175t, b; 178bl, br; 180t, bl, br; 181tl, um, tr, br; 185t, br; 187t; 188b; 190bl; 191b; 192b; 193; 194t; 195; 196t; 197; 198t, bl, br; 199b; 200b; 201tl, tr, b; 202t; 203t, b; 204t, b; 205t; 206br; 208t; 209b; 210t, b; 213t, bl, br; 214t, b; 216t, b; 219bl; 221t; 222; 223tl, tr; 224; 225b; 227tl, tr, br; 233t, b; 250bl; 252; 253; 255; *M. Allen* 44b; 56tr; 95tr, bl; 118bl; *Archive Manuel de Falla* 226bl; *Arthur Reynolds Collection* 168b; 169t, b; 181bl; *Milein Cosman* 218b; *Mike Evans* 236t, b; *David Farrell* 225t; 238t; 251tr; *Betty Freeman* 231tl; 239t; 251tl; *Joanne Harris* 63t; 202b; *Matti Kolho* 161r; 223b; *Kurt Weill Foundation* 211b; *S. Lauterwasser* 165br; *Andre LeCoz* 244b; *Nigel Luckhurst* 234b; 248b; *Suzie Maeder* 239b; 240b; 243t; *Peter Mares* 135tr; *R. Meek* 24t; *B. Morris* 99tr; 134b; 139t; 146br; *Kate Mount* 17t; 231tr; 237b; *Wladimir Polak* 235b; *Private Collection* 65b; 82b; 106b; 199t; 208br; 226t; *Mary Robert* 17bl; *Zsuzsi Roboz* 200t; *Celene Rosen* 9tl; 52bl; *Royal Academy of Music* 64b; 94t; 144b; 160bl; *G. Salter* 74br; 75b; 158br; 235t; 241b; *D. Smirnov* 250br; *Richard H. Smith* 244t; 247b; *Horst Tappe* 218t; *Greg Tomin* 232t, bl; *Guy Vivien* 190br; *Toby Wales* 231b.
Performing Arts Library: 189tr; *Clive Barda* 105b; 209t; 237t; 245t, b; 247t; 248t; 249t, bl; 251bl, br; *Ben Christopher* 251bm; *Fritz Curzon* 17br; 134t; *Linda Rich* 219br; 220t.
The Stock Market: 205b; 228–9.
Wendy Thompson: 25b; 57tl; *British Library* 81br; *Editions des Musées Nationaux* 46bl; *Harold T. Storey* 159t.

Index

Notes

Notes

Notes

Notes

Notes

Notes

Notes

Notes

Notes

Notes

Notes

Notes

Notes

NOTES

Notes

Notes

Notes

Notes

Notes

Notes

Notes

Notes

Notes

Notes

Notes

NOTES

Notes

Notes

Notes

Notes